The English Housewife

GERVASE MARKHAM

The English Housewife

Containing the inward and outward virtues which ought to be in a complete woman; as her skill in physic, cookery, banqueting-stuff, distillation, perfumes, wool, hemp, flax, dairies, brewing, baking, and all other things belonging to a household

Edited by
Michael R. Best

McGill-Queen's University Press
Kingston and Montreal

© McGill-Queen's University Press 1986
ISBN 0-7735-0582-2
Legal deposit third quarter 1986
Bibliothèque nationale du Québec
Printed in Canada

This book has been published with the help of a grant from
the Canadian Federation for the Humanities, using funds provided by
the Social Sciences and Humanities Research Council of Canada.

Publication has also been assisted by the Canada Council
under its block grant program.

Printed on acid-free paper

Canadian Cataloguing in Publication Data

Markham, Gervase, 1568?-1637
The English housewife
Bibliography: p.
Includes index.
ISBN 0-7735-0582-2
1. Home economics – Early works to 1800.
I. Best, Michael R., 1939-   . II. Title.
TX144.M37 1986   640   C86-093718-6

To my family

Contents

CHAPTER V

Of wool, hemp, flax, and cloth, and dyeing of colours, of each several substance, with all the knowledges belonging thereto 146

CHAPTER VI

Of dairies, butter, cheese, and the necessary things belonging to that office 166

CHAPTER VII

The office of the maltster, and the several secrets and knowledges belonging to the making of malt 180

CHAPTER VIII

Of the excellency of oats, and the many singular virtues and uses of them in a family 199

CHAPTER IX

Of the office of the brew-house, and the bake-house, and the necessary things belonging to the same 204

Preface

The English Housewife is the most comprehensive, the most practical, and the most readable of the many books of instruction written for women in the early seventeenth century. Markham's book describes the activities of a large rural household, and we must assume that the women who read it were predominantly those of superior social status; it seems likely that barely one in ten women of the time was literate. The comprehensiveness of *The English Housewife* is achieved despite the social limitations of its intended audience. It is wide-ranging in its record of the multitude of day-to-day household activities, and at the same time precise in the careful particularity of its advice. Markham did not make a name for himself as a writer, but as a compiler, editor, observer, and recorder he wrote works which, like *The English Housewife*, remain valuable social documents, much quoted by scholars of early seventeenth-century history and literature. The present edition is intended to bring Markham's record of the activities and responsibilities of the housewife of his time to a wider audience.

Gervase Markham acknowledged his debt to others when writing of his books on husbandry: "I am but only a public notary who records the most true and infallible experience of the best knowing husbands in this land." Those best knowing scholars who have assisted in the production of this edition deserve no less a recognition: Terry Best, Patrick White, Anne Field, Jean Butler, and the many friends and colleagues who read the Introduction and offered advice much appreciated – Ed Berry, Connie Rooke, John Bean, Bob Schuler, Patrick Grant, Alan Brissenden, Tim Mares, John Money, and David Bevington.

Particular thanks are due to the University of Victoria, the Social Sciences and Humanities Research Council of Canada, and the Canadian Federation for the Humanities for financial support of the project; they have proven to be more enlightened patrons than Gervase Markham ever found.

Introduction

Gervase Markham

HIS LIFE (1568?–1637)

The life of Gervase Markham documents in many ways the varied world he records in his written works. Like many of his contemporaries, Markham was caught between a love for old, established values, and a fascination for things new. He was a younger son from a noble family in decline, and believed in the old, chivalrous virtues, particularly in the ideal of an orderly hierarchical society led by an aristocracy that was noble in action as well as in birth; yet he was fascinated by new ways of doing things, and was a natural though unscientific experimenter. During his life he appears to have become progressively more puritan in his views; yet he retained an obvious delight in the "feather light"[1] study of poetry, and would have been much distressed by the puritan Commonwealth, with its closing of the theatres, for which he had written two plays, and its attack on the power of the nobility, about which he had written much that was laudatory.

During the lifetime of Gervase, a family quarrel and a profligate elder brother brought about "a headlong decline in the Markham fortune."[2] In the fifteenth century the family owned five estates, but a split in the family reduced the fortune of Gervase's father, Robert, a prominent soldier, courtier, and politician; and when Gervase's elder brother died some time before 1618 the last of the estates had to be sold.

Gervase, the third son, was born in 1568, ten years after the accession of Elizabeth I and four years after the birth of Shakespeare. Direct information about his life is sketchy, but his brother Francis (the second son) left a brief autobiography, from which we may gather an unusually full picture of the life of a younger son of a not-so-wealthy gentleman. Francis' education involved attendance at several noteworthy institutions.[3] After his early years, he lived a hand-to-mouth existence, moving from the study of law to the experience of military service, and to the life of the court as occasion demanded, always in pursuit of a wealthy widow or a generous patron. When Francis finally succeeded in marrying, it seems that it was scarcely to his advantage, since he was forced still to live by his wit and charm:

I grew acquainted with a widow, Mrs. Dorothy Lovell, whose daughter Mary I married January 3, 1608 ... I raffled with 10 ladies ... each venturing £20 for a jewel worth £100. I won and got that help. I was poor.

Francis continued to seek financial security, but his fortunes fluctuated on the borderline of respectability and genteel poverty for the rest of his life.

Gervase must have led a life scarcely more secure than that of his elder brother, though he seems to have avoided Francis' extremes of adventuring and gambling. Writing at the age of fifty-two, Gervase summed up his life's major activities in an epigrammatic defence of his experience in the field of husbandry: "Now for myself, although a piece of my life was scholar, a piece soldier, and all horseman; yet did I for nine years apply myself to the plough, followed it with earnestness."[4] Of his education – the piece of his life as a scholar – we can surmise from his writings that he was well read; he translated several works from French,[5] he wrote many works which reveal a thorough reading of literature both classical and modern, and he began his career as writer by trying his hand at most of the popular literary forms of the day. As soldier, Gervase spent much of his youth in and out of service; late in life he wrote of his military career that he had "hitherto served his country in ... Ireland and in other places in the place of a captain, and [had] in those services received divers grievous wounds in his body whereby [he] was disabled to follow that course of life."[6]

Gervase was also active at least on the fringe of the circle at court, for there is a reference to "the younger Markham" who performed before the Queen some time in 1600; he "did several gallant feats on a horse before the gate, leaping down and kissing his sword, then mounting swiftly on the saddle, and passing a lance with much skill."[7] This episode is a pleasing confirmation that Gervase's interest in horses was far from being limited to the writing of theoretical treatises on the subject; he was, indeed, "all horseman." Francis' memoir indicates that the Markhams were closely allied with followers of the Earl of Essex, and it may be no coincidence that Gervase seems to have given up any hope of military or courtly advancement from the time of the downfall of Essex in 1601, very soon after his promising appearance before the Queen.

The direction of his life seems to have undergone a distinct change at this time, for it was also in 1601 that Gervase, responding to an ill-tempered letter written to his father by a member of a feuding branch of the family in which he was described as a "poetical lying knave," avowed that he had given up poetry, and regretted his time spent on it:

You have charged me ... [with] the title of a poetical lying knave, to which I thus answer: for my love to poetry, if it be an error, I confess myself faulty, and have, with as great heartiness as ever I grieved for any sin committed against the Highest, mourned for mine hours misspent in that feather-light study; yet can I name many noble personages who with greater desire, and more fervency have continued and boasted in the humour, which, though in other it be excellent, in myself I loathe and utterly abhor it.[8]

The attitude to poetry expressed in this letter is curiously mixed. In his own life he sees the writing of poetry to be a sin, and he expresses this attitude in language strong enough to align him with puritan polemicists writing against literature; but in other writers, possibly those of nobler birth, he finds the "humour" of poetry to be "excellent." To complicate matters further, there is abundant evidence that he continued to write poetry for many years, though his longest poem remained unpublished.[9] Markham is pulled in two apparently contradictory directions: he seems to feel that his youthful enthusiasm for literature was somehow mis-directed, his time frivolously rather than wisely spent; yet it is impossible for him, as an admirer of such figures as Sir Philip Sidney, whose *Arcadia* he imitated, to go so far as to reject poetry altogether. When we add to the evidence provided by this letter the devotion demonstrated by Mark-ham's many specifically religious works (some of which, ironically, were poems), and the nature of his advice on religious matters scattered throughout his practical works, we are led to the conclusion that he was increasingly inclined towards that kind of austerity in religion and life which we associate with the movement towards puritanism, though it is clear that in politics he remained staunchly royalist.[10]

The apparent change in Markham's life in 1601 coincided with his marriage, on 23 February of that year, to Mary Gelsthorpe. It is probable that the married couple spent the next nine years as husbandman and housewife. (The husbandman was a small landowner or farmer whose living depended on the land.) The extent of his earnestness as he followed the plough may be judged from the fact that he published little new in this period. The evidence of his books on husbandry suggests that he spent the time learning and experimenting. No doubt he read all he could on the subject of husbandry; two such books available to him he later edited with additions intended to make them more useful to the English reader: *The Whole Art of Husbandry* by Conrad Heresbach (Markham's edition appeared in 1634), and *Maison Rustique, or, The Countrey Farme*, first translated from the French of Charles Estienne and Jean Liebault by Richard Surflet in 1600. The sections of *Maison Rustique* which deal with the duties of the housewife were almost certainly the inspiration of *The English Housewife* (see below).

The life of husbandman, while it furnished Gervase with much material for his books, does not seem to have made a sufficient living for his family. The evidence is that he became increasingly poor as he grew older. He must have been frustrated indeed by the lack of copyright protection afforded writers at the time; the author was paid for his manuscript by the publisher, but received no further payments, no matter how many editions of the book appeared. It is little wonder that the popularity of his books on horses and cattle led Markham (and, Poynter suggests, publishers eager to cash in on his popularity) to reissue some of his material in different forms. When no less than five of Markham's books on diseases of horses (and related subjects) were on the market simultaneously, and another in the offing, the Stationers called a halt to the process by requiring Markham's signature on a memorandum dated 14 July 1617:

Memorandum, that I Gervase Markham of London, gent., do promise hereafter never to write any more book or books to be printed of the diseases or cures of any cattle, as horse, ox, cow, sheep, swine, goats, etc.[11]

Another scheme for raising money, more respectable than Francis' gamble for the "jewel worth £100," was a wager Gervase undertook in 1622, at the age of fifty-four, "desirous" (he later wrote) "by some honest endeavour to raise unto himself some means whereas to live in his old years."[12] He undertook to go "on foot" from London to Berwick without going over "any apparent bridge great or small whatsoever," and not to use "directly or indirectly any boat, ship or other engine for water whatsoever." He completed the journey successfully, but had to go to the Court of Requests five years later to enforce payment from the thirty-nine acquaintances (mostly actors) with whom he had made the bet. His plea to the court included the information that he had "grown poor" because of his "many children and great charge of household." There is no indication that his circumstances improved in the next ten years before he died, in 1637.

Markham's literary reputation has never been high. Despite a mention by Francis Meres in 1598,[13] Markham's contemporaries were not avid readers of his literary efforts; only one such work, *The Dumbe Knight* (a play), reached a second edition, so far as we know.[14] At best it can be said that he inhabited the fringes of the literary world, praised by some friends, but otherwise attracting little attention (unless, as one unlikely theory suggests, he was the "rival poet" of Shakespeare's sonnets, and was satirized in the figure of Don Armado in *Love's Labour's Lost*).[15] Probably the most flattering contemporary judgement of Markham's poetry was the inclusion of passages from two of his poems in several "miscellanies," collections of memorable or morally admirable quotations, published between 1597 and 1600. The best-known of these anthologies, *England's Parnassus* (1600), wrongly attributed a passage taken from Markham's poem *Devoreux* to Christopher Marlowe; it is an entertaining reminder of the inexactitude of the art of criticism to discover that these lines have been highly praised by modern critics, although the rest of Markham's poetry, unattributed to Marlowe, has otherwise been met with yawns by those few who have read it.[16] Markham was aware, however, that as a poet he was but a "prentice to the Muses." The reader concerned with Markham principally as the author of *The English Housewife* will be most interested in the energy, the variety, and the sincerity of his poetic writings; he published, for the most part, narrative poems on historical, political, romantic, and religious topics.[17] In addition, there remains the long, unpublished poem "The Newe Metamorphosis," written between 1600 and 1615. Markham is also recorded as the author of two plays, each written in collaboration (or perhaps revised by other writers), and a number of prose works as varied as his poetical writings.

The tendency to experiment widely, which is so noticeable in Markham's literary works, becomes even more evident in his practical writings. Any summary tends to become a mere catalogue, simply because there are so many interests to record;[18] the danger is that Markham's pervasive curiosity and the genuine fascination which his subjects obviously held for him will be forgotten.

The catalogue: four books on horses; six on husbandry, including two editions of works by other writers; four on military discipline; four on various country sports and recreations, including one edition of an earlier work; and one on housewifery. Two collections of his works, one of those on husbandry and one on military affairs, were issued in his lifetime; and there were also four abridgements of his popular works, two issued during his life, two issued after his death. The catalogue scarcely does justice to the breadth of Markham's interests, for within each category he deals with widely different subjects (see for example the notes summarizing the contents of *Cheape and Good Husbandry* [chapter vi, paragraph 5] and *The English Husbandman* [vi, 12]); it is also fair to say that, with the exception of frequent lists of remedies for the diseases of animals, his books are not repetitive, even when several deal with the same general subject.

HIS TECHNIQUE AS WRITER

The total sum of lucidly conveyed information about the habits, the work, and the recreation of the country gentleman in the early seventeenth century contained in Markham's works is formidable indeed. Markham's particular strength was his ability to record the daily minutiae of the life he observed around him, not as a passive onlooker, but as one exploring and experimenting; he was not simply passing on information in the manner of an encyclopaedist. His sustained and active curiosity is evident not only in the variety of subjects he chose to write upon, but in the seriousness with which he treated each topic, and above all in the attention he gave to detail. His concern for accuracy is most clearly to be seen in his love for technical terms, for he was always concerned to use the right words for any activity he was discussing. The editor of Markham becomes very quickly aware of the extensive use to which the editors of the *Oxford English Dictionary* put his works, for he is always careful either to explain the technical words he uses or to put them in contexts where their meaning is clear.[19] So concerned was Markham to use the most correct term wherever possible that his revision of *The English Housewife* for its second printing included changes in which a general or imprecise word was replaced by a more specialized one: for example, he substituted "cheese heck" for the less accurate "cheese press" (see vi, 39).

Markham's vocabulary is a reminder of a world we have lost as activities have moved away from the house to the factory; he writes of "bolters, searces, ranges, and meal sieves of all sorts both fine and coarse" (ix, 18), revealing an array of different, now forgotten utensils for the different stages in sifting flour and meal. Markham also seems to enjoy the way different words will be used for the same object, with the result that his style sometimes acquires a biblical flavour ("will and testament") when he provides alternatives: he speaks of "lets and hindrances" in making malt "good and perfect," and extends the pattern as he expounds the "art, skill and knowledge" (vii, 25) of malt-making – an art which involves the use of "garners, hutches, or holds" (vii, 20), care about the "poise and weight" (vii, 24) of water used, and so on. Markham seldom employs figures of speech in *The English Housewife*, but his language achieves strength by its directness, by its high proportion of concrete nouns, and, at times, by proverbial and near-proverbial statements of practical or moral advice.[20] The final edition of *The English Housewife* in which Markham had a hand (1631) contains two passages added to acknowledge his debt to the manuscripts of others in the chapters on medicine and wine (i, 8 and iv, 1 of this edition).

In writing and compiling *The English Housewife*, Markham worked from many disparate sources, selecting, rewording, and rearranging his material and adding original matter in a way which is confusing to the modern reader, who is inclined to think in terms of plagiarism when sources are unacknowledged.[21] It is well known that sixteenth- and seventeenth-century attitudes towards originality and the use of sources were very different from our own – the use Shakespeare makes of earlier plays and plots is an obvious example – but even by the standards of his own day, the range of sources used by Markham in *The English Housewife* is remarkable, partly, no doubt, because he was writing in an area less familiar to him than the care of horses or the management of farm lands. Since he does acknowledge at least some of the sources he used,[22] it is probably more accurate to think of him as an editor who made some original contributions to his material, rather than as a writer claiming originality but guilty in fact of plagiarism.

The printer of the first edition of *The English Housewife* (1615), Roger Jackson, inserted a note to the "gentle reader," suggesting that Markham had not written or even "collected" the book, but had simply organized it:

this is no collection of his whose name is prefixed to this work, but an approved manuscript which he hath happily light on, belonging sometime to an honourable personage of this kingdom ... This only hath he done, digested the things of this book in a good method, placing everything of the same kind together ...

The second edition (1623) contains two comments by Markham which confirm his editorial role, though he makes clear the fact that he contributed material to the book, as well as reorganizing those parts which were taken from the "approved manuscript." In the dedication he writes:

I do not assume to myself (though I am not altogether ignorant in ability to judge of these things) the full invention and scope of this whole work; for it is true ...

that much of it was a manuscript which many years ago belonged to an honourable Countess, one of the greatest glories of our kingdom, and were the opinions of the greatest physicians which then lived ...

A close examination of Markham's sources reveals that he was in fact working from several manuscripts, reorganizing them logically, as Roger Jackson indicated. The chapter on medicine is thus transformed to "good method" between the first and second editions, for example; the recipes are grouped under headings, and the organization of the headings is logical, proceeding from diseases of the head to those of the feet. In a similarly logical manner, the chapter on cookery is organized according to the order of serving dishes to the table, from soups to vegetables to roast meats to pies (see note to ii, 191). Since Markham's sources were themselves compilations from yet earlier sources, and since in the process of arranging and editing his manuscripts Markham added original material, *The English Housewife* combines comments and recipes of widely varying origin and antiquity within a few lines. It is a tribute to Markham's care in preparing his final manuscript for publication that the seams seldom show, and that the style is consistent throughout.

Three examples will illustrate something of the variety of Markham's editorial techniques. In the chapter on wines, taken from a single source, Markham's only contribution was to rearrange the material; in the chapter on medicine one source in particular allows us to see in fascinating detail the way in which remedies were compiled and in some cases modified with experience; and in the complicated relationship between *The English Housewife* and the translation by Richard Surflet of the French work on farming, *Maison Rustique*, by Charles Estienne and Jean Liebault, we see Markham's own opinions asserting themselves in reaction to a source which he admired, but with which he also, at times, strongly disagreed.

Chapter iv of the present edition, on the care of wines, first appeared without acknowledgement of its source in the second edition of *The English Housewife*. In the third extant edition, however, Markham added a passage in which he specifically defined his role as that of editor:

I do not assume to myself this knowledge of the vintner's secrets, but ingeniously confess that one professed skilful in the trade, having rudely written, and more rudely disclosed this secret, and preferring it to the stationer, it came to me to be polished, which I have done ... [See iv, 1.]

The manuscript to which he refers, or a copy of it, was earlier in the hands of Sir Hugh Platt, who discusses it in *A Jewell House of Art and*

Nature (1594): "I can assure you I have almost the whole art as it is this day in use amongst the Vintners, written in a pretty volume called *Secreta de pampinei*" (p. 65). Platt then goes on to discuss some of the methods, recorded in his manuscript, of "tricking" or "compassing" the wine, noticing with more disapproval than Markham the way in which actual adulteration of the wine is advocated (see iv, 3 and 4, and the notes to these passages). An incomplete version of the manuscript Markham worked from is preserved in the British Museum as a part of Sloane 3692 (fols. 26–30v); a comparison of this manuscript with the chapter in *The English Housewife* reveals the extent of Markham's changes.

Markham's own description of his editorial technique as "polishing" the manuscript is accurate. He contributes nothing of substance himself, being content simply with polishing the style and reorganizing the contents of the manuscript so that items dealing with the same topic were, on the whole, dealt with together rather than being scattered at random.[23] Organizational tidiness of this kind is, indeed, one of the qualities that distinguishes *The English Housewife* from other handbooks of its kind, and is a characteristic of all Markham's works on practical matters.

The chapter on medicine furnishes us with a further glimpse of a mind absorbing and categorizing information, this time in a rather more complex way. We cannot be certain that the work was done by Markham himself, though there is a high probability that it was done at least by a member of his family. A large number of remedies recorded by Markham in the first edition of *The English Housewife* were derived from the first herbal printed in English, the popular "Banckes" herbal (1525).[24] Several recipes in *The English Housewife* were taken almost verbatim from the Banckes herbal, the only modifications resulting once again from an attempt to polish the style. But the most interesting use of the source is found in a large number of remedies which were compiled from the herbal rather than simply transcribed. Markham, or whoever compiled the remedies, must have read systematically through the herbal, noting all the herbs which were described as beneficial for the frenzy, for dim or sore eyes, for the dropsy, and so on; he then devised a recipe for each sickness by including each herb which was recorded as effective in its treatment. He thus produced some good examples of polypharmacy, or "shotgun medicine": put enough ingredients in the medication and one of them may hit the target.[25]

Markham trusted the Banckes herbal enough to use many recipes derived from it on his horses; in fact, one further source of the remedies in the chapter on medicines is Markham's own medical advice concerning equestrian diseases, scattered (and often repeated with modifications which suggest actual testing) throughout his books on the care of horses. One such recipe is introduced simply enough in Banckes, where the herb shepherd's purse, drunk with red wine, is recommended as a cure for diarrhoea. In the popular *Cavelarice* (1607) this mixture is prescribed as a cure for "looseness" in a horse in the same paragraph as a remedy from some other source, involving a combination of bean flour, tanner's bark, and milk.[26] In *Markham's Maister-peece* (1610) the two remedies are combined, specific quantities are prescribed, and a further ingredient is added as an afterthought: "If you do add into it a little cinnamon, it is not amiss" (p. 150). Finally, in *The English Housewife* (1615) two versions of the recipe occur: i, 105 "to staunch blood" and i, 130 "for the bloody flux." The second of these, the most sophisticated version of them all, gives precise quantities, instructions for preparation, and includes all the accumulated ingredients except the bean flour. The evolution of this remedy, and of others like it, is a strong indication that at least some of the medical material includes Markham's own experience, and that he was ready to go beyond the role of compiler and editor when he had specific knowledge of the subject under consideration.

That Markham is much more than simply an editor of already existing works can be seen in the interesting and complex relationship between *The English Housewife* and the translation by Richard Surflet of a popular French work on farming, *L'agriculture et maison rustique* (2 parts, Paris, 1569–70) by Charles Estienne (anglicized as Stevens) and Jean Liebault. Surflet's translation, *Maison Rustique or The Countrie Farme*, appeared in 1600, and must have attracted Markham's attention by the time he was writing the "Epistle to the general and gentle reader" in *The English Husbandman* (1613), where he commented on the lack of literature on farming dealing with specifically English conditions: "[a man] translates Libault and Stevens, a work of infinite excellency, yet only proper to the French, and not to us." As its name implies, *The English Housewife* was an attempt to fill this gap for the English reader; but while he was in part reacting against *The Countrie Farme* because of its French qualities, he was also very much indebted to it, as almost every chapter of *The English Housewife* bears witness. The interaction between the two works continued until 1623. In 1615 the first edition of *The English Housewife* appeared, its general organization derived from *The Countrie Farme* and including some specific passages borrowed from it. In 1616 a version of *The Countrie Farme* edited by Markham himself was published; his contribution was mainly in the form of additional passages, some of which were condensed versions of material he had originally published in *The English Housewife*. Finally, in 1623 the second edition of *The English Housewife* appeared, containing two new chapters which are in effect expanded and detailed versions of passages he had earlier added to his edition of *The Countrie Farme*.

Of the many sections of *The Countrie Farme* which are related to *The English Housewife* there are three of particular interest. Markham had already written about wool, hemp, flax, and cloth (chapter v of this edition), and he obviously disapproved of the instructions given on these subjects by Estienne and Liebault; at the conclusion of their rather unenthusiastic comments about hemp, Markham introduced his own judgement, in a passage which was a condensed version of the paragraphs already published in *The English Housewife* on the same subject, with this remark: "This is the opinion of the French, but not the opinion of the better experienced" (p. 566). Two further passages in *The Countrie Farme* stirred Markham's scorn, in each case stimulating an extensive addition, which in turn became a full chapter in the second edition of *The English Housewife*. One of these was on barley and the making of malt, the other an indignant rejection of the "French opinion" on the use of oatmeal. Estienne and Liebault were distinctly lukewarm in their discussion of oatmeal, speaking rather half-heartedly of "the profit coming of them for the feeding of great cattle, as also of men in the time of necessity ... oats be not used to make bread of, except in the time of great dearth." (Dr Johnson would have approved – see the note to viii, 7.) Markham dismisses this opinion with some vigour: "This much of the French opinion of oats, who indeed are but half knowing, or not so much, in the excellency of the grain; but to come to their knowledge who have the full proof and trial thereof, you shall understand that it is a grain of no less worth and estimation than any ... other" (p. 558). Hence it was by a reaction against the opinion expressed in *The Countrie Farme* that Markham came to write the enthusiastic, almost polemical chapter "Of the excellency of oats, and the many singular virtues and uses of them in a family," which first appeared in the second edition of *The English Housewife*.

Markham's use of his sources was complex and varied; at times in *The English Housewife* he was simply an editor, polishing and reorganizing, but he was always interested in modifying the material he was working with if his own experience was in any way able to contribute, and there are many occasions when he chose to write purely from his own knowledge. In *The English Husbandman* Markham describes with accuracy and modesty his method as writer on practical affairs: "I am but only a public notary who record[s] the most true and infallible experience of the best knowing husbands in this land." He goes on to enunciate the principles which he used as editor and writer to select what was worth recording in the experience he observed:

I am not altogether unseen in those mysteries I write of: for it is well known I followed the profession of husbandman so long myself as well might make one worthy to be a graduate in the vocation; wherein my simplicity was not such but I both observed well those which were esteemed famous in the profession, and preserved to myself those rules which I found infallible by experience.

Markham's writings can be seen as an indication of the extent to which an experimental attitude was operating at the grass roots even while it was achieving theoretical respectability in the work of his more famous contemporary, Francis Bacon. Markham was no slavish copier of received opinion; both as writer and as editor he approached his subjects with a balanced scepticism,[27] transmitting the opinions of those "esteemed famous" in whatever profession he was writing about, but always prepared to test them by experience, and to approve or criticize them accordingly.

The Housewife

HER CHARACTER

Writing in a convention which allowed him freedom of imagination, Markham described what he saw as the ideal wife.[28] *Hobsons Horse-load of Letters* is a collection of fictional letters intended to be used as models for various occasions; one letter is written by a young man to his friend, telling of his recent marriage, and of his good fortune in finding an ideal partner (Part ii, 1617, letter 25). The young man's love is both idealistic and realistic, combining the visual infatuation we associate with courtly love with a frank sexual attraction: "I have her, enjoy her, eat with her, lie with her, and sometimes sleep with her; my eyes still unwilling to yield themselves any respite from gazing ..." We need not find an appreciation of the wife's sexuality a surprise, despite Markham's tendency towards the puritan in his religious outlook; puritan handbooks on marriage were in many ways more liberal than conventional teaching in their treatment of sex in marriage.[29] The young man's comment is also a reminder that in *The English Housewife* Markham chose not to discuss one occupation which must have occupied women for the greater part of their lives: the bearing and rearing of children.[30]

The young bridegroom in *Hobsons Horse-load of Letters* is, however, unconcerned with the problems of raising a family as he dwells on his bride's virtues. He goes on to say that beauty is not the only quality she has to offer: "She is not all sail, beautiful flags and tackling, but freighted with rich merchandise, to which th'other serve but as necessary instruments." Markham's admonition to his housewife that her clothes be "altogether without toyish garnishes," and "made as well to preserve the health as adorn the person" (i, 5) is echoed by the young man, who boasts that his wife's apparel is "rather to cover her body than to set out her body, which is adorned with nothing but plainness, and her mind suitable to that, free from artificial guile or glozing [deception]." Artificial guile in maintaining beauty is a common theme in many medical and culinary works published before *The English Housewife*, but Markham provides very few recipes for cosmetics.

The proverbial tendency of wives to gossip is forsworn both by Markham's housewife, who is to be "wise in discourse, but not frequent therein" (i, 7), and by the young man's wife in *Hobsons Horse-load*, of whom he writes, "I never heard a woman discourse so well and so little, often sparing herself from needful speeches, lest she should get a habit of gossiping. The home is her circle, from which she seldom stirs but to her devotions, and never without me, in whom she seems to live." If we feel that the young bridegroom is a shade too complacent, Markham provides a partial antidote for his reader through the next letter in the collection, a misogynistic reply from a bachelor friend. He does not, however, provide model letters written from the wife's point of view.

The introductory paragraphs to *The English Housewife* present a man's ideal of womankind similar to the young man's view of his wife. The housewife, very much the equal partner of the husbandman in her contribution to the domestic economy, is nonetheless subordinate to him.[31] The housewife's "mild sufference" (i, 4) towards her husband is to be an outward sign of her inward spiritual humility. Markham stresses the importance of religion by putting it first among the virtues he discusses; he would no doubt have thoroughly approved of the typical day spent by Lady Margaret Hoby, a puritan, writing in the early years of the seventeenth century:

After private prayers I broke my fast, was busy in the kitchen till dinner time, then I prayed; after dined; all the afternoon I was busied about taking of accounts and other things so that through idleness distractions had no advantage; and at night I betook myself to private examination and prayer: then I went to supper after public prayers, then to private, and so to my chamber, with much comfort, I thank God.[32]

While cautioning the housewife against excessive zeal, or "violence of spirit" (i, 2), Markham characteristically justifies the value of religion in practical terms by suggesting that the religious household will produce servants more faithful and godly favours more plentiful: "and therefore a small time morning and evening bestowed in prayers ... will prove no lost time at the week's end" (i, 3). Virtue is rewarded by increased efficiency.[33] A similar sentiment is expressed in Markham's advice on the

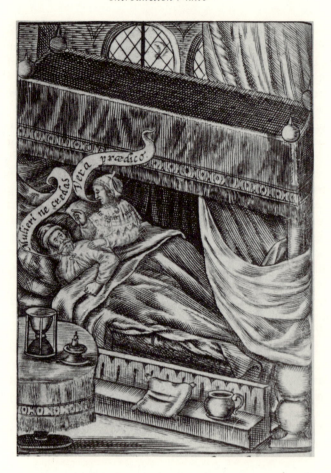

Thomas Heywood exploited the stereotype of the shrew who keeps her
husband awake by nagging. The woman is maintaining "I proclaim the truth,"
while the husband mutters "Don't believe women." The illustration is
accompanied by these verses:
When wives preach 'tis not in the husband's power
To have their lectures end within an hour;
If he with patience stay till they have done,
She'll not conclude till twice the glass have run.
The illustration is from Heywood's *A Curtaine Lecture.*

use of one of the by-products of the dairy: "The best use of buttermilk for the able housewife is charitably to bestow it on the poor neighbours, whose wants do daily cry out for sustenance: and no doubt but she shall find the profit thereof in a divine place, as well as in her earthly business" (vi, 3). Markham goes on to describe what the housewife should do with the buttermilk if "her own wants command her to use it for her own good" (see vi, 33). A similar product, the whey left after the making of cheese, may profitably be used either "to bestow on the poor" or "to nourish and bring up ... swine" (vi, 45).[34]

Frugality of this kind is obviously a virtue Markham admires. In his introductory remarks he argues for a balance between prodigality and covetousness, increase and consumption (i, 4), but the practical advice he gives tends to emphasize increase or preservation rather than generosity. The "stubble or after-crop" of wheat, rye, or barley is recommended as a fuel for the drying of malt, being "less chargeable" than other fuels (vii, 19); the water used for steeping barley in the first stage of making malt is to be used as "very good swine's meat," and "may not be lost by any good housewife" (vii, 25). The same is true of the dust left after the winnowing of the malt (vii, 28); and we are reminded that the "coarse hulls or chaff" left after the milling of oatmeal make "an excellent good horse provender" (viii, 8). Elsewhere we learn that in the preparation of hemp and flax even the coarsest fibres have their uses (v, 39), and it must surely have been the impulse to economize that persuaded Markham to include in the second edition of *The English Housewife* the chapter on "ordering, preserving, and helping" of wines – what in the vintner was scandalous adulteration was admirable ingenuity in the frugal housewife. It is only fair to add that the chapter on food provides us with some notable examples of generosity, even prodigality, particularly in the passages concerning banquets and great feasts (ii, 191, etc.). Although the housewife is instructed to shun food which is strange, rare, or foreign (i, 6), recipes abound which spectacularly contradict this advice;[35] in the same vein Markham directs the housewife to ensure that her dishes "proceed more from the provision of her own yard, than the furniture of the markets," yet almost every recipe he records requires rich seasonings which could only be imported.[36]

If Markham's housewife was to be expansively Elizabethan in the food she prepared, she was also to be aware that abstinence was at times of medicinal value (see i, 157), and that drink was to be treated carefully, particularly when given to the servants (see below, in the discussion of "Malting and brewing"). As well as being a model of sobriety, the housewife was to be "cleanly" in all things (i, 5 and 6). In the dairy, for example, "sweet and neat keeping" was of the greatest importance: "though cleanliness be such an ornament to a housewife, that if she want any part thereof she loseth both that and all good names else, yet in this action it must be more seriously employed than in any other" (vi, 19). In the kitchen she must be "cleanly both in body and garments," and she must manage not to be "butter-fingered, sweet-toothed, nor faint-hearted; for the first will let everything fall, and second will consume what it should increase, and the last will lose time with too much niceness" (ii, 10). A similar caution appears in the chapter on malting, where Markham singles out "the neat and fine keeping of the kiln" as the greater part of "the housewife's art," and goes on to describe "sluttishness and sloth" as "the only great imputations hanging over a housewife" (vii, 17).

A concise summary of the character and competence of the ideal housewife is given by the poet George Herbert in his prose work *A Priest to the Temple*. In a list of priorities which echoes the organization of chapters in *The English Housewife*, Herbert enumerates the three qualities the parson's wife should have:

first, a training up of her children and maids in the fear of God, with prayers and catechizing, and all religious duties. Secondly, a curing and healing of all wounds and sores with her own hands; which skill either she brought with her, or he takes care she shall learn it of some religious neighbour. Thirdly, a providing for her family in such sort, as that neither they want a competent sustentation [sustenance], nor her husband be brought in debt.[37]

HER STATUS

Markham's attitude towards the housewife (both his subject and the audience for which his book was written) was as practical as his attitude towards the knowledge he was communicating. He includes some conventional words of advice, placing her in the accepted position of subservience to her husband, but he is concerned almost exclusively throughout the book with her practical rather than her theoretical role; and in her practical role it is clear that he sees her playing a vital part in an economic partnership between husband and wife.

The English Housewife appeared originally as the second volume of a two-volume work; the first volume was devoted to the various pastimes of the husbandman ("riding great horses ... hunting, hawking, coursing of greyhounds ... shooting, bowling, tennis ...").[38] Markham's acceptance of the traditional status of women is revealed when he writes at the beginning of *The English Housewife* that, having completed his discussion of "the perfect husbandman, who is the father and master of the family," it is appropriate that he "descend" to a discussion of "the office of our

English housewife, who is the mother and mistress of the family" (i, 1). In the orderly hierarchy of Markham's society, the wife is properly to be considered after the husband, since her rank is more lowly. The wife was expected to seek fulfilment through her husband, supporting him, following his lead, but never asserting herself against him: "coveting less to direct than to be directed" (i, 4). Even when her husband behaved irresponsibly, she was "with mild sufferance rather to call him home from his error, than with the strength of anger to abate the least spark of his evil" (i, 4). Popular literature of the period – particularly the drama – offers ample evidence that women were in fact prepared to be far less passive, in love or in anger, than the ideal Markham implies; that ideal was, nonetheless, what his housewife would have heard preached from the pulpit, and would have read in popular books of religious instruction.[39]

In the practical world Markham describes, however, it is clear that the housewife's role is far from being passive and subservient; she is an active and indispensable partner in the domestic economy. Though he is careful, where possible, to generalize his information, Markham's model in the companion volumes *The English Housewife* and *The English Husbandman* is the household and farm of the self-sufficient landowner, of the kind we may imagine he himself wished to be. *The English Husbandman* opens with an epistle directed "To the gentle and general reader," a phrase which could be equally well applied to the audience of *The English Housewife*. Markham intended to reach at one end the gentry, and at the other the more "general" reader, possibly the wife of a wage earner, more interested in "ordinary wholesome boiled meats which are of use in every goodman's house" (ii, 40), than in "banqueting stuff and conceited dishes" (ii, 146).[40]

Within the ideal economic unit of the self-sufficient estate, Markham's tidy mind dictates that the duties of husband and wife should be divided by giving to the man the external activities and to the woman those "within the house" (i, 1) The division, though traditional,[41] is neater than the facts allow, for Markham himself allows the housewife to work outside in the growing of hemp and flax. In addition, there were several activities outdoors which Markham does not mention; the housewife would have spent some time in the yard looking after the poultry and the pigs, and further time would have been spent outside the house assisting in the fields, particularly at harvest-time. The housewife would also have been responsible for selling produce from the estate at market, and often she would have been the one who purchased any items the estate could not provide.

An earlier writer than Markham laid stress on the mutual accountability of husband and wife when it came to such commercial transactions. The wife, after her day at the market, was "to make a true reckoning and account to her husband what she hath received and what she hath paid. And if the husband go to the market to buy or sell as they oft do, he then to show his wife in like manner; for if one of them should use to deceive the other, he deceiveth himself, and he is not likely to thrive, and therefore they must be true either to other."[42] The economic partnership is neatly complemented by the religious; since man and wife are one flesh, to deceive the spouse is to deceive one's self. The importance of the wife in the domestic economy can scarcely be exaggerated. Not only was she responsible for the physical well-being of the family, as she is instructed in the chapters in *The English Housewife* on medicine and cookery, but she was actively involved in the productivity of the estate, as the later chapters testify: under her guidance were produced vegetables from the garden; woollen, linen, and hempen thread; dairy products; and malt, together with its end-products of beer and ale. If we add her activities in the yard, omitted by Markham, there would also have been eggs and various fowl for eating.

The wife's economic importance assured her of a status which, in practical terms, was close to being that of an equal partner with her husband. It follows, interestingly, that not only was the social status of the wife far higher than that of the unmarried woman, but, in a progression almost the reverse of the pattern of more recent times, the unmarried woman was accustomed to a life of menial domestic labour as a servant, whereas the wife assumed an almost managerial role, supervising the activities of the maids in the kitchen, the dairy, or the nursery.[43] Markham's description of "all or most" of "the worthy knowledges which do belong to her vocation" (i, 7) is eloquent testimony not only to the housewife's versatility, but to the extent of her responsibilities as she performed her many duties.

HER DUTIES

Skill in medicine

A satirical pamphlet written by Robert Greene about twenty years before *The English Housewife* shows incidentally how important the housewife's role was in the medical care of the family.[44] Cloth-breeches, a homely country fellow, and Velvet-breeches, a courtier, are choosing a jury to decide which of them is the more worthy. Cloth-breeches rejects both the surgeon and the apothecary because they will be biased in favour of Velvet-breeches, who provides them with their livelihoods. Cloth-breeches does not become involved in "brawls to make wounds," and he does not frequent whorehouses, so he has little use for the surgeon; he is even less enthusiastic about the wares offered by the apothecary:

And for you, M. Apothecary, alas, I look not once in seven year in your shop, without it be to buy a pennyworth of wormseed[45] to give my child to drink, or a little treacle to drive out the measles, or perhaps some dregs [punningly for drugs] and powders to give my sick horse a drench [dose] withal; but for myself, if I be ill at ease I take kitchen physic; I make my wife my doctor and my garden my apothecary's shop ...

Markham would certainly have approved the judgement of Greene's fictional character.[46] Cloth-breeches scorns an excessive dependence on the apothecary, and although some of the remedies used by Velvet-breeches appear in the medical chapter of *The English Housewife*, Markham would have enjoyed the sentiment if not the direct language as Cloth-breeches continues:

whereas queasy Master Velvet-breeches cannot have a fart awry but he must have his purgatives, pills, and clysters [enemas], or evacuate by electuaries [medicinal pastes]; he must, if the least spot of morphew come on his face, have his oil of tartar, his *lac virginis* ["virgin's milk," a cosmetic], his camphor dissolved in verjuice [apple vinegar – see iii, 31] to make the fool as fair, forsooth, as if he were to play Maid Marian in a May-game or morris dance ...

Markham recommends camphor in vinegar for the morphew (scaly skin), though he is silent about *lac virginis*. Cloth-breeches further attacks the apothecary, and the courtier, for trafficking in aphrodisiacs (one of which is eryngo – see ii, 115 and note), and attempting to cover a "stinking breath" by perfumes (see i, 69).

The decision of the grand jury – twenty-four are chosen, all of honest trades and callings[47] – is of course that Cloth-breeches is "most worthy," since he is "by many hundred years more ancient ... [an] equal with the nobility, a friend to gentlemen and yeomen, and a patron of the poor; a true subject, a good housekeeper, and [in] general as honest as he is ancient."

In order for Markham's housewife to be "a good housekeeper" she had to care for the "health and soundness of body" of her family; the long chapter on medicine makes it clear that Markham would have agreed with Cloth-breeches' belief in "kitchen physic." The actual remedies he records would have required a visit to the apothecary's somewhat oftener than once in seven years, but on the whole, compared to other medical works of the period, they are relatively "wholesome" (i, 8), and seldom as extreme as those sought by Velvet-breeches.[48]

The housewife is assured that she will not be asked to deal with the "depth and secrets of this most excellent art of physic," receiving instruction only in "some ordinary rules and medicines which may avail for the benefit of her family ... for the curing of those ordinary sicknesses which daily perturb the health of men and women" (i, 8). Nevertheless, the list of diseases and disorders is dauntingly long and, at times, horrifyingly detailed. Markham moves systematically from a discussion of general fevers to "particular sicknesses" (i, 56), beginning at the head and moving downwards, via the stomach, liver, belly and guts (i, 136), kidneys and bladder, to the diseases of the private parts (i, 169); he concludes with further general disorders not exclusively associated with particular parts of the body – burns, scalds, wounds, and aches.[49]

As in other popular medical works of the period, most of Markham's remedies belong to a tradition of medicine which dates back to such medical authorities of antiquity as Hippocrates, Dioscorides, Pliny, and Galen. The recipes taken from the Banckes herbal (1525; see above) certainly belong to this tradition, and there are many others similar in kind to those contained in late medieval medical manuscripts.[50] Perhaps because the "depth and secrets" of the art of physic were not the housewife's province, there are few remedies of a highly complex or dramatic nature. Markham does, however, cite two contemporary "authorities," Doctors Burket and Bomelius (see i, 8) as sources of the manuscript, and there are some recipes which make use of the elaborate compound medicines frequently recommended in medical text books: *unguentum aureum* (i, 205), *unguentum basilicon* (i, 195), *unguentum apostolorum* (i, 212), *balsamum cephalium* (i, 205), the remarkable cure-all, mithridate (i, 14 and iii, 16), and so on.

Markham's mention of Doctors Burket and Bomelius may well have been intended more to impress his readers than to record indebtedness, for both were figures of some fame (or notoriety) in an earlier generation. Dr "Burket" (more properly Burcot)[51] was originally a mining engineer from Germany, where his name was Burchard Cranach or Kranich; he had arrived in England by 1554, and was involved in a number of mining ventures, none of which appears to have been particularly successful. He then took up the profession of physician under the name of Burcot, and may have been the physician credited with curing the young Queen Elizabeth of smallpox.[52] Burcot's reputation with the progressive and energetic physician William Bullein was not so high, however, for in his *Dialogue Against the Fever Pestilence* (London, second ed., 1573) Bullein satirized him under the anagram of Dr Tocrub.[53] Markham's other authority, Eliseus Bomelius, was a remarkably similar figure; his popular reputation seems to have been high, but more informed opinion was critical. Bomelius was born in Holland, gained an M.D. from Cambridge, served a term of imprisonment for practising medicine without a licence, and died (1574?) in Russia. William Clowes, one of the most distinguished surgeons of Markham's day, mentions Bomelius in a context which is particularly unflattering; Clowes describes a charlatan from whom he inherited a disastrous case:

Then rises out of his chair fleering and jeering this miraculous Surgeon, gloriously glittering like the man in the moon, with his bracelets about his arms ... his fingers full of rings, a silver case with instruments hanging at his girdle and a gilt spatula sticking in his hat ... And now here he did begin to brag and boast as though all the keys of knowledge did hang at his girdle. For, he said, he had attained unto the deep knowledge of the making [of] a certain Quintessence which he learned beyond the seas of his master, one Bomelius, a great magician.[54]

In due course, Clowes was able to cure the charlatan's patient.

It is an interesting coincidence, connected no doubt with the popular appeal gained by both doctors, that Bomelius was called (however scornfully) "a great magician," while Burcot is alleged in at least two references, contemporary and near-contemporary, to have dabbled in the conjuring arts.[55] The same was said of many other figures in the period, some of whom were genuinely original thinkers; almost any student of natural philosophy would have spent enough time in his laboratory to gain a reputation as a magician.[56] It is unlikely that any of the recipes in *The English Housewife* came from the laboratory of either Burcot or Bomelius, though it is possible that the doctors' documents were in part the means by which traditional remedies were transmitted. If they were specifically responsible for any recipes, the most likely candidates are the elaborate "waters" prepared by distillation, of which there are examples both in the medical chapter and in the chapter (iii) specifically on distillation. Many of these distilled waters would have been simple perfumes derived from herbs high in essential oils, but occasionally the recipes preserve alchemical or magical rituals: the injunction to repeat a process nine times (iii, 15), or to steep ingredients in "the urine of a man child" and "the woman's milk that nourisheth a man child" (iii, 14; in each case the association with the male would be expected to give any effect greater potency).

Magical effects more associated with folk traditions also surface on occasion, as when a recipe (for gall stones) calls not simply for milk, but for "new milk of a red cow" (i, 155; see also i, 188 and note). The same

recipe for gall stones recalls another long-established belief when it recommends saxifrage as one of the herbs to be added to the milk; saxifrage
(the name is from Latin and means "rock-breaking") grows habitually in
cracks in rocks, and was therefore thought not only to break the stones
it grew in, but also to break stones in humans. A plant's appearance or
habit of growth was taken to give a "sign" of its medical effect, a belief
known as the "doctrine of signatures." Other well-known examples are
found in the text: saffron, because of its yellow colour, is "the most
present cure" for jaundice (i, 106); and euphrasy, also known as eye-
bright, was recommended in herbals for diseases of the eye because the
flower, with its black spot in the middle, resembles an eye (see i, 80).
"Sympathetic magic" is the term given to such beliefs, based on the
assumption that the appearance of an object reveals its innate powers.

A further, closely related belief which lay behind the choice of many
herbs and other substances in Markham's remedies was the principle of
antagonism. Humans, like everything else in the universe, were understood to be composed of four elements – earth, air, fire, and water – and
in their bodies the elements formed four corresponding humours, themselves expressing combinations of the four primary qualities: hot, cold,
dry, and moist. Disease resulted when the humours (and hence the qual-
ites) were unbalanced; the logical way to redress the imbalance was to
administer substances which had opposing or antagonistic qualities in
abundance. On the most literal level, "any scald or burning" could be
cured by oil and "snow water" - water which, having once been snow,
would keep its cold property the better. Less obviously, herbs which
were thought to be "cold" were to be used for fevers, while those which
were thought to be "hot" were given when the disease made the patient
sluggish. Hemlock, because of its poisonously sedative effect, was considered to be extremely cold, and was therefore used to treat the "hot
gout," fortunately only as an ointment (i, 190); radish water, on the other
hand, because radish is hot to the taste, was thought to induce sexual
heat, to "multiply and provoke lust" (iii, 16; see also ii, 115 and note).
Less pleasant to our sensibility is the extension of this principle to the
dung of animals noted for their sexual heat (i, 101 and note). The source
of excess heat in humans was the liver, seat of the choleric humour (hot
and dry); Markham explains in passing that "great heat and inflammation
of the liver" gives rise to such sicknesses as "pimples and redness of the
face" (i, 99) and ringworm (i, 112).

The same logic that sees excess of nourishment produce too much heat,
and thereby provoke "disease or putrefaction" (vi, 8; said here of cows,
but the principle applies to humans as well), sees "inflammation of the

blood" as the cause of fever (i, 15) and leads finally to the widespread practice of blood letting, as a cure for such supposed excess. Markham is unusually sparing in this regard, perhaps because bleeding would have been one of the "secrets of this most excellent art of physic ... far beyond the capacity of the most skilful woman" (i, 8).[57] Certainly in his books on the diseases of animals he recommends bleeding more freely. In *The English Housewife* he follows convention in recommending bleeding for a patient infected with the plague (i, 20), and he also suggests that a remedy for leprosy will be more successful if the leper "have some part of his corrupt blood taken away" first; but his readers would have been more likely to survive his remedy for the "green sickness" (anaemia in the adolescent girl, see i, 170) than the remedies in many of the medical books of the period, since blood letting was often the first step recommended.

There are other examples of the restraint and relative good sense of the remedies Markham selected for the housewife's use. Astrological medicine was at the time widespread, and had many academic and learned defenders,[58] yet there are very few astrological references in Markham's recipes, and when they do appear they are likely to be treated with caution. In recording a remedy for "the falling sickness" (epilepsy) gathered from the Banckes herbal, a document which Markham normally trusted, Markham includes instructions from his source concerning the phase of the moon and the astrological sign when a plant is to be picked – "morning and evening during the wane of the moon, or when she is in the sign of Virgo ..." – but he concludes the recipe with a distinct scepticism: "though this medicine be somewhat doubtful" (i, 37). A similar response is elicited when he passes on a folk remedy to "dry up milk" in a woman's breasts: "some are of opinion, that for a woman to milk her breasts upon the earth will cause the milk to dry" (i, 172; a similar logic led to the belief that masturbation would cause sterility), for he concludes carefully, "but I refer it to trial."

While no final judgement on the possible value of the herbal lore which Markham was in large measure transmitting is possible, since herbal medicine is still a subject of controversy, it is fair to say that Markham's medical advice is at worst unlikely to be harmful, at best practical and sensible (see the instructions on the application of tourniquets, i, 114, for example). He reminds the housewife that diet should be "wholesome and cleanly" (i, 6) at the outset, and later advocates, apart from specific medicaments, the general virtues of exercise in avoiding disease (i, 100) and abstinence in curing it (i, 157). Many of his recipes point out, in passing, the need for adequate nourishment and patience in the treatment of disorders; in the treatment of broken bones various herbs are to be administered, particularly of course "knitwort" (comfrey), but the instructions for splints, plaster, and diet are all of a practical good sense.

Although no claim could be made that Markham's medical advice shares the growing enlightenment of the best medical minds of the period, the general tenor of the chapter is less actively destructive than many comparable works. The sheer length and elaborateness of many of the recipes is an indication of the energy and concern expended by the housewife on the care of those under her charge. The preparations may not often have had direct influence on the disease being treated, but at least it can be said that for the most part Markham's housewife would have interfered little with the course of nature; in the constant fight against disease, she would have received advice which assured that she did not, unwittingly, join battle on the wrong side. The chapter on the whole is a sobering reminder of an often unequal struggle against "griefs," or disorders, no longer so grievous.[59]

Skill in the kitchen

Diet. It is appropriate that the chapter on cooking follows the chapter on medicine, for the medical writers of Markham's day, from the most popular to the most learned, were very much aware of the importance of diet.[60] Markham's division of the two subjects into different chapters is uncharacteristic of cookery books of the period, which habitually introduce medical remedies into the midst of recipes of a purely culinary nature. Conversely, a learned work on diet such as *Health's Improvement* (1655) by Thomas Muffett switches rapidly and naturally between medical comment and advice in the preparation of specific foods; on capons Muffett writes:

[A capon] helpeth appetite, openeth the breast, cleaneth the voice, fatteneth lean men, nourisheth all men, restoreth sick men, hurteth none but the idle, tasteth pleasantly, digesteth easily ... Concerning the preparation of them, I commend them roasted for moist stomachs; but being boiled with sweet marrow in white broth [see Markham ii, 483], they are of speedier, though not of stronger, nourishment.

Markham's categories are tidier and more logical than those found in other books of the period, but even they overlap at times. The "cordial caudle" he recommends for "consumption" is a variant on the simple soups (pottages) for which he gives recipes in the second chapter (ii, 43, 44); and at the end of a curious recipe, as much a practical joke as a dish, for a pudding disguised as a leg of lamb (ii, 67), he adds: "If into this pudding also you beat the inward pith [marrow] of an ox's back, it is both good in taste, and excellent sovereign for any disease, ache, or flux in the reins [flow from the kidneys] whatsoever."

Despite such awareness of the link between eating habits and health there can be no doubt that unavoidable inadequacies in diet and unfortunate fashions in food would have contributed to ill health in the housewife's family. The difficult time was the winter, when the garden and orchard were unproductive, and when fewer animals could be sustained on winter pastures.[61] Food in winter depended heavily on salted meats, particularly bacon (see "collops and eggs," ii, 22), salt fish (see the recipes for ling and herring, ii, 120 and 121), and "white meats" or dairy products. There are also a number of recipes for pickling and preserving fruits, vegetables, and butter (ii, 16, 17, 131, 147; vi, 29). When all else failed, tainted meat could be "recovered" by marinating it (ii, 126).

Lent, coming at the end of the winter, would have made the task of providing adequate nutrition and variety even harder. The pies made from salt ling cod and herring are singled out by Markham as "especial Lenten dishes"; in addition, the otherwise rather curious dishes "To roast a pound of butter well" (ii, 71) and "To roast a pudding on a spit" were devised to provide some relief from normal Lenten fare. The pudding disguised as a leg of mutton, mentioned above, may have sharpened the appetite of diners on fast days with a delicious sense of temptation resisted. A more ancient means of varying Lenten meals is mentioned in one of the letters written by Margaret Paston to her husband, in which she mentions her purchases of fish: "As for herring, I have bought an barrel-load for four shillings, four pence; I can get none eel yet. As for beaver, there is promised me some, but I might not get it yet."[62] The beaver became extinct in Britain largely because, on the authority of Pliny, its tail (but not the rest of the animal) was believed to be fish.[63] Fish were eaten all year round on fast days, "those days whereon eating of flesh is especially forbidden by the laws of the realm." The laws were retained for practical rather than for religious reasons: "[this] order is taken only to the end our numbers of cattle may be better increased, and that abundance of fish which the sea yieldeth were generally received."[64] Fish were also harvested from fresh-water sources, both from rivers and from specially constructed ponds in which they were farmed.[65]

In addition to the dietary problems posed by fast days and the difficulty of preserving food for winter, there was a prevailing suspicion concerning fresh fruit, an indifference towards vegetables, and a remarkable love for sugar. It was a commonplace in medical works of the period that fresh fruits were to be regarded with suspicion, "by reason that they fill the body with crude and waterish humours, that dispose the blood unto putrefaction."[66] Markham, not surprisingly, mentions only cooked fruits (see ii, 129 ff.). However, in its extensive treatment of salads and cooked vegetables *The English Housewife* is less conventional. Other cookery books of the period record the grand "compound sallat" (ii, 13), but little else; this may in part be because the preparation of vegetables was considered too basic to be worth mentioning, but there is much evidence to suggest that, particularly in wealthier households, the meals were made up largely of bread, meat, and puddings.[67]

One effect of a diet which neglected fresh fruit and vegetables was that the English were "often molested with scurvy, said to have first crept into England with the Norman conquest."[68] Markham does not mention scurvy specifically, but several symptoms for which he provides remedies would often have been the result of scurvy – stinking breath (i, 42, 69) and loose teeth (i, 67), for example.[69] The English were known to suffer from poor teeth; a visitor to England in 1598 said of the sixty-four-year-old Queen Elizabeth that her "teeth [were] black, a defect the English seem subject to from their too great use of sugar."[70] The price of sugar fell with its greater availability,[71] and by 1676 Sarah Fell was able to record the purchase of no less than a hundredweight of brown sugar in her household accounts (p. 315).

Cookery. An excess of sugar in the housewife's cookery is probably the first characteristic the modern cook will notice in Markham's recipes. Almost any dish was likely to be seasoned with sugar: salads (ii, 11, 12, 13); omelettes, fritters, and pancakes (ii, 25, 26, 27); broth (ii, 47, 48); boiled meat (ii, 50, 54, 57); stewed fish (ii, 55); roast meats (ii, 66, 70, 74); meat pies (ii, 114, 115, 116); and of course puddings, tarts, and all manner of "banqueting stuff and conceited dishes" (ii, 146). It comes almost as a relief to read in John Evelyn's *Aceteria* (1699) that "now sugar is almost wholly banished from all, except the more effeminate palates, as too much palling, and taking from the grateful acid now in use" (pp. 33–4).

Markham's housewife prepared food which was not only sweet, but, it seems, highly seasoned. Virtually every recipe requires that a number of herbs or spices – frequently both herbs and spices – be added. The housewife's garden would of course have supplied the herbs, and, like sugar, spices had become more available and somewhat cheaper with the development of the spice trade.[72] However, though many different spices are recommended for a typical recipe, there is no reason to believe that the quantities used were large; prices were still high enough to discourage extravagance.[73] It is sometimes said that the use of spices was stimulated by the need to mask the flavour of meat that was "far from fresh,"[74] but if this were so it is hard to see why spiced meat dishes declined in favour

over the next 200 years without any improvement in techniques for preserving meat. It is more likely that spices were used so ubiquitously for
the same reason that sugar appeared in so many recipes; they were suddenly available to the general public because of the increase of trade, and
it was a period in which there was an increased receptivity to new things
– new ideas, new religions, new political systems, and, it seems, new
flavours.[75] The frequency with which certain combinations of spices were
used suggests that the cook may have prepared a blend of ground spices
to add to the dishes, along the lines of the powders "fort" and "douce"
of medieval cookery; a jar containing some combination of powdered
cloves, mace, cinnamon, nutmeg, and ginger would have been used in
many recipes.

Markham's general instructions on seasoning explain that the cook can
readily correct the flavour of a dish if it is unsatisfactory, "altering the
taste by the alternation of the compounds as she shall see occasion: and
when a broth is too sweet, to sharpen it with verjuice [crab-apple vinegar,
see iii, 31]; when too tart, to sweeten it with sugar; when flat and wallowish [insipid], to quicken it with oranges and lemons; and when too
bitter, to make it pleasant with herbs and spices" (ii, 53). It is not surprising, in view of the quantities of sugar used, that verjuice, lemons,
and vinegar are recommended so frequently.

The seventeenth-century taste for extravagant flavours is admirably
documented in the "excellent sallat ... which indeed is usual at great feasts
and upon princes' tables" (ii, 13). Sweet flavours were to be provided by
raisins, figs, currants, "good store of sugar," and "more sugar"; sour,
bitter, and hot or spicy flavours were intermingled by the addition of
almonds, capers, olives, sage, oranges, lemons, and pickled cucumbers;
the base of the sallat was to be spinach, "cabbage lettuce" (head lettuce),
and "red cauliflower" (red broccoli). The ingredients seem to have been
chosen more for their expense and rarity than for any logic of the combination of flavours; almost everything in the sallat was imported, and
even the basic greens were chosen because of their relative rarity. It was
of such extravagant dishes that William Harrison wrote disapprovingly:
"the kind of meat [food] which is obtained with most difficulty and cost
is commonly taken for the most delicate, and thereupon each guest will
soonest desire to feed."[76]

Not all of Markham's recipes are so elaborate. He is careful to include,
often in introductory remarks of his own added to each section, instructions for the "general" housewife who would normally be concerned to
offer simpler fare. Simple sallats (ii, 11), poached eggs and bacon (ii, 22),
"ordinary" boiled meats (ii, 40), and the plain art of roasting meat are
all treated at some length. The English were, even in Markham's day,

famed for their roasts: "they are more polite in eating than the French, devouring less bread, but more meat, which they roast in perfection."[77] In the later chapter on oatmeal, writing more obviously from his own experience rather than transcribing the recipes of others, Markham has words of high praise for such simple country food as oatcakes, haggis, "washbrew," "flummery," "girtbrew" (viii, 9), and "whole [oatmeal] grits boiled in water till they burst, and then mixed with butter, and eaten with spoons, which ... seamen call simply by the name of loblolly" (viii, 10). The same paragraph echoes a substantial section of the chapter on cookery when Markham praises oatmeal sausages, or "puddings" (viii, 10; see ii, 32–9). The section of the final chapter which deals with baking is similarly concerned with instructions for simpler and more basic food.

The recipes for simple dishes, however, seem in large measure to be aimed at the poorer end of the spectrum of readers Markham had in mind; he does, after all, caution the housewife that she who is ignorant in the "pretty and curious secrets" of preparing food for a banquet is "but the half part of a complete housewife" (ii, 146). The seventeenth-century taste for sugar and spice dominates these dishes, but on the whole they are inventive only in the ingenuity used in devising different colours and decorative shapes (see ii, 138 and 140–2). The same ingenuity of design and sameness of flavour was found in the most elaborate banquets of the period. In 1591 the Earl of Hertford provided a lavish four-day entertainment for Queen Elizabeth, on progress through Hampshire; on the evening of the third day there was a display of fireworks and a banquet which included the following "sugar-work":

Her Majesty's arms in sugar-work ...
Castles, forts, ordinance, drummers, trumpeters, and soldiers of all sorts, in sugar-work.
Lions, unicorns, bears, horses, camels, bulls rams, dogs, tigers, elephants, antelopes, dromedaries, apes, and all other beasts in sugar-work.
Eagles, falcons, cranes, bustards, heronshows, cocks, owls, and all that fly, in sugar-work.
Snakes, adders, vipers, frogs, toads, and all kind of worms, in sugar-work.
Mermaids, whales, dolphins, congers, sturgeons, pikes, carps, breams, and all sorts of fishes, in sugar-work.[78]

Near the opposite end of the social spectrum, a humbler feast was to be prepared by Perdita for the shearing festival in *The Winter's Tale*; the Clown rehearses his shopping list just before he is robbed by Autolycus:

Let me see, what am I to buy for our sheep-shearing feast? Three pound of sugar, five pound of rice – what will this sister of mine do with rice? But my father hath made her mistress of the feast, and she lays it on ... I must have saffron to colour the warden pies [see ii, 130]; mace, dates, none, that's out of my note; nutmegs, seven; a race [root] of ginger, but that I may beg; four pounds of prunes, and as many raisins o' th' sun. (iv.iii.37–50.)

Perdita, for whom "nothing does or seems / But smacks of something greater than herself" (iv.iv.157–8), is apparently providing fare more noble than the shearers were accustomed to.

Striking a mean between the royal feast and the shearer's festival is the attractive section of *The English Housewife* on banquets, a part contributed by Markham rather than derived from his manuscript. Here he describes "the order or setting forth of a banquet" (ii, 190), and in particular the "humble feast ... which any goodman may keep in his family for the entertainment of his true and worthy friends" (ii, 192). Only sixteen "full dishes" (dishes "not empty or for show") are called for, with sixteen more fanciful concoctions, for a total of thirty-two dishes in all, a meal "which will be both frugal in the spender, contentment to the guest, and much pleasure and delight to the beholders."

The modern reader tempted to try some of Markham's recipes[79] will want to begin with something even more modest than this humble feast. It is important to realize that the instructions would have been written initially by a cook already fully accomplished, and would similarly have been intended for those who were familiar with basic techniques; for this reason, few precise instructions concerning quantities or methods were given. Today's recipes give meticulously precise quantities, but only the most insecure cook is likely to follow them exactly, as experience teaches how to adjust proportions "according to the fancy of the cook, or the will of the householder" (ii, 52). There is much in Markham's recipes to stimulate the culinary imagination; though few would venture upon "puddings of a calf's mugget [entrails]" (ii, 37), "a galantine or sauce for a swan, bittern, shoveller, or large fowl" (ii, 88), or roast cow's udder (ii, 77), there are many dishes well worth experimenting with. Notes to this section of *The English Housewife* are not primarily intended to provide a means of translating the recipes into versions which accord with modern taste; however, where a cookery book of Markham's period includes a similar recipe and provides more information on quantities or methods, the notes record the extra information in the hope that it will be of assistance. Unusual herbs and spices are identified in the Glossary.

Markham's sallats and pottages, with substitutions where necessary, are excellent. We are less accustomed to boiled meat, but some original pot roasts will result if the quantity of water is substantially reduced (see particularly the recipe for "a mallard smored," ii, 54). By use of an oven rotisserie or a barbecue some of the quality of his roast meats can be recaptured; the sauces to accompany meat are on the whole too sweet for modern taste, but there are several simple enough to reproduce (see ii, 81-4 for example). "Carbonadoes" were similar to our barbecued meats, though Markham obviously disliked the taste of smoke on the meat (see ii, 97), a taste now sufficiently sought after that artificial smoke flavour can be added to oven-cooked food. Baked meats were usually cooked in a tough pastry which stood on its own without the benefit of a pie dish, but many of the pie recipes can be adapted to slow-cooked casseroles or pot roasts (see in particular the "olive pie" [ii, 114], which has caught the attention of several cooks modernizing Markham). The fruit pies are little different from today's pies, though the "pippin pie" (ii, 129) made with whole cooking apples, is unusual and well worth a trial.

Skill in other housewifely secrets

Distillation. George Digby, Earl of Bristol,[80] begins one scene of his melodramatic tragi-comedy *Elvira, or, The Worst Not Always True* (1667) with a picturesque discovery:

[Stage direction] Here is to open a curious scene of a laboratory in perspective, with a fountain in it, some stills, many shelves with pots of porcelain and glasses, with pictures above them, the room paved with black and white marble with a prospect through pillars, at the end discovering the full moon, and by its light a perspective of orange trees, and towards that further end Silvia appears at a table shifting flowers.

"Silvia" is the heroine Elvira in disguise as a lady's maid: that the work in the laboratory was not limited to the maid is shown by the instructions she has earlier received from her mistress, instructions which also make clear to the modern reader what "shifting" flowers involved. Silvia is asked

> ... to gather store of
> Fresh orange flowers, and then carefully
> To shift the oils in the perfuming room
> As in the several ranges you shall see
> The old begin to wither; to do it well
> Will take you up some hours; but 'tis a work
> I oft perform myself.[81]

The extraction of perfume by infusion (or maceration) in oil was one of the simplest of techniques employed by the woman in her preparation of cosmetic and medicinal oils and waters (see i, 249 ff.).

Almost a hundred years before Digby provided this dramatic picture of the woman in charge of the mysteries of distillation and perfuming, Thomas Tusser epigrammatically located distillation as the job of the housewife; under "May's duties" he instructs her:

> *Wife as you will*
> *Now ply your still ...*
> The knowledge of stilling is one pretty feat,
> The waters be wholesome, the charges not great.
> What timely thou gettest, while summer doth last,
> Think winter will help thee to spend it as fast.[82]

Markham's chapter on distillation overlaps considerably with the chapter on household medicine, and there is little further to add by way of background here.[83] Knowledge of the art of distillation was made generally available in Europe by the publication in 1500 of the *Liber de Arte Distillandi* by Hieronymus von Braunschweig (Brunschwig, Brunschwygk); a larger version followed in 1512, and a translation into English by Lawrence Andrewe appeared in 1527. Braunschweig's aim was to popularize a technique hitherto known only to initiates: "Howbeit that the learned and expert masters of the science of alchemy have a knowlege, yet it is not open to all manner of peoples, whereof I shall make the first rehearsal" (sig. A1). The effect of distillation in the preparation of medicines was "a purifying of the gross from the subtle, and the subtle from the gross ... to the extent that the corruptible shall be made incorruptible and ... the material immaterial" (sig. A1); hence distillation would be expected to concentrate the virtues (real or supposed) of any herbs or other substances used. Distillation does indeed achieve this end in many cases: the fact that alcohol in particular could be concentrated added to a general belief in the medicinal value of distillates, as the many recipes for aqua vitae attest (iii, 6–10, 12, 14, 15). It is the connection with medicine rather than with alchemy which must have made the still one of the "necessaries" in the housewife's closet.

Her equipment would probably have been simple, though the books on distillation from the period are full of illustrations of complex and elaborate stills. Braunschweig gives instructions on distillation in a "common distillatory" which give a clear idea of the instruments and technique involved:

Ye shall lay sand under the pan of [the still]four inches of thickness. Thereupon ye shall set your pan of earth[enware] either leaded or glazed ... or else of copper ... Then lay therein such things as ye shall distil and set the helm upon it, then make a long small linen cloth wet in thin clay ... with the same cloth you shall stop [seal] your stillatory between the helmet and the pan. Then set a glass before it that the pipe [of the helm] hang in the glass; then distil. (Sig. B4–B4v.)

The helm or limbeck in which the distillate condensed. From Hieronymous Braunschweig, *Liber de arte distillandi*, trans. Laurence Andrewe, sig. A2v.

The helm, also known as the alembic or limbeck, was usually cone-shaped, with a spout coming from the lower lip to drain off the condensed liquid. Varying heats were used for distillation, ranging from the warmth of horse dung or the mild heat of the sun to the heat of fire insulated by ashes or sand (as in the example quoted); the hottest was achieved when the glass was "set boldly ... upon the fire and nothing between the fire and it but only an iron grate or an iron trivet" (sig. A1v).

After recording recipes for medicinal waters, Markham goes on to give instructions on the preparation of various perfumes. What is surprising about this chapter is that it omits all recipes for cosmetics, common in other books on medicine, cookery, and "secrets." No doubt Markham's puritan inclination led him to delete most recipes of this kind which he may have found in his sources, though his housewife, after diligent search through the earlier chapter on medicine, would have been able to keep her teeth white (i, 64 and 66), her eyes clear (i, 73), her face free from pimples (i, 198), and her hands smooth (i, 252); she could also have taken "a general bath for clearing the skin and comforting the body" (i, 242).

Care of wine. Markham justifies his inclusion of the chapter on wine by claiming that "It is necessary that our English housewife be skilful in the election [choice], preservation and curing of all sorts of wines, because they be usual charges under her hands, and by the least neglect must turn her husband to much loss" (iv, 2). Certainly, in larger estates, there would have been considerable quantities of wine to care for. The archives of Sir William Petre (?1505–72) of Ingatestone Hall record that on various occasions the wine-cellar held between 300 and 600 gallons of wine, mostly in hogsheads and puncheons (casks containing roughly sixty to eighty gallons).[84] In the seventeenth century the more austere establishment of the Fells (Margaret Fell was a leader in the Quaker movement) nonetheless recorded various expenses for wine, usually for runlets, smaller casks of a capacity of about eighteen gallons.[85]

Although these recorded quantities of wine seem large, they scarcely live up to the expectations of the chapter on wine in *The English House-wife*, where the recipes for the most part deal with the butt or pipe (126 gallons), or the tun (252 gallons). The source of Markham's chapter is discussed above; it is clear that he incorporated into a housewife's handbook a practical treatise on wine devised for the professional vintner.[86] That the vintner may not have been wholly honest is shown by the recipes for the adulteration of wine (iv, 3, 10, 11, and 35; see notes also).

The probability is that if she were confronted with a cask of wine that had gone sour or cloudy the housewife would indeed have employed techniques such as Markham records, though on a more modest level. Cookery books of the eighteenth century and after give what is perhaps a more accurate picture of the housewife's activities in the care of wine: Elizabeth Raffald's *The Experienced House-keeper* (London, 1769), for example, gives recipes for making home-made fruit wines, for curing any such wine that becomes acid, and for "fining" or clarifying wine.[87] Modern wine-makers, amateur or professional, use techniques similar to those recorded by Markham, but prefer to speak of albumen rather than egg-white, casein rather than skim milk, and so on (see iv, 3 and notes to "parel" and "milk").

It is difficult to identify some of the wines mentioned by Markham, for the Englishman's thirst for rich, sweet wine caused importers to go far beyond the traditional trade with France, to Alsace (iv, 8), the Rhine (iv, 18), Spain (iv, 2, 15), Crete (iv, 10, 11), the Canary Islands (iv, 21), and perhaps to Italy (iv, 36) and Cyprus (iv, 38). Such was the preference for sweet wines that they were often drunk with sugar to make them sweeter – one of Falstaff's many sobriquets was "Sir John Sack-and-sugar" (1 Henry IV, 1.ii.114).

Wool, hemp, flax; spinning, weaving, and dyeing. By the time Markham was writing, the textile industry had already become sufficiently established that much of the work in preparing cloth was done outside the home.[88] The instructions Markham gives both for dyeing and for weaving are prefaced by remarks which indicate that he did not expect the housewife to acquire skill in these crafts, but believed the knowledge to be useful, if for no other reason than to prevent fraud on the part of the tradesman:

Now as touching the warping of cloth [setting up threads on the loom in preparation for weaving], which is both the skill and action of the weaver, yet must not our English housewife be ignorant therein, but though the doing of the thing be not proper unto her, yet what is done must not be beyond her knowledge, both to bridle the falsehood of unconscionable workmen, and for her own satisfaction when she is rid of the doubt of another's evil doing. (See v, 21 and the passage by Greene quoted in the note; on dyeing see v, 4.)

Apart from weaving, the further stages of the preparation of cloth by beating and trimming it were carried out by the fuller and shearman (see v, 22). Even the job of spinning was often beyond the resources of the housewife, particularly if she had a large amount of fibre ready for spinning; the fibre, or "tear," was farmed out to others, often the wives or daughters of labourers.[89] Here too Markham advises caution: the fibre is to be weighed before it is sent out, and the housewife is to allow "an ounce and a half for waste at the most" (v, 47).

Preparation of the fibre of flax and hemp was the work of the housewife and her women. Almost a century after Markham's work, a Frenchman, Louis Crommelin, was highly critical of the skill of Irish housewives in the preparation of flax:

The manner of preparing flax in this kingdom ... was (and still is in many places) extremely pernicious and ruinous. First it is managed by women altogether ignorant as to the choice of their seed or oil ... They do not know when or how to pull their flax ... [and] they have no judgement when or how to water or grass their flax, so as to give it a natural colour.[90]

If the women were ignorant it was not Markham's fault, for he gives detailed instructions for all processes criticized by Crommelin. One of the most energetic activities of the housewife was "braking" and "swingling" the flax and hemp, two stages in separating the fibre from the waste material in the stalk (see v, 34 and 38); once again a later writer, Lionel Slator, inveighed against the inefficiency of the women's methods: "What must [Ireland] lose by the barbarous methods followed by the housewives? who have neither tools nor skill to use them if they had them."[91] Perhaps both Crommelin and Slator, with their obvious desire that men take over the job of beating hemp and flax, would have approved of the trickery of the chaste wife two centuries earlier, who captured her three suitors in turn and set each free only on completion of a task; the first was put to work braking, the second swingling, and the third spinning.[92]

The dairy

The dairy was certainly worth looking at ... such coolness, such purity, such fresh fragrance of new pressed cheese, of firm butter, of wooden vessels perpetually bathed in pure water; such soft colouring of red earthenware and creamy surfaces, brown wood and polished tin, grey limestone and rich orange-red rust on the iron weights and hooks and hinges.

Dairies changed little in the 200 years after *The English Housewife*, with the result that this description by George Eliot of the dairy at the Hall Farm in *Adam Bede*[93] would probably have won Markham's approval, though he might have been surprised by the rather idealistic atmosphere created by Eliot's romantic prose. Markham would certainly have approved of the emphasis on purity and cleanliness:

Touching the well ordering of milk after it is come home to the dairy, the main point belonging thereunto is the housewife's cleanliness in the sweet and neat keeping of the dairy house; where not the least mote of any filth may by any means appear, but all things either to the eye or nose so void of sourness or sluttishness, that a prince's bed chamber must not exceed it. (vi, 16)

The emphasis on cleanliness is typical of Markham's estimate of the ideal housewife's character, and reminds us that the chapter on the dairy, like most of the later chapters in *The English Housewife*, was written from his own experience and observation. Apart from a brief "lesson for dairy maid Cisley" by Thomas Tusser (pp. 100–1), there is nothing of any substance written in English on management of the dairy before Markham, no doubt because such feminine concerns as the dairy were ignored by writers more interested in masculine pursuits. The influence of Markham's views was considerable; his remarks on the choice of "stock wherewith to furnish dairies" (vi, 2–5), for example, were unquestioned for over a hundred years.[94]

The respect accorded Markham's views on the dairy was, on the whole, well merited. We may find little significance in a "crumpled horn" (vi, 4) as a sign of a good milch cow, but in the sections where he deals with the care of utensils, the churning and "potting" of butter (vi, 29), and the making and pressing of cheese, Markham offered his housewife excellent advice. To us he communicates no less effectively than George Eliot a picture of a domestic industry which provided not only a nourishing mainstay in the diet of the family, but also an extra source of revenue for the estate; the churning of butter was reserved for Tuesday and Friday to prepare for market days on Wednesday and Saturday, and to provide for the fast-days, Wednesday, Friday, and Saturday (see vi, 22).[95] A rustic character in Lodge and Greene's *A Looking Glass for London and England* cogently sums up the value of the cow in the ordinary man's diet: "Why, sir, alas, my cow is a commonwealth to me, for first, sir, she allows me, my wife and son, for to banquet ourselves withal: butter, cheese, whey, curds, cream, sod [boiled] milk, raw milk, sour milk, sweet milk and buttermilk."[96]

The productivity of the dairy was such that even a modest establishment would have employed a dairymaid. One of the few times Markham assumes that the housewife would be assisted by a servant is in this section (vi, 16); elsewhere, even in the "ordering of great feasts" when he refers to the various servants who would normally be employed, he conscientiously ensures that he "allow[s] no officer but our housewife to whom we only speak in this book" (ii, 191). Markham's milk maid is to "do nothing rashly or suddenly about the cow, which may affright or amaze her, but as she came gently, so with all gentleness she shall depart" (vi, 15). The image is so seductive that anyone but the severely practical Markham would have elaborated; George Eliot, with the advantage of the writer of fiction, concludes her description of the dairy, quoted above, by introducing the "distractingly pretty" Hetty, "rounding her dimpled arm to lift a pound of butter out of the scale."

Malting and brewing. Markham's introduction to the chapter on malting is unusual in that he takes some pains to justify his view that the office of the maltster belongs properly to the woman: "though we have many excellent men maltsters, yet it is properly the work and care of the woman, for it is a house work, and done altogether within doors, where generally lieth her charge" (vii, 1). Markham may have been more influenced by the trend than he realized, however, because the chapter on malting is the only place where he mixes (or confuses) male and female pronouns. The making of malt and the brewing of beer was increasingly becoming centralized in the large towns during Markham's time,[97] largely because of the considerable economic gains to be made by both maltster and brewer, an advantage Markham takes pleasure in describing: "to the fruitful husbandman ... [malt] is an excellent merchandise, and a commodity of so great trade, that not alone especial towns and counties are maintained thereby, but also the whole kingdom, and divers others of our neighbouring nations" (vii, 1).

We can be sure that Markham would have deplored the increasing monopoly of the large malt-houses and breweries, despite the prosperity they reflected, for he was consistently concerned that the housewife and husbandman should be as self-sufficient as possible. As in the passages

English country housewives carry the produce of their gardens and yards to market. From Georgius Braun and Franz Hohenberg, *Civitates Orbis Terrarum*, vol. 5, plate 1.

on dyeing and weaving, we are aware that Markham is hankering after days and ways which will not return. The absence of treatises on malting earlier than Markham's, like a similar absence of works on the brewery, the dairy, the preparation of hemp and flax, and the bakehouse, may indicate that, as women's work, it was a subject of little interest to male writers. The literature of the period, however, is rich in reference to malting and brewing. However much Markham may have regretted the mass production methods of "men maltsters" turning the malt with a shovel rather than by hand (vii, 21), the malt man was well enough established that he could appear as a character in a popular song. The ballad "Sir John Barleycorn" is detailed in its reference to the process of malting and brewing. "Sir John Barleycorn" is to die, but he proves difficult to kill. The processes of planting, growing, harvesting, and threshing the barley are described: Sir John is buried, then assaulted with "harrows strong"; the grain sprouts of course, and after further attempts to kill him with "hooks and sickles" he reaches the stage which concerns Markham in chapter vii, and it is here that the malting of Sir John is done by the malt man rather than a housewife.

> And then they knit him in a sack,
>   Which grieved him full sore,
> They steeped him in vat, God wot,
>   For three days' space and more.[98]
>
> Then they took him up again,
>   And laid him for to dry;
> They cast him on a chamber floor,
>   And swore that he should die.
>
> They rubbed him and they stirred him,
>   And still they did him turn,
> The Malt-man swore that he should die,
>   His body he would burn.
>
> They spitefully took him up again,
>   And threw him on a kill [kiln],
> So dried him there with fire hot
>   And thus they wrought their will.

The malting may have been done by a man, but the final moral – or admonition – of the ballad shows that brewing was still the province of the wife:

All you good wives that brew good ale,
God turn you from all tears;
But if you put too much water in,
The Devil put out your eyes.[99]

Another early account of the brewing of ale presents a somewhat less savoury image. John Skelton's Breughel-like picture of the ale-house run by Elinour Rumming includes, together with a parade of the remarkable characters who form Elinour's clientele (all women, incidentally), a description of the vat in which her "nappy" (heady) ale is made so potent:

The hens run in the wash-vat;
For they go to roost
Straight over the ale-joust [jug],
And dung, when it comes
In the ale-tuns [barrels].
Then Elinour taketh
The wash-bowl and shaketh
The hen's dung away,
And skimmeth it into a tray
Whereas the yeast is,
With her mangy fisties;
And sometimes she blens
The dung of her hens
And the ale together,
And sayeth, "Gossip, come hither,
This ale shall be thicker,
And flower [ferment] the more quicker."[100]

Markham's beer was less colourful in its ingredients than Elinour's, but he is certainly not understating the importance of beer to the household when he claims that it is "the drink, by which the household is nourished and sustained" (vii, 1; see also ix, 4). Water, as a drink, was justifiably suspect, so ale and beer were the staple drinks, even of young children.[101] Beer and ale would have provided valuable calories, minerals, and vitamins in the diet of the time,[102] quite apart from any effect the alcohol may have had in lightening the burdens of the day. It is characteristic of Markham's somewhat austere standards – the opposite of Elinour Rumming's – that while he approved of the nourishment provided by ale and beer, he was suspicious of its side effects, and deplored the fact that it was "in every house more generally spent than bread, being indeed (but how well I know not) the very substance of all entertainment" (ix, 1). He preferred the "labouring man" to drink the whey or "whig" left after the making of butter or cheese (vi, 34 and 35). The labouring man may not have shared Markham's opinion, especially in the winter, when "Both foot and hand, go cold," and a preference for ale could surely be excused:

> Back and side go bare, go bare;
>   Both foot and hand go cold;
> But belly, God send thee good ale enough,
>   Whether it be new or old!
>
> I cannot eat but little meat,
>   My stomach is not good;
> But sure I think that I can drink
>   With him that wears a hood [i.e. a friar].
>
> Though I go bare, take ye no care,
>   I am nothing acold,
> I stuff my skin so full within
>   Of jolly good ale and old.[103]

Other duties. Markham's account of the housewife's activities is so complete that it seems scarcely possible that there were housewifely duties which he did not mention. Nonetheless, partly because Markham chose to limit the housewife's sphere of activities to those "within the house" (i, 1), there are some he omitted. John Fitzherbert, in his *Boke of Husbandry* (London, 1525) includes "A lesson for the wife," in which after a brief homily on the evils of idleness, he summarizes her duties. The passage reminds us again that Markham chose not to include the activities of the mother with those of the housewife:

when thou art up and ready, then first sweep thy house, dress up thy dish-board, and set all things in good order within thy house; milk thy kine, feed thy calves, sile [strain] up thy milk, take up thy children and array them, and provide for thy husband's breakfast, dinner, supper, and for thy children and servants, and take thy part with them. And to ordain corn and malt to the mill, to bake and brew withal when need is ... Thou must make butter and cheese when thou may; serve thy swine, both morning and evening, and give thy pullen [fowl] meat in the morning, and when time of the year cometh, thou must take heed how thy hen, ducks and geese do lay, and to gather up their eggs; and when they wax broody to set them thereas no beasts, swine or other vermin hurt them ... And in the beginning of March, or a little before, is time for a wife to make her garden ... And also in March is time to sow flax and hemp ... and thereof may they make sheets, board-cloths [table-cloths], towels, shirts, smocks, and such other necessaries; and therefore let thy distaff be always ready for a pastime, that thou be not idle ...

With his list of activities only half over, it is with some sympathy that Fitzherbert interrupts his account by remarking, "It may fortune sometimes that thou shalt have so many things to do that thou shalt not well know where is best to begin." He continues nonetheless:

It is a wife's occupation to winnow all manner of corn, to make malt, [to] wash and wring, to make hay, to shear corn; and in time of need to help her husband to fill the muck wain or dung cart, [to] drive the plough, to load hay, corn and such other. (Sigs. I1v–I3.)

There is much here that is familiar, but, in addition to his mention of the children, Fitzherbert manages to add several activities to the housewife's duties: caring for pigs, hens, and geese, and assisting the husbandman, when needed, in the field. Markham had already written on poultry and pigs in *The English Husbandman*, so no doubt he felt it unnecessary to include further information on those subjects in *The English Housewife*. The same desire not to repeat himself[104] led to the rather sketchy and derivative passage on the kitchen garden, for he also has a larger and rather more useful treatment of gardens in *The English Husbandman*.[105] To these already extensive duties some writers add even more: the making of candles (Tusser, p. 174, "Wife, make thine own candle, / Spare penny to handle"), and the care of bees.[106]

If the sheer volume of the work expected of the housewife seemed excessive to Fitzherbert, it will seem even more so to a modern reader. An awareness of the burden placed on the housewife is perhaps a necessary corrective to the aura of the romantic and the curious which we now tend to associate with "the world we have lost";[107] the truth of the housewife's life of unremitting labour should never be far from the mind of the reader of *The English Housewife*. In addition to her domestic duties, she was faced with regular pregnancies, the constant presence of disease, and for the smaller landowner or the labourer, the threat of poverty. Markham's own life is a reminder of the difficulty of sustaining an adequate standard of living despite a combination of intelligence and hard work.

Whether the family was wealthy or poor, however, Fitzherbert reminds us again of the economic importance of the housewife. She is "Also to go or ride to the market to sell butter, cheese, milk, eggs, capons, hens, pigs, geese, and all manner of corn. And also to buy all manner of necessary things belonging to a household." Fitzherbert follows this passage with an injunction (quoted above) to the housewife and husbandman both to keep their accounts carefully, and to "be true either to other." There is ample historical evidence to show that some housewives not only kept accounts – witness the conscientiousness of Sarah Fell, whose records have several times been quoted in the notes – but sometimes took over the management of the whole estate, either because of her skill or because her husband was absent or dead.[108]

Women worked beside the men in the fields at harvest. From *The Roxburghe Ballads*, ed. Charles Hindley (London, 1874), vol. ii, p. 182.

The contribution that the housewife made to the domestic economy, and, within limits, the freedom she enjoyed, made her very much the partner of her husband; that she was required by her religious teaching to acknowledge her husband as her superior did not mean that she contributed less to the partnership. Indeed, by Markham's time something close to an effective equality in the marriage was taught in some books of religious instruction; William Whately's influential and popular book on marriage, *A Bride-bush* (1619), includes a passage which makes the familiar distinction in duties between husband and wife and goes on to stress their mutual interdependence:

In husband and wife the next point to godliness and honesty, is good husbandry and good housewifery ... He without doors, she within; he abroad, she at home; he in such things as befit his sex, she (in those that beseem hers), must be content to unite their pains for their profit, and to undergo the labour of getting their living in the sweat of their brows, and of eating the labour of their hands. Neither must be an idlesby, a do-naught, a loiterer; neither must be like a lame or gouty leg, that hath all the attendance, and performeth no service for it: but they must be partners in painstaking, as two oxen that draw in one yoke. [109]

Whately and Markham are both, in their different ways, examples of an awareness of the importance of the woman's role.

With the exception of cookery, earlier writers ignored women's work. Earlier works on medicine and distillation are clearly intended for male practitioners of those arts, and there are no publications before *The English Housewife* which deal with the activities he discusses in his other chapters. Even the later works referred to in the notes to these chapters are likely to be arguing that the job should be done by men. [110] Markham's housewife was in many ways in a period of participation in the life around her unequalled before our present century; though ranked below her husband in the ordered hierarchy of society, her status had been raised by changes in religious and social attitudes, and her economic importance had not yet been reduced by the steady shift away from home industry as men increasingly took over the medical care of the family, the brewing, baking, spinning, and eventually the dairy, leaving the housewife merely a *femme de ménage*, washing, cleaning, cooking, and making purchases of finished products with money earned by her husband. We are fortunate that in *The English Housewife* Markham has preserved so much detail of the Renaissance housewife's activities while she was still fully active.

This Edition

THE NOTES

The notes in this edition of *The English Housewife* have been prepared with both the non-specialist and the scholar in mind. The notes are intended to assist the modern reader by providing further information where appropriate. The glossary explains words which may be unfamiliar, and identifies (where possible) the many herbs mentioned by Markham, particularly in the chapters on medicine, cookery, and distillation.

Paragraphs have been numbered in this edition; cross-references to Markham's text and the notes to the text are given by chapter and paragraph number (ii, 12, for example). Works printed before 1800 are referred to in the notes by short title only; full descriptions will be found in the Bibliography. Where possible, passages from early works are identified by page or folio numbers; otherwise the binder's signature is given.

Modern works are identified fully in the notes. They are not included in the Bibliography unless they are mentioned often enough that a short title is used; all modern works of relevance to Markham and *The English Housewife* are recorded by subject in the appropriate note to the Introduction.

THE TEXT

The first edition of *The English Housewife* was published in 1615 as Book ii of *Countrey Contentments* (Poynter 23.1; *STC* 17342), "Printed at London by John Beale, for Roger Jackson." The first book of *Countrey Contentments* was *The Husbandmans Recreations* (see note to i, 1). Two further surviving editions of *The English Housewife* appeared in Markham's lifetime, both of which were revised by him. According to Poynter, all editions after 1615 appeared as a part of the collection *A Way to Get Wealth*, first published in 1623 (Poynter 31.4; *STC* 17395.3); the revised *STC*, however, retains separate entries for editions up to 1637. After the second edition of 1623, a further edition, revised by Markham, was published in 1631 (Poynter 34.5; *STC* 17353 and 17396). Though the edition of 1637 (Poynter 34.6; *STC* 17354 and 17397) claimed to be "now the fifth time much augmented, purged, and made most profitable and necessary for all men" it follows the edition of 1631. The present text, which uses the 1631 edition as copy-text, is the result of detailed collation of the British Library copies of the editions of 1615 (*1*), 1623 (*2*), and 1631 (*3*); the edition of 1638 was consulted on microfilm, and, to provide a check on later emendations, an edition of 1658 (Poynter 34.8) in the library of the University of Victoria was collated with *1*, *2*, and *3* above.

Edition *2* introduced substantial revisions and additions to *1*, and also a number of corruptions; edition *3*, which was the subject of further minor revisions, corrected some of the errors of both *1* and *2*, but introduced some further misreadings. Major additions and reorganizations in the two later editions are summarized in the table opposite (for specific material added, see the list at the end of the Collation).

In addition to the large-scale revisions recorded below, each edition was in places revised in detail. Some of the revisions involved corrections of errors (for corrections in *2* see Collation, i, 18, i, 42, and ix, 15, for example; for corrections in *3* see Collation, i, 29, i, 143, ii, 131, etc.). On occasion a later edition wrongly corrects an earlier (see Collation i,

1 (1615)	*2* (1623)	*3* (1631)
Chapter I (Medicine)	Systematically reorganized; many remedies *added*.	Follows 2.
Chapter II (Cookery, Distillations)	Many remedies *added* throughout; further section on wines *added*.	Follows 2, but subdivided thus: Chapter II (Cookery) Chapter III (Distillations) Chapter IV (Wines)
Chapter III (Wool, etc.)	Follows *1*.	Follows 2, but becomes Chapter V
Chapter IV (Dairy)	Follows *1*.	Follows 2, but becomes Chapter VI
	Chapter V (Malt) *added*.	Follows 2, but becomes Chapter VII
	Chapter VI (Oats) *added*.	Follows 2, but (misnumbered) Chapter VI.
Chapter V (Brewing, etc.)	Follows *1*, but becomes Chapter VIII	Follows 2, but misnumbered Chapter VIII

20 "pour it into," i, 195, iii, 16); the correct reading is revealed by the first edition, or by the source. Some obscurities persist in all editions, obviously because Markham was following a corrupt manuscript and was unaware of the correct reading; again these are occasionally to be corrected by reference to a source (see Collation and notes to the text on "euphrasy," i, 80; "dauke," i, 117; "dittander," i, 175; "In the month of April ... ," ii, 5; "hearing," iii, 16; and "will not," iv, 4).

In preparing *3* Markham occasionally introduced changes for what were apparently purely stylistic reasons (e.g., i, 88; ii, 25), though these often involved substantive changes of emphasis (ii, 34, for example). He also modernized or modified the vocabulary of earlier editions: "dewition" becomes "decoction" (i, 20; i, 34; i, 179), "walm" becomes "boil" (ii, 49), and "cheese press" becomes "cheese heck" (vi, 39). This edition takes *3*, Markham's final version, as copy-text, and accordingly follows all revisions unless they introduce ambiguity, or remove language of significant interest ("dewition," a word possibly invented by Markham, and unrecorded in the *OED*, is a good example). Frequently Markham's stylistic revisions in *3* involved the omission of words or phrases he evidently found repetitive; sometimes, however, an ingredient in a recipe is omitted, in which case the earlier reading has been retained, and the omission noted (see i, 253, ii, 29, ii, 28, iii, 6, etc.). Each later edition introduced inaccuracies, and by no means all of those introduced in 2 were corrected in 3. For errors in 2 followed by 3, see i, 22 ("live"), i, 188, and ii, 66 ("a loin"), for example; for errors introduced by 3, see i, 148, ii, 50, ii, 126 and vi, 27.

Except for words which have changed significantly in meaning ("sallat" rather than "salad," for example) the spelling has been modernized throughout. The punctuation has been modified only if the original meaning would have been unclear to the modern reader. Paragraph headings have been taken from the marginal side-notes in the original; paragraph numbers have been added in this edition for convenience of reference.

Summary of Sources and Close Parallels

The nature of much of the material that Markham was transcribing – medical remedies and cooking recipes – is such that an exact source can seldom be claimed with absolute confidence. Many cooks today have a card-index of recipes collected from friends and from printed sources, and it is obvious that much the same interchange, with its inevitable introduction of slight modifications both deliberate and accidental, was the rule in Markham's day.[111] Hence even close verbal parallels may indicate the use of a common source rather than a direct relationship; hence also a parallel passage which appears in a later text than Markham's may not indicate a direct borrowing, and may thus assist in solving textual problems, since it may represent a more accurate transcription of a common source rather than an emendation of Markham (two possible examples of this occur in the chapter on wine, see notes to iv, 21 and 24).

The present list, then, is a compilation of close parallels and sources. I have no doubt that more could be uncovered.

Chapter I. Markham in the 1631 edition of *The English Housewife* specifically mentions as sources for this chapter (or for the additions to it), "Dr Burket and Dr Bomelius," who he says passed on the remedies in a manuscript to "a great worthy Countess of this land" (see i, 8). No trace has been found of the Countess, but for Drs Burket (Burcot) and Bomelius, see above pp. xxx–xxxi. There is no evidence that either actually contributed to the manuscript Markham was using.

Known sources are basically three: the Banckes herbal (see above, p. xix), other works of Markham himself, and a long tradition of medicine which surfaces in several other works of the period, and of which early examples have been printed by George Henslowe, *Medical Works of the Fourteenth Century* (London, 1899), and W.R. Dawson, *A Leechbook, or Collection of Medical Recipes of the Fifteenth Century* (London, 1934).

1. Passages taken or compiled from the Banckes herbal (in some cases, indicated in the notes, only part of the paragraph comes from Banckes): paragraphs 30, 32, 33, 36, 37, 47–51, 53–5, 89–93, 98–100, 105, 109, 117, 118, 130, 134, 151, 156, 166, 168, 171, 176, 187, 188, 190, 197, 203, 206.

2. Passages which also appear in Markham's other works (with three exceptions, marked with an asterisk, all were taken initially from the Banckes herbal): *Cavelarice* (1607), paragraphs 31*, 48, 151; *Markham's Maister-peece* (1610), paragraphs 48, 195*; *Cheape and Good Husbandry* (1612), paragraphs 47, 90, 105, 134, 203, 206; *Countrey Contentments*, bk. i, *The Husbandmans Recreations* (1615), paragraph 196*.

3. Others: Paragraphs 66–9 appear both in Dawson and Henslowe (see above) as well as Thomas Moulton; paragraph 75 appears twice in Dawson, and in Moulton; paragraphs 56 and 214 in Dawson only; paragraphs 80 and 149 in Henslowe only; paragraph 79 is also found in *The Treasury of Healthe* (c. 1550) by Pope John xxi (Petrus Hispanus), translated by Humphrey Lloyd; paragraph 152 occurs in *A Booke of Soveraigne Approved Medicines and Remedies* (1577) and the manuscript published as *Arcana Fairfaxiana*, ed. George Weddell (Newcastle-on-Tyne, 1890).

Chapter II. Many of the recipes recorded in the chapter on cookery had appeared in various forms in previous books (and manuscripts) on cookery, as one would expect, for there is bound to be some unanimity on the way to prepare a basic dish like "white broth," for example (see ii, 48 and note). But a careful check of extant printed cookery books published before 1623 reveals that only three of these were possibly used by Markham: *A Book of Cookrye* (London, 1584), "gathered" by A.W. (paragraphs 33 and 79); *A New Booke of Cookerie* (London, 1617), by John Murrell (paragraphs 17, and 101–7); and *Delightes for Ladies* (London, 1602), by Sir Hugh Platt (paragraph 189, and iii, 8 below). For the rest, the best guess is that Markham used some kind of manuscript where recipes had been collected and modified for many years; he may have received the manuscript from his own family, or from the "Countess" he mentions both in the Introduction and in i, 8.[112] Paragraphs 3–9 on the kitchen garden were transcribed from a table in Surflet's *The Countrie Farme.*

Chapter III. This chapter illustrates how closely related were the arts of medicine, cookery, and perfumery, for we find the Banckes herbal,

The Countrie Farme, and Platt's *Delightes for Ladies* included in the sources. The passage from the Banckes herbal is interesting, for it shows that a late edition was used, since the passage on the "virtues" of waters (see paragraphs 16–21) appears only in editions of Banckes, 1552–60. The borrowing from Banckes is also evidence that Markham may have possessed the herbal himself, since the passages in the medical section which use the herbal appeared in the edition of 1615, whereas paragraphs 16–21 of chapter iii appeared first in 1623. Reference to this source also solves one difficult textual problem (see iii, 16, note to "hearing"). *The Countrie Farme* is used as a source for paragraph 22, and a passage almost identical to paragraph 8 is found in *Delightes for Ladies* (see notes to the text). Further parallels exist between paragraph 5 and *The Pathway to Health* by Peter Levens (London, 1582), between paragraph 34 and *A Closet for Ladies and Gentlewomen* (London, 1608), and between a part of paragraph 16 and Dawson, *Leechbook*, p. 301.

Chapter IV. The manuscript tradition, from which this chapter was taken, is discussed on pp. xvii–xix above, and in my article "The Mystery of Vintners," *Agricultural History*, l (April, 1976), 362–76.

Chapters V–IX. No sources or parallels have been located for these chapters.

The English Housewife

THE
ENGLISH
Huf-wife,

Contayning,

The inward and outward vertues which
ought to be in a compleat woman.

As, her skill in Physicke, Cookery, Banqueting-
stuffe, Diftillation, Perfumes, VVooll, Hemp, Flax,
Dayries, Brewing, Baking, *and all other things
belonging to an Houshould.*

*A Worke very profitable and neceffarie, gathered for
the generall good of this kingdome.*

Printed at London by *Iohn Beale*, for *Roger Iackfon*,
and are to bee fold at his fhop neere the great
Cunduit in Fleet-ftreete. 1615.

DEDICATION

*To the right honourable and most
excellentest of all ladies,
Frances, Countess Dowager of Exeter*

Howsoever (Right Honourable and most virtuous Lady)[1] this book may
come to your noble goodness clothed in an old name or garment, yet
doubtless (excellent madam) it is full of many new virtues which will ever
admire and serve you; and though it can add nothing to your own rare
and unparalleled knowledge, yet may it to those noble good ones (which
will endeavour any small spark of your imitation) bring such a light, as
may make them shine with a great deal of charity. I do not assume to
myself (though I am not altogether ignorant in ability to judge of these
things) the full invention and scope of this whole work; for it is true
(great Lady) that much of it was a manuscript which many years ago
belonged to an honourable Countess, one of the greatest glories of our
Kingdom, and were the opinions of the greatest physicians which then
lived; which being now approved by one not inferior to any of that
profession, I was the rather emboldened to send it to your blessed hand,
knowing you to be a Mistress so full of honourable piety and goodness,
that although this imperfect offer may come unto you weak and disable,
yet your noble virtue will support it, and make it so strong in the world,
that I doubt not but it shall do service to all those which will serve you,
whilst myself and my poor prayers shall to my last gasp labour to attend
you.

The true admirer of your noble virtues,
Gervase Markham.

CHAPTER I

Of the inward virtues of the mind which ought to be in every housewife. And first of her general knowledges both in physic and surgery, with plain approved medicines for health of the household, also the extraction of excellent oils for those purposes

1 Having already in a summary briefness passed through those outward parts of husbandry which belong unto the perfect husbandman,[1]* who is the father and master of the family, and whose office and employments are ever for the most part abroad, or removed from the house, as in the field or yard; it is now meet that we descend[2] in as orderly a method as we can to the office of our English housewife, who is the mother and mistress of the family, and hath her most general employments within the house; where from the general example of her virtues, and the most approved skill of her knowledges, those of her family may both learn to serve God, and sustain man in that godly and profitable sort which is required of every true Christian.

2   *A housewife must be religious.*
    First then to speak of the inward virtues of her mind; she ought, above all things, to be of an upright and sincere religion, and in the same both zealous and constant; giving by her example an incitement and spur unto all her family to pursue the same steps, and to utter forth by the instruction of her life those virtuous fruits of good living, which shall be pleasing both to God and his creatures; I do not mean that herein she should utter forth that violence of spirit[3] which many of our (vainly accounted pure) women do, drawing a contempt upon the ordinary ministry, and thinking nothing lawful but the fantasies of their own inventions, usurping to themselves a power of preaching and interpreting the holy word, to which

---

* Additional notes will be found on pp. 237–89. Unfamiliar words not provided
  with a note are explained in the glossary.

The title-page of Richard Brathwait's *The English Gentlewoman* expresses symbolically the conventional ideal of feminine behaviour touched on by Markham: "Grace my guide, glory my goal." Apparel is to be "Comely, not gaudy"; behaviour (she sets an example to her children) "Loving modesty, living beauty"; "Civil compliment my best accomplishment"; "Virgin decency virtue's livery" (she rejects beads and feathers); "Honour" is "virtue's harbour"; gentility (a family tree is illustrated) is not enough, as "desert crowns descent"; fancy is avoided as she looks at her husband's picture, "My choice admits no change"; and in estimation, "My prize is her own praise."

they ought to be but hearers and believers, or at the most but modest persuaders; this is not the office either of good housewife or good woman. But let our English housewife be a godly, constant, and religious woman, learning from the worthy preacher, and her husband, those good examples which she shall with all careful diligence see exercised amongst her servants.

3   In which practice of hers, what particular rules are to be observed, I leave her to learn of them who are professed divines,[4] and have purposely written of this argument; only thus much I will say, which each one's experience will teach him to be true, that the more careful the master and mistress are to bring up their servants in the daily exercises of religion toward God, the more faithful they shall find them in all their businesses towards men, and procure God's favour the more plentifully on all the household: and therefore a small time morning and evening bestowed in prayers, and other exercises of religion, will prove no lost time at the week's end.

4

She must be temperate.

Next unto this sanctity and holiness of life, it is meet that our English housewife be a woman of great modesty and temperance as well inwardly as outwardly: inwardly, as in her behaviour and carriage towards her husband, wherein she shall shun all violence of rage, passion, and humour, coveting less to direct than to be directed, appearing ever unto him pleasant, amiable, and delightful; and though occasion, mishaps, or the misgovernment of his will may induce her to contrary thoughts, yet virtuously to suppress them, and with a mild sufferance rather to call him home from his error, than with the strength of anger to abate the least spark of his evil, calling into her mind that evil and uncomely language is deformed though uttered even to servants, but most monstrous and ugly when it appears before the presence of a husband: outwardly, as in her apparel and diet, both which she shall proportion according to the competency of her husband's estate and calling, making her circle rather strait[5] than large, for it is a rule if we extend to the uttermost we take away increase, if we go a hair breadth beyond we enter into consumption, but if we preserve any part, we build strong forts against the adversities of fortune, provided that such preservation be honest and conscionable; for as lavish prodigality is brutish, so miserable covetousness is hellish.

5

Of her garments.

Let therefore the housewife's garments be comely, cleanly and strong, made as well to preserve the health as adorn the person, altogether without toyish garnishes, or the gloss of light colours, and as far from the vanity of new and fantastic fashions, as near to the comely imitations of modest matrons.

6   *Of her diet.*

Let her diet be wholesome and cleanly, prepared at due hours, and cooked with care and diligence; let it be rather to satisfy nature than our affections, and apter to kill hunger than revive new appetites; let it proceed more from the provision of her own yard, than the furniture of the markets, and let it be rather esteemed for the familiar acquaintance she hath with it, than for the strangeness and rarity it bringeth from other countries.

7   *Her general virtues.*

To conclude, our English housewife must be of chaste thought, stout courage, patient, untired, watchful, diligent, witty, pleasant, constant in friendship, full of good neighbourhood, wise in discourse, but not frequent therein, sharp and quick of speech, but not bitter or talkative, secret in her affairs, comfortable in her counsels, and generally skilful in all the worthy knowledges which do belong to her vocation; of all or most parts whereof I now in the ensuing discourse intend to speak more largely.

8   *Of her virtues in physic.*

To begin then with one of the most principal virtues which doth belong to our English housewife; you shall understand that sith the preservation and care of the family touching their health and soundness of body consisteth most in her diligence, it is meet that she have a physical[6] kind of knowledge; how to administer many wholesome receipts or medicines for the good of their healths, as well to prevent the first occasion of sickness as to take away the effects and evil of the same when it hath made seizure on the body. Indeed we must confess that the depth and secrets of this most excellent art of physic is far beyond the capacity of the most skilful woman, as lodging only in the breast of the learned professors; yet that our housewife may from them receive some ordinary rules and medicines which may avail for the benefit of her family, is (in our common experience) no derogation at all to that worthy art. Neither do I intend here to load her mind with all the symptoms, accidents,[7] and effects which go before or after every sickness, as though I would have her to assume the name of a practitioner, but only relate unto her some approved medicines, and old doctrines which have been gathered together by two excellent and famous physicians (*Dr Burket, Dr Bomelius*),[8] and in a manuscript given to a great worthy Countess of this land (for far be it from me to attribute this goodness unto mine own knowledge), and delivered by common experience, for the curing of those ordinary sicknesses which daily perturb the health of men and women.

9   *Of fevers in general.*[9]

First then to speak of fevers or agues, the housewife shall know those kinds thereof which are most familiar and ordinary, as the *quotidian* or daily ague, the *tertian* or every other day ague, the *quartan* or every third day's ague, the *pestilent*, which keepeth no order in his fits, but is more dangerous and mortal, and lastly the *accidental* fever which proceedeth from the receipt of some wound or other painful perturbation of the spirits. There be sundry other fevers which, coming from consumptions[10] and other long continued sicknesses, do altogether surpass our housewife's capacity.

10   *Of the quotidian.*

First then for the quotidian fever (whose fits always last above twelve hours), you shall take a new laid egg, and opening the crown you shall put out the white, then fill up the shell with very good aqua vitae,[11] and stir it and the yolk very well together, and then as soon as you feel your cold fit begin to come upon you, sup up the egg, and either labour till you sweat, or else, laying great store of clothes upon you, put yourself in a sweat in your bed; and thus do whilst your fits continue, and for your drink let it be only cool posset ale.[12]

11   *Of the single tertian.*

For a single tertian fever, or each other day's ague; take a quart of posset ale, the curd being well drained from the same, and put thereinto a good handful of dandelion, and then, setting it upon the fire, boil it till a fourth part be consumed, then as soon as your cold fit beginneth drink a good draught thereof, and then either labour till you sweat,[13] or else force yourself to sweat in your bed, but labour is much the better provided that you take not cold after it, and thus do whilst your fits continue, and in all your sickness let your drink be posset ale thus boiled with the same herb.

12   *Of the accidental fever.*

For the accidental fever which cometh by means of some dangerous wound received, although for the most part it is an ill sign if it be strong and continuing, yet many times it abateth, and the party recovereth when the wound is well tended and comforted with such sovereign balms[14] and hot oils as are most fit to be applied to the member so grieved or injured:

therefore in this fever you must respect the wound from whence the accident doth proceed, and as it recovereth, so you shall see the fever waste and diminish.

13   *Of the fever hectic.*

For the hectic fever, which is also a very dangerous sickness, you shall take the oil of violets, and mix it with a good quantity of the powder of white poppy seed finely searced, and therewith anoint the small and reins of the patient's back, evening and morning, and it will not only give ease to the fever, but also purge and cleanse away the dry scalings which is engendered either by this or any other fever whatsoever.

14   *For the quartan or for any fever.*

For any fever whatsoever, whose fit beginneth with a cold. Take a spoonful and a half of dragon water,[15] a spoonful of rose-water,[16] a spoonful of running water, a spoonful of aqua vitae, and a spoonful of vinegar, half a spoonful of mithridate[17] or less, and beat all these well together, and let the party drink it before his fit begin.

15   *Of thirst in fevers.*

It is to be understood that all fevers of what kind soever they be, and these infectious diseases as the pestilence, plague, and such like, are through the inflammation of the blood, incivilly[18] much subject to drought; so that, should the party drink so much as he desired, neither could his body contain it, nor could the great abundance of drink do other than weaken his stomach, and bring his body to a certain destruction. Wherefore, when any man is so overpressed with desire of drink, you shall give him at convenient times, either posset ale made with cold herbs;[19] as sorrel, purslane, violet leaves, lettuce,[20] spinach, and such like, or else a julep[21] made as hereafter said in the pestilent fever, or some almond milk: and betwixt those times, because the use of these drinks will grow wearisome and loathsome to the patient, you shall suffer him to gargle in his mouth good wholesome beer or ale, which the patient best liketh, and having gargled it in his mouth, to spit it out again, and then to take more, and thus to do as oft as he pleaseth, till his mouth be cooled, provided that by no means he suffer any of the drink to go down: and this will much better assuage the heat of his thirst than if he drank; and when appetite desireth drink to go down, then let him take either his julep, or his almond milk.

16   *For an ague sore.*

To make a poultice to cure any ague sore,[22] take elder leaves and seethe them in milk till they be soft, then take them up and strain them; and then boil it again till it be thick, and so use it to the sore as occasion shall serve.

17
[*Another.*]

To cure an ague sore by bringing it to a head: take alexanders and chop them small, then beat therewithal a little oatmeal, then seethe them well in milk, then take beer and put into it and there will rise a curd; then take the curd and lay it to the sore as hot as the party can endure it.

18
For the quartan fever.

For the quartan fever or third day ague, which is of all fevers the longest lasting, and many times dangerous, because many times consumptions, black jaundice,[23] and such like mortal sicknesses follow it: you shall take mithridate and spread it upon a lemon slice, cut of a reasonable thickness, and so as the lemon be covered with the mithridate; then bind it to the pulse of the sick man's wrist of his arm about an hour before his fit doth begin, and then let him go to his bed made warm, and with hot cloths laid to the soles of his feet, and store of cloths laid upon him, let him try if he can force himself to sweat; which if he do, then half an hour after he hath sweat, he shall take hot posset ale brewed with a little mithridate, and drink a good draught thereof, and so rest till his fit be passed over.

19
To make one sweat.

But if he be hard to sweat, then with the said posset ale also you shall mix a few bruised aniseeds, and that will bring sweat upon him: and thus you shall do every fit till they begin to cease, or that sweat come naturally of its own accord, which is a true and manifest sign that the sickness decreaseth.

20
Of the pestilent fever.

For the pestilent fever,[24] which is a continual sickness full of infection, and mortality, you shall cause the party first to be let blood,[25] if his strength will bear it: then you shall give him cool juleps made of endive or succory[26] water, the syrup of violets, conserve of barberries, and the juice of lemons, well mixed and symbolized together. Also you shall give him to drink almond milk made with the dewition[27] of cool herbs, as violet leaves, strawberry leaves, French mallows,[28] purslane, and such like; and if the party's mouth shall through the heat of his stomach or liver inflame or grow sore, you shall wash it with the syrup of mulberries; and that will not only heal it, but also strengthen his stomach. If (as it is most common in this sickness) the party shall grow costive, you shall give him a suppository made of honey, boiled to the height[29] of hardness, which you shall know by cooling a drop thereof, and so if you find it hard, you shall then know that the honey is boiled sufficiently; then put salt to it, and so pour it into water, and work it into a roll in the manner of a suppository,[30] and so administer it, and it most assuredly bringeth no hurt, but ease to the party, of what age or strength soever he be. During his sickness, you shall keep him from all manner of strong drinks, or hot spices, and then there is no doubt of his recovery.

21 ### A preservative against the plague.

To preserve your body from the infection of the plague, you shall take a quart of old ale, and after it hath risen upon the fire and hath been scummed, you shall put thereinto of *aristolochia longa*,[31] of angelica,[32] and of celandine of each half a handful, and boil them well therein; then strain the drink through a clean cloth, and dissolve therein a dram of the best mithridate, as much ivory finely powdered and searced, and six spoonful of dragon water, then put it up in a close glass; and every morning fasting take five spoonful thereof, and after bite and chaw in your mouth the dried root of angelica, or smell, as on a nosegay, to the tasselled end of a ship rope, and they will surely preserve you from infection.

22 ### For infection of the plague.

But if you be infected with the plague, and feel the assured signs thereof, as pain in the head, drought, burning, weakness of stomach and such like, then you shall take a dram of the best mithridate, and dissolve it in three or four spoonful of dragon water, and immediately drink it off, and then with hot cloths or bricks made extreme hot, and laid to the soles of your feet after they have been wrapped in woollen cloths, compel the sick party to sweat, which if he do, keep him moderately therein till the sore begin to rise; then to the same apply a live pigeon cut in two parts, or else a plaster[33] made of the yolk of an egg, honey, herb of grace[34] chopped exceeding small, and wheat flour, which in very short space will not only ripen, but also break the same without any other incision; then after it hath run a day or two you shall apply a plaster of melilot[35] unto it until it be whole.

23 ### [ADDITION.] For the pestilence.

Take featherfew, maleselon,[36] scabious, and mugwort,[37] of each a like, bruise them and mix them with old ale, and let the sick drink thereof six spoonful, and it will expel the corruption.

Another.

24 Take yarrow,[38] tansy, featherfew, of each a handful, and bruise them well together, then let the sick party make water into the herbs, then strain them, and give it the sick to drink.

A preservative against the pestilence.

25 Take of sage, rue, briar leaves, elder leaves, of each a handful, stamp them and strain them with a quart of white wine, and put thereto a little ginger, and a good spoonful of the best treacle, and drink thereof morning and evening.

To draw a plague botch to any place you will.

26 Take smallage, mallows,[39] wormwood, and rue, stamp them well together, and fry them in oil olive till they be thick, plasterwise apply it to the place where you would have it rise, and let it lie until it break, then to heal it up, take the juice of smallage, wheat flour, and milk, and boil them to a poultice, and apply it morning and evening till it be whole.

A cordial for any infection at the heart.

27 Take of borage, langdebeef,[40] and calamint, of each a good handful, of hart's-tongue, red mint, violets, and marigolds, of each half a handful, boil them in white wine, or fair running water, then add a pennyworth of the best saffron, and as much sugar, and boil them over again well, then strain it into an earthen pot, and drink thereof morning and evening, to the quantity of seven spoonfuls.

Against too violent sweating.

28 Take linseed, and lettuce, and bruise it well, then apply it to the stomach, and remove it once in four hours.

For the headache.

29 For the headache, you shall take of rose-water, of the juice of camomile, of woman's milk, and of strong wine vinegar, of each two spoonful; mix them together well upon a chafing-dish of coals, then take of a piece of a dry rose cake[41] and steep it therein, and as soon as it hath drunk up the liquor and is thoroughly hot, take a couple of sound nutmegs grated to powder, and strew them upon the rose cake; then breaking it into two parts, bind it on each side upon the temples of the head, and so let the party lie down to rest, and the pain will in a short space be taken from him.

30
For the frenzy.

For frenzy[42] or inflammation of the cauls of the brain, you shall cause the juice of beets to be with a syringe squirted up into the patient's nostrils, which will purge and cleanse his head exceedingly; and then give him to drink posset ale, in which violet leaf and lettuce hath been boiled, and it will suddenly bring him to a very temperate mildness, and make the passion of frenzy forsake him.

31
For the lethargy.

For the lethargy[43] or extreme drowsiness, you shall by all violent means, either by noise or other disturbances, force perforce keep the party from sleeping; and whensoever he calleth for drink, you shall give him white wine and hyssop water of each a little quantity mixed together, and not suffer him to sleep above four hours in four and twenty, till he come to his former wakefulness, which as soon as he hath recovered, you shall then forthwith purge his head with the juice of beets squirted up into his nostrils as is before showed.

32
To provoke sleep.

But if any of the family be troubled with too much watchfulness, so that they cannot by any means take rest, then to provoke the party to sleep, you shall take of saffron a dram dried, and beaten to powder, and as much lettuce seed also dried, and beaten to powder, and twice as much white poppy seed beaten also to powder, and mix these with woman's milk till it be a thick salve, and then bind it to the temples of the head and it will soon cause the party to sleep; and let it lie on not above four hours.

33
For the swimming of the head.

For the swimming or dizzying in the head, you shall take of *agnus castus*,[44] of broomwort,[45] and of camomile dried, of each two drams;[46] mix it with the juice of ivy, oil of roses[47] and white wine, of each a like quantity, till it come to a thick salve: and then bind it to the temples of the head, and it will in short space take away the grief.

34
For the palsy.

For the apoplexy or palsy[48] the strong scent or smell of a fox is exceeding sovereign, or to drink every morning half a pint of the dewition of lavender, and to rub the head every morning and evening exceeding hard with a very clean coarse cloth, whereby the humours[49] may be dissolved and dispersed into the outward parts of the body: by all means for this infirmity keep your feet safe from cold or wet, and also the nape of your neck, for from those parts it first getteth the strength of evil and un-avoidable pains.

For a new cough.

35 For a cough or cold but lately taken, you shall take a spoonful of sugar finely beaten and searced, and drop into it of the best aqua vitae, until all the sugar be wet through, and can receive no more moisture. Then, being ready to lie down to rest, take and swallow the spoonful of sugar down; and so cover you warm in your bed, and it will soon break and dissolve the cold.

For an old cough.

36 But if the cough be more old and inveterate, and more inwardly fixed to the lungs, take of the powder of betony, of the powder of caraway seeds, of the powder of skirret dried, of the powder of hound's-tongue, and of pepper, finely beaten, of each two drams, and mixing them well with clarified honey, make an electuary[50] thereof and drink it morning and evening for nine days together. Then take of sugar candy coarsely beaten an ounce, of liquorice finely pared and trimmed and cut into very little small slices as much, of aniseeds and coriander seeds half an ounce; mix all these together, and keep them in a paper in your pocket, and ever in the day time when the cough offendeth you, take as much of this dredge,[51] as you can hold between your thumb and fingers, and eat it, and it will give ease to your grief. And in the night when the cough or rheum offendeth you, take as much of the juice of liquorice as two good barley corns, and let it melt in your mouth, and it will give you ease.

For the falling sickness.

37 Although the falling sickness be seldom or never to be cured, yet if the party which is troubled with the same will but morning and evening during the wane of the moon, or when she is in the sign Virgo, eat the berries of the herb asterion,[52] or bear the herbs about him next to his bare skin, it is likely he shall find much ease and fall very seldom, though this medicine be somewhat doubtful.

For the falling evil.

38 For the falling evil, take, if it be a man, a female mole, if a woman a male mole, and take them in March, or else April, when they go to the buck:[53] then dry it in an oven, and make powder of it whole as you take it out of the earth; then give the sick person of this powder to drink evening and morning for nine or ten days together.

39
Of an oil to help hearing.

To take away deafness, take a grey eel with a white belly and put her into a sweet earthen pot quick,[54] and stop the pot very close with an earthen cover, or some such hard substance: then dig a deep hole in a horse dunghill,[55] and set it therein, and cover it with the dung, and so let it remain a fortnight, and then take it out and clear out the oil which will come of it, and drop it into the imperfect ear, or both if both be imperfect.

40
For the rheum.

To stay the flux of the rheum,[56] take sage and dry it before the fire, and rub it to powder: then take bay salt[57] and dry it and beat it to powder; and take a nutmeg and grate it, and mix them all together, and put them in a long linen bag, then heat it upon a tile stone, and lay it to the nape of the neck.

41
For a stinking breath.

For a stinking breath, take oak buds when they are newly budded out, and distil them; then let the party grieved nine mornings and nine evenings drink of it, then forbear a while, and after take it again.

42
A vomit for an ill breath.

To make a vomit for a strong stinking breath, you must take of *antimonium*[58] the weight of three barley corns, and beat it very small, and mix it with conserve of roses and give the patient to eat in the morning; then let him take nine days together the juice of mints and sage, then give him a gentle purgation, and let him use the juice of mint and sage longer. This medicine must be given in the spring of the year, but if the infirmity come for want of digestion in the stomach, then take mints, coarse marjoram,[59] and wormwood, and chop them small and boil them in malmsey till it be thick, and make a plaster of it, and lay it to the stomach.

43
For the toothache.

For the toothache, take a handful of daisy roots, and wash them very clean and dry them with a cloth, and then stamp them, and when you have stamped them a good while, take the quantity of half a nutshell full of bay salt, and strew it amongst the roots, and then when they are very well beaten, strain them through a clean cloth: then grate some *cattham aromaticus*,[60] and mix it good and stiff with the juice of the roots, and when you have done so, put it into a quill and snuff it up into your nose, and you shall find ease.

Another.

44 Another for the toothache: take small sage, rue, smallage, featherfew, wormwood and mints, of each of them half a handful, then stamp them well all together, putting thereto four drams of vinegar, and one dram of bay salt, with a pennyworth of good aqua vitae; stir them well together, then put it between two linen clouts of the bigness of your cheek, temples, and jaw, and quilt it in manner of a coarse embroidery; then set it upon a chafing-dish of coals, and as hot as you may abide it, lay it over that side where the pain is, and lay you down upon that side, and as it cools warm it again, or else have another ready warm to lay on.

A drink for a pearl in the eye.

45 To make a drink to destroy any pearl or film in the eye: take a good handful of marigold plants, and a handful of fennel, as much of may-weed,[61] and beat them together, then strain them with a pint of beer, then put it into a pot and stop it close that the strength may not go out; then let the offended party drink thereof when he is in bed, and lie of that side on which the pearl is, and likewise drink of it in the morning next his heart when he is risen.

For pain in the eyes.

46 For pain in the eyes, take milk when it comes new from the cow, and having siled it into a clean vessel, cover it with a pewter dish, and the next morning take off the dish and you shall see a dew upon the same, and with that dew wash the pained eyes, and it will ease them.

For dim eyes.

47 For dim eyes:[62] take wormwood, beaten with the gall of a bull, and then strain it and anoint the eyes therewith, and it will clear them exceedingly.

For sore eyes.

48 For sore eyes,[63] or bloodshotten eyes: take the white of an egg beaten to oil, as much rose-water, and as much of the juice of houseleek, mix them well together, then dip flat pledgets of flax therein, and lay them upon the sore eyes, and as they dry, so renew them again, and wet them, and thus do till the eyes be well.

For watery eyes.

49 For watery eyes, take the juice of affodil, myrrh, and saffron, of each a little, and mix it with twice so much white wine, then boil it over the fire, then strain it and wash the eyes therewith, and it is a present help.

50   *For a canker.*

For a canker or any sore mouth: take chervil and beat it to a salve with old ale and alum[64] water, and anoint the sore therewith, and it will cure it.

51   *A swelled mouth.*

For any swelling in the mouth: take the juice of wormwood, camomile, and skirret,[65] and mix them with honey, and bathe the swelling therewith, and it will cure it.

52   *For the quinsy.*

For the quinsy,[66] or quinancy, give the party to drink the herb mouse-ear steeped in ale or beer, and look where you see a swine rub himself, and there upon the same place rub a slate stone, and then with it slate all the swelling, and it will cure it.

53   *Against drunkenness.*

If you would not be drunk, take the powder of betony and coleworts[67] mixed together; and eat it every morning fasting, as much as will lie upon a sixpence, and it will preserve a man from drunkenness.

54   *To quicken the wit.*

To quicken a man's wits, spirits, and memory; let him take langdebeef, which is gathered in June or July, and beating it in a clean mortar, let him drink the juice thereof with warm water, and he shall find the benefit.

55   *For the King's evil.*

If a man be troubled with the King's evil,[68] let him take the red dock[69] and seethe it in wine till it be very tender, then strain it, and so drink a good draught thereof, and he shall find great ease from the same: especially if he do continue the use thereof.

56   *ADDITIONS to the particular sicknesses, and first of the head and the parts thereof and the lungs. [For the Headache.]*

·Take frankincense,[70] doves' dung, and wheat flour, of each an ounce, and mix them well with the white of an egg, then plasterwise apply it where the pain is.·

57   *[Another.]*

The oil of lilies if the head be anointed therewith, is good for any pain therein.

58
Another.

Take rue, and steep it in vinegar a day and a night, the rue being first well bruised, then with the same anoint the head twice or thrice a day.

59
For the headache and to stay bleeding at the nose.

Take the white of an egg and beat it to oil, then put to it rose-water, and the powder of alabaster,[71] then take flax and dip it therein and lay it to the temples, and renew it two or three times a day.

60
To draw out bones broken in the head.

Take agrimony[72] and bruise it, and plasterwise apply it to the wound, and let the party drink the juice of betony, and it will expel the bones, and heal the wound.

61
For the falling of the mould of the head.[73]

Take the leaves of agrimony, and boil them in honey, till it be thick like a plaster, and then apply it to the wound of the head warm.

62
For the squinancy.[74]

Take a table napkin or any linen cloth, and wet it in cold water, and when you go to bed apply it to the swelling and lie upright; thus do three or four times in a night till the swelling wastes.

63
For the toothache.

Take two or three dock roots, and as many daisy roots, and boil them in water till they be soft, then take them out of the water, and boil them well over again in oil olive, then strain them through a clean cloth, and anoint the pained tooth therewith, and keep your mouth close, and it will not only take away the pain, but also ease any megrim or grief in the head.

64
To make teeth white.

Take a saucer of strong vinegar, and two spoonfuls of the powder of roche alum,[75] a spoonful of white salt, and a spoonful of honey; seethe all these till it be as thin as water, then put it into a close vial and keep it, and when occasion serves wash your teeth therewith, with a rough cloth, and rub them soundly, but not to bleed.

65
To draw teeth without iron.

Take some of the green of the elder tree, or the apples of oak trees and with either of these rub the teeth and gums and it will loosen them so as you may take them out.

66 *For teeth that are yellow.*

Take sage and salt, of each alike, and stamp them well together, then bake it till it be hard, and make a fine powder thereof, then therewith rub the teeth evening and morning and it will take away all yellowness.[76]

67 *For teeth that are loose.*

First let them blood, then take hartshorn[77] or ivory, and red pimpernel, and bruise them well together, then put it into a linen cloth and lay it to the teeth, and it will fasten them.

68 *For any venom in the ear.*

Take the juice of lovage and drop it into the ear, and it will cure any venom, and kill any worm, earwig, or other vermin.

69 *For a stinking breath which cometh from the stomach.*

Take two ounces of cumin[78] and beat it in a mortar to fine powder, then boil it in wine from a pottle to a quart, then drink thereof morning and evening as hot as you can suffer it: or otherwise take an ounce of wild thyme, and being clean washed cut it small and then powder it, then put to it half an ounce of pepper in fine powder, and as much cumin; mix them all well together, and boil them in a pottle of white wine till half be consumed, and after meat (but not before) use to drink thereof hot; also once in the afternoon and at your going to bed, and it will purge the breath.

70 *For stinking nostrils.*

Take red nettles[79] and burn them to powder, then add as much of the powder of pepper, and mix them well together, and snuff thereof up into the nose, and thus do divers times a day.

71 *For a canker in the nose.*

Take old ale, and having boiled it on the fire, and cleansed it, add thereto a pretty quantity of life honey[80] and as much alum, then with a syringe or such like wash the sores therewith very warm.

72 *A red water for any canker.*

Take a gallon of running water, and boil it to a pottle, then put to it a handful of red sage, a handful of celandine, a handful of honeysuckles, a handful of woodbine leaves and flowers, then take a pennyworth of grains[81] made into fine powder, and boil all very well together, then put to it a quart of the best life honey of a year old, and a pound of roche alum, let all boil together till it come to a pottle, then strain it and put it into a close vessel, and therewith dress and anoint the sores as occasion serves; it will heal any canker or ulcer, and cleanse any wound. It is best to be made at midsummer.

To clear the eyes.

73
Take the flowers and roots of primrose clean washed in running water, then boil them in fair running water the space of an hour, then put thereto a pretty quantity of white copperas, and then strain all through a linen cloth and so let it stand a while, and there will an oil appear upon the water; with that oil anoint the lids and the brows of your eyes, and the temples of your head, and with the water wash your eyes, and it is most sovereign.

Another for the sight.

74
Take fifteen seeds of juniper, and as many gromwell seeds, five branches of fennel, beat them all together, then boil them in a pint of old ale till three parts be wasted, then strain it into a glass, and drop thereof three drops into each eye at night, and wash your eyes every morning for the space of fifteen days with your own water, and it will clear any decayed sight whatsoever.

For sore eyes.

75
Take red snails, and seethe them in fair water, and then gather the oil that ariseth thereof, and therewith anoint your eyes morning and evening.[82]

For sick eyes.

76
Take a gallon or two of the dregs of strong ale, and put thereto a handful or two of cumin, and as much salt, and then distil it in a limbeck,[83] and the water is most precious to wash eyes with.

For bleared eyes.

77
Take celandine, rue, chervil, plantain,[84] and anise, of each alike, and as much fennel as of all the rest, stamp them all well together, then let it stand two days and two nights, then strain it very well and anoint your eyes morning and evening therewith.

For the pin and web[85] in the eye.

78
Take an egg, and roast it extreme hard, then take the white being very hot and lap in it as much white copperas as a pease and then violently strain it through a fine cloth, then put a good drop thereof into the eye, and it is most sovereign.

79   *A powder for the pin and the web in the eye.*
Take two drams of prepared tutia, of sandragon[86] one dram, of sugar a dram, bray them all very well together till they be exceeding small, then take of the powder and blow a little thereof into the eye, and it is sovereign.

"Eyebright." From John Gerarde,
*The Herball, or General Historie of
Plantes*, p. 537.

80   *A precious water for the eyes.*[87]
Take of red rose leaves, of smallage, of maidenhair, euphrasy,[88] endive, succory, red fennel, hillwort,[89] and celandine, of each half a quarter of a pound, wash them clean and lay them in steep in white wine a whole day, then still them in an ordinary still, and the first water will be like gold, the second like silver, and the third like balm; any of these is most precious for sore eyes, and hath recovered sight lost for the space of ten years, having been used but four days.

81   *To make hair to grow.*
Take the leaves of willow and boil them well in oil and therewith anoint the place where you would have any hair to grow, whether upon head or beard.

82   *Another.*
Take treacle water and honey, boil them together, and wet a cloth

therein, and lay it where you would have hair to grow, and it will come speedily.

For a pimpled or red-saucy[90] face.

Take nine or ten eggs and roast them very hard, then put away the yolks, and bray the whites very small with three or four ounces of white copperas till it be come to perfect ointment, then with it anoint the face morning and evening for the space of a week and more.

For the rheum.

Take the rind of hyssop,[91] and boil it or burn it and let the fume or smoke go into the mouth and it will stay any rheum falling from the head.

For hoarseness in the throat.

Take a pint of running water, and three spoonfuls of honey, and boil them together and skim off the filth, then put thereto an ounce of small raisins, and strain it well through a cloth, and so drink it morning and evening.

For a dangerous cough.

Take aqua vitae and salt, and mix it with strong old ale and then heat it on the fire, and therewith wash the soles of the feet when you go to bed.

For the dry cough.

Take of clean wheat and of clean barley of each a like quantity, and put them into a gallon and a half of fair water, and boil them till they burst, then strain it into a clean vessel, and add thereto a quartern[92] of fine liquorice powder, and two pennyworth of gum arabic, then boil it over again and strain it, and keep it in a sweet vessel, and drink thereof morning and evening.

For the phthisic.[93]

Take the best wort[94] and let it stand till it be yellow, then boil it and after let it cool, then put to it a little quantity of barm and saffron, and so drink of it every morning and evening while it lasteth; otherwise take horehound,[95] violet leaves, and hyssop, of each a good handful, seethe them in water, and put thereto a little saffron, liquorice, and sugar candy; after they have boiled a good while, then strain it into an earthen vessel, and let the sick drink thereof six spoonful at a time morning and evening;

or lastly, take the lungs of a fox, and lay it in rose-water, or boil it in rose-water, then take it out and dry it in some hot place without the sun, then beat it to powder with sugar candy and eat of this powder morning and evening.

89   *For griefs in the stomach.*

To ease pain in the stomach, take endive, mints, of each a like quantity, and steep them in white wine the space of a day, then straining it and adding thereto a little cinnamon and pepper, give it to the sick person to drink; and if you add thereto a little of the powder of horse-mint[96] and calamint, it will comfort the stomach exceedingly, and occasion swift and good digestion.

90   *For spitting of blood.*

For spitting of blood, whether it proceed of inward bruises, over-straining or such like, you shall take some pitch, and a little spermaceti,[97] and mix it with old ale and drink it, and it will stay the flux of blood: but if by means of the bruise any outward grief remain, then you shall take of the herb brockelhemp,[98] and frying it with sheep's tallow lay it hot to the grieved place, and it will take away the anguish.

91   *For vomiting.*

To stay the flux of vomiting take wormwood, and sour bread toasted, of each a like quantity, and beat them well in a mortar, then add to them as much of the juice of mints and the juice of plantain as will bring it to a thick salve; then fry them all together in a frying pan, and when it is hot lay it plasterwise to the mouth of the stomach,[99] then let the party drink a little white wine and chervil water mixed together, and then, steeping sour toasted bread in very strong vinegar, wrap it in a fine cloth and let the sick party smell thereto, and it will stay the excess of vomiting, and both comfort and strengthen the stomach.

92   *To force one to vomit.*

If you would compel one to vomit, take half a spoonful of stonecrop,[100] and mix it with three spoonful of white wine and give it to the party to drink, and it will make him vomit presently, but do this seldom and to strong bodies, for otherwise it is dangerous.

93   *For the iliaca passio.*

For the *iliaca passio*,[101] take of polypody[102] an ounce, and stamp it, then boil it with prunes and violets in fennel water or aniseed water, taking thereof a good quantity, then strain it and let the party every morning and evening drink a good draught thereof.

ADDITIONS to the diseases of the stomach. For the stomach.

If the stomach be troubled with wind or other pain, take cumin and beat it to powder, and mix with it red wine, and drink it at night when you go to bed, divers nights together.

For the iliaca passio.

Take brooklime roots and leaves and wash them clean and dry them in the sun, so dry that you may make powder thereof, then take of the powder a good quantity, and the like of treacle, and put them in a cup with a pretty quantity of strong old ale, and stir them well together, and drink thereof first and last morning and evening for the space of three or four days, and if need do require, use the same in the broths you do eat, for it is very sovereign.

For pain in the breast.

Take hartshorn or ivory beaten to fine powder, and as much cinnamon in powder, mix them with vinegar, and drink thereof to the quantity of seven or eight spoonfuls.

For the mother.[103]

Take the water of mouse-ear, and drink thereof the quantity of an ounce and a half or two ounces, twice or thrice a day, or otherwise take a little nutmeg, a little cinnamon, a little cloves, a little mace, and a very little ginger, and the flowers of lavender; beat all unto a fine powder, and when the passion of the mother cometh, take a chafing-dish of good quick coals, and bend the patient forward and cast of the powder into the chafing-dish so as she may receive the smoke both in at her nose and mouth, and it is a present cure.

Obstructions of the liver.

Against obstructions in the liver, take aniseeds, amees,[104] burnet, camomile, and the greater centaury,[105] and boil them in white wine with a little honey, and drink it every morning and it will cure the obstructions, and cleanse the liver from all imperfection.

Against the heat of the liver.

Against the heat and inflammation of the liver, take endive dried to powder, and the meal of lupin seeds, and, mixing it with honey and the juice of wormwood, make a cake thereof and eat it, and it will assuage the great heat and inflammation of the liver, and take away the pimples and redness of the face which proceedeth from the same.

100   *For the pleurisy.*

To prevent a pleurisy a good while before it come, there is no better way than to use much the exercise of ringing[106] or to stretch your arms upward, so as they may bear the weight of your body, and so to swing your body up and down a good space: but having caught a pleurisy and feeling the gripes, stitches, and pangs thereof, you shall presently cause the party to be let blood,[107] and then take the herb althea or hollyhock,[108] and boil it with vinegar and linseed till it be thick plasterwise, and then spread it upon a piece of alum leather, and lay it to the side that is grieved, and it will help it.

101   *A plaster for a stitch.*

To help a stitch in the side or elsewhere, take doves' dung,[109] [and] red rose leaves and put them into a bag, and quilt it: then thoroughly heat it upon a chafing-dish of coals with vinegar in a platter; then lay it unto the pained place as hot as may be suffered, and when it cooleth heat it again.

102   *Another.*

Otherwise take marigolds a handful and seethe them in milk, then take beer and make a posset of it, and let the party drink of it as hot as may be, and lay the curd to the pained place. Also to take an old acorn and grate it like a nutmeg into a pint of old ale and drink it off is approved most good for any stitch whatsoever.

103   *Heat in the liver.*

For any extraordinary heat or inflammation in the liver, take barberries and boil them in clarified whey and drink them and they will cure it.

104   *For the consumption.*

If you will make a cordial caudle[110] for a consumption or any other weakness: take a quart of running water, a piece of mutton, and a piece of veal, and put them with the water into a pot, then take of sorrel, violet leaves, spinach, endive, succory, sage, hyssop, of each a good quantity; then take prunes and raisins, and put them all into the broth, and seethe them from a quart to a pint, then strain the yolk of an egg and a little saffron thereinto, putting in sugar, whole mace, and a little white wine, so seethe them a while together, and let the party drink it as warm as may be.

To staunch blood.

05 To staunch blood, take the herb shepherd's purse (if it may be gotten) distilled at the apothecary's, and drink an ounce thereof at a time morning and evening, and it will stay any flux of blood natural or unnatural; but if you cannot get the distilled water, then boil a handful of the herb with cinnamon, and a little sugar, in claret wine, and boil it from a quart to a pint, and drink it as oft as you please: also if you but rub the herb between your hands, you shall see it will soon make the blood return.

For the yellow jaundice.

06 For the yellow jaundice, take two pennyworth of the best English saffron,[111] dry it and grind it to an exceeding fine powder, then mix it with the pap of a roasted apple, and give it the diseased party to swallow down in the manner of a pill; and do thus divers mornings together, and without doubt it is the most present cure that can be for the same, as hath been often times proved.

For the yellow jaundice.

07 For the yellow jaundice take pimpernel, and chick-weed, stamp them and strain them into poset ale, and let the party drink thereof morning and evening.

For a desperate yellow jaundice.

08 For the yellow jaundice which is desperate and almost past cure: take sheep's dung new made and put it into a cup of beer or ale, and close the cup fast and let it stand so all night, and in the morning take a draught of the clearest of the drink, and give it to the sick party.

For the black jaundice.

09 For the black jaundice[112] take the herb called pennyroyal, and either boil it in white wine, or drink the juice thereof simply by itself to the quantity of three or four spoonful at a time, and it will cure the black jaundice.

ADDITIONS to the diseases of the liver. For wasting of the liver.

10 Take of hyssop, parsley, and hart's-tongue, of each a like quantity, and seethe them in wort till they be soft, then let it stand till it be cold, and then drink thereof first and last, morning and evening.

A restorative for the liver.

11 Take fennel roots, and parsley roots, of each a like, wash them clean, and peel off the upper bark and cast away the pith within, then mince

them small, then put them to three pints of water, and set them over the fire; then take figs, and shred them small, liquorice and break it small, and put them to the herbs, and let all boil very well, then take sorrel and stamp it and put it to the rest, and let it boil till some part be wasted, then take a good quantity of honey and put to it and boil a while, then take it from the fire and clarify it through a strainer into a glass vessel and stop it very close, then give the sick to drink thereof morning and evening.

112   *To heal a ringworm coming of heat from the liver.*

Take the stalk of Saint Mary,[113] garlic, and burn it or lay it upon a hot tile stone until it be very dry, and then beat it into powder, and rub the sore therewith till it be whole.

113   *To staunch blood.*

Take wool in the walkmill[114] that cometh from the cloth and flyeth about like down and beat it into powder, then take thereof and mix it with the white of an egg and wheat flour, and stamp them together, then lay it on a linen cloth or lint and apply it to the bleeding place, and it will staunch it.

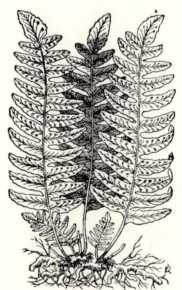

"Polypody of the oak." From John Gerarde, *The Herball, or General Historie of Plantes*, p. 974.

114   *For great danger in bleeding.*

If a man bleed and have no present help, if the wound be on the foot, bind him about the ankle, if in the legs bind him about the knee, if it be on the hand bind him about the wrist, if it be on the arm bind him about the brawn of the arm, with a good list,[115] and the blood will presently staunch.

15

For a stitch.

Take good store of cinnamon grated and put it into posset ale very hot and drink it, and it is a present cure.

16

A bath for the dropsy.[116]

Take a gallon of running water, and put to it as much salt as will make the water salt as the sea water, then boil it a good while, and bathe the legs therein as hot as may be suffered.

"Branched asphodill." From John Gerarde, *The Herball, or General Historie of Plantes*, p. 86.

"Purple circled daffodil." From John Gerarde, *The Herball*, p. 108.

17

For the dropsy.

For the dropsy, take *agnus castus*, fennel, affodil, dauke,[117] wallwort, lupins,[118] and wormwood, of each a handful, and boil them in a gallon of white wine until a fourth part be consumed: then strain it and drink morning and evening half a pint thereof, and it will cure the dropsy; but you must be careful that you take not daffodil for affodil.[119]

118   *Pain in the spleen.*

For pain in the spleen,[120] take *agnus castus*, agrimony, aniseeds, centaury the great, and wormwood, of each half a handful, and boil them in a gallon of white wine, then strain it and let the patient drink divers mornings together half a pint thereof: and at his usual meals let him neither drink ale, beer, nor wine, but such as hath had the herb tamarisk[121] steeped in the same, or for want of the herb, let him drink out of a cup made of tamarisk wood, and he shall surely find remedy.

119   *For pain in the side.*

For any pain in the side, take mugwort and red sage, and dry them between two tile stones, and then put it in a bag, and lay it to your side as hot as can be endured.

120   *For fatness and short breath.*

To help him that is exceeding fat, pursy, and short breathed: take honey clarified, and bread unleavened and make toasts of it, and dip the toasts into the clarified honey, and eat this divers times with your meat.

121   *ADDITIONS to the diseases of the spleen: for the spleen.*

Take a lump of iron or steel, and heat it red hot, and quench it in wine, then give the wine to the sick party to drink.

122   *For the stopping of the spleen.*

Take fennel seeds and the roots, boil them in water, and after it is cleansed put to it honey and give it the party to drink, then seethe the herb in oil and wine together, and plasterwise apply it to the side.

123   *For the hardness of the spleen.*

Make a plaster of wormwood boiled in oil, or make an ointment of the juice of wormwood, of vinegar, armeniac,[122] wax, and oil, mixed and melted together, and anoint the side therewith, either in the sun, or before the fire.

124   *Diseases of the heart: for the passion of the heart.*

Take the powder of galingale, and mix it with the juice of borage, and let the offended party drink it with sweet wine.

125   *For heart sickness.*

Take rosemary and sage, of each a handful, and seethe them in white wine or strong ale, and then let the patient drink it lukewarm.

6 *For fatness about the heart.*

Take the juice of fennel mixed with honey, and seethe them together till it be hard, and then eat it evening and morning, and it will consume away the fatness.

7 *For the wind colic.*

For the wind colic,[123] which is a disease both general and cruel, there be a world of remedies, yet none more approved than this which I will repeat: you shall take a nutmeg sound and large, and divide it equally into four quarters: then the first morning as soon as you rise eat a quarter thereof, the second morning eat two quarters, the third eat three quarters, and the fourth morning eat a whole nutmeg, and so having made your stomach and taste familiar therewith, eat every morning whilst the colic offendeth you a whole nutmeg dry without any composition, and fast ever an hour at least after it, and you shall find a most unspeakable profit which will arise from the same.

8 *The wind colic.*

For the wind colic, take a good handful of clean wheat meal as it cometh from the mill, and two eggs and a little wine vinegar, and a little aqua vitae, and mingle them all together cold and make a cake of it and bake it on a gridiron with a soft fire, and turn it often and tend it with basting of aqua vitae with a feather; then lay it somewhat higher than the pain is, rather than lower.

9 *For the lax.*

For the lax or extreme scouring of the belly, take the seeds of the wood rose, or briar rose, beat it to powder and mix a dram thereof with an ounce of the conserve of sloes[124] and eat it, and it will in short space bind and make the belly hard.

0 *For the bloody flux.*

For the bloody flux, take a quart of red wine and boil therein a handful of shepherd's-purse till the herb be very soft: then strain it, and add thereto a quarter of an ounce of cinnamon, and as much of dried tanner's bark taken from the ooze,[125] and both beaten to fine powder, then give the party half a pint thereof to drink morning and evening, it being made very warm, and it will cure him.

1 *To stay a lax.*

To stay a sore lax, take plantain water and cinnamon finely beaten, and the flowers of pomegranates, and boil them well together, then take sugar, and the yolk of an egg, and make a caudle of it, and give it the grieved party.

132   *For the flux.*

For the flux take a stag's pizzle[126] dried, and grate it, and give it in any drink, either in beer, ale, or wine, and it is most sovereign for any flux whatsoever: so is the jaw bones of a pike, the teeth and all dried and beaten to powder, and so given the party diseased in any drink whatsoever.

133   *For the worst flux.*

To cure the worst bloody flux that may be, take a quart of red wine, and a spoonful of cumin seed, boil them together until half be consumed, then take knot-grass and shepherd's-purse, and plantain, and stamp them severally, and then strain them and take of the juice of each of them a good spoonful, and put them to the wine, and so seethe them again a little: then drink it luke warm, half overnight, and half the next morning; and if it fall out to be in winter, so that you cannot get the herbs; then take the water of them distilled, of each three spoonfuls, and use it as before.

134   *For costiveness.*

For extreme costiveness, or binding in the body, so as a man cannot avoid[127] his excrements, take aniseeds, fenugreek,[128] linseed, and the powder of peony, of each half an ounce, and boil them in a quart of white wine, then drink a good draught thereof, and it will make a man go to the stool orderly and at great ease.

135   *For worms.*

For worms in the belly, either of child or man, take aloes socotrine,[129] as much as half a hazel nut, and wrap it in the pap of a roasted apple, and so let the offended party swallow it in manner of a pill fasting in the morning, or else mix it with three or four spoonful of muscadine,[130] and so let the party drink it; and it is a present cure: but if the child be either so young, or the man so weak with sickness that you dare not administer anything inwardly, then you shall dissolve your aloes in the oil of savin,[131] making it salve-like thick, then plasterwise spread it upon sheep's leather, and lay it upon the navel and mouth of the stomach of the grieved party, and it will give him ease; so will also unset leeks chopped small and fried with sweet butter, and then in a linen bag apply it hot to the navel of the grieved party.

36 *ADDITIONS to the diseases of the belly and guts. For the greatest lax.*
 Take a quart of red wine and put to it three yolks of eggs, and a pennyworth of long pepper[132] and grains, and boil it well and drink it as hot as can be suffered, or otherwise take an ounce of the inner bark of an oak, and a pennyworth of long pepper, and boil them in a pint and better of new milk, and drink it hot first and last morning and evening.

37   *For the bloody flux.*
 Take an egg and make a little hole in the top, and put out the white, then fill it up again with aqua vitae, stirring the egg and aqua vitae till it be hard, then let the party eat the egg and it will cure him, or otherwise take a pint of red wine and nine yolks of eggs, and twenty peppercorns small beaten; let them seethe till they be thick, then take it off and give the diseased party to eat nine spoonful morning and evening.

38   *For an easy lax.*
 Take of rue and beets a like quantity, bruise them and take the juice, mix it with clarified honey, and boil it in red wine, and drink it warm first and last morning and evening.

39   *To have two stools a day and no more.*
 Take mercury,[133] cinquefoil,[134] and mallows, and when you make pottage or broth with other herbs, let these herbs before named have most strength in the pottage, and eating thereon it will give you two stools and no more.

40   *For hardness of the belly or womb.*
 Take two spoonful of the juice of ivy leaves, and drink it three times a day, and it will dissolve the hardness.

41   *Against costiveness.*
 Take the barks of the roots of the elder tree and stamp it, and mix it with old ale, and drink thereof a good hearty draught.

42   *For the wind colic.*
 Take the crumbs of white bread, and steep it in milk with alum and add sugar unto it and eat it, and it will open the belly.

43   *For the stopping of the womb.*
 Take the kernels of three peach stones, and bruise them, seven corns of case pepper,[135] and of sliced ginger a greater quantity than of the pepper,

pound all together grossly and put it into a spoonful of sack (which is the best) or else white wine or strong ale, and drink it off in a great spoon, then fast two hours after and walk up and down if you can, if otherwise, keep yourself warm, and beware of melancholy. It may be taken at all times.

144 ### For the rupture.

Take of daisies, comfrey,[136] polypody of the oak,[137] and avens,[138] of each half a handful, two roots of osmund, boil them in strong ale and honey, and drink thereof morning, noon, and night, and it will heal any reasonable rupture. Or otherwise take of smallage, comfrey, setwall, polypody that grows on the ground like fern, daisies, and morel,[139] of each a like, stamp them very small, and boil them well in barm, until it be thick like a poultice, and so keep it in a close vessel, and when you have occasion to use it, make it as hot as the party can suffer it, and lay it to the place grieved, then, with a truss, truss him up close, and let him be careful for straining of himself, and in a few days it will knit, during which cure give him to drink a draught of red wine, and put therein a good quantity of the flour of vetches finely bolted, stirring it well together, and then fast an hour after.

145 ### For the stone.[140]

For the violent pain of the stone, make a posset of milk and sack, then take of the curd, and put a handful of camomile flowers into the drink, then put it into a pewter pot and let it stand upon hot embers, so that it may diffuse or dissolve: and then drink it as occasion shall serve.

146 ### Another.

Other for this grief take the stone of an ox gall, and dry it in an oven, then beat it to powder, and take of it the quantity of a hazel nut with a draught of good old ale or white wine.

147 ### The colic and stone.

For the colic and stone, take hawthorn berries, the berries of sweet briars, and ashen keys,[141] and dry them every one severally until you make them into powder, then put a little quantity of every one of them together; then if you think good put to it the powder of liquorice and aniseeds, to the intent that the patient may the better take it, then put in a quantity of this powder in a draught of white wine, and drink it fasting.

148 ### Another.

Otherwise you may take smallage seed, parsley, lovage, saxifrage,[142] and broom seed, of every one of them a like quantity, beat them into a powder, and when you feel a fit of either of the diseases, eat of this powder a spoonful at a time either in pottage, or else in the broth of a chicken, and so fast two or three hours after.

A powder for the colic and stone.

To make a powder for the colic and stone, take fennel, parsley seed, aniseed, and caraway seed, of each the weight of six pence, of gromwell seed, saxifrage seed, the roots of filipendula, and liquorice, of each the weight of twelve pence, of galingale, spikenard, and cinnamon, of each the weight of eight pence, of senna[143] the weight of seventeen shillings, good weight; beat them all to powder and searce it, which will weigh in all twenty five shillings and six pence. This powder is to be given in white wine and sugar in the morning fasting, and so to continue fasting two hours after; and to take of it at one time the weight of ten pence or twelve pence.

Another.

Other physicians for the stone take a quart of Rhenish[144] or white wine, and two lemons, and pare the upper rind thin, and slice them into the wine, and as much white soap as the weight of a groat, and boil them to a pint, and put thereto sugar according to your discretion; and so drink it keeping yourself warm in your bed, and lying upon your back.

For the stone in the reins.

For the stone in the reins, take amees, camomile, maidenhair, sparrow-tongue,[145] and filipendula, of each a like quantity; dry it in an oven, and then beat it to powder, and every morning drink half a spoonful thereof with a good draught of white wine, and it will help.

For the stone in the bladder.

For the stone in the bladder, take a radish root and slit it cross twice, then put it into a pint of white wine, and stop the vessel exceeding close; then let it stand all one night, and the next morning drink it off fasting, and thus do divers mornings together and it will help.

A powder for the stone in the bladder.

For the stone in the bladder take the kernels of sloes and dry them on a tile stone, then beat them to powder, then take the roots of alexanders, parsley, pellitory,[146] and hollyhock, of every of their roots a like quantity, and seethe them all in white wine, or else in the broth of a young chicken: then strain them into a clean vessel, and when you drink of it, put into it half a spoonful of the powder of sloe kernels. Also if you take the oil of scorpion,[147] it is very good to anoint the member, and the tender part of the belly against the bladder.

154   *A bath for the stone.*

To make a bath for the stone, take mallows, hollyhock, and lily roots, and linseed, pellitory of the wall, and seethe them in the broth of a sheep's head, and bathe the reins of the back therewith oftentimes, for it will open the straitness of the water conduits, that the stone may have issue, and assuage the pain, and bring out the gravel with the urine: but yet in more effect, when a plaster is made and laid unto the reins and belly immediately after the bathing.

155   *A water for the stone.*

To make a water for the stone, take a gallon of new milk of a red cow, and put therein a handful of pellitory of the wall, and a handful of wild thyme, and a handful of saxifrage and a handful of parsley, and two or three radish roots sliced and a quantity of filipendula roots; let them lie in the milk a night, and in the morning put the milk with the herbs into a still, and distil them with a moderate fire of charcoal or such like: then when you are to use the water, take a draught of Rhenish wine or white wine, and put into it five spoonful of the distilled water, and a little sugar and nutmeg sliced, and then drink of it; the next day meddle not with it, but the third day do as you did the first day, and so every other day for a week's space.

156   *Difficulty of urine.*

For the difficulty of urine, or hardness to make water, take smallage, dill, aniseeds, and burnet, of each a like quantity, and dry them and beat them to fine powder, and drink half a spoonful thereof with a good draught of white wine.

157   *For hot urine.*

If the urine be hot and burning, the party shall use every morning to drink a good draught of new milk and sugar well mixed together, and by all means to abstain from beer that is old, hard, and tart, and from all meats and sauces which are sour or sharp.

158   *For the strangury.*

For the strangury,[148] take saxifrage, polypody of the oak, the roots of beans, and a quantity of raisins, of every one three handful or more, and then take two gallons of good wine, or else wine lees, and put it into a serpentary and make thereof a good quantity, and give the sick thereof to drink morning and evening a spoonful at once.

For pissing in bed.

For them that cannot hold their water in the night time take a kid's hoof and dry it and beat it into powder, and give it to the patient to drink, either in beer or ale four or five times.

For the rupture.

For the rupture or burstness in men, take comfrey and fern osmund, and beat them together with yellow wax and deer's suet until it come unto a salve, and then apply it unto the broken place and it will knit it; also it shall be good for the party to take comfrey roots, and roast them in hot embers as you roast wardens, and let the party eat them, for they are very sovereign for the rupture, especially being eaten in a morning fasting, and by all means let him wear a strong truss till he be whole.

ADDITIONS to the diseases of the reins and bladder.

Take goat's claws[149] and burn them, in a new earthen pot, to powder, then put of the powder into broth or pottage and eat it therein, or otherwise take rue, gromwell, and parsley, and stamp them together and mix it with wine and drink it.

For he that cannot hold his water.

Take *agnus castus*, and castoreum[150] and seethe them together in wine and drink thereof, also seethe them in vinegar and hot lap it about the privy parts and it will help.

For the gonorrhoea or shedding of seed.

Take malmsey[151] and butter, and warm it and wash the reins of the back, whereupon you find pain, then take oil of mace and anoint the back therewith.

For weakness in the back.

First wash the reins of the back with warm white wine, then anoint all the back with the ointment called *perstuaneto*.[152]

For heat in the reins. For comforting and strengthening of the back.

Take a leg of beef, a handful of fennel roots, a handful of parsley roots, two roots of comfrey, one pound of raisins of the sun, a pound of damask prunes, and a quarter of a pound of dates; put all these together and boil them very soft with six leaves of nep,[153] six leaves of clary, twelve leaves of betony of the wood, and a little hart's-tongue: when they are sod very soft, take them and stamp them very small and strain them into the same broth again with a quart of sack[154] and a pennyworth of large mace, and of this drink at your pleasure.

166   *For the haemorrhoids.*

For the haemorrhoids, which is a troublesome and a sore grief, take of dill, dog-fennel, and pellitory of Spain,[155] of each half a handful, and beat it in a mortar with sheep's suet and black soap till it come to a salve, and then lay it plasterwise to the sore, and it will give the grief ease.

167   *For the piles or haemorrhoids.*

For the piles or haemorrhoids, take half a pint of ale, and a good quantity of pepper, and as much alum as a walnut; boil all this together till it be as thick as birdlime or thicker: this done, take the juice of white violets, and the juice of houseleek, and when it is almost cold, put in the juice and strain them all together, and with this ointment anoint the sore place twice a day. Others for this grief take lead and grate it small, and lay it upon the sores: or else take mussels dried and beat to powder, and lay it on the sores.

168   *For the falling of the fundament.*[156]

If a man's fundament fall down through some cold taken or other cause, let it be forthwith put up again: then take the powder of town-cresses dried, and strew it gently upon the fundament, and anoint the reins of the back with honey, and then above it strew the powder of cumin and calafine mixed together, and ease will come thereby.

169   *ADDITIONS to the diseases of the private parts. For the haemorrhoids.*

Take a great handful of orpines, and bruise them between your hands till they be like a salve, and then lay them upon a cloth and bind them fast to the fundament.

170   *For the green sickness.*

To help the green sickness, take a pottle of white wine and a handful of rosemary, a handful of wormwood, an ounce of *carduus benedictus* seed, and a dram of cloves: all these must be put into the white wine in a jug, and covered very close, and lie in steep a day and a night before the party drink of it, then let her drink of it every morning and two hours before supper: and so take it for a fortnight, and let her stir as much as she can, the more the better, and as early as she can. Otherwise for this sickness take hyssop, fennel, and pennyroyal, of these three one good handful; take two ounces of currants, seethe these in a pint of fair water to the half, then strain the herbs from the liquor, and put thereto two ounces of fine sugar, and two spoonfuls of white wine vinegar, and let the party drink every morning four spoonfuls thereof and walk upon it.

71

To increase a woman's milk.

To increase a woman's milk, you shall boil in strong posset ale good store of coleworts, and cause her to drink every meal of the same; also if she use to eat boiled coleworts with her meat, it will wonderfully increase her milk also.

72

To dry up milk.

To dry up woman's milk, take red sage, and having stamped it and strained the juice from the same, add thereunto as much wine vinegar, and stir them well together, then warming it on a flat dish over a few coals, steep therein a sheet of brown paper; then making a hole in the midst thereof for the nipple of the breast to go through, cover all the breast over with the paper, and remove it as occasion shall serve, but be very careful it be laid very hot to. Some are of opinion, that for a woman to milk her breasts upon the earth will cause her milk to dry, but I refer it to trial.

73

A poultice for sore breasts in women.

To help women's sore breasts, when they are swelled or else inflamed: take violet leaves and cut them small, and seethe them in milk or running water with wheat bran, or wheat bread crumbs; then lay it to the sore as hot as the party can endure it.

74

For ease in child bearing.

If a woman have a strong and hard labour: take four spoonful of another woman's milk, and give it the woman to drink in her labour, and she shall be delivered presently.

75

Child dead in the womb.

If a woman by mischance have her child dead within her she shall take dittander, felwort, and pennyroyal, and stamp them, and take of each a spoonful of the juice, and mix it with old wine and give it her to drink, and she shall soon be delivered without danger.

176   *Aptness to conceive.*
To make a woman apt to conceive, let her either drink mugwort steeped in wine, or else the powder thereof mixed with wine, as shall best please her taste.

177   *ADDITIONS to women's infirmities. To cease women's flowers.*
Take the powder of coral fine ground and eat it in a rear[157] egg, and it will stay the flux.

178   *Against the flowers.*
Against the flowers withholden in women, make a pessary of the juice of mugwort or the water that it is sodden in and apply it, but if it be for the flux of the flowers, take the juice of plantain and drink it in red wine.

179   *For the matrix.*
Take a fomentation made of the water wherein the leaves and flowers of tutsan[158] is sodden, to drink up the superfluities of the matrix; it cleanseth the entrance; but this herb would be gathered in harvest. If a woman have pain in the matrix, set on the fire water that amomum[159] hath been sodden in and of the dewition make a pessary and it will give ease.

180   *A general purge for a woman in child bed.*
Take two or three eggs and they must be neither roast nor raw, but between both, and then take butter that salt never came in, and put it into the eggs and sup them off, and eat a piece of brown bread to them and drink a draught of small ale.[160]

181   *To deliver the dead birth.*
Take the root of *aristolochia rotunda*[161] and boil it in wine and oil; make a fomentation thereof and it helps.

182   *To increase milk.*
Take the buds and tender crops of bryony,[162] and boil them in broth or pottage, and let the woman eat thereof; it is sovereign.

183   *For a woman that is new brought in bed, and soundeth*[163] *much.*
Take mugwort, motherwort,[164] and mints, the quantity of a handful in

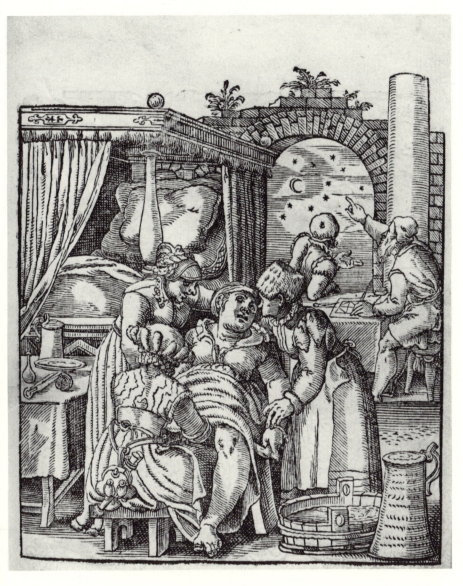

A woman, assisted by midwife and friends, gives birth; the men in the background are casting the child's horoscope. From Jost Amman, *Kunnst vnd Lehrbüchlein*

all, seethe them together in a pint of malmsey and give her to drink thereof two or three spoonful at a time, and it will appease her swounding.

184   *To provoke sleep.*

Take henbane[165] stamped and mixed with vinegar and apply it plasterwise over all the forehead, and it will cause sleep.

185   *For sore breasts.*

Take sage, smallage, mallows, and plantain, of each an handful, beat them all well in a mortar, then put to them oatmeal and milk, and spread it on a fine linen cloth an inch thick, and lay it to the breast or breasts, or otherwise take white bread leaven and strain it with cream, and put thereto two or three yolks of eggs, salt, oil, or oil of roses, and put it upon a soft fire till it be lukewarm, and so apply it to the breast.

186   *For morphew of both kinds.*

For the morphew,[166] whether it be white or black, take of the litharge of gold[167] a dram, of unwrought brimstone two drams; beat them into fine powder, then take of the oil of roses, and swine's grease, of each a like quantity, and grind them all together with half a dram of camphor and a little vinegar, and anoint the same therewith morning and evening.

187   *To breed hair.*

To breed hair, take southernwood[168] and burn it to ashes, and mix it well with common oil, then anoint the bald place therewith morning and evening, and it will breed hair exceedingly.

188   *For the gout.*

For the gout, take *aristolochia rotunda*, althea, betony, and the roots of wild nep,[169] and the root of the wild dock cut into thin pieces after the upper rind is taken away, of each a like quantity, boil them all in running water till they be soft and thick: then stamp them in a mortar as small as may be, and put thereto a little quantity of chimney soot, and a pint or better of new milk of a cow which is all of one entire colour,[170] and as much of the urine of a man that is fasting, and having stirred them all well together, boil them once again on the fire; then, as hot as the party can suffer it, apply it to the grieved place, and it will give him ease.

189   *For the sciatica.*

For the sciatica, take of mustard seed a good handful, and as much in weight of honey, and as much in weight of figs, and crumbs of white bread half so much, then with strong vinegar beat it in a mortar till it come to a salve, then apply it to the grieved place and it will give the party ease; so will also a plaster of oxycrate,[171] if it be continually worn upon the same.

[*For the hot gout.*]

90

For the hot gout,[172] take five or six spoonful of the juice of hemlock, and as much swine's grease finely clarified, and beating them well together anoint the sore place with the same, and it will give sudden ease.

For any pain or swelling, or the stinging of venomous beasts.

91

To help all manner of swellings or aches, in what part of the body soever it be, or the stinging of any venomous beast, as adder, snake, or such like, take horehound, smallage, porrets, small mallows,[173] and wild tansy, of each a like quantity, and bruise them or cut them small: then seethe them all together in a pan with milk, oatmeal, and as much sheep's suet, or deer's suet, as a hen's egg, and let it boil till it be a thick plaster, then lay it upon a blue woollen cloth, and lay it to the grief as hot as one can suffer it.

For swellings in the legs or feet.

92

For any swelling in the legs or feet, take a good handful of water cresses and shred them small, and put them in an earthen pot, and put thereto thick wine lees, and wheat bran, and sheep's suet, of each of them a like quantity, and let them boil together until they be thick, then take a linen cloth and bind it about the sore or swelling as hot as the party grieved can endure it, and let it remain on a whole night and a day without removing; and when you take it away lay to a fresh plaster, hot as before, and it will take away both the pain and the swelling. Other surgeons for this grief take honey and beer and heat them together and therewith bathe the swelling both morning and evening.

A water to wash a sore with.

93

To wash any sore or ulcer, take running water and bole armeniac[174] and camphor, and boil them together, and dip in a cloth, and lay it to the sore as hot as may be endured; also plantain water is good to kill the heat of any sore; or if you take woodbine leaves and bruise them small, it will heal a sore; or if you wash a sore with verjuice[175] that hath been burned or scalded, it is a present remedy.

A poultice for a sore.

94

There be divers others which for this grief take the green of goose dung and boil it in fresh butter, then strain it very clean and use it. Also sallat oil and snow water, beaten together, will cure any scald or burning.

195   *For any old sore.*

To cure any old sore[176] how grievous soever it be, take of new milk three quarts, a good handful of plantain, and let it boil till a pint be consumed: then add three ounces of alum made into powder, and one ounce and a half of white sugar candy powdered. Also then let it boil a little till it have a hard curd, then strain it; with this warm, bathe the ulcer, and all the member about it; then dry it, and lay upon the ulcer *unguentum basilicon*[177] spread on lint, and your *de minio*[178] plaster over it, for this strengtheneth and killeth the itch: but if you find this is not sharp enough, then take of milk a quart, alum in powder two ounces, vinegar a spoonful; when the milk doth seethe, put in the alum and vinegar, then take of the curd, and use the rest as was before said, and it will cure it.

196   *For any scabs or itch.*

For scabs or itch take *unguentum* [of] populeon,[179] and therewith anoint the party and it will help; but if it be more strong and rank, take an ounce of nerval[180] and three pennyworth of quicksilver, and beat and work them together till you see that assuredly the quicksilver is killed,[181] then let the party anoint therewith only the palms of his hands, the boughts at his elbows, his armpits, and hams, and it will cure all his body.[182]

197   *For the leprosy.*

To cure the leprosy, take the juice of coleworts, and mix it with alum and strong ale, and anoint the leper therewith morning and evening, and it will cleanse him wonderfully, especially if he be purged first, and have some part of his corrupt blood taken away.

198   *To take away pimples.*

To take away either pimples from the face, or any other part of the body, take virgin wax, and spermaceti, of each a like quantity, and boil them together, and dip in a fine linen cloth, and as it cools dip it well of both sides, then lay it upon another fair cloth upon a table, and then fold up a cloth in your hands, and all to sleight[183] it with the cloth, then take as much as will cover the grieved place.

199   *For any burning.*

For any burning, take six new laid eggs and roast them very hard, and

"Beautifying." From the title-page of *The Accomplished Lady's Delight in Preserving, Physick, Beautifying and Cookery.*

take out the yolks thereof, and put them into an earthen pot, and set it over the fire on hot embers, and then whilst the eggs look black, stir them with a slice till they come to an oil, which oil take and clarify and put into a glass by itself, and therewith anoint any burning, and it will cure it.

Privy parts burned.

If any man have his privy parts burned, take the ashes of a fine linen cloth in good quantity, and put it into the former oil of eggs, and anoint the sore member therewith, and it will cure it.

For any scalding.

For any scalding with hot water, oil, or otherwise: take thick cream, and set it on the fire, and put into it the green which grows on a stone wall;[184] take also yarrow, the green of elder bark, and fire grass,[185] and chop them small, then put them into the cream, and stir it well till it come to an oil salve, then strain it and anoint the sore with it.

A poultice to dry a sore.

To dry up any sore, take smallage, groundsel, wild mallows, and violet leaves: chop them small and boil them in milk with bruised oatmeal and sheep's suet, and so apply it to the sore.

To eat away dead flesh.

To eat away dead flesh, take stubwort, and fold it up in a red dock leaf, or red wort[186] leaf, and so roast it in the hot embers and lay it hot to any sore, and it will fret away all the dead flesh; or otherwise, if you strew upon the sore a little precipitate[187] it will eat away the dead flesh.

204   *A water to heal wounds.*

To make a water to heal all manner of wounds, you shall take iuphwort[188] flowers, leaves, and roots, and in March or April when the flowers are at the best, distil it, then with that water bathe the wound, and lay a linen cloth well therewith in the wound, and it will heal it.

205   *To heal any wound.*

To heal any wound or cut in any flesh or part of the body: first if it be fit to be stitched, stitch it up, and then take *unguentum aureum,*[189] and lay it upon a pledget of lint as big as the wound, and then over it lay a *de minio* plaster made of sallat oil and red lead, and so dress it at least once in four and twenty hours; but if it be a hollow wound, as some thrust in the body or other member, then you shall take *balsamum cephalicum,*[190] and, warming it on a chafing-dish of coals, dip the tent therein, and so put into the wound, then lay your plaster *de minio* over it, and do thus at least once a day till it be whole.

206   *For sinews cut or shrunk.*

If a man's sinews be cut or shrunk, he shall go to the root of the wild nep which is like woodbine, and make a hole in the midst of the root, then cover it well again that no air go out nor in, nor rain nor other moisture: thus let it abide a day and a night, then go and open it, and you shall find therein a certain liquor: then take out the liquor and put it into a clean glass, and do thus every day whilst you find any moisture in the hole, and this must only be done in the months of April and May: then anoint the sore therewith against the fire, then wet a linen cloth in the same liquor, and lap it about the sore, and the virtue will soon be perceived.

207   *To break any impostume.*

To break any impostume, and to ripe it only, take the green[191] melilot plaster, and lay it thereunto, and it is sufficient.

208   *ADDITIONS, to general infirmities of surgery, and first of burnings and scaldings. For burning or scalding with either liquor or gunpowder.*

Take plantain water, or sallat oil and running water beaten together, and therewith anoint the sore with a feather till the fire be taken out, then take the white of eggs and beat them to oil, which done take a hare skin and clip the hair into the oil and make it as thick as you may spread it upon a fine linen cloth, and so lay it upon the sore and remove it not, until it be whole, and if any rise up of itself, clip it away with your shears, and if it be not perfectly whole, then take a little of the ointment and lay it to the same place again, or otherwise take half a bushel of glovers' shreds[192] of all sorts, and so much of running water as shall be thought convenient to seethe them, and put thereto a good quarter of a pound of barrow's grease, and then take half a bushel of the down of cats' tails[193] and boil them all together, continually stirring them, till they be sodden that they may be strained into an earthen pot or glass, and with it anoint the sore. Or else take of caprifoil,[194] mouse-ear, ground ivy, and hen's dung of the reddest or of the yellowest, and fry them with May butter all together until it be brown, then strain it through a clean cloth, and anoint the sore therewith.

09   *For burnings or scaldings on the face.*
Take the middle rind of the elm tree, and lay it two or three hours in fair running water till it wax ropy like glue, and then anoint the sore therewith.[195] Or otherwise, take sheep's tallow and sheep's dung and mix them together till they come to a salve, and then apply it to the sore.

10   *An ointment for burning.*
Take plantain leaves, daisy leaves, the green bark of elders, and green germanders, stamp them all together with fresh butter or with oil, then strain it through a linen cloth, and with a feather anoint the sore till it be whole.

"Ragwort." From John Gerarde, *The Herball, or General Historie of Plantes,* p. 218.

11   *Ulcers and sores. A salve for any old sore.*
Take of oil olive a pint, turpentine a pound, unwrought wax half a pound, resin a quarter of a pound, sheep's suet two pound, then take of

orpines, smallage, ragwort,[196] plantain, and sicklewort, of each a good handful, chop all the herbs very small, and boil them in a pan all together upon a soaking fire, and stir them exceeding much till they be well incorporate together, then take it from the fire and strain all through a strong canvas cloth into clean pots or glasses and use it as your occasion shall serve, either to anoint, tent, or plaster. Otherwise take poplar buds, and elder buds, stamp and strain them, then put thereto a little Venice turpentine, wax, and resin, and so boil them together, and therewith dress the sore, or else take two handful of plantain leaves, bray them small, and strain out the juice, then put to it as much woman's milk, a spoonful of honey, a yolk of an egg, and as much wheat flour as you think will bring it to a salve, then make a plaster thereof and lay it unto the sore, renewing it once in four and twenty hours.

212
To take away dead flesh.

Take an ounce of *unguentum apostolorum*,[197] and an ounce of *unguentum Aegyptiacum*,[198] and put them together in a pot, being first well wrought together in a bladder, and if the flesh be weak, put to it a little fine white sugar, and therewith dress the sore, or otherwise take only precipitate in fine powder, and strew it on the sore.

213
A water for a sore.

Take a gallon of smith's slake water,[199] two handfuls of sage, a pint of honey, a quart of ale, two ounces of alum, and a little white copperas; seethe them all together till half be consumed, then strain it, and put it into a clean vessel, and therewith wash the sore. Or otherwise take clean running water and put therein roche alum and madder,[200] and let them boil till the alum and the madder be consumed, then take the clearest of the water and therewith wash the sore. Or else take sage, fennel, and cinquefoil, of each a good handful, boil them in a gallon of running water till they be tender, then strain the liquor from the herbs, and put to it a quarter of a pound of roche alum, and let it seethe again a little till the alum be melted, then take it from the fire and use it thus: dip lint in it warm and lay it to the sore, and if it be hollow apply more lint, then make a little bolster of linen cloth, and wet it well in the water, then wring out the water, and so bind on the bolster close.

214
A black plaster[201] to heal old sores and kill inflammation.

Take a pint of sallat oil and put into it six ounces of red lead, and a little ceruse or white lead, then set it over a gentle fire, and let it boil a long season stirring it well till it be stiff, which you shall try in this order; let it drop from your stick or slice upon the bottom of a saucer, and so stand until it be cold, and then if it be well boiled, it will be stiff and very black; then take it off and let it stand a little, and after strain it through a cloth into a basin, but first anoint the basin with sallat oil, and also your fingers, and so make it up into rolls plasterwise, and spread it and apply it as occasion shall serve.

An ointment to ripen sores.
15

Take mallows and beets, and seethe them in water, then dry away the water from them, and beat the herbs well with old boar's grease, and so apply it to the aposthume hot.

For the stinging of any adder or venomous thing.
16

Take a handful of rue and stamp it with rusty bacon till it come to a perfect salve, and therewith dress the sore till it be whole.

For any venoming.
17

If the party be outwardly venomed, take sage[202] and bruise it well and apply it to the sore, renewing it at least twice a day, but if it be inwardly, then let the party drink the juice of sage either in wine or ale morning and evening.

For a ringworm.
18

Take celandine early in the morning,[203] and bruise it well, and then apply it to the sore, and renewing it twice or thrice a day.

For the itch.
19

Take of camphor one dram, of quicksilver four pennyworth killed well with vinegar, then mix it with two pennyworth of oil de bay,[204] and therewith anoint the body. Or otherwise take red onions and seethe them in running water a good while, then bruise the onions small, and with the water they were sodden in, strain them in, then wash the infected place with the same.

For the dried scab.[205]
220

Take a great quantity of the herb bennet,[206] and as much of red nettles, pound them well and strain them, and with the juice wash the patient naked before the fire, and so let it drink in, and wash him again, and do so divers days till he be whole.

To kill the itch, tetter, or serpigo.[207]
221

Take a pennyworth of white copperas, and as much green copperas, a quarter of an ounce of white mercury,[208] a halfpennyworth of alum and burn it, and set all over the fire with a pint of fair water, and a quarter of a pint of wine vinegar, boil all these together till they come to half a pint, and then anoint the sore therewith.

222   *To take away the scars of the small pox.*

Take barrow's grease a pretty quantity, and take an apple and pare it and take the core clean out, then chop your apple and your barrow's grease together, and set it over the fire that it may melt but not boil, then take it from the fire, and put thereto a pretty quantity of rose-water and stir all together till it be cold, and keep it in a clean vessel, and then anoint the face therewith.

223   *For the French or Spanish pox.*[209]

Take quicksilver and kill it with fasting spittle, then take verdigris,[210] arabic,[211] turpentine, oil olive, and populeon, and mix them together to one entire ointment, and anoint the sores therewith, and keep the party exceeding warm. Or otherwise, take of alum burned, of resin, frankincense, populeon, oil of roses, oil de bay, oil olive, green copperas, verdigris, white lead, mercury sublimate,[212] of each a pretty quantity but of alum most, then beat to powder the simples that are hard, and melt your oils, and cast in your powders and stir all well together, then strain them through a cloth, and apply it warm to the sores; or else take of capon's grease that hath touched no water, the juice of rue and the fine powder of pepper, and mix them together to an ointment, and apply it round about the sores, but let it not come into the sores, and it will dry them up.

224   *To put out the French or Spanish pox.*

Take of treacle half a pennyworth, of long pepper as much, and of grains as much, a little ginger, and a little quantity of liquorice, warm them with strong ale, and let the party drink it off, and lie down in his bed and take a good sweat: and then when the sores arise, use some of the ointment before rehearsed.

225   *To make the scabs of the French pox to fall away.*

Take the juice of red fennel, and the juice of sengreen, and stone honey,[213] and mix them very well together till it be thick, and with it anoint the party, but before you do anoint him you shall make this water: take sage and seethe it in very fair water from a gallon to a pottle, and put therein a quantity of honey and some alum, and let them boil a little together; when you have strained the herbs from the water, then put in your honey and your alum, and therewth wash the pox first, and let it dry in well, and then lay on the aforesaid ointment.

26   *ADDITIONS, to green wounds. A defensative for a green wound.*

Take the oil of the white of an egg, wheat flour, a little honey and Venice turpentine, take and stir all these together, and so use it about the wound but not within, and if the wound do bleed, then add to this salve a little quantity of bole armeniac.[214]

For some of the more elaborate medicines advised by Markham, a visit to the apothecary would have been necessary. From Hans Sachs, *Eygentliche Beschreibung aller Stande auf Erden,* sig. Div.

A salve for a green wound.

227   Take opopanax[215] and galbanum,[216] of each an ounce, *ammoniacum,*[217] and bedlynd[218] of each two ounces, of litharge of gold one pound and a half, new wax half a pound, *lapis calaminaris*[219] one ounce, turpentine four ounces, myrrh two ounces, oil de bay one ounce, *thus* one ounce, *aristolochia*[220] roots two ounces, oil of roses two ounces, sallat oil two pound; all the hard simples must be beaten to fine powder and searced:

take also three pints of right[221] wine vinegar, and put your four gums into the vinegar a whole day before till the gums be dissolved, then set it over the fire and let it boil very softly till your vinegar be as good as boiled away, then take an earthen pot with a wide mouth and put your oil in and your wax, but your wax must be scraped before you put it in, then by a little at once put in your litharge and stir it exceedingly, then put in all your gums and all the rest, but let your turpentine be last, and so let it boil till you see it grow to be thick, then pour it into a basin of water and work it with oil of roses for sticking to your hands, and make it up in rolls plasterwise, and here is to be noted, that your oil of roses must not be boiled with the rest, but [added] after it is taken from the fire, a little before the turpentine.

228   *A water to heal any green wound, cut, or sore.*

Take three good handful of sage, and as much of honeysuckle leaves and the flowers clean picked, then take one pound of roche alum, and a quarter of a pound of right English honey clarified clean, half a penny-worth of grains, and two gallons of running water, then put all the said things into the water, and let them seethe till half be consumed, then take it from the fire till it be almost cold and strain it through a clean cloth, and put it up in a glass, and then either on tent or pledget use as you have occasion.

229   *To staunch blood and draw sinews together.*

Take a quart of rye flour and temper it with running water, and make dough thereof, then according to the bigness of the wound lay it in with the defensative plaster before rehearsed[222] over it, and every dressing make it less and less till the wound be closed.

230   *A made oil for shrinking of sinews.*

Take a quart of neat's-foot oil,[223] a quart of ox galls, a quart of aqua vitae, and a quart of rose-water, a handful of rosemary stripped, and boil all these together till half be consumed, then press and strain it, and use it according as you find occasion.

231   *For a wound in the guts.*

Take honey, pitch, and butter, and seethe them together, and anoint the hurt against[224] the fire, and tent the sore with the same.

232   *For pricking with a thorn.*

Take groundsel and stamp it, and seethe it with sweet milk till it be thick, then temper it with black soap[225] and lay it to the sore.

233

To gather flesh in wounds.

Take resin, a quarter of a pound, of wax three ounces, of oil of roses one ounce and a half, seethe all them together in a pint of white wine till it come to skimming, then take it from the fire and put thereto two ounces of Venice turpentine, and apply it to the wound or sore.

234

ADDITIONS, for ache or swellings. For the sciatica.

Take mustard made with strong vinegar, the crumbs of brown bread, with a quantity of honey and six figs mixed, temper all together well and lay it upon a cloth plasterwise, put a thin cloth between the plaster and the flesh and lay it to the place grieved as oft as need requires.

235

A yellow cerecloth[226] for any pain or swelling.

Take a pound of fine resin, of oil de bay two ounces, of populeon as much, of frankincense half a pound, of oil of spike[227] two ounces, of oil of camomile two ounces, of oil of roses two ounces, of wax half a pound, of turpentine a quarter of a pound, melt them and stir them well together and then dip linen cloths therein, and apply the cerecloth as you shall have occasion, and note the more oil you use, the more suppler the cerecloth is, and the less oil the stiffer it will be.

236

For bruises swelled.

Take a little black soap, salt, and honey, and beat them well together, and spread it on a brown paper and apply it to the bruise.

237

For swelled legs.

Take mallows and seethe them in the dregs of good ale or milk, and make a plaster thereof, and apply it to the place swelled.

238

For any ache.

Take, in the month of May, henbane and bruise it well and put it into an earthen pot and put thereto a pint of sallat oil and set it in the sun till it be all one substance, then anoint the ache therewith.

239

A plaster for any pain or ache in the joints.

Take half a pound of unwrought wax, as much resin, one ounce of galbanum, a quarter of a pound of litharge of gold, three quarters of white lead beaten to powder and searced, then take a pint of neat's-foot oil and set it on the fire in a small vessel which may contain the rest, and when it is all molten, then put in the powders and stir it fast with a slice, and try it upon the bottom of a saucer; when it beginneth to be somewhat hard, then take it from the fire, and anoint a fair board with neat's-foot oil, and as [soon as] you may handle it for heat, work it up in rolls, and it will keep five or six years, being wrapped up close in papers; and when you will use it, spread of it thin upon new lockram or leather somewhat bigger than the grief, and so if the grief remove, follow it, renewing it morning and evening, and let it be somewhat warm when it is laid on, and beware of taking cold, and drinking hot wines.

240   *ADDITIONS, to grief in the bones. For bones out of joint or sinews sprung or strained.*

Take four or five yolks of eggs, hard sodden[228] or roasted, and take the branches of great morel,[229] and the berries in summer, and in winter the roots, and bray all well together in a mortar with sheep's milk, and then fry it until it be very thick and so make a plaster thereof, and lay it about the sore and it will take away both pain and swelling.

241   *A bath for broken joints.*

Take a gallon of standing lye, put to it of plantain and knotgrass, of each two handful, of wormwood and comfrey, of each a handful, and boil all these together in the lye a good while, and when it is lukewarm bathe the broken member therewith, and take the buds of elder gathered in March, and stripped downward, and a little boil them in water, then eat them in oil and very little wine vinegar, a good quantity at a time in the morning ever before meat, or an hour before the patient go to dinner, and it much avails to the knitting of bones.

242   *A general bath for clearing the skin and comforting the body.*

Take rosemary, featherfew, organy,[230] pellitory of the wall, fennel, mallows, violet leaves, and nettles; boil all these together, and when it is well sodden put to it two or three gallons of milk, then let the party stand or sit in it an hour or two, the bath reaching up to the stomach, and when they come out they must go to bed and sweat; beware taking of cold.

243   *A sovereign help for broken bones.*

Make a plaster of wheat flour and the whites of eggs, and spread it on a double linen cloth, then lay the plaster on an even board, and lay the broken limb thereon, and set it even according to nature, and lap the plaster about it and splint it, and give him to drink knitwort,[231] the juice thereof, twice and no more, for the third time it will unknit, but give him to drink nine days each day twice the juice of comfrey, daisies, and osmund in stale ale and it shall knit it, and let the foresaid plaster lie to ten days at the least, and when you take it away do thus; take horehound, red fennel, hound's-tongue, wallwort, and pellitory, and seethe them, then unroll the member and take away the splints, and then bathe the linen and the plaster about the member in this bath, until it have soaked so long that it come gently away of itself, then take the aforesaid plaster and lay thereto five or six days very hot, and let each plaster lie a day and a night and always splint it well, and after cherish it with the ointments before rehearsed for broken bones, and keep the party from unwholesome meats and drinks till he be whole, and if the hurt be on his arm let him bear a ball of green herbs in his hand to prevent the shrinking of the hand and sinews.

For any fever.

Take sage, ragwort, yarrow, unset leeks, of each a like quantity, stamp them with bay salt and apply them to the wrists of the hands.

To expel heat in a fever.

Blanch almonds in the cold water, and make milk[232] of them (but it must not seethe) then put to it sugar, and in the extremity of heat, see that you drink thereof.

The royal medicine for fevers.

Take three spoonful of ale and a little saffron, and bruise and strain it thereto, then add a quarter of a spoonful of fine treacle and mix it together, and drink it when the fit comes.

Another.

Take two roots of crowfoot[233] that grows in a marsh ground, which have no little roots about them, to the number of twenty or more, and a little of the earth that is about them, and do not wash them, and add a little quantity of salt, and mix all well together and lay it on linen cloths and bind it about your thumbs betwixt the first and the nether joint, and let it lie nine days unremoved, and it will expel the fever.

An approved medicine for the greatest lax or flux.

Take a right pomwater[234] the greatest you can get, or else two little ones, roast them very tender to pap, then take away the skin and the core and use only the pap, and the like quantity of chalk finely scraped, mix them both together upon a trencher before the fire, and work them well to a plaster, then spread it upon a linen cloth warmed very hot as may be suffered, and so bind it to the navel for twenty four hours; use this medicine twice or thrice or more until the lax be stayed.

249   *Of oil of swallows.*

To make the oil of swallows, take lavender cotton, spike, knotgrass, ribwort, balm, valerian, rosemary tops, woodbine tops, vine strings, French mallows, the tops of alecost,[235] strawberry strings, tutsan, plantain, walnut tree leaves, the tops of young bays, hyssop, violet leaves, sage of virtue,[236] fine Roman wormwood,[237] of each of them a handful, camomile and red roses, of each two handful, twenty quick swallows, and beat them all together in a great mortar, and put to them a quart of neat's-foot oil, or May butter, and grind them all well together with two ounces of cloves well beaten, then put them all together in an earthen pot, and stop it very close that no air come into it, and set it nine days in a cellar or cold place, then open your pot and put into it half a pound of white or yellow wax cut very small, and a pint of oil or butter, then set your pot close stopped into a pan of water, and let it boil six or eight hours, and then strain it. This oil is exceeding sovereign for any broken bones, bones out of joint, or any pain or grief either in the bones or sinews.[238]

250   *To make oil of camomile.*

To make oil of camomile,[239] take a quart of sallat oil and put it into a glass, then take a handful of camomile and bruise it, and put it into the oil, and let them stand in the same twelve days, only you must shift it every three days, that is to strain it from the old camomile, and put in as much of new; and that oil is very sovereign for any grief proceeding from cold[240] causes.

251   *To make oil of lavender.*

To make oil of lavender, take a pint of sallat oil and put it into a glass, then put to it a handful of lavender, and let it stand in the same twelve days, and use it in all respects as you did your oil of camomile.

252   *To make smooth hands.*

To make an oil which shall make the skin of the hands very smooth, take almonds and beat them to oil, then take whole cloves and put them both together into a glass, and set it in the sun five or six days; then strain it, and with the same anoint your hands every night when you go to bed, and otherwise as you have convenient leisure.

253   *To make Doctor Stevens' water.*

To make that sovereign water which was first invented by Doctor Stevens,[241] in the same form as he delivered the receipt to the Archbishop of Canterbury, a little before the death of the said doctor: take a gallon of good Gascon wine,[242] then take ginger, galingale, cinnamon, nutmegs, grains, cloves bruised, fennel seeds, caraway seeds, origanum,[243] of every of them a like quantity, that is to say a dram; then take sage, wild marjoram, pennyroyal, mints, red roses, thyme, pellitory, rosemary, wild thyme, camomile, lavender, of each of them a handful, then bray the spices small, and bruise the herbs and put all into the wine, and let it stand so twelve hours, only stir it divers times; then distil it by a limbeck, and keep the first water by itself, for that is the best, then keep the second water for that is good, and for the last neglect it not, for it is very wholesome though the worst of the three. Now for the virtue of this water it is this, it comforteth the spirits and vital parts, and helpeth all inward diseases that cometh of cold, it is good against the shaking of the palsy, and cureth the contraction of sinews, and helpeth the conception of women that be barren; it killeth the worms in the body, it cureth the cold cough, it helpeth the toothache, it comforteth the stomach and cureth the old dropsy, it helpeth the stone in the bladder and in the reins, it helpeth a stinking breath; and whosoever useth this water moderately and not too often, preserveth him in good liking, and will make him seem young in old age. With this water Doctor Stevens preserved his own life until such extreme age, that he could neither go nor ride, and he continued his life being bed-rid five years, when other physicians did judge he could not live one year, which he did confess a little before his death, saying: that if he were sick at any time, he never used anything but this water only. And also the Archbishop of Canterbury used it, and found such goodness in it that he lived till he was not able to drink of a cup, but sucked his drink through a hollow pipe of silver. This water will be much the better if it be set in the sun all summer.

A restorative of rosa solis.

To make a cordial *rosa solis*:[244] take *rosa solis*, and in any wise touch not the leaves thereof in the gathering, nor wash it; take thereof four good handfuls, then take two good pints of aqua vitae, and put them both in a glass or pewter pot of three or four pints, and then stop the same hard and just, and so let it stand three days and three nights; and the third day strain it through a clean cloth into another glass or pewter pot, and put thereto half a pound of sugar beaten small, four ounces of fine liquorice beaten into powder, half a pound of sound dates, the stones being taken out, and cut them, make them clean, and then mince them small; and mix all these together and stop the glass or pot close and just, and after distil it through a limbeck, then drink of it at night to bedward half a spoonful with ale or beer (but ale is the better), as much in the morning fasting; for there is not the weakest body in the world that wanteth nature or strength, or that is in a consumption, but it will restore him again, and cause him to be strong and lusty, and to have a marvellous hungry stomach, provided always that this *rosa solis* be gathered (as near as you possibly can) at the full of the moon when the sun shineth before noon, and let the roots of them be cut away.

255   *ADDITIONS to the oils. To make oil of roses or violets.*
Take the flowers of roses or violets, and break them small and put them into sallat oil, and let them stand in the same ten or twelve days, and then press it. Or otherwise take a quart of oil olive, and put thereto six spoonfuls of clean water, and stir it well with a slice, till it wax as white as milk, then take two pound of red rose leaves and cut the white of the ends of the leaves away, and put the roses into the oil, and then put it into a double glass and set it in the sun all the summer time, and it is sovereign for any scalding or burning with water or oil. Or else take red roses new plucked, a pound or two, and cut the white ends of the leaves away, then take May butter[245] and melt it over the fire with two pound of oil olive, and when it is clarified put in your roses and put it all in a vessel of glass or of earthen[ware], and stop it well about that no air enter in nor out, and set it in another vessel with water and let it boil half a day or more, and then take it forth and strain or press it through a cloth, and put it into glass bottles; this is good for all manner of unkind heats.

256   *To make oil of nutmegs.*
Take two or three pound of nutmegs and cut them small and bruise them well, then put them into a pan and beat them and stir them about; which done, put them into a canvas or strong linen bag, and close them in a press and press them, and get out all the liquor of them which will be like manna,[246] then scrape it from the canvas bag as much as you can with a knife, then put it into some vessel of glass and stop it well, but set it not in the sun for it will wax clean of itself within ten or fifteen days, and it is worth thrice so much as the nutmegs themselves, and the oil hath very great virtue in comforting the stomach and inward parts, and assuaging the pain of the mother and sciatica.

257   *To make perfect oil of spike.*
Take the flowers of spike, and wash them only in oil olive and then stamp them well, then put them in a canvas bag and press them in a press as hard as you can, and take that which cometh out, carefully, and put

it into a strong vessel of glass, and set it not in the sun for it will clear of itself and wax fair and bright and will have a very sharp odour of the spike; and thus you may make oil of other herbs of like nature, as lavender, camomile, and such like.

8

To make oil of mastic.

Take an ounce of mastic,[247] and an ounce of olibanum[248] pounded as small as is possible, and boil them in oil olive (a quart) to a third part, then press it and put it into a glass, and after ten or twelve days it will be perfect: it is exceeding good for any cold grief.

9

Thus having in a summary manner passed over all the most physical and surgical notes which ought to burden the mind of our English housewife, being as much as is needful for the preservation of the health of her family; and having in this chapter showed all the inward virtues wherewith she should be adorned, I will now return to her more outward and active knowledges, wherein, albeit the mind be as much occupied as before, yet is the body a great deal more in use: neither can the work be well effected by rule or direction.

CHAPTER II

*Of the outward and active knowledge of the
housewife; and first of her skill in cookery; as sallats
of all sorts, with flesh, fish, sauces, pastry, banqueting
stuff, and ordering of great feasts*

1   To speak then of the outward and active knowledges which belong to
our English housewife, I hold the first and most principal to be a perfect
skill and knowledge in cookery, together with all the secrets belonging
to the same, because it is a duty really belonging to a woman; and she
that is utterly ignorant therein may not by the laws of strict justice
challenge the freedom of marriage, because indeed she can then but perform half her vow;[1] for she may love and obey, but she cannot serve and
keep him with that true duty which is ever expected.

2   *She must know all herbs.*
To proceed then to this knowledge of cookery, you shall understand
that the first step thereunto is to have knowledge of all sorts of herbs
belonging to the kitchen, whether they be for the pot, for sallats, for
sauces, for servings, or for any other seasoning, or adorning; which skill
of knowledge of the herbs she must get by her own true labour and
experience, and not by my relation, which would be much too tedious;
and for the use of them, she shall see it in the composition of dishes and
meats hereafter following. She shall also know the time of the year,
month, and moon, in which all herbs are to be sown; and when they are
in their best flourishing, that, gathering all herbs in their height of goodness, she may have the prime use of the same. And because I will enable,
and not burden her memory, I will here give her a short epitome of all
that knowledge.

3   *Her skill in the garden.*
First then,[2] let our English housewife know that she may at all times

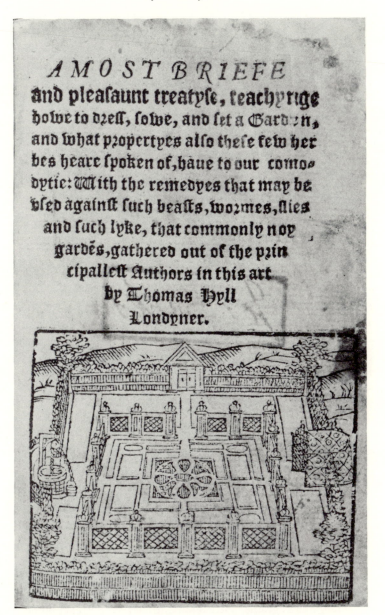

The housewife's garden was both productive and decorative. Title-page from Thomas Hill, *A Most Briefe and Pleasaunt Treatyse, Teaching Howe to Dress, Sowe, and Set a Garden.*

of the month and moon, generally sow asparagus, coleworts,[3] spinach, lettuce, parsnips, radish, and chives.

4   In February, in the new of the moon, she may sow spike, garlic, borage, bugloss,[4] chervil,[5] coriander, gourds, cresses, marjoram, *palma Christi*,[6] flower-gentle, white poppy, purslane, radish, rocket, rosemary, sorrel, double marigolds,[7] and thyme. The moon full, she may sow aniseeds musked,[8] violets, bleets,[9] skirrets,[10] white succory,[11] fennel, and parsley. The moon old, sow holy thistle, cole cabbage,[12] white cole, green cole, cucumbers, hartshorn,[13] dyer's grain, cabbage-lettuce,[14] melons, onions, parsnips, lark-heel, burnet,[15] and leeks.

5   In March, the moon new, sow garlic, borage, bugloss, chervil, coriander, gourds, marjoram, white poppy, purslane, radish, sorrel, double marigolds, thyme, violets. At the full moon, aniseeds, bleets, skirrets, succory,[16] fennel, apples of love,[17] and marvellous apples.[18] At the wane, artichokes, basil, blessed thistle, cole cabbage, white cole, green cole, citrons, cucumbers, hartshorn, samphire,[19] spinach, gillyflowers, hyssop, cabbage-lettuce, melons, muggets,[20] onions, flower-gentle, burnet, leeks and savory. In the month of April, the moon being new, sow marjoram, flower-gentle, thyme, violets; in the full of the moon, apples of love, and marvellous apples; and in the wane, artichokes, holy thistle, cabbage-cole, citrons, hartshorn, samphire, gillyflowers, [muggets],[21] and parsnips. In May, the moon old, sow blessed thistle. In June, the moon new, sow gourds and radishes. The moon old, sow cucumbers, melons, parsnips. In July, the moon at full, sow white succory, and the moon old, sow cabbage-lettuce. Lastly, in August, the moon at full, sow white succory.

6   *Transplanting of herbs.*

Also she must know that herbs growing of seeds may be transplanted at all times, except chervil, orach,[22] spinach, and parsley, which are not good being once transplanted, observing ever to transplant in moist and rainy weather.

7   *Choice of seeds.*

Also she must know that the choice of seeds are twofold, of which some grow best being new, as cucumbers and leeks, and some being old, as coriander, parsley, savory, beets, origanum, cresses, spinach and poppy; you must keep [from the] cold:[23] lettuce, artichokes, basil, holy thistle, cabbage, cole, dyer's grains, and melons, fifteen days after they put forth of the earth.

8   *Prosperity of seeds.*

Also seeds prosper better being sown in temperate weather than in hot, cold, or dry days.

"Oval" and "maze" garden-knots, or designs. From part six of *A Way to Get Wealth, The Country Housewifes Garden*, by William Lawson, p. 84.

9   *Gathering of seeds.*

Seeds must be gathered in fair weather, at the wane of the moon, and kept, some in boxes of wood, some in bags of leather, and some in vessels of earth, and after to be well cleansed and dried in the sun or shadow; othersome, as onions, chibols,[24] and leeks, must be kept in their husks. Lastly, she must know that it is best to plant in the last quarter of the moon; to gather grafts in the last but one, and to graft two days after the change; and thus much for her knowledge briefly of herbs, and how she shall have them continually for her use in the kitchen.

10   *Of cookery and the parts thereof.*

It resteth now that I proceed unto cookery itself, which is the dressing and ordering of meat, in good and wholesome manner; to which, when our housewife shall address herself, she shall well understand, that these qualities must ever accompany it: first, she must be cleanly both in body and garments, she must have a quick eye, a curious[25] nose, a perfect taste, and a ready ear (she must not be butter-fingered, sweet-toothed, nor faint-hearted; for the first will let everything fall, the second will consume what it should increase, and the last will lose time with too much niceness). Now for the substance of the art itself, I will divide it into five parts: the first, sallats and fricassees;[26] the second, boiled meats and broths; the third, roast meats, and carbonadoes;[27] the fourth, baked meats and pies; and the fifth, banqueting and made dishes, with other conceits[28] and secrets.

11   *Of sallats. Simple sallats.*

First then to speak of sallats,[29] there be some simple, and some compounded; some only to furnish out the table, and some both for use and adornation: your simple sallats are chibols peeled, washed clean, and half of the green tops cut clean away, so served on a fruit dish; or chives, scallions, radish roots, boiled carrots, skirrets,[30] and turnips, with such like served up simply; also, all young lettuce, cabbage lettuce, purslane,[31] and divers other herbs which may be served simply without anything but a little vinegar, sallat oil, and sugar; onions boiled,[32] and stripped from their rind and served up with vinegar, oil and pepper is a good simple sallat; so is samphire, bean cods, asparagus, and cucumbers, served in likewise with oil, vinegar, and pepper, with a world of others, too tedious to nominate.

12   *Of compound sallats.*

Your compound sallats[33] are first the young buds and knots of all manner of wholesome herbs at their first springing; as red sage, mints, lettuce, violets, marigolds, spinach, and many other mixed together, and then served up to the table with vinegar, sallat oil and sugar.

Another compound sallat.

3   To compound an excellent sallat, and which indeed is usual at great feasts, and upon princes' tables: take a good quantity of blanched almonds, and with your shredding knife cut them grossly; then take as many raisins of the sun, clean washed and the stones picked out, as many figs shred like the almonds, as many capers, twice so many olives, and as many currants as of all the rest, clean washed, a good handful of the small tender leaves of red sage and spinach; mix all these well together with good store of sugar, and lay them in the bottom of a great dish; then put unto them vinegar and oil, and scrape more sugar over all; then take oranges and lemons, and, paring away the outward peels, cut them into thin slices, then with those slices cover the sallat all over; which done, take the fine thin leaf of the red cauliflower,[34] and with them cover the oranges and lemons all over; then over those red leaves lay another course of old olives, and the slices of well pickled cucumbers, together with the very inward heart of your cabbage lettuce cut into slices; then adorn the sides of the dish, and the top of the sallat with more slices of lemons and oranges, and so serve it up.[35]

An excellent boiled sallat.

4   To make an excellent compound boiled sallat:[36] take of spinach[37] well washed two or three handfuls, and put it into fair water, and boil it till it be exceeding soft, and tender as pap; then put it into a colander and drain the water from it; which done, with the backside of your chopping knife chop it, and bruise it as small as may be: then put it into a pipkin with a good lump of sweet butter, and boil it over again; then take a good handful of currants clean washed, and put to it, and stir them well together; then put to as much vinegar as will make it reasonable tart, and then with sugar season it according to the taste of the master of the house, and so serve it upon sippets.[38]

Of preserving of sallats.

5   Your preserved sallats are of two kinds, either pickled, as are cucumbers, samphire, purslane, broom,[39] and such like, or preserved with vinegar, as violets, primrose, cowslips, gillyflowers[40] of all kinds, broom flowers, and for the most part any wholesome flower whatsoever.

[Of pickling sallats.]

6   Now for the pickling of sallats, they are only boiled, and then drained

from the water, spread upon a table, and good store of salt thrown over them, then when they are thorough cold, make a pickle with water, salt, and a little vinegar, and with the same pot them up in close earthen pots, and serve them forth as occasion shall serve.

17 *[Of preserving sallats.]*

Now for preserving sallats, you shall take any of the flowers before said after they have been picked clean from their stalks, and the white ends (of them which have any) clean cut away, and washed and dried, and, taking a glass pot like a gallipot, or for want thereof a gallipot itself; and first strew a little sugar in the bottom, then lay a layer of the flowers, then cover that layer over with sugar, then lay another layer of the flowers, and another of sugar; and thus do one above another till the pot be filled, ever and anon pressing them hard down with your hand: this done, you shall take of the best and sharpest vinegar you can get (and if the vinegar be distilled vinegar, the flowers will keep their colours the better) and with it fill up your pot till the vinegar swim aloft, and no more can be received; then stop up the pot close, and set them in a dry temperate place, and use them at pleasure, for they will last all the year.

18 *The making of strange sallats.*

Now for the compounding of sallats of these pickled and preserved things, though they may be served up simply of themselves, and are both good and dainty, yet for better curiosity, and the finer adorning of the table, you shall thus use them: first, if you would set forth any red flower that you know or have seen, you shall take your pots of preserved gilly-flowers, and suiting the colours answerable to the flower you shall proportion it forth, and lay the shape of the flower in a fruit dish; then with your purslane leaves make the green coffin of the flower, and with the purslane stalks, make the stalk of the flower, and the divisions of the leaves and branches; then with the thin slices of cucumbers make their leaves in true proportions, jagged or otherwise: and thus you may set forth some full blown, some half blown, and some in the bud, which will be pretty and curious. And if you will set forth yellow flowers, take the pots of primroses and cowslips, if blue flowers then the pots of violets, or bugloss flowers; and these sallats are both for show and use, for they are more excellent to taste than to look on.

19 *Sallats for show only.*

Now for sallats for show only,[41] and the adorning and setting out of a table with numbers of dishes, they be those which are made of carrot roots of sundry colours well boiled,[42] and cut out into many shapes and proportions, as some into knots, some in the manner of scutcheons and arms,[43] some like birds, and some like wild beasts, according to the art and cunning of the workman; and these for the most part are seasoned with vinegar, oil, and a little pepper. A world of other sallats there are, which time and experience may bring to our housewife's eye, but the composition of them and the serving of them differeth nothing from these already rehearsed.

Of fricassees and quelquechoses.

Now to proceed to your fricassees, or *quelquechoses*,[44] which are dishes of many compositions and ingredients, as flesh, fish, eggs, herbs, and many other things, all being prepared and made ready in a frying pan; they are likewise of two sorts, simple, and compound.

Of simple fricassees.

Your simple fricassees are eggs and collops fried, whether the collops be of bacon, ling,[45] beef, or young pork, the frying whereof is so ordinary, that it needeth not any relation, or the frying of any flesh or fish simple of itself with butter or sweet oil.

Best collops and eggs.

To have the best collops and eggs, you shall take the whitest and youngest bacon; and, cutting away the sward,[46] cut the collops into thin slices; lay them in a dish, and put hot water unto them, and so let them stand an hour or two, for that will take away the extreme saltness; then drain away the water clean, and put them into a dry pewter dish, and lay them one by one, and set them before the heat of the fire, so as they may toast, and turn them so as they may toast sufficiently through and through: which done, take your eggs and break them into a dish, and put a spoonful of vinegar unto them, then set on a clean skillet with fair water on the fire, and as soon as the water boileth put in the eggs, and let them take a boil or two, then with a spoon try if they be hard enough, and then take them up, and trim them, and dry them; and then, dishing up the collops, lay the eggs upon them, and so serve them up: and in this sort you may poach eggs when you please, for it is the best way and most wholesome.

Of the compound fricassees.

Now the compound fricassees are those which consist of many things, as tansies,[47] fritters, pancakes, and any *quelquechose* whatsoever, being things of great request and estimation in France, Spain, and Italy, and the most curious nations.

24   *To make the best tansy.*

First then for making the best tansy,[48] you shall take a certain number of eggs, according to the bigness of your frying pan, and break them into a dish, abating ever the white of every third egg; then with a spoon you shall cleanse away the little white chicken knots which stick unto the yolks; then with a little cream[49] beat them exceedingly together: then take of green wheat blades, violet leaves, strawberry leaves, spinach, and succory, of each a like quantity, and a few walnut tree buds; chop and beat all these very well, and then strain out the juice, and, mixing it with a little more cream, put it to the eggs, and stir all well together; then put in a few crumbs of bread, fine grated bread, cinnamon, nutmeg and salt, then put some sweet butter into the frying pan, and so soon as it is dissolved or melted, put in the tansy, and fry it brown without burning, and with a dish turn it in the pan as occasion shall serve; then serve it up, having strewed good store of sugar upon it, for to put in sugar before will make it heavy.[50] Some use to put of the herb tansy[51] into it, but the walnut tree buds do give the better taste or relish; and therefore when you please for to use the one, do not use the other.

25   *The best fritters.*

To make the best fritters, take a pint of cream and warm it; then take eight eggs, only abate four of the whites, and beat them well in a dish, and so mix them with the cream, then put in a little cloves, mace, nutmeg, and saffron, and stir them well together; then put in two spoonful of the best ale barm, and a little salt, and stir it again; then make it thick according unto your pleasure with wheat flour; which done, set it within the air of the fire, that it may rise and swell; which when it doth, you shall beat it in once or twice, then put into it a penny pot of sack: all this being done, you shall take a pound or two of very sweet seam, and put it into a pan, and set it over the fire, and when it is molten and begins to bubble, you shall take the fritter batter, and, setting it by you, put thick slices of well-pared apples into the batter; and then taking the apples and batter out together with a spoon put it into the boiling seam, and boil your fritters crisp and brown: and when you find the strength of your seam consume or decay, you shall renew it with more seam; and of all sorts of seam that which is made of the beef suet is the best and strongest: when your fritters are made, strew good store of sugar and cinnamon upon them, being fair dished, and so serve them up.

26   *The best pancake.*

To make the best pancake, take two or three eggs, and break them into a dish, and beat them well; then add unto them a pretty quantity of

A German view of the kitchen: wife, husband, and cat prepare the meal. From the title-page of Marx Rumpolt, *Ein new Kochbuch*.

fair running water,[52] and beat all well together; then put in cloves, mace, cinnamon, and nutmeg, and season it with salt: which done, make it thick as you think good with fine wheat flour; then fry the cakes as thin as may be with sweet butter, or sweet seam, and make them brown, and so serve them up with sugar strewed upon them. There be some which mix pancakes with new milk or cream,[53] but that makes them tough, cloying, and not crisp, pleasant and savoury as running water.

Veal toasts.

To make the best veal toasts,[54] take the kidney fat, and all of a loin of veal roasted, and shred it as small as is possible; then take a couple of eggs and beat them very well; which done, take spinach, succory, violet leaves, and marigold leaves, and beat them, and strain out the juice, and mix it with the eggs: then put it to your veal, and stir it exceedingly well in a dish; then put to good store of currants clean washed and picked, cloves, mace, cinnamon, nutmeg, sugar, and salt, and mix them all perfectly well together; then take a manchet and cut it into toasts, and toast them well before the fire; then with a spoon lay upon the toasts in a good thickness the veal, prepared as beforesaid: which done, put into your frying pan good store of sweet butter, and when it is well melted and very hot, put your toasts into the same with the bread side upward, and the flesh side downward; and as soon as you see they are fried brown, lay upon the upperside of the toasts which are bare more of the flesh meat, and then turn them, and fry that side brown also: then take them out of the pan and dish them up, and strew sugar upon them, and so serve them forth. There be some cooks which will do this but upon one side of the toasts, but to do it on both is much better. If you add cream it is not amiss.

28 *To make the best panperdy.*

To make the best panperdy,[55] take a dozen eggs, and break them, and beat them very well, then put unto them cloves, mace, cinnamon, nutmeg, and good store of sugar, with as much salt as shall season it: then take a manchet, and cut it into thick slices like toasts; which done, take your frying pan, and put into it good store of sweet butter, and, being melted, lay in your slices of bread, then pour upon them one half of your eggs; then when that is fried, with a dish turn your slices of bread upward, and then pour on them the other half of your eggs, and so turn them till both sides be brown; then dish it up, and serve it with sugar strewed upon it.

29 *To make any quelquechose.*

To make a *quelquechose*, which is a mixture of many things together; take eggs and break them, and do away the one half of the whites, and after they are beaten put to them a good quantity of sweet cream, currants, cinnamon, cloves, mace, salt, and a little ginger, spinach, endive, and marigold flowers grossly chopped, and beat them all very well together; then take pig's pettitoes sliced, and grossly chopped, and mix them with the eggs, and with your hand stir them exceeding well together; then put sweet butter in your frying pan, and, being melted, put in all the rest, and fry it brown without burning, ever and anon turning it till it be fried enough; then dish it up upon a flat plate, and cover it with sugar,[56] and so serve it forth. Only herein is to be observed, that your pettitoes must be very well boiled before you put them into the fricassee.

30 And in this manner as you make this *quelquechose*, so you may make any other, whether it be of flesh, small birds, sweet roots, oysters, mussels, cockles, giblets, lemons, oranges, or any fruit, pulse, or other sallat herb whatsoever; of which to speak severally were a labour infinite, because they vary with men's opinions. Only the composition

Kitchen activities: crust for a pie is being raised on the left, roast meats and pottage prepared on the right. From the title-page of *The Accomplished Lady's Delight in Preserving, Physick, Beautifying and Cookery.*

and work is no other than this before prescribed; and who can do these need no further instruction for the rest. And thus much for sallats and fricassees.

31   *ADDITIONS to the housewife's cookery. To make fritters.*
     To make fritters another way, take flour, milk, barm, grated bread, small raisins, cinnamon, sugar, cloves, mace, pepper, saffron, and salt; stir all these together very well with a strong spoon, or small ladle; then let it stand more than a quarter of an hour that it may rise, then beat it in again, and thus let it rise and be beat in twice or thrice at least; then take it and bake them in sweet and strong seam, as hath been before showed; and when they are served up to the table, see you strew upon them good store of sugar, cinnamon, and ginger.

32   *To make the best white puddings.*[57]
     Take a pint of the best, thickest, and sweetest cream, and boil it, then whilst it is hot, put thereunto a good quantity of fair great oatmeal grits[58] very sweet and clean picked, and formerly steeped in milk twelve hours at least, and let it soak in this cream another night; then put thereto at least eight yolks of eggs, a little pepper, cloves, mace, saffron, currants, dates, sugar, salt, and great store of swine's suet, or for want thereof, great store of beef suet, and then fill it up in the farmes[59] according to the order of good housewifery, and then boil them on a soft and gentle fire, and as they swell, prick them with a great pin, or small awl, to keep them that they burst not: and when you serve them to the table (which

must be not till they be a day old), first boil them a little, then take them out and toast them brown before the fire, and so serve them, trimming the edge of the dish either with salt or sugar.

33 *Puddings of a hog's liver.*

Take the liver of a fat hog and parboil it, then shred it small, and after, beat it in a mortar very fine; then mix it with the thickest and sweetest cream, and strain it very well through an ordinary strainer; then put thereto six yolks of eggs, and two whites, and the grated crumbs of near hand a penny white loaf, with good store of currants, dates, cloves, mace, sugar, saffron, salt, and the best swine suet, or beef suet, but beef suet is the more wholesome, and less loosening; then after it hath stood a while, fill it into the farmes, and boil them, as before showed; and when you serve them to the table, first boil them a little, then lay them on a gridiron over the coals, and broil them gently, but scorch them not, nor in any wise break their skins, which is to be prevented by oft turning and tossing them on the gridiron, and keeping a slow fire.

34 *To make bread puddings.*

Take the yolks and whites of a dozen or fourteen eggs, and, having beat them very well, put to them the fine powder of cloves, mace, nutmegs, sugar, cinnamon, saffron, and salt; then take the quantity of two loaves of white grated bread, dates (very small shred) and great store of currants, with good plenty either of sheep's, hog's, or beef suet beaten and cut small; then when all is mixed and stirred well together, and hath stood a while to settle, then fill it into the farmes as hath been before showed, and in like manner boil them, cook them, and serve them to the table.

35 *Rice puddings.*

Take half a pound of rice, and steep it in new milk a whole night, and in the morning drain it, and let the milk drop away; then take a quart of the best, sweetest, and thickest cream, and put the rice into it, and boil it a little; then set it to cool an hour or two, and after put in the yolks of half a dozen eggs, a little pepper, cloves, mace, currants, dates, sugar, and salt; and having mixed them well together, put in great store of beef suet well beaten, and small shred, and so put it into the farmes, and boil them as before showed, and serve them after a day old.

36 *Another of liver.*

Take the best hog's liver you can get, and boil it extremely till it be as hard as a stone; then lay it to cool, and, being cold, upon a bread-grater grate it all to powder; then sift it through a fine meal-sieve, and put to it the crumbs of (at least) two penny loaves of white bread, and boil all in the thickest and sweetest cream you have till it be very thick; then let it cool, and put to it the yolks of half a dozen eggs, a little pepper cloves, mace, currants, dates small shred, cinnamon, ginger, a little nutmeg, good store of sugar, a little saffron, salt, and of beef and swine's suet great plenty, then fill it into the farmes, and boil them as before showed.

Puddings of a calf's mugget.

37
 Take a calf's mugget, clean and sweet dressed, and boil it well; then shred it as small as is possible, then take of strawberry leaves, of endive, spinach, succory, and sorrel, of each a pretty quantity, and chop them as small as is possible, and then mix them with the mugget; then take the yolks of half a dozen eggs, and three whites, and beat them into it also; and if you find it is too stiff,[60] then make it thinner with a little cream warmed on the fire; then put in a little pepper, cloves, mace, cinnamon, ginger, sugar, currants, dates, and salt, and work all together, with casting in little pieces of sweet butter one after another, till it have received good store of butter; then put it up into the calf's bag, sheep's bag, or hog's bag, and then boil it well,[61] and so serve it up.

A blood pudding.

38
 Take the blood of a hog whilst it is warm, and steep in it a quart, or more, of great oatmeal grits, and at the end of three days with your hands take the grits out of the blood, and drain them clean; then put to those grits more than a quart of the best cream warmed on the fire; then take mother of thyme, parsley, spinach, succory, endive, sorrel, and strawberry leaves, of each a few chopped exceeding small, and mix them with the grits, and also a little fennel seed finely beaten; then add a little pepper, cloves and mace, salt, and great store of suet finely shred, and well beaten; then therewith fill your farmes, and boil them, as hath been before described.

Links.[62]

39
 Take the largest of your chines[63] of pork, and that which is called a list,[64] and first with your knife cut the lean thereof into thin slices, and then shred small those slices, and then spread it over the bottom of a dish or wooden platter; then take the fat of the chine and the list, and cut it in the very self same manner, and spread it upon the lean, and then cut more lean, and spread it on the fat, and thus do one lean upon another till all the pork be shred, observing to begin and end with the lean; then

with your sharp knife scotch it through and through divers ways, and mix it all well together: then take good store of sage, and shred it exceeding small, and mix it with the flesh, then give it a good season of pepper and salt; then take the farmes made as long as is possible, and not cut in pieces as for puddings, and first blow them well to make the meat slip, and then fill them: which done, with threads divide them into several links as you please, then hang them up in the corner of some chimney clean kept, where they may take air of the fire, and let them dry there at least four days before any be eaten; and when they are served up, let them be either fried or broiled on the gridiron, or else roasted about a capon.[65]

40   *Of boiled meats ordinary.*

It resteth now that we speak of boiled meats and broths, which, forasmuch as our housewife is intended to be general, one that can as well feed the poor as the rich,[66] we will first begin with those ordinary wholesome boiled meats, which are of use in every goodman's[67] house: therefore to make the best ordinary pottage, you shall take a rack of mutton cut into pieces, or a leg of mutton cut into pieces; for this meat and these joints are the best, although any other joint, or any fresh beef will likewise make good pottage: and, having washed your meat well, put it into a clean pot with fair water, and set it on the fire; then take violet leaves, endive, succory, strawberry leaves, spinach, langdebeef, marigold flowers, scallions, and a little parsley, and chop them very small together; then take half so much oatmeal well beaten as there is herbs, and mix it with the herbs, and chop all very well together: then when the pot is ready to boil, scum it very well, and then put in your herbs, and so let it boil with a quick fire, stirring the meat oft in the pot, till the meat be boiled enough, and that the herbs and water are mixed together without any separation, which will be after the consumption of more than a third part: then season them with salt, and serve them up with the meat either with sippets or without.

41   *Pottage without sight of herbs.*

Some desire to have their pottage green, yet no herbs to be seen in this case. You must take your herbs and oatmeal, and, after it is chopped, put it into a stone mortar, or bowl, and with a wooden pestle beat it exceedingly; then with some of the warm liquor in the pot strain it as hard as may be, and so put it in and boil it.

42   *Pottage without herbs.*

Others desire to have pottage without any herbs at all, and then you must only take oatmeal beaten, and good store of onions, and put them

A kitchen scene, with women preparing pottage (in foreground), vegetables, and pastry. From Nicholas de Bonnefons, *The French Gardiner*, p. 263.

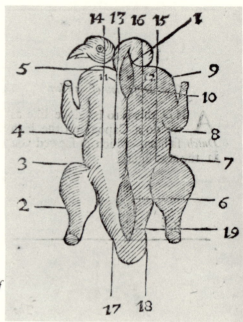

"The dissection of a boiled hen."
From Giles Rose, *A Perfect School of Instructions for the Officers of the Mouth*, p. 39.

in, and boil them together; and thus doing you must take a greater quantity of oatmeal than before.

43   *Pottage with whole herbs.*

If you will make pottage of the best and daintiest kind, you shall take mutton, veal, or kid, and having broke the bones, but not cut the flesh in pieces, and washed it, put it into a pot with fair water; after it is ready to boil, and is thoroughly scummed, you shall put in a good handful or two of small oatmeal, and then take whole lettuce, of the best and most inward leaves, whole spinach, whole endive, whole succory, and whole leaves of cauliflower, or the inward parts of white cabbage, with two or three sliced onions; and put all into the pot and boil them well together till the meat be enough, and the herbs so soft as may be, and stir them oft well together; and then season it with salt and as much verjuice[68] as will only turn the taste of the pottage; and so serve them up, covering the meat with the whole herbs, and adorning the dish with sippets.

44   *To make ordinary stewed broth.*

To make ordinary stewed broth, you shall take a neck of veal, or a leg, or marrow bones of beef, or a pullet, or mutton, and, after the meat is washed, put it into a pot with fair water, and, being ready to boil, scum it well; then you shall take a couple of manchets, and, paring away the crust, cut it into thick slices and lay them in a dish, and cover them with hot broth out of the pot; when they are steeped, put them and some of the broth into a strainer, and strain it, and then put it into the pot; then take half a pound of prunes, half a pound of raisins, and a quarter of a pound of currants clean picked and washed, with a little whole mace and two or three bruised cloves, and put them into the pot and stir all well together, and so let them boil till the meat be enough; then if you will alter the colour of the broth, put in a little turnsole,[69] or red sanders,[70] and so serve it upon sippets, and the fruit uppermost.

A fine boiled meat.

45

To make an excellent boiled meat: take four pieces of a rack of mutton, and wash them clean and put them into a pot well scoured with fair water; then take a good quantity of wine and verjuice and put into it; then slice a handful of onions and put them in also, and so let them boil a good while; then take a piece of sweet butter with ginger and salt and put it to also, and then make the broth thick with grated bread, and so serve it up with sippets.

To boil a mallard.

46

To boil a mallard curiously,[71] take the mallard when it is fair dressed, washed, and trussed, and put it on a spit and roast it till you can get the gravy out of it; then take it from the spit and boil it, then take the best of the broth into a pipkin, and the gravy which you saved, with a piece of sweet butter and currants, vinegar, sugar, pepper, and grated bread: thus boil all these together, and when the mallard is boiled sufficiently, lay it on a dish with sippets, and the broth upon it, and so serve it forth.

To make an excellent olla podrida.

47

To make an excellent *olla podrida*,[72] which is the only principal dish of boiled meat which is esteemed in all Spain, you shall take a very large vessel, pot or kettle, and, filling it with water, you shall set it on the fire, and first put in good thick gobbets of well fed beef, and, being ready to boil, scum your pot; when the beef is half boiled, you shall put in potato roots, turnips, and skirrets: also like gobbets of the best mutton, and the best pork; after they have boiled a while, you shall put in the like gobbets of venison, red and fallow,[73] if you have them; then the like gobbets of veal, kid, and lamb; a little space after these, the foreparts of a fat pig, and a crammed pullet; then put in spinach, endive, succory, marigold leaves and flowers, lettuce, violet leaves, strawberry leaves, bugloss, and scallions, all whole and unchopped; then when they have boiled a while, put in a partridge and a chicken chopped in pieces, with quails, rails,[74] black birds,[75] larks, sparrows, and other small birds, all being well and tenderly boiled; season up the broth with good store of sugar, cloves, mace, cinnamon, ginger, and nutmeg mixed together in a good quantity of verjuice and salt, and so stir up the pot well from the bottom, then dish it up upon great chargers, or long Spanish dishes made in the fashion of our English wooden trays, with good store of sippets in the bottom; then cover the meat all over with prunes, raisins, currants, and blanched almonds, boiled in a thing by themselves; then cover the fruit and the whole boiled herbs with slices of oranges and lemons, and lay the roots round about the sides of the dish, and strew good store of sugar over all, and so serve it forth.

48   *To make the best white broth.*

To make the best white broth,[76] whether it be with veal, capon, chickens, or any other fowl or fish: first boil the flesh or fish by itself, then take the value of a quart of strong mutton broth, or fat kid broth, and put it into a pipkin by itself, and put into it a bunch of thyme, marjoram, spinach, and endive bound together; then when it seethes put in a pretty quantity of beef marrow, and the marrow of mutton, with some whole mace and a few bruised cloves; then put in a pint of white wine with a few whole slices of ginger; after these have boiled a while together, take blanched almonds, and, having beaten them together in a mortar with some of the broth, strain them and put it in also; then in another pipkin boil currants, prunes, raisins, and whole cinnamon in verjuice and sugar, with a few sliced dates; and boil them till the verjuice be most part consumed, or at least come to a syrup; then drain the fruit from the syrup, and if you see it be high coloured, make it white with sweet cream warmed, and so mix it with your wine broth; then take out the capon or the other flesh or fish, and dish it up dry in a clean dish; then pour the broth upon it, and lay the fruit on the top of the meat, and adorn the side of the dish with very dainty sippets; first [trim it with] oranges, lemons, and sugar, and so serve it forth to the table.

49   *To boil any wild fowl.*

To boil any wild fowl, as mallard, teal, widgeon,[77] or such like: first boil the fowl by itself,[78] then take a quart of strong mutton broth, and put it into a pipkin, and boil it; then put into it good store of sliced onions, a bunch of sweet pot herbs, and a lump of sweet butter; after it hath boiled well, season it with verjuice, salt, and sugar, and a little whole pepper; which done, take up your fowl and break it up according to the fashion of carving,[79] and stick a few cloves about it; then put it into the broth with onions, and there let it take a walm[80] or two, and so serve it and the broth forth upon sippets:[81] some use to thicken it with toasts of bread steeped and strained, but that is as please the cook.

To boil a leg of mutton.

50
To boil a leg of mutton, or any other joint of meat whatsoever; first, after you have washed it clean, parboil it a little, then spit it and give it half a dozen turns before the fire, then draw it when it begins to drop,[82] and press it between two dishes, and save the gravy; then slash it with your knife, and give it half a dozen turns more, and then press it again, and thus do as often as you can force any moisture to come from it; then mixing mutton broth, white wine, and verjuice together, boil the mutton therein till it be tender, and that most part of the liquor is clean consumed; then having all that while kept the gravy you took from the mutton stewing gently upon a chafing-dish and coals, you shall add unto it good store of salt, sugar, cinnamon, and ginger, with some lemon slices, and a little of an orange peel, with a few fine white bread crumbs: then, taking up the mutton, put the remainder of the broth in which it lay to the gravy, and then serve it up with sippets, laying the lemon slices uppermost, and trimming the dish about with sugar.

An excellent way to boil chickens.

51
If you will boil chickens, young turkeys,[83] peahens, or any house fowl daintily, you shall, after you have trimmed them, drawn them, trussed them, and washed them, fill their bellies as full of parsley as they can hold; then boil them with salt and water only till they be enough: then take a dish and put into it verjuice, and butter, and salt, and when the butter is melted, take the parsley out of the chickens' bellies, and mince it very small, and put it to the verjuice and butter, and stir it well together; then lay in the chickens, and trim the dish with sippets, and so serve it forth.

A broth for any fresh fish.

52
If you will make broth for any fresh fish whatsoever, whether it be pike, bream,[84] carp, eel, barbel,[85] or such like: you shall boil water, verjuice, and salt together with a handful of sliced onions; then you shall thicken it with two or three spoonful of ale barm; then put in a good quantity of whole barberries, both branches and other, as also pretty store of currants: then when it is boiled enough, dish up your fish, and pour your broth unto it, laying the fruit and onions uppermost. Some to this broth will put prunes and dates sliced, but it is according to the fancy of the cook, or the will of the householder.

Many early illustrations of the kitchen show men, professional cooks, in charge. From M. Marnette, *The Perfect Cook*.

53   Thus I have from these few precedents showed you the true art and making of all sorts of boiled meats, and broths; and though men may coin strange names, and feign strange art, yet be assured she that can do these, may make any other whatsoever; altering the taste by the alteration of the compounds as she shall see occasion: and when a broth is too sweet, to sharpen it with verjuice; when too tart, to sweeten it with sugar; when flat and wallowish, to quicken it with oranges and lemons; and when too bitter, to make it pleasant with herbs and spices.

54
ADDITIONS to boiled meats.
A mallard smored,⁸⁶ or a hare, or old cony.

    Take a mallard when it is clean dressed, washed, and trussed, and parboil it in water till it be scummed and purified; then take it up, and put it into a pipkin with the neck downward, and the tail upward, standing as it were upright; then fill the pipkin half full with that water in which the mallard was parboiled, and fill up the other half with white wine; then peel and slice thin a good quantity of onions, and put them in with whole fine herbs, according to the time of the year, as lettuce, strawberry leaves, violet leaves, vine leaves, spinach, endive, succory, and such like, which have no bitter or hard taste, and a pretty quantity of currants and dates sliced; then cover it close, and set it on a gentle fire, and let it stew, and smore till the herbs and onions be soft, and the mallard enough; then take out the mallard, and carve it as it were to go to the table; then to the broth put a good lump of butter, sugar, cinnamon; and if it be in summer, so many gooseberries as will give it a sharp taste, but in the winter as much wine vinegar; then heat it on the fire, and stir all well together; then lay the mallard in a dish with sippets, and pour all this broth upon it; then trim the edges of the dish with sugar, and so serve it up. And in this manner you may also smore the hinder parts of a hare, or a whole old cony, being trussed up close together.

55
To stew a pike.

    After your pike is dressed and opened in the back, and laid flat, as if it were to fry, then lay it in a large dish for the purpose, able to receive it; then put as much white wine to it as will cover it all over; then set it on a chafing-dish and coals to boil very gently, and if any scum arise, take it away; then put to it currants, sugar, cinnamon, barberries, and as many prunes as will serve to garnish the dish; then cover it close with another dish, and let it stew till the fruit be soft, and the pike enough; then put to it a good lump of sweet butter; then with a fine scummer take up the fish and lay it in a clean dish with sippets; then take a couple of yolks of eggs, the film taken away, and beat them well together with

a spoonful or two of cream, and as soon as the pike is taken out, put it into the broth; and stir it exceedingly to keep it from curding; then pour the broth upon the pike, and trim the sides of the dish with sugar, prunes, and barberries, slices of oranges or lemons, and so serve it up. And thus may you also stew rochets,[87] gurnets, or almost any sea fish, or fresh fish.

To stew a lamb's head and purtenance.

56

Take a lamb's head and purtenance[88] clean washed and picked and put it into a pipkin with fair water, and let it boil, and scum it clean; then put in currants and a few sliced dates, and a bunch of the best farcing herbs tied up together, and so let it boil well till the meat be enough: then take up the lamb's head and purtenance, and put it into a clean dish with sippets; then put in a good lump of butter, and beat the yolks of two eggs with a little cream, and put it to the broth with sugar, cinnamon, and a spoonful or two of verjuice, and whole mace, and as many prunes as will garnish the dish, which should be put in when it is but half boiled, and so pour it upon the lamb's head and purtenance, and adorn the sides of the dish with sugar, prunes, barberries, oranges, and lemons, and in no case forget not to season well with salt, and so serve it up.

A breast of mutton stewed.

57

Take a very good breast of mutton chopped into sundry large pieces, and when it is clean washed, put it into a pipkin with fair water, and set it on the fire to boil; then scum it very well, then put in of the finest parsnips cut into large pieces as long as one's hand, and clean washed and scraped; then good store of the best onions, and all manner of sweet pleasant pot herbs[89] and lettuce, all grossly chopped, and good store of pepper and salt, and then cover it, and let it stew till the mutton be enough; then take up the mutton, and lay it in a clean dish with sippets, and to the broth put a little wine vinegar, and so pour it on the mutton with the parsnips whole, and adorn the sides of the dish with sugar, and so serve it up: and as you do with the breast, so may you do with any other joint of mutton.

To stew a neat's foot.

58

Take a neat's foot that is very well boiled[90] (for the tenderer it is, the better it is) and cleave it in two, and with a clean cloth dry it well from the souse-drink;[91] then lay it in a deep earthen platter, and cover it with verjuice; then set it on a chafing-dish and coals, and put to it a few currants, and as many prunes as will garnish the dish; then cover it, and let it boil well, many times stirring it up with your knife, for fear it stick

to the bottom of the dish; then when it is sufficiently stewed, which will appear by the tenderness of the meat and softness of the fruit, then put in a good lump of butter, great store of sugar and cinnamon, and let it boil a little after; then put it altogether into a clean dish with sippets, and adorn the sides of the dish with sugar and prunes, and so serve it up. And thus for broths and boiled meats.

59   *Of roast meats. Observations in roast meats.*

To proceed then to roast meats,[92] it is to be understood that in the general knowledge thereof are to be observed these few rules. First, the cleanly keeping and scouring of the spits and cob-irons; next, the neat picking and washing of meat before it is spitted,

60   *Spitting of roast meats.*

then the spitting and broaching of meat, which must be done so strongly and firmly that the meat may by no means either shrink from the spit, or else turn about the spit: and yet ever to observe that the spit do not go through any principal part of the meat, but such as is of least account and estimation: and if it be birds or fowl which you spit, then to let the spit go through the hollow of the body of the fowl, and so fasten it with picks or skewers under the wings, about the thighs of the fowl, and at the feet or rump, according to your manner of trussing and dressing them.

61   *Temperature of fire.*

Then to know the temperatures of fires for every meat, and which must have a slow fire, yet a good one, taking leisure in roasting, as chines of beef, swans,[93] turkeys, peacocks,[94] bustards, and generally any great large fowl, or any other joints of mutton, veal, pork, kid, lamb, or such like, whether it be venison, red or fallow, which indeed would lie long at the fire, and soak[95] well in the roasting; and which would have a quick and sharp fire without scorching, as pigs, pullets, pheasants, partridge, quail, and all sorts of middle sized or lesser fowl, and all small birds, or compound roast meats, as olives of veal,[96] haslets, a pound of butter roasted,[97] or puddings simple of themselves; and many other such like, which indeed would be suddenly and quickly despatched, because it is intended in cookery that one of these dishes must be made ready whilst the other is in eating.

62   *The complexions of meat.*

Then to know the complexions of meats, as which must be pale and white roasted (yet thoroughly roasted), as mutton, veal, lamb, kid, capon,

pullet, pheasant, partridge, quail, and all sorts of middle and small land or water fowl, and all small birds; and which must be brown roasted, as beef, venison, pork, swan, geese, pigs, crane, bustards, and any large fowl, or other thing whose flesh is black.

63

The best bastings for meats.

Then to know the best bastings for meat, which is sweet butter, sweet oil, barrelled butter, or fine rendered up seam, with cinnamon, cloves, and mace. There be some that will baste only with water, and salt, and nothing else; yet it is but opinion, and that must be the world's master always.

64

The best dredging.

Then the best dredging,[98] which is either fine white bread crumbs well grated, or else a little very fine white meal, and the crumbs very well mixed together.

"The dissection of a sucking pig." From Giles Rose, *A Perfect School of Instructions for the Officers of the Mouth*, p. 79.

65

To know when meat is enough.

Lastly to know when meat is roasted enough; for as too much rareness is unwholesome, so too much dryness is not nourishing. Therefore to know when it is in the perfect height, and is neither too moist nor too dry, you shall observe these signs first in your large joints of meat; when the steam or smoke of the meat ascendeth, either upright or else goeth from the fire, when it beginneth a little to shrink from the spit, or when the gravy which droppeth from it is clear without bloodiness, then is the meat enough. If it be a pig, when the eyes are fallen out, and the body leaveth piping; for the first is when it is half roasted, and would be singed to make the coat rise and crackle, and the latter when it is fully enough and would be drawn: or if it be any kind of fowl you roast, when the thighs are tender, or the hinder parts of the pinions, at the setting on of the wings, are without blood, then be sure that your meat is fully enough roasted: yet for a better and more certain assuredness, you may thrust your knife into the thickest parts of the meat, and draw it out again, and if it bring out white gravy without any bloodiness, then assuredly it is enough, and may be drawn with all speed convenient, after it hath been well basted with butter not formerly melted, then dredged as aforesaid, then basted over the dredging, and so suffered to take two or three turns, to make crisp the dredging, then dish it in a fair dish with salt sprinkled over it, and so serve it forth. Thus you see the general form of roasting all kind of meat: therefore now I will return to some particular dishes, together with their several sauces.

66   *Roasting mutton with oysters.*

If you will roast mutton with oysters; take a shoulder, a loin, or a leg, and after it is washed parboil it a little; then take the greatest oysters, and, having opened them into a dish, drain the gravy clean from them twice or thrice, then parboil them a little: then take spinach, endive, succory, strawberry leaves, violet leaves, and a little parsley, with some scallions; chop these very small together: then take your oysters very dry drained, and mix them with an half part of these herbs; then take your meat and with these oysters and herbs farce or stop it,[99] leaving no place empty, then spit it and roast it; and whilst it is in roasting take good store of verjuice and butter, and a little salt, and set it in a dish on a chafing-dish and coals; and when it begins to boil, put in the remainder of your herbs without oysters, and a good quantity of currants, with cinnamon, and the yolk of a couple of eggs: and after they are well boiled and stirred together, season it up according to taste with sugar; then put in a few lemon slices, and the meat being enough, draw it and lay it upon this sauce removed into a clean dish, the edges thereof being trimmed about with sugar, and so serve it forth.

67   *To roast a leg of mutton otherwise.*

To roast a leg of mutton after an outlandish fashion,[100] you shall take it after it is washed, and cut out all the flesh from the bone, leaving only the outmost skin entirely whole and fast to the bone; then take thick cream and the yolk of eggs and beat them exceedingly well together; then put to cinnamon, mace, and a little nutmeg, with salt, then take bread crumbs finely grated and searced, with good store of currants, and, as you mix them with the cream, put in sugar, and so make it into a good stiffness. Now if you would have it look green, put in the juice of sweet herbs, as spinach, violet leaves, endive, etc. If you would have it yellow, then put in a little saffron strained, and with this fill up the skin of your leg of mutton in the same shape and form that it was before, and stick the outside of the skin thick with cloves, and so roast it thoroughly and baste it very well, then after it is dredged serve it up as a leg of mutton with this pudding, for indeed it is no other: you may stop any other joint of meat,[101] as breast or loin, or the belly of any fowl boiled or roast, or rabbit, or any meat else which hath skin or emptiness. If into this pudding also you beat the inward pith of an ox's back, it is both good in taste, and excellent sovereign for any disease, ache or flux in the reins whatsoever.

68 ### *To roast a gigot of mutton.*

To roast a gigot of mutton, which is the leg splatted, and half part of the loin together; you shall, after it is washed, stop it with cloves, so spit it, and lay it to the fire, and tend it well with basting: then you shall take vinegar, butter, and currants, and set them on the fire in a dish or pipkin; then when it boils you shall put in sweet herbs finely chopped, with the yolk of a couple of eggs, and so let them boil together; then the meat being half roasted you shall pare off some part of the leanest and brownest, then shred it very small and put it into the pipkin also; then season it up with sugar, cinnamon, ginger, and salt, and so put it into a clean dish: then draw the gigot of mutton and lay it on the sauce, and throw salt on the top, and so serve it up.

69 ### *To roast olives[102] of veal.*

You shall take a leg of veal and cut the flesh from the bones, and cut it out into thin long slices; then take sweet herbs and the white parts of scallions, and chop them well together with the yolks of eggs, then roll it up within the slices of veal, and so spit them and roast them; then boil verjuice, butter, sugar, cinnamon, currants, and sweet herbs together, and, being seasoned with a little salt, serve the olives up upon that sauce with salt cast over them.

70 ### *To roast a pig.*

To roast a pig curiously,[103] you shall not scald it, but draw[104] it with the hair on, then, having washed it, spit it and lay it to the fire so as it may not scorch, then being a quarter roasted, and the skin blistered from

the flesh, with your hand pull away the hair and skin, and leave all the
fat and flesh perfectly bare: then with your knife scotch all the flesh down
to the bones, then baste it exceedingly with sweet butter and cream, being
no more but warm; then dredge it with fine bread crumbs, currants,
sugar, and salt mixed together, and thus apply dredging upon basting,
and basting upon dredging, till you have covered all the flesh a full inch
deep: then the meat being fully roasted, draw it and serve it up whole.

1
To roast a pound of butter well.

To roast a pound of butter curiously and well,[105] you shall take a pound
of sweet butter and beat it stiff with sugar, and the yolks of eggs; then
clap it roundwise about a spit, and lay it before a soft fire, and presently
dredge it with the dredging before appointed for the pig; then as it warmeth
or melteth, so apply it with dredging till the butter be overcomed and
no more will melt to fall from it, then roast it brown, and so draw it,
and serve it out, the dish being as neatly trimmed with sugar as may be.

2
To roast a pudding on a spit.

To roast a pudding on a spit, you shall mix the pudding before spoken
of[106] in the leg of mutton, neither omitting herbs, nor saffron, and put
to a little sweet butter and mix it very stiff: then fold it about the spit,
and have ready in another dish some of the same mixture well seasoned,
but a great deal thinner and no butter at all in it, and when the pudding
doth begin to roast, and that the butter appears, then with a spoon cover
it all over with the thinner mixture, and so let it roast; then if you see
no more butter appear, then baste it as you did the pig and lay more of
the mixture on, and so continue till all be spent: and then roast it brown,
and so serve it up.

3
To roast a chine of beef, loin of mutton, lark, and capon at one fire, and at one instant.

If you will roast a chine of beef, a loin of mutton, a capon, and a lark,
all at one instant and at one fire, and have all ready together and none
burnt: you shall first take your chine of beef and parboil it more than
half through; then first take your capon, being large and fat, and spit it
next the hand of the turner,[107] with the legs from the fire, then spit the
chine of beef, then the lark, and lastly the loin of mutton, and place the
lark so as it may be covered over with the beef, and the fat part of the
loin of mutton, without any part disclosed; then baste your capon, and
your loin of mutton, with cold water, and salt, the chine of beef with
boiling lard: then when you see the beef is almost fully enough, which

you shall hasten by scotching and opening of it, then with a clean cloth you shall wipe the mutton and capon all over, and then baste it with sweet butter till all be enough roasted; then with your knife lay the lark open which by this time will be stewed between the beef and mutton, and, basting it also, dredge all together; draw them and serve them up.

74   *To roast venison.*

If you will roast any venison, after you have washed it, and cleansed all the blood from it,[108] you shall stick it with cloves all over on the outside; and if it be lean you shall lard it either with mutton lard, or pork lard, but mutton is the best: then spit it and roast it by a soaking fire, then take vinegar, bread crumbs, and some of the gravy which comes from the venison, and boil them well in a dish; then season it with sugar, cinnamon, ginger, and salt, and serve the venison forth upon the sauce when it is roasted enough.

75   *How to roast fresh sturgeon.*

If you will roast a piece of fresh sturgeon, which is a dainty dish, you shall first stop it all over with cloves, then spit it, and let it roast at great leisure, plying it continually with basting, which will take away the hardness: then when it is enough, you shall draw it, and serve it upon venison sauce with salt only thrown upon it.

76   *Ordering of meats to be roasted.*

The roasting of all sorts of meats differeth nothing but in the fires, speed, and leisure as is aforesaid, except these compound dishes, of which I have given you sufficient precedents, and by them you may perform any work whatsoever: but for the ordering, preparing, and trussing your meats for the spit or table, in that there is much difference; for in all joints of meat except a shoulder of mutton, you shall crush and break the bones well; from pigs and rabbits you shall cut off the feet before you spit them, and the heads when you serve them to table, and the pig you shall chine, and divide into two parts; capons, pheasants, chickens, and turkeys you shall roast with the pinions folded up, and the legs extended; hens, stock-doves, and house-doves, you shall roast with the pinions folded up, and the legs cut off by the knees, and thrust into the bodies; quails, partridges, and all sorts of small birds shall have their pinions cut away, and the legs extended; all sorts of waterfowl shall have their pinions cut away, and their legs turned backward; woodcocks,[109] snipes, and stints shall be roasted with their heads and necks on, and their legs thrust into their bodies, and shovellers[110] and bitterns[111] shall have no necks but their heads only.

7   *[ADDITION.] To roast a cow's udder.*

Take a cow's udder, and first boil it well, then stick it thick all over with cloves: then, when it is cold, spit it, and lay it to the fire, and apply it very well with basting of sweet butter, and when it is sufficiently roasted, and brown, then dredge it, and draw it from the fire; take vinegar and butter, and put it on a chafing-dish and coals and boil it with white bread crumbs, till it be thick: then put to it good store of sugar and cinnamon, and, putting it in a clean dish, lay the cow's udder therein, and trim the sides of the dish with sugar, and so serve it up.

8   *To roast a fillet of veal.*

Take an excellent good leg of veal, and cut the thick part thereof a handful and more from the knuckle: then take the thick part (which is the fillet) and farce it in every part all over with strawberry leaves, violet leaves, sorrel, spinach, endive, and succory grossly chopped together, and good store of onions: then lay it to the fire and roast it very sufficiently and brown, casting good store of salt upon it, and basting it well with sweet butter: then take of the former herbs much finer chopped than they were for farcing, and put them into a pipkin with vinegar, and clean washed currants, and boil them well together: then when the herbs are sufficiently boiled and soft, take the yolks of four very hard boiled eggs, and shred them very small, and put them into the pipkin also with sugar and cinnamon, and some of the gravy which drops from the veal, and boil it over again, and then put it into a clean dish, and the fillet, being dredged and drawn, lay upon it, and trim the side of the dish with sugar, and so serve it up.

9   *Of sauces, and first for a roast capon or turkey.*

To make an excellent sauce for a roast capon, you shall take onions, and, having sliced and peeled them, boil them in fair water with pepper, salt, and a few bread crumbs: then put unto it a spoonful or two of claret wine, the juice of an orange, and three or four slices of a lemon peel; all these shred together, and so pour it upon the capon being broke up.

0   *Sauce for a hen or pullet.*

To make sauce for an old hen or pullet, take a good quantity of beer and salt, and mix them well together with a few fine bread crumbs, and boil them on a chafing-dish and coals, then take the yolks of three or four hard eggs, and, being shred small, put it to the beer, and boil it also: then, the hen being almost enough, take three or four spoonful of the gravy which comes from her and put it to also, and boil all together to an indifferent thickness: which done, suffer it to boil no more, but only keep it warm on the fire, and put into it the juice of two or three oranges, and the slices of lemon peels, all shred small, and the slices of oranges also having the upper rind taken away: then, the hen being broken up, take the brawns[112] thereof, and, shredding them small, put it into the sauce also; and, stirring all well together, put it hot into a clean warm dish, and lay the hen (broke up) in the same.

81   *Sauce for chickens.*

The sauce for chickens is divers, according to men's tastes: for some will only have butter, verjuice, and a little parsley rolled in their bellies mixed together: others will have butter, verjuice, and sugar boiled together with toasts of bread: and others will have thick sippets with the juice of sorrel and sugar mixed together.

82   *Sauce for a pheasant or partridge.*

The best sauce for a pheasant is water, onions sliced, pepper and a little salt mixed together, and but stewed upon the coals, and then poured upon the pheasant or partridge being broken up, and some will put thereto the juice or slices of an orange or lemon, or both: but it is according to taste, and indeed more proper for a pheasant than a partridge.

83   *Sauce for a quail, rail, or big bird.*

Sauce for a quail, rail, or any fat big bird,[113] is claret wine and salt mixed together with the gravy of the bird; and a few fine bread crumbs well boiled together, and either a sage leaf or bay leaf crushed among it according to men's tastes.

84   *Sauce for pigeons.*

The best sauce for pigeons, stockdoves, or such like, is vinegar and butter melted together, and parsley roasted in their bellies, or vine leaves roasted and mixed well together.

85   *A general sauce for wild fowl.*

The most general sauce for ordinary wild fowl roasted,[114] as ducks, mallard, widgeon, teal, snipe, sheldrake, plovers, pulers,[115] gulls,[116] and such like, is only mustard and vinegar, or mustard and verjuice mixed together, or else an onion, water, and pepper, and some (especially in the court) use only butter melted, and not anything else.

86   *Sauce for green geese.*

The best sauce for green geese[117] is the juice of sorrel and sugar, mixed together with a few scalded feaberries,[118] and served upon sippets; or else the belly of the green goose filled with feaberries, and so roasted, and then the same mixed with verjuice, butter, sugar, and cinnamon, and so served up upon sippets.

Sauce for a stubble goose.

87

The same for a stubble goose[119] is divers, according to men's minds; for some will take the pap of roasted apples, and, mixing it with vinegar, boil them together on the fire with some of the gravy of the goose, and a few barberries and bread crumbs, and when it is boiled to a good thickness, season it with sugar and a little cinnamon, and so serve it up; some will add a little mustard and onions unto it, and some will not roast the apples, but pare them and slice them; and that is the nearer way, but not the better. Others will fill the belly of the goose full of onions shred, and oatmeal grits, and being roasted enough, mix it with the gravy of the goose, and sweet herbs well boiled together, and seasoned with a little verjuice.

A galantine or sauce for a swan, bittern, shoveller, or large fowl.

88

To make a galantine[120] or sauce for a swan, bittern, shoveller, hern,[121] crane, or any large fowl, take the blood of the same fowl, and, being stirred well, boil it on the fire, then when it comes to be thick, put unto it vinegar, a good quantity, with a few fine bread crumbs, and so boil it over again: then, being come to good thickness, season it with sugar and cinnamon so as it may taste pretty and sharp upon the cinnamon, and then serve it up in saucers as you do mustard: for this is called a chawdron[122] or galantine, and is a sauce almost for any fowl whatsoever.

Sauce for a pig.

89

To make sauce for a pig, some take sage and roast it in the belly of the pig, then, boiling verjuice, butter, and currants together, take and chop the sage small, and, mixing the brains of the pig with it, put all together, and so serve it up.

Sauce for veal.

90

To make a sauce for a joint of veal, take all kind of sweet pot herbs, and, chopping them very small with the yolks of two or three eggs, boil them in vinegar and butter, with a few bread crumbs and good store of currants; then season it with sugar and cinnamon, and a clove or two crushed, and so pour it upon the veal, with the slices of oranges and lemons about the dish.

ADDITIONS unto sauces. Sops[123] for chickens.

91

Take oranges and slice them thin, and put unto them white wine and rose-water, the powder of mace, ginger, and sugar, and set the same upon a chafing-dish and coals, and when it is half boiled put to it a good lump of butter, and then lay good store of sippets of fine white bread therein, and so serve your chickens upon them, and trim the sides of the dish with sugar.

92   *Sauce for a turkey.*

Take fair water, and set it over the fire, then slice good store of onions and put into it, and also pepper and salt, and good store of the gravy that comes from the turkey, and boil them very well together: then put to it a few fine crumbs of grated bread to thicken it; a very little sugar and some vinegar, and so serve it up with the turkey: or otherwise, take grated white bread and boil it in white wine till it be thick as a galantine, and in the boiling put in good store of sugar and cinnamon, and then with a little turnsole make it of a high murrey colour, and so serve it in saucers with the turkey in the manner of a galantine.

93   *The best galantine.*

Take the blood of a swan, or any other great fowl, and put it into a dish; then take stewed prunes and put them into a strainer, and strain them into the blood; then set it on a chafing-dish and coals, and let it boil, ever stirring it till it come to be thick, and season it very well with sugar and cinnamon, and so serve it in saucers with the fowl: but this sauce must be served cold.

94   *Sauce for a mallard.*

Take good store of onions, peel them, and slice them, and put them into vinegar, and boil them very well till they be tender; then put into it a good lump of sweet butter, and season it well with sugar and cinnamon, and so serve it up with the fowl.

95   *Of carbonadoes.*

Charbonadoes, or carbonadoes, which is meat broiled upon the coals (and the invention thereof first brought out of France, as appears by the name) are of divers kinds according to men's pleasures: for there is no meat either boiled or roasted whatsoever, but may afterwards be broiled, if the master thereof be disposed;

96   *What is to be carbonadoed.*

yet the general dishes for the most part which are used to be carbonadoed are a breast of mutton half boiled, a shoulder of mutton half roasted, the legs, wings, and carcasses of capon, turkey, goose, or any other fowl whatsoever, especially land fowl. And lastly, the uppermost thick skin which covereth the ribs of beef, and is called (being broiled) the Inns of Court[124] goose, and is indeed a dish used most for wantonness, sometimes to please appetite: to which may also be added the broiling of pigs' heads, or the brains of any fowl whatsoever after it is roasted and dressed.

The manner of carbonadoes.

7 Now for the manner of carbonadoing, it is in this sort; you shall first take the meat you must carbonado, and scotch it both above and below, then sprinkle good store of salt upon it, and baste it all over with sweet butter melted, which done, take your broiling iron; I do not mean a gridiron (though it be much used for this purpose) because the smoke of the coals, occasioned by the dropping of the meat, will ascend about it, and make it stink;[125] but a plate iron made with hooks and pricks, on which you may hang the meat, and set it close before the fire, and so the plate heating the meat behind as the fire doth before, it will both the sooner and with more neatness be ready: then having turned it, and basted it till it be very brown, dredge it, and serve it up with vinegar and butter.

Of the toasting of mutton.

8 Touching the toasting of mutton, venison, or any other joint of meat, which is the most excellentest of all carbonadoes, you shall take the fattest and largest that can possibly be got (for lean meat is loss of labour, and little meat not worth your time), and, having scotched it, and cast salt upon it, you shall set it on a strong fork, with a dripping pan underneath it, before the face of a quick fire, yet so far off, that it may by no means scorch, but toast at leisure; then with that which falls from it, and with no other basting, see that you baste it continually, turning it ever and anon many times, and so oft that it may soak and brown at great leisure, and as oft as you baste it, so oft sprinkle salt upon it, and as you see it toast so scotch it deeper and deeper, especially in the thickest and most fleshy parts where the blood most resteth: and when you see that no more blood droppeth from it, but the gravy is clear and white; then shall you serve it up either with venison sauce, or with vinegar, pepper and sugar, cinnamon, and the juice of an orange mixed together, and warmed with some of the gravy.[126]

ADDITIONS[127] unto carbonadoes. A rasher of mutton or lamb.

9 Take mutton or lamb that hath been either roasted, or but parboiled, and with your knife scotch it many ways; then lay it in a deep dish, and put to it a pint of white wine, and a little whole mace, a little sliced nutmeg and some sugar, with a lump of sweet butter, and stew it so till

it be very tender: then take it forth, and brown it on the gridiron, and then laying sippets in the former broth serve it up.

100 ### To carbonado tongues.

Take any tongue, whether of beef, mutton, calves, red deer or fallow, and, being well boiled, peel them, cleave them, and scotch them many ways; then take three or four eggs broken, some sugar, cinnamon, and nutmeg, and, having beaten it well together, put to it a lemon cut in thin slices, and another clean peeled, and cut into little four-square bits, and then take the tongue and lay it in; and then having melted good store of butter in a frying pan put the tongue and the rest therein, and so fry it brown, and then dish it, and scrape sugar upon it, and serve it up.

101 ### *ADDITIONS* for dressing of fish. To souse any fresh fish.

Take any fresh fish whatsoever (as pike, bream, carp, barbel, chevin, and such like) and draw it, but scale it not; then take out the liver and the refuse, and, having opened it, wash it; then take a pottle of fair water, a pretty quantity of white wine, good store of salt, and some vinegar, with a little bunch of sweet herbs, and set it on the fire, and as soon as it begins to boil, put in your fish, and having boiled a little, take it up into a fair vessel, then put into the liquor some gross pepper, and slit ginger; and when it is boiled well together with more salt, set it by to cool, and then put your fish into it, and when you serve it up, lay fennel thereupon.

102 ### How to boil small fish.

To boil small fish, as roaches, daces,[128] gudgeon, or flounders, boil white wine and water together with a bunch of choice herbs, and a little whole mace; when all is boiled well together, put in your fish, and scum it well: then put in the sole[129] of a manchet, a good quantity of sweet butter, and season it with pepper and verjuice, and so serve it in upon sippets, and adorn the sides of the dish with sugar.

103 ### To boil a gurnet or rochet.

First, draw your fish, and either split it open in the back, or joint it in the back, and truss it round, then wash it clean, and boil it in water and salt, with a bunch of sweet herbs: then take it up into a large dish, and pour unto it verjuice, nutmeg, butter, and pepper, and, letting it stew a little, thicken it with the yolks of eggs: then, hot, remove it into another dish, and garnish it with slices of oranges and lemons, barberries, prunes, and sugar, and so serve it up.

Modus vendendi Lupos pisces apud

"The English method of selling pike." From Georgius Braun and Franz
Hohenberg, *Civitates Orbis Terrarum*, vol. 5, plate 1.

To bake a carp.

4
After you have drawn, washed, and scalded a fair large carp, season it
with pepper, salt and nutmeg, and then put it into a coffin[130] with good
store of sweet butter,[131] and then cast on raisins of the sun, the juice of
lemons, and some slices of orange peels; and then, sprinkling on a little
vinegar, close it up and bake it.

How to bake a tench.

5
First, let your tench blood in the tail, then scour it, wash it, and scald
it: then, having dried it, take the fine crumbs of bread, sweet cream, the
yolks of eggs,[132] currants clean washed, a few sweet herbs chopped small,
season it with nutmegs and pepper, and make it into a stiff paste,[133] and
put it into the belly of the tench: then season the fish on the outside with
pepper, salt, and nutmeg, and so put it into a deep coffin with sweet

butter, and so close up the pie and bake it: then when it is enough, draw it, and open it, and put into it a good piece of a preserved orange minced: then take vinegar, nutmeg, butter, sugar, and the yolk of a new laid egg, and boil it on a chafing-dish and coals, always stirring it to keep it from curding; then pour it into the pie, shake it well, and so serve it up.

106   *How to stew a trout.*

Take a large trout, fair trimmed, and wash it, and put it into a deep pewter dish, then take half a pint of sweet wine, with a lump of butter, and a little whole mace, parsley, savory and thyme, mince then all small, and put them into the trout's belly, and so let it stew a quarter of an hour:[134] then mince the yolk of an hard egg, and strew it on the trout, and, laying the herbs about it, and scraping on sugar, serve it up.

107   *How to bake eels.*

After you have drawn your eels, chop them into small pieces of three or four inches, and season them with pepper, salt, and ginger, and so put them into a coffin with a good lump of butter, great raisins, onions small chopped, and so close it, bake it, and serve it up.

108   *Of the pastry and baked meats.*

Next to these already rehearsed, our English housewife must be skilful in pastry, and know how and in what manner to bake all sorts of meat, and what paste is fit for every meat, and how to handle and compound such pastes. As, for example, red deer venison, wild boar, gammons of bacon, swans, elks, porpoise, and such like standing dishes, which must be kept long, would be baked in a moist, thick, tough, coarse, and long lasting crust, and therefore of all other your rye paste is best for that purpose: your turkey, capon, pheasant, partridge, veal, peacocks, lamb, and all sorts of water fowl which are to come to the table more than once (yet not many days) would be baked in a good white crust, somewhat thick; therefore your wheat is fit for them: your chickens, calves' feet, olives, potatoes, quinces, fallow deer, and such like, which are most commonly eaten hot, would be in the finest, shortest[135] and thinnest crust; therefore your fine wheat flour which is a little baked in the oven before it be kneaded is the best for that purpose.

109   *Of the mixture of pastes.*

To speak then of the mixture and kneading of pastes, you shall understand that your rye paste would be kneaded only with hot water and a little butter, or sweet seam and rye flour very finely sifted, and it would be made tough and stiff that it may stand well in the raising,[136] for the

An ornamental peacock pie is in the foreground (right) of the pastry cook's kitchen; as well as plentiful game hanging and lying near, there are various bowls and rolling pins visible; in the background a peel is being used to put pies or bread deep in the oven. From François P. La Varenne, *The French Pastery-cooke*.

coffin thereof must ever be very deep: your coarse wheat crust would be kneaded with hot water, or mutton broth and good store of butter, and the paste made stiff and tough because that coffin must be deep also; your fine wheat crust must be kneaded with as much butter as water, and the paste made reasonable lithe and gentle, into which you must put three or four eggs or more according to the quantity you blend together, for they will give it a sufficient stiffening.[137]

110   *Of puff paste.*

   Now for the making of puff paste of the best kind, you shall take the finest wheat flour after it hath been a little baked in a pot in the oven, and blend it well with eggs, whites and yolks all together, after the paste is well kneaded, roll out a part thereof as thin as you please, and then spread cold sweet butter over the same, then upon the same butter roll another leaf of the paste as before; and spread it with butter also; and thus roll leaf upon leaf with butter between till it be as thick as you think good:[138] and with it either cover any baked meat, or make paste for venison, Florentine,[139] tart or what dish else you please and so bake it. There be some that to this paste use sugar, but it is certain it will hinder the rising thereof; and therefore when your puffed paste is baked, you shall dissolve sugar into rose-water, and drop it into the paste as much as it will by any means receive, and then set it a little while in the oven after and it will be sweet enough.

111   *Of baking red deer, or fallow, or anything to keep cold.*

   When you bake red deer, you shall first parboil it and take out the bones, then you shall if it be lean lard it, if fat save the charge, then put it into a press to squeeze out the blood; then for a night lay it in a mere sauce[140] made of vinegar, small drink,[141] and salt, and then taking it forth season it well with pepper finely beaten, and salt, well mixed together, and see that you lay good store thereof, both upon and in every open and hollow place of the venison; but by no means cut any slashes to put in the pepper, for it will of itself sink fast enough into the flesh, and be more pleasant in the eating: then having raised the coffin, lay in the bottom a thick course of butter, then lay the flesh thereon and cover it all over with butter, and so bake it as much as if you did bake great brown bread; then when you draw it, melt more butter, with three or four spoonful of vinegar, and twice so much claret wine, and at a vent hole on the top of the lid pour in the same till it can receive no more, and so let it stand and cool; and in this sort you may bake fallow deer, or swan, or whatsoever else you please to keep cold, the mere sauce only being left out which is only proper to red deer.

To bake beef, or mutton for venison.

And if to your mere sauce you add a little turnsole, and therein steep beef, or ram mutton; you may also in the same manner take the first for red deer venison, and the latter for fallow, and a very good judgement shall not be able to say otherwise than that it is of itself perfect venison, both in taste, colour, and the manner of cutting.

To bake a custard or doucet.

To bake an excellent custard or doucet[142] you shall take good store of eggs, and, putting away one quarter of the whites, beat them exceeding well in a basin, and then mix with them the sweetest and thickest cream you can get, for if it be anything thin, the custard will be wheyish; then season it with salt, sugar, cinnamon, cloves, mace, and a little nutmeg; which done raise your coffins of good tough wheat paste,[143] being the second sort before spoke of, and if you please raise it in pretty works, or angular forms, which you may do by fixing the upper part of the crust to the nether with the yolks of eggs: then when the coffins are ready, strew the bottoms a good thickness over with currants and sugar; then set them into the oven, and fill them up with the confection before blended, and so drawing them, adorn all the tops with caraway comfits, and the slices of dates pricked right up, and so serve them up to the table. To prevent the wheyishness of the custard, dissolve into the first confection a little isinglass and all will be firm.

To bake an olive pie.

To make an excellent olive pie[144] take sweet herbs as violet leaves,[145] strawberry leaves, spinach, succory, endive, thyme, and sorrel, and chop them as small as may be, and if there be a scallion or two amongst them it will give the better taste; then take the yolks of hard eggs with currants, cinnamon, cloves, and mace, and chop them amongst the herbs also; then having cut out long olives[146] of a leg of veal, roll up more than three parts of the herbs so mixed within the olives, together with a good deal of sweet butter; then having raised your crust of the finest and best paste, strew in the bottom the remainder of the herbs, with a few great raisins having the stones picked out; then put in the olives and cover them with great raisins and a few prunes; then over all lay good store of butter and so bake them; then being sufficiently baked, take claret wine, sugar, cinnamon, and two or three spoonful of wine vinegar and boil them together, and then drawing the pie, at a vent in the top of the lid put in the same, and then set it into the oven again a little space, and so serve it forth.

115   *To make a marrow bone pie.*

To bake the best marrow bone pie, after you have mixed the crusts of the best sort of pastes, and raised the coffin in such manner as you please, you shall first in the bottom thereof lay a course of marrow of beef mixed with currants; then upon it a lay[er] of the souls of artichokes, after they have been boiled, and are divided from the thistle; then cover them over with marrow, currants, and great raisins, the stones picked out; then lay a course of potatoes cut in thick slices, after they have been boiled soft, and are clean peeled; then cover them with marrow, currants, great raisins, sugar, and cinnamon: then lay a layer of candied eryngo[147] roots mixed very thick with the slices of dates: then cover it with marrow, currants, great raisins, sugar, cinnamon, and dates, with a few damask prunes, and so bake it: and after it is baked pour into it as long as it will receive it white wine, rose-water, sugar, cinnamon, and vinegar, mixed together, and candy all the cover with rose-water and sugar only; and so set it into the oven a little, and after serve it forth.

116   *To bake a chicken pie.*

To bake a chicken pie; after you have trussed your chickens, broken their legs and breast bones, and raised your crust of the best paste, you shall lay them in the coffin close together with their bodies full of butter. Then lay upon them, and underneath them, currants, great raisins, prunes, cinnamon, sugar, whole mace, and salt: then cover all with great store of butter, and so bake it; after, pour into it the same liquor you did in your marrow bone pie, with the yolks of two or three eggs beaten amongst it, and so serve it forth.

117   *ADDITIONS to the pastry. Venison of hares.*

To make good red deer venison of hares, take a hare or two, or three, as you can or please, and pick all the flesh from the bones; then put it into a mortar either of wood or stone, and with a wooden pestle let a strong person beat it exceedingly, and ever as it is beating, let one sprinkle in vinegar and some salt; then when it is sufficiently beaten, take it out of the mortar, and put it into boiling water and parboil it: when it is parboiled, take it and lay it on a table in a round lump, and lay a board over it, and with weights press it as hard as may be: then, the water being pressed out of it, season it well with pepper and salt: then lard it with the fat of bacon so thick as may be: then bake it as you bake other red deer, which is formerly declared.[148]

118   *To bake a hare pie.*

Take a hare and pick off all the flesh from the bones, and only reserve the head, then parboil it well: which done, take it out and let it cool; as soon as it is cold, take at least a pound and a half of raisins of the sun, and take out the stones, then mix them with a good quantity of mutton suet, and with a sharp shredding knife shred it as small as you would do for a chewet:[149] then put to it currants and whole raisins, cloves and mace, cinnamon and salt: then, having raised the coffin longwise to the proportion of a hare, first lay in the head, and then the aforesaid meat, and lay the meat in the true portion of a hare, with neck, shoulders, and legs, and then cover the coffin and bake it as other baked meats of that nature.

A gammon of bacon pie.

Take a gammon of bacon and only wash it clean, and then boil it on a soft gentle fire till it be boiled as tender as is possible, ever and anon fleeting it clean, that by all means it may boil white: then take off the sward, and farce it very well with all manner of sweet and pleasant farcing herbs: then strew store of pepper over it, and prick it thick with cloves: then lay it into a coffin made of the same proportion, and lay good store of butter round about it, and upon it, and strew pepper upon the butter, that as it melts, the pepper may fall upon the bacon: then cover it, and make the proportion of a pig's head in paste upon it, and then bake it as you bake red deer, or things of the like nature, only the paste would be of wheat meal.

A herring pie.

Take white pickled herrings of one night's watering,[150] and boil them a little: then peel off the skin, and take only the backs of them, and pick the fish clean from the bones, then take good store of raisins of the sun, and stone them, and put them to the fish: then take a warden or two, and pare it, and slice it in small slices from the core, and put it likewise to the fish: then with a very sharp shredding knife shred all as small and fine as may be: then put to it good store of currants, sugar, cinnamon, sliced dates, and so put it into the coffin with good store of very sweet butter, and so cover it, and leave only a round vent hole on the top of the lid, and so bake it like pies of that nature. When it is sufficiently baked, draw it out, and take claret wine and a little verjuice, sugar, cinnamon, and sweet butter, and boil them together; then put it in at the vent hole, and shake the pie a little, and put it again into the oven for a little space, and so serve it up, the lid being candied over with sugar, and the sides of the dish trimmed with sugar.

A ling pie.

Take a jowl of the best ling that is not much watered, and is well sodden and cold, but whilst it is hot take off the skin, and pare it clean underneath, and pick out the bones clean from the fish: then cut it into gross bits and let it lie: then take the yolks of a dozen eggs boiled exceeding hard, and put them to the fish, and shred all together as small as is possible: then take all manner of the best and finest pot herbs, and chop them wonderful small, and mix them also with the fish; then season it with pepper, cloves, and mace, and so lay it into a coffin with great store of sweet butter, so as it may swim therein, and then cover it, and leave a vent hole open in the top: when it is baked, draw it, and take verjuice, sugar, cinnamon, and butter, and boil them together, and first with a feather anoint all the lid over with that liquor, and then scrape good store of sugar upon it; then pour the rest of the liquor in at the vent hole, and then set it into the oven again for a very little space, and serve it up as pies of the same nature[151] and both these pies of fish before rehearsed are especial Lenten dishes.

122   *A Norfolk fool.*[152]

Take a pint of the sweetest and thickest cream that can be gotten, and set it on the fire in a very clean scoured skillet, and put into it sugar, cinnamon, and a nutmeg cut into four quarters, and so boil it well: then take the yolks of four eggs, and take off the films, and beat them well with a little sweet cream: then take the four quarters of the nutmeg out of the cream, then put in the eggs, and stir it exceedingly, till it be thick: then take a fine manchet, and cut it into thin shives, as much as will cover a dish bottom, and, holding it in your hand, pour half the cream into the dish: then lay your bread over it, then cover the bread with the rest of the cream, and so let it stand till it be cold: then strew it over with caraway comfits, and prick up some cinnamon comfits, and some sliced dates; or for want thereof, scrape all over it some sugar, and trim the sides of the dish with sugar, and so serve it up.

123   *A trifle.*

Take a pint of the best and thickest cream, and set it on the fire in a clean skillet, and put into it sugar, cinnamon, and a nutmeg cut into four quarters, and so boil it well: then put it into the dish you intend to serve it in, and let it stand to cool till it be no more than lukewarm: then put in a spoonful of the best earning, and stir it well about, and so let it stand till it be cold, and then strew sugar upon it, and so serve it up, and this you may serve either in dish, glass, or other plate.

124   *A calves' foot pie.*

Take calves' feet well boiled, and pick all the meat from the bones: then being cold shred it as small as you can, then season it with cloves and mace, and put in good store of currants, raisins, and prunes: then put it into the coffin with good store of sweet butter, then break in whole sticks of cinnamon, and a nutmeg sliced into four quarters, and season it before with salt: then close up the coffin, and only leave a vent hole. When it is baked, draw it, and at the vent hole put in the same liquor you did in the ling pie, and trim the lid after the same manner, and so serve it up.

5

Oyster pie.

Take of the greatest oysters drawn from the shells, and parboil them in verjuice: then put them into a colander, and let all the moisture run from them, till they be as dry as is possible: then raise up the coffin of the pie, and lay them in: then put to them good store of currants and fine powdered sugar, with whole mace, whole cloves, whole cinnamon, and a nutmeg sliced, dates cut, and good store of sweet butter: then cover it, and only leave a vent hole: when it is baked, then draw it, and take white wine, and white wine vinegar, sugar, cinnamon, and sweet butter, and melt it together; then first trim the lid therewith, and candy it with sugar; then pour the rest in at the vent hole, and shake it well, and so set it into the oven again for a little space, and so serve it up, the dish edges trimmed with sugar. Now some use to put to this pie onions sliced and shred, but that is referred to discretion, and to the pleasure of the taste.

6

To recover venison that is tainted.

Take strong ale, and put to it of wine vinegar as much as will make it sharp: then set it on the fire, and boil it well, and scum it, and make of it a strong brine with bay-salt,[153] or other salt: then take it off, and let it stand till it be cold, then put your venison into it, and let it lie in it full twelve hours: then take it out from that mere sauce, and press it well; then parboil it, and season it with pepper and salt, and bake it, as hath been before shewed in this chapter.[154]

7

A chewet pie.

Take the brawns and the wings of capons and chickens after they have been roasted, and pull away the skin; then shred them with fine mutton suet very small; then season it with cloves, mace, cinnamon, sugar, and salt: then put to raisins of the sun and currants, and sliced dates, and orange peels, and, being well mixed together, put it into small coffins made for the purpose, and strew on the top of them good store of caraway comfits: then cover them, and bake them with a gentle heat, and these chewets you may also make of roasted veal,[155] seasoned as before showed, and of all parts the loin is the best.

128   *A minced pie.*

Take a leg of mutton, and cut the best of the flesh from the bone, and parboil it well: then put to it three pound of the best mutton suet, and shred it very small: then spread it abroad, and season it with pepper and salt, cloves and mace: then put in good store[156] of currants, great raisins, and prunes clean washed and picked, a few dates sliced, and some orange peels sliced: then, being all well mixed together, put it into a coffin, or into divers coffins, and so bake them: and when they are served up open the lids, and strew store of sugar on the top of the meat, and upon the lid. And in this sort you may also bake beef or veal; only the beef would not be parboiled, and the veal will ask a double quantity of suet.

129   *A pippin pie.*

Take of the fairest and best pippins, and pare them, and make a hole in the top of them; then prick in each hole a clove or two, then put them into the coffin, then break in whole sticks of cinnamon, and slices of orange peels and dates, and on the top of every pippin a little piece of sweet butter: then fill the coffin, and cover the pippins over with sugar; then close up the pie, and bake it,[157] as you bake pies of the like nature, and when it is baked anoint the lid over with store of sweet butter, and then strew sugar upon it a good thickness, and set it into the oven again for a little space, as whilst the meat is in dishing up, and then serve it.

130   *A warden pie, or quince pie.*

Take of the fairest and best wardens,[158] and pare them, and take out the hard cores on the top, and cut the sharp ends at the bottom flat; then boil them in white wine and sugar, until the syrup grow thick: then take the wardens from the syrup into a clean dish, and let them cool; then set them into the coffin, and prick cloves in the tops, with whole sticks of cinnamon, and great store of sugar, as for pippins; then cover it, and only reserve a vent hole, so set it in the oven and bake it: when it is baked, draw it forth, and take the first syrup in which the wardens were boiled, and taste it, and if it be not sweet enough, then put in more sugar and some rose-water, and boil it again a little, then pour it in at the vent hole, and shake the pie well; then take sweet butter and rose-water melted, and with it anoint the pie lid all over, and then strew upon it store of sugar, and so set it into the oven again a little space, and then serve it up. And in this manner you may also bake quinces.[159]

131   *To preserve quinces to bake all the year.*

Take the best and sweetest wort,[160] and put to it good store of sugar; then pare and core the quinces clean, and put them therein, and boil them till they grow tender: then take out the quinces and let them cool, and let the pickle in which they were boiled stand to cool also; then strain it through a range or sieve, then put the quinces into a sweet earthen pot, then pour the pickle or syrup unto them, so as all the quinces may be quite covered all over; then stop up the pot close, and set it in a dry place, and once in six or seven weeks look unto it; and if you see it shrink, or do begin to hoar or mould, then pour out the pickle or syrup, and, renewing it, boil it over again, and as before put it to the quinces being cold, and thus you may preserve them for the use of baking, or otherwise, all the year.

A pippin tart.

Take pippins of the fairest, and pare them, and then divide them just in the halves, and take out the cores clean: then, having rolled out the coffin flat, and raised up a small verge of an inch or more high, lay in the pippins with the hollow side downward, as close one to another as may be: then lay here and there a clove, and here and there a whole stick of cinnamon, and a little bit of butter; then cover all clean over with sugar, and so cover the coffin, and bake it according to the manner of tarts; and, when it is baked, then draw it out, and, having boiled butter and rose-water together, anoint all the lid over therewith, and then scrape or strew on it good store of sugar, and so set it in the oven again, and after serve it up.

A codling tart.

Take green apples from the tree, and coddle[161] them in scalding water without breaking; then peel the thin skin from them, and so divide them in halves, and cut out the cores, and so lay them into the coffin, and do in everything as you did in the pippin tart; and before you cover it when the sugar is cast in, see you sprinkle upon it good store of rose-water, then close it, and do as before showed.

A codling pie.

Take codlings as before said, and peel them, and divide them in halves, and core them, and lay a layer thereof in the bottom of the pie: then scatter here and there a clove, and here and there a piece of whole cinnamon; then cover them all over with sugar, then lay another layer of codlings, and do as before said, and so another, till the coffin be all filled; then cover all with sugar, and here and there a clove and a cinnamon stick, and if you will a sliced orange peel and a date; then cover it, and bake it as the pies of that nature: when it is baked, draw it out of the oven, and take of the thickest and best cream with good store of sugar,

Number 53, a peel and malkin, used in baking (see ix, 18); 54, a haunch of
venison; 55, a platter with a round pie; 56, (top) a manchet, and a loaf of
bread; 57, a roasted pullet and a haunch of veal; 58, a spitted pig, a cup, and a
jug; 59, a quart and a pot; 60, a "twiggen" basket with apples, 68 and 72, a
wine piercer and a tun with a round bung (see chapter iv). From Randle
Holme, *The Academy of Armory*, vol. ii, 284.

and give it one boil or two on the fire: then open the pie, and put the
cream therein, and mash the codlings all about; then cover it, and, having
trimmed the lid (as was before showed in the like pies and tarts), set it
into the oven again for half an hour, and so serve it forth.

135   *A cherry tart.*
    Take the fairest cherries you can get, and pick them clean from leaves
and stalks; then spread out your coffin as for your pippin tart, and cover
the bottom with sugar; then cover the sugar all over with cherries, then
cover those cherries with sugar, some sticks of cinnamon, and here and
there a clove; then lay in more cherries, and so more sugar, cinnamon,
and cloves till the coffin be filled up: then cover it, and bake it in all
points as the codling and pippin tart, and so serve it; and in the same
manner you may make tarts of gooseberries, strawberries, raspberries,
bilberries, or any other berry whatsoever.

6 *A rice tart.*

Take rice that is clean picked, and boil it in sweet cream, till it be very soft; then let it stand and cool, and put into it good store of cinnamon and sugar, and the yolks of a couple of eggs, and some currants; stir and beat all well together: then, having made the coffin in the manner before said for other tarts, put the rice therein, and spread it all over the coffin; then break many little bits of sweet butter upon it all over, and scrape some sugar over it also; then cover the tart, and bake it, and trim it in all points as hath been before showed, and so serve it up.

7 *A Florentine.*[162]

Take the kidneys of veal after it hath been well roasted, and is cold; then shred it as fine as is possible: then take all sorts of sweet pot herbs or farcing herbs, which have no bitter or strong taste, and chop them as small as may be, and, putting the veal into a large dish, put the herbs unto it, and good store of clean washed currants, sugar, cinnamon, the yolks of four eggs, a little sweet cream warmed, and the fine grated crumbs of a halfpenny loaf, and salt, and mix all exceeding well together; then take a deep pewter dish, and in it lay your paste very thin rolled out, which paste you must mingle thus: take of the finest wheat flour a quart, and a quarter so much sugar, and a little cinnamon; then break into it a couple of eggs, then take sweet cream and butter melted on the fire, and with it knead the paste, and, as was before said, having spread butter all about the dish's sides, and rolled out the paste thin, lay it into the dish; then put in the veal, and break pieces of sweet butter upon it, and scrape sugar over it; then roll out another paste reasonable thick, and with it cover the dish all over, closing the two pastes with the beaten whites of eggs very fast together: then with your knife cut the lid into divers pretty works according to your fancy: then set it in the oven and bake it with pies and tarts of like nature: when it is baked, draw it, and trim the lid with sugar, as hath been showed in tarts, and so serve it up in your second courses.

8 *A prune tart.*

Take of the fairest damask prunes you can get, and put them in a clean pipkin with fair water,[163] sugar, unbruised cinnamon, and a branch or two of rosemary; and, if you have bread to bake, stew them in the oven with your bread, if otherwise, stew them on the fire; when they are stewed, then bruise them all to mash in their syrup, and strain them into a clean dish; then boil it over again with sugar, cinnamon, and rose-water till it be as thick as marmalade; then set it to cool, then make a reasonable tough paste with fine flour, water, and a little butter, and roll it out very thin; then, having patterns of paper cut in divers proportions, as beasts, birds, arms, knots, flowers, and such like, lay the patterns on the paste, and so cut them accordingly; then with your fingers pinch up the edges of the paste, and set the work in good proportion: then prick it well all over for rising, and set it on a clean sheet of large paper, and so set it into the oven, and bake it hard: then draw it, and set it by to cool: and thus you may do by a whole oven full at one time, as your occasion of expense is: then against[164] the time of service comes, take off the confection of prunes before rehearsed, and with your knife, or a spoon fill the coffin according to the thickness of the verge: then strew it over all with caraway comfits, and prick long comfits upright in it, and so, taking the paper from the bottom, serve it on a plate in a dish or charger, according to the bigness of the tart, and at the second course, and this tart carrieth the colour black.

139   *Apple tart.*

Take apples and pare them, and slice them thin from the core into a pipkin with white wine, good store of sugar, cinnamon, a few sanders, and rose-water, and boil it till it be thick; then cool it, and strain it, and beat it very well together with a spoon; then put it into the coffin as you did the prune tart, and adorn it also in the same manner; and this tart you may fill thicker or thinner, as you please to raise the edge of the coffin; and it carrieth the colour red.

140   *A spinach tart.*

Take good store of spinach, and boil it in a pipkin with white wine till it be very soft as pap; then take it, and strain it well into a pewter dish, not leaving any part unstrained: then put to it rose-water, great store of sugar and cinnamon, and boil it till it be as thick as marmalade; then let it cool, and after fill your coffin, and adorn it, and serve it in all points as you did your prune tart, and this carrieth the colour green.

141   *A yellow tart.*

Take the yolks of eggs, and break away the films, and beat them well with a little cream; then take of the sweetest and thickest cream that can be got, and set it on the fire in a clean skillet, and put into it sugar, cinnamon, and rose-water, and then boil it well: when it is boiled, and still boiling, stir it well, and as you stir it, put in the eggs, and so boil it till it curdle; then take it from the fire and put it into a strainer, and first let the thin whey run away into a by-dish, then strain the rest very well, and beat it well with a spoon, and so put it into the tart coffin, and adorn it as you did your prune tart, and so serve it: this carrieth the colour yellow.

A white tart.

2
Take the whites of eggs and beat them with rose-water, and a little sweet cream: then set on the fire good thick sweet cream, and put into it sugar, cinnamon, rose-water, and boil it well, and as it boils stir it exceedingly, and in the stirring put in the whites of eggs; then boil it till it curdle, and after do in all things as you did to the yellow tart, and this carrieth the colour white, and it is a very pure white, and therefore would be adorned with red caraway comfits, and as this, so with blanched almonds[165] like white tarts, and full as pure. Now you may (if you please) put all these several colours, and several stuffs into one tart, as thus: if the tart be in the proportion of a beast, the body may be of one colour, the eyes of another, the teeth of another, and the talons of another; and so of birds, the body of one colour, the eyes another, the legs of another, and every feather in the wings of a several colour according to fancy; and so likewise in arms,[166] the field of one colour, the charge of another, according to the form of the coat-armour; as for the mantles, trails, and devices about arms, they may be set out with several colours of preserves, conserves, marmalades, and goodinyakes,[167] as you shall find occasion or invention, and so likewise of knots,[168] one trail of one colour, and another of another, and so of as many as you please.

An herb tart.

3
Take sorrel, spinach, parsley, and boil them in water till they be very soft as pap; then take them up, and press the water clean from them, then take good store of yolks of eggs boiled very hard, and, chopping them with the herbs exceedingly small, then put in good store of currants, sugar, and cinnamon, and stir all well together; then put them into a deep tart coffin with good store of sweet butter, and cover it, and bake it like a pippin tart, and adorn the lid after the baking in that manner also, and so serve it up.

To bake a pudding pie.

44
Take a quart of the best cream, and set [it] on the fire, and slice a loaf of the lightest white bread into thin slices, and put into it, and let it stand on the fire till the milk begin to rise: then take it off, and put it into a basin, and let it stand till it be cold: then put in the yolks of four eggs, and two whites, good store of currants, sugar, cinnamon, cloves, mace, and plenty of sheep's suet finely shred, and a good season of salt; then

trim your pot very well round about with butter, and so put in your pudding, and bake it sufficiently, then when you serve, strew sugar upon it.

145   *A whitepot.*

Take the best and sweetest cream, and boil it with good store of sugar, and cinnamon, and a little rose-water, then take it from the fire and put into it clean picked rice, but not so much as to make it thick, and let it steep therein till it be cold; then put in the yolks of six eggs, and two whites, currants, sugar, cinnamon, and rose-water, and salt, then put it into a pan, or pot, as thin as if it were a custard; and so bake it and serve it in the pot it is baked in, trimming the top with sugar or comfits. [169]

146   *Of banqueting stuff and conceited dishes.*

There are a world of other baked meats and pies, but forasmuch as whosoever can do these may do all the rest, because herein is contained all the art of seasonings, I will trouble you with no further repetitions; but proceed to the manner of making of banqueting stuff and conceited dishes, with other pretty and curious secrets, necessary for the under-standing of our English housewife: for albeit they are not of general use, yet in their true times they are so needful for adornation that whosoever is ignorant therein is lame, and but the half part of a complete housewife.

147   *To make paste of quinces.*

To make paste of quinces:[170] first boil your quinces whole, and when they are soft pare them and cut the quince from the core; then take the finest sugar you can get finely beaten and searced, and put in a little rose-water and boil it together till it be thick; then put in the cut quinces and so boil them together till it be stiff enough to mould, and when it is cold, then roll it and print it. A pound of quinces will take a pound of sugar, or near thereabouts.

148   *To make thin quince cakes.*

To make thin quince cakes, take your quince when it is boiled soft as beforesaid, and dry it upon a pewter plate with a soft heat, and be ever stirring of it with a slice till it be hard; then take searced sugar quantity for quantity and strew it into the quince, as you beat it in a wooden or stone mortar; and so roll them thin and print them. [171]

149   *To preserve quinces.*

To preserve quinces; first pare your quinces and take out the cores and boil the cores and parings altogether in fair water, and when they begin

to be soft, take them out and strain your liquor, and put the weight of
your quinces in sugar, and boil the quinces in the syrup till they be
tender; then take them up and boil your syrup till it be thick. If you will
have your quinces red, cover them in the boiling, and if you will have
them white do not cover them.

To make hippocras.

To make hippocras,[172] take a pottle of wine, two ounces of good cinnamon, half an ounce of ginger, nine cloves, and six pepper corns, and
a nutmeg, and bruise them and put them into the wine with some rosemary
flowers, and so let them steep all night, and then put in sugar a pound
at least; and when it is well settled, let it run through a woollen bag made
for that purpose: thus if your wine be claret, the hippocras will be red;
if white, then of that colour also.

To make jelly.

To make the best jelly, take calves' feet and wash them and scald off
the hair as clean as you can get it; then split them and take out the fat
and lay them in water, and shift[173] them: then boil them in fair water
until it will jelly, which you shall know by now and then cooling a
spoonful of the broth; when it will jelly then strain it, and when it is
cold then put in a pint of sack and whole cinnamon and ginger sliced,
and sugar and a little rose-water, and boil all well together again: then
beat the white of an egg and put it into it,[174] and let it have one boil more:
then put in a branch of rosemary into the bottom of your jelly bag, and
let it run through once or twice, and if you will have it coloured, then
put in a little turnsole. Also if you want calves' feet you may make as
good jelly if you take the like quantity of isinglass, and so use no calves'
feet at all.

To make leach.

To make the best leach,[175] take isinglass and lay it two hours in water,
and shift it and boil it in fair water and let it cool: then take almonds and
lay them in cold water till they will blanch: and then stamp them and
put to new milk, and strain them and put in whole mace and ginger sliced,
and boil them till it taste well of the spice; then put in your isinglass and
sugar, and a little rose-water: and then let them all run through a strainer.

To make gingerbread.

Take claret wine and colour it with turnsole, and put in sugar and set
it to the fire; then take wheat bread finely grated and sifted, and liquorice,
aniseeds, ginger, and cinnamon beaten very small and searced; and put

your bread and your spice all together, and put them into the wine and boil it and stir it till it be thick; then mould it and print it at your pleasure, and let it stand neither too moist nor too warm. [176]

154   *Marmalade of quinces red.*

To make red marmalade of quinces; take a pound of quinces and cut them in halves, and take out the cores and pare them; then take a pound of sugar and a quart of fair water and put them all into a pan, and let them boil with a soft fire, and sometimes turn them and keep them covered with a pewter dish, so that the steam or air may come a little out; the longer they are in boiling the better colour they will have; and when they be soft take a knife and cut them cross upon the top, it will make the syrup go through that they may be all of a like colour: then set a little of your syrup to cool, and when it beginneth to be thick then break your quinces, with a slice or a spoon, so small as you can in the pan, and then strew a little fine sugar in your box's[177] bottom, and so put it up.

155   *Marmalade white.*

To make white marmalade you must in all points use your quinces as is beforesaid; only you must take but a pint of water to a pound of quinces, and a pound of sugar, and boil them as fast as you can, and cover them not at all.

156   *To make jumbles.*

To make the best jumbles, take the whites of three eggs and beat them well, and take off the veil;[178] then take a little milk and a pound of fine wheat flour and sugar together finely sifted, and a few aniseeds well rubbed and dried; and then work all together as stiff as you can work it, and so make them in what forms you please, and bake them in a soft oven upon white papers. [179]

157   *To make biscuit bread.*

To make biscuit bread, take a pound of fine flour, and a pound of sugar finely beaten and searced, and mix them together; then take eight eggs and put[180] four yolks and beat them very well together; then strew in your flour and sugar as you are beating[181] of it, by a little at once; it will take very near an hour's beating: then take half an ounce of aniseeds, coriander seeds, and let them be dried and rubbed very clean, and put them in; then rub your biscuit pans with cold sweet butter as thin as you can, and so put it in and bake it in an oven: but if you would have thin cakes, then take fruit dishes and rub them in like sort with butter, and so bake your cakes on them, and when they are almost baked, turn them and thrust them down close with your hand. Some to this biscuit bread will add a little cream, and it is not amiss, but excellent good also.

To make finer jumbles.

58   To make jumbles more fine and curious than the former, and nearer to the taste of the macaroon; take a pound of sugar, beat it fine; then take as much fine wheat flour and mix them together, then take two whites and one yolk of an egg, half a quarter of a pound of blanched almonds; then beat them very fine all together with half a dish of sweet butter, and a spoonful of rose-water, and so work it with a little cream till it come to a very stiff paste, then roll them forth as you please:[182] and hereto you shall also, if you please, add a few dried aniseeds finely rubbed and strewed into the paste, and also coriander seed.

To make dry sugar leach.

59   To make dry sugar leach, blanch your almonds and beat them with a little rose-water and the white of one egg, and you must beat it with a great deal of sugar, and work it as you would work a piece of paste: then roll it and print it as you did other things, only be sure to strew sugar in the print for fear of cleaving to.

To make leach Lombard.

60   To make leach Lombard, take half a pound of blanched almonds, two ounces of cinnamon beaten and searced, half a pound of sugar; then beat your almonds, and strew in your sugar and cinnamon till it come to a paste, then roll it and print it as aforesaid.

To make fresh cheese.

61   To make an excellent fresh cheese, take a pottle of milk as it comes from the cow, and a pint of cream: then take a spoonful of rennet or earning and put it unto it, and let it stand two hours; then stir it up and put it into a fine cloth, and let the whey drain from it: then put it into a bowl and take the yolk of an egg, a spoonful of rose-water, and bray them together with a very little salt, with sugar and nutmegs; and when all these are brayed together and searced, mix it with the curd, and then put it into a cheese vat with a very fine cloth.

How to make coarse ginger bread.

62   To make coarse gingerbread, take a quart of honey and set it on the coals and refine it: then take a pennyworth of ginger, as much pepper, as much liquorice; and a quarter of a pound of aniseeds, and a pennyworth of sanders: all these must be beaten and searced, and so put into the

honey: then put in a quarter of a pint of claret wine or old ale: then take three penny manchets finely grated and strew it amongst the rest, and stir it till it come to a stiff paste, and then make it into cakes and dry them gently.

163 *How to make quince cakes ordinary.*

To make ordinary quince cakes, take a good piece of a preserved quince, and beat it in a mortar, and work it up into a very stiff paste with fine searced sugar: then print it and dry them gently.

164 *How to make cinnamon sticks.*

To make most artificial cinnamon sticks, take an ounce of cinnamon and pound it, and half a pound of sugar: then take some gum dragon[183] and put it in steep in rose-water, then take thereof to the quantity of a hazel nut, and work it out and print it, and roll it in form of a cinnamon stick.

165 *How to make cinnamon water.*

To make cinnamon water take a pottle of the best ale and a pottle of sack lees, a pound of cinnamon sliced fine, and put them together, and let them stand two days; then distil them in a limbeck[184] or glass still.

166 *How to make wormwood water.*

To make wormwood water take two gallons of good ale, a pound of aniseeds, half a pound of liquorice, and beat them very fine; and then take two good handfuls of the crops of wormwood, and put them into the ale and let them stand all night, and then distil them in a limbeck with a moderate fire.

167 *To make sweet water.*

To make sweet water of the best kind, take a thousand damask roses, two good handfuls of lavender knops,[185] a three-pennyweight of mace, two ounces of cloves bruised, a quart of running water: put a little water into the bottom of an earthen pot, and then put in your roses and lavender with the spices by little and little, and in the putting in always knead them down with your fist, and so continue it until you have wrought up all your roses and lavender, and in the working between put in always a little of your water; then stop your pot close, and let it stand four days, in which time every morning and evening put in your hand, and pull from the bottom of your pot the said roses, working it for a time: and then distil it, and hang in the glass of water a grain or two of musk wrapped in a piece of sarcenet or fine cloth.

68

Another way.

Others to make sweet water, take of ireos[186] two ounces, of calamus[187] half an ounce, of cypress roots half an ounce, of yellow sanders nine drams, of cloves bruised one ounce, of benjamin[188] one ounce, of storax and calamint one ounce, and of musk twelve grains, and, infusing all these in rose-water, distil it.

69

To make date leach.

To make an excellent date leach, take dates, and take out the stones and the white rind, and beat them with sugar, cinnamon, and ginger very finely: then work it as you would work a piece of paste, and then print them as you please.

70

To make sugar plate.

To make a kind of sugar plate, take gum dragon, and lay it in rose-water two days: then take the powder of fair hips[189] and sugar, and the juice of an orange; beat all these together in a mortar, then take it out and work it with your hand, and print it at your pleasure.

71

To make spice cakes.

To make excellent spice cakes, take half a peck[190] of very fine wheat flour; take almost one pound of sweet butter, and some good milk and cream mixed together; set it on the fire, and put in your butter, and a good deal of sugar, and let it melt together: then strain saffron into your milk a good quantity; then take seven or eight spoonfuls of good ale barm,[191] and eight eggs with two yolks and mix them together, then put your milk to it when it is somewhat cold, and into your flour put salt, aniseeds bruised, cloves, and mace, and a good deal of cinnamon: then work all together good and stiff, that you need not work in any flour after; then put in a little rose-water cold, then rub it well in the thing you knead it in, and work it thoroughly: if it be not sweet enough, scrape in a little more sugar, and pull it all in pieces, and hurl in a good quantity of currants, and so work all together again, and bake your cake as you see cause in a gentle warm oven.

72

To make Banbury cake.

To make a very good Banbury[192] cake, take four pounds of currants, and wash and pick them very clean, and dry them in a cloth: then take three eggs and put away one yolk, and beat them, and strain them with good barm, putting thereto cloves, mace, cinnamon, and nutmegs; then take a pint of cream, and as much morning's milk and set it on the fire till the cold be taken away; then take flour and put in good store of cold butter and sugar, then put in your eggs, barm, and meal and work them all together an hour or more; then save a part of the paste, and the rest break in pieces and work in your currants; which done, mould your cake of what quantity you please; and then with that paste which hath not any currants cover it very thin both underneath and aloft. And so bake it according to the bigness.

173   *To make the best marchpane.*

To make the best marchpane, take the best Jordan almonds and blanch them in warm water, then put them into a stone mortar, and with a wooden pestle beat them to pap, then take of the finest refined sugar well searced, and with it, and damask rose-water, beat it[193] to a good stiff paste, allowing almost to every Jordan almond three spoonful of sugar;[194] then when it is brought thus to a paste, lay it upon a fair table, and, strewing searced sugar under it, mould it like leaven; then with a rolling pin roll it forth, and lay it upon wafers[195] washed with rose-water; then pinch it about the sides, and put it into what form you please; then strew searced sugar all over it; which done, wash it over with rose-water and sugar mixed together, for that will make the ice; then adorn it with comfits, gilding, or whatsoever devices you please, and so set it into a hot[196] stove, and there bake it crispy, and so serve it forth. Some use to mix with the paste cinnamon and ginger finely searced, but I refer that to your particular taste.

174   *To make a paste of Genoa, or any other paste.*

To make paste of Genoa, you shall take quinces after they have been boiled soft, and beat them in a mortar with refined sugar,[197] cinnamon, and ginger finely searced, and damask rose-water till it come to a stiff paste; and then roll it forth and print it, and so bake it in a stove;[198] and in this sort you may make paste of pears, apples, wardens, plums of all kinds, cherries, barberries, or what other fruit you please.

175   *To make any conserve.*

To make conserve of any fruit you please, you shall take the fruit you intend to make conserve of; and if it be stone fruit you shall take out the stones; if other fruit, take away the paring and core, and then boil them in fair running water to a reasonable height;[199] then drain them from thence, and put them into a fresh vessel with claret wine, or white wine, according to the colour of the fruit: and so boil them to a thick pap all to mashing, breaking, and stirring them together; then to every pound of pap put to a pound of sugar, and so stir them all well together, and, being very hot, strain them through fair strainers, and so pot it up.

76   *To make conserve of flowers.*

To make conserve of flowers, as roses, violets, gillyflowers, and such like; you shall take the flowers from the stalks, and with a pair of shears cut away the white ends at the roots thereof, and then put them into a stone mortar or wooden brake,²⁰⁰ and there crush or beat them till they be come to a soft substance; and then to every pound thereof, take a pound of fine refined sugar well searced and beat it all together, till it come to one entire body, and then pot it up, and use it as occasion shall serve.

77   *To make wafers.*

To make the best wafers, take the finest wheat flour you can get, and mix it with cream, the yolks of eggs, rose-water, sugar, and cinnamon till it be a little thicker than pancake batter; and then, warming your wafer irons on a charcoal fire, anoint them first with sweet butter, and then lay on your batter and press it, and bake it white or brown at your pleasure.

78   *To make marmalade of oranges.*

To make an excellent marmalade of oranges, take the oranges, and with a knife pare off as thin as is possible the uppermost rind of the orange; yet in such sort as by no means you alter the colour of the orange; then steep them in fair water, changing the water twice a day, till you find no bitterness of taste therein; then take them forth, and first boil them in fair running water, and, when they are soft, remove them into rose-water, and boil them therein till they break: then to every pound of the pulp put a pound of refined sugar, and so, having mashed and stirred them all well together, strain it through very fair strainers into boxes, and so use it as you shall see occasion.

79   *ADDITIONS to banqueting stuff. To make fine cakes.*

Take a pottle of fine flour, and a pound of butter, a pound of sugar, a little mace, and good store of water to mingle the flour into a stiff paste, and a good season of salt, and so knead it, and roll out the cake thin and bake them on papers.

80   *Fine bread.*

Take a quarter of a pound of fine sugar well beaten, and as much flour finely bolted, with a quantity of aniseeds a little bruised, and mingle all together; then take two eggs and beat them very well, whites and all; then put in the mingled stuff aforesaid, and beat all together a good while, then put it into a mould, wiping the bottom ever first with butter to make

A family meal. From *The Roxburghe Ballads*, ed. Charles Hindley (London, 1874), vol. i., p. 116.

it come out easily, and in the baking turn it once or twice as you shall have occasion, and so serve it whole, or in slices at your pleasure.

181   *To preserve quinces for kitchen service.*

Take sweet apples and stamp them as you do for cider, then press them through a bag as you do verjuice;[201] then put it into a firkin wherein you will keep your quinces, and then gather your quinces, and wipe them clean, and neither core them nor pare them, but only take the blacks from the tops, and so put them into the firkin of cider, and therein you may keep them all the year very fair, and take them not out of the liquor, but as you are ready to use them, whether it be for pies, or any other purpose, and then pare them, and core them as you think good.

182   *To make hippocras.*[202]

Take a gallon of claret or white wine, and put therein four ounces of ginger, an ounce and a half of nutmegs, of cloves one quarter, of sugar four pound; let all this stand together in a pot at least twelve hours, then take it, and put it into a clean bag made for the purpose, so that the wine may come with good leisure from the spices.

To preserve quinces.

3

Take quinces and wipe them very clean, and then core them, and as you core them, put the cores straight into fair water, and let the cores and the water boil; when the water boileth, put in the quinces unpared, and let them boil till they be tender, and then take them out and pare them, and ever as you pare them, put them straight into sugar finely beaten: then take the water they were sodden in, and strain it through a fair cloth, and take as much of the same water as you think will make syrup enough for the quinces, and put in some of your sugar and let it boil a while, and then put in your quinces, and let them boil a while, and turn them, and cast a good deal of sugar upon them; they must seethe apace, and ever as you turn them cover them still with sugar, till you have bestowed all your sugar; and when you think that your quinces are tender enough, take them forth, and if your syrup be not stiff enough, you may seethe it again after the quinces are forth. To every pound of quinces you must take more than a pound of sugar, for the more sugar you take, the fairer your quinces will be, and the better and longer they will be preserved.

Conserve of quinces.

4

Take two gallons of fair water, and set it on the fire, and when it is lukewarm, beat the whites of five or six eggs, and put them into the water, and stir it well, and then let the water seethe, and when it riseth up all on a curd, then scum it off.[203] Take quinces and pare them, and quarter them, and cut out the cores: then take as many pound of your quinces as of your sugar, and put them into your liquor, and let it boil till your liquor be as high coloured as French wine, and when they be very tender, then take a fair new canvas cloth fair washed, and strain your quinces through it, with some of your liquor (if they will not go through easily), then if you will make it very pleasant, take a little musk, and lay it in rose-water, and put it thereto; then take and seethe it, until it be of such substance that, when it is cold, it will cut with a knife; and then put it into a fair box, and if you please, lay leaf gold thereon.

To keep quinces all the year.

5

Take all the parings of your quinces that you make your conserve withal, and three or four other quinces, and cut them in pieces, and boil the same parings, and the other pieces in two or three gallons of water, and so let them boil till all the strength be sodden out of the said quinces and parings, and if any scum arise whilst it boils, take it away: then let the said water run through a strainer into a fair vessel, and set it on the fire again, and take your quinces that you will keep, and wipe them clean, and cut off the uttermost part of the said quinces, and pick out the kernels and cores as clean as you can, and put them into the said liquor, and so let them boil till they be a little soft, and then take them from the fire, and let them stand till they be cold: then take a little barrel, and put into the said barrel the water that your quinces be sodden in; then take up your quinces with a ladle, and put them into your barrel, and stop your barrel close that no air come into them, till you have fit occasion to use them; and be sure to take such quinces as are neither bruised nor rotten.

186   *Fine ginger cakes.*

Take of the best sugar, and when it is beaten searce it very fine, and [take] of the best ginger and cinnamon; then take a little gum dragon and lay it in rose-water all night, then pour the water from it, and put the same, with a little white of an egg well beaten, into a brass mortar, the sugar, ginger, cinnamon and all together, and beat them together till you may work it like paste; then take it and drive it forth into cakes, and print them, and lay them before the fire, or in a very warm stove to bake. Or otherwise take sugar and ginger (as is before said), cinnamon and gum dragon excepted, instead whereof take only the whites of eggs, and so do as was before showed you.

187   *To make suckets.*

Take curds, the parings of lemons, of oranges or pomecitrons, or indeed any half ripe green fruit, and boil them till they be tender, in sweet wort; then make a syrup in this sort: take three pound of sugar, and the whites of four eggs, and a gallon of water; then swinge and beat the water and the eggs together, and then put in your sugar, and set it on the fire, and let it have an easy fire, and so let it boil six or seven walms, and then strain it through a cloth, and let it seethe again till it fall from the spoon, and then put it into the rinds of fruits. [204]

188   *Coarse gingerbread.*

Take a quart of honey clarified, and seethe it till it be brown, and if it be thick put to it a dish of water: then take fine crumbs of white bread grated, and put to it, and stir it well, and when it is almost cold, put to it the powder of ginger, cloves, cinnamon, and a little liquorice and aniseeds; then knead it, and put it into moulds and print it: some use to put to it also a little pepper, but that is according unto taste and pleasure.

189   *To candy any root, fruit, or flower.*

Dissolve sugar, or sugar-candy in rose-water, boil it to a height, [205] put in your roots, fruits, or flowers, the syrup being cold, then rest a little;

after take them out and boil the syrup the third time²⁰⁶ to a hardness, putting in more sugar, but not rose-water; put in the roots, etc., the syrup being cold, and let them stand till they candy.

Ordering of banquets.

Thus having showed you how to preserve, conserve, candy, and make pastes of all kinds, in which four heads consists the whole art of banqueting dishes, I will now proceed to the ordering or setting forth of a banquet; wherein you shall observe that marchpanes have the first place, the middle place, and last place; your preserved fruits shall be dished up first, your pastes next, your wet suckets²⁰⁷ after them, then your dried suckets, then your marmalades and goodinyakes,²⁰⁸ then your comfits of all kinds; next, your pears, apples, wardens baked, raw or roasted, and your oranges and lemons sliced; and lastly your wafer cakes. Thus you shall order them in the closet;²⁰⁹ but when they go to the table, you shall first send forth a dish made for show only, as beast, bird, fish, or fowl, according to invention: then your marchpane, then preserved fruit, then a paste, then a wet sucket, then a dry sucket, marmalade, comfits, apples, pears, wardens, oranges, and lemons sliced; and then wafers, and another dish of preserved fruits, and so consequently all the rest before: no two dishes of one kind going or standing together, and this will not only appear delicate to the eye, but invite the appetite with the much variety thereof.

[ADDITION.] Ordering of great feasts and proportion of expense.

Now we have drawn our housewife into these several knowledges of cookery, inasmuch as in her is contained all the inward offices of household, we will proceed to declare the manner of serving and setting forth of meat for a great feast, and from it derive meaner, making a due proportion of all things:²¹⁰ for what avails it our good housewife to be never so skilful in the parts of cookery, if she want skill to marshal the dishes, and set every one in his due place, giving precedency according to fashion and custom; it is like to a fencer leading a band of men in rout,²¹¹ who knows the use of the weapon, but not how to put men in order. It is then to be understood, that it is the office of the clerk of the kitchen²¹² (whose place our housewife must many times supply) to order the meat at the dresser, and deliver it unto the sewer,²¹³ who is to deliver it to the gentlemen and yeomen waiters to bear to the table. Now because we allow no officer but our housewife, to whom we only speak in this book, she shall first marshal her sallats, delivering the grand sallat first, which is evermore compound;²¹⁴ then green sallats, then boiled sallats, then some smaller compound sallats. Next unto sallats she shall deliver forth all her

A table setting. Note the wooden trenchers (plates) and the fork (upper right); the fork was introduced to England from Italy in Markham's lifetime. From Vincenzo Cervio, *Il Trinciante*, p. 94.

fricassees, the simple first, as collops, rashers, and such like; then compound fricassees; after them all her boiled meats in their degrees, as simple broths, stewed broth, and the boilings of sundry fowls. Next them all sorts of roast meats, of which the greatest first, as chine of beef or sirloin, the gigot or legs of mutton, goose, swan, veal, pig, capon, and such like. Then baked meats, the hot first, as fallow deer in pasty, chicken, or calf's-foot pie and doucet. Then cold baked meats, pheasant, partridges, turkey, goose, woodcock, and such like. Then lastly, carbonadoes both simple and compound. And being thus marshalled from the dresser, the sewer, upon the placing them on the table, shall not set them down as he received them, but, setting the sallats extravagantly about the table, mix the fricassees about them; then the boiled meats amongst the fricassees, roast meats amongst the boiled, baked meats amongst the roast, and carbonadoes amongst the baked; so that before every trencher may stand a sallat, a fricassee, a boiled meat, a roast meat, a baked meat, and a carbonado, which will both give a most comely beauty to the table, and very great contentment to the guest. So likewise in the second course she shall first prefer the lesser wild fowl, as mallard, teal, snipe, plover, woodcock, and such like: then the lesser land fowl; as chicken, pigeons, partridge, rail, turkey, chickens, young peahens, and such like. Then the greater wild fowl; as bittern, hern, shoveller, crane, bustard,[215] and such like. Then the greater land fowls; as peacocks, pheasant, pewits, gulls, and such like. Then hot baked meats; as marrow-bone pie, quince pie, Florentine, and tarts.

92   Then cold baked meats, as red deer, hare pie, gammon of bacon pie, wild boar, roe pie, and such like, and these also shall be marshalled at the table as the first course, not one kind all together, but each several sort mixed together, as a lesser wild fowl and a lesser land fowl; a great wild fowl, and a great land fowl; a hot baked meat, and a cold: and for made dishes and *quelquechoses*, which rely on the invention of the cook, they are to be thrust in, into every place that is empty, and so sprinkled over all the table: and this is the best method for the extraordinary great feasts of princes. But in case it be for much more humble means, then less care and fewer dishes may discharge it; yet, before I proceed to that lower rate, you shall understand that in these great feasts of princes, though I have mentioned nothing but flesh, yet is not fish to be exempted; for it is a beauty and an honour unto every feast, and is to be placed amongst all the several services, as thus; as amongst your sallats all sorts of soused fish that lives in the fresh water; amongst your fricassees all manner of fried fish; amongst your boiled meats, all fish in broths; amongst your roast meats, all fish served hot, but dry; amongst the baked meats, all fish baked, and sea fish that is soused, as sturgeon and the like; and amongst your carbonadoes, fish that is broiled. As for your second course, to it belongeth all manner of shell-fish, either in the shell, or without; the hot to go up with the hot meat, and the cold with the cold. And thus shall the feast be royal, and the service worthy.

93   Now for a more humble feast,[216] or an ordinary proportion which any goodman may keep in his family for the entertainment of his true and worthy friends, it must hold limitation with his provision, and the season of the year; for summer affords what winter wants, and winter is master of that which summer can but with difficulty have: it is good then for him that intends to feast, to set down the full number of his full dishes, that is, dishes of meat that are of substance, and not empty or for show; and of these sixteen is a good proportion for one course unto one mess,[217] as thus for example; first, a shield of brawn[218] with mustard; secondly, a boiled capon; thirdly, a boiled piece of beef; fourthly, a chine of beef roasted; fifthly, a neat's tongue roasted; sixthly, a pig roasted; seventhly, chewets baked; eighthly, a goose roasted; ninthly, a swan roasted; tenthly, a turkey roasted; the eleventh, a haunch of venison roasted; the twelfth,

a pasty of venison; the thirteenth, a kid with a pudding in the belly; the fourteenth, an olive pie; the fifteenth, a couple of capons; the sixteenth, a custard or doucets. Now to these full dishes may be added in sallats, fricassees, *quelquechoses*, and devised paste, as many dishes more, which make the full service no less than two and thirty dishes, which is as much as can conveniently stand on one table, and in one mess; and after this manner you may proportion both your second and third course, holding fullness in one half of the dishes, and show in the other, which will be both frugal in the spender, contentment to the guest,[219] and much pleasure and delight to the beholders. And thus much touching the ordering of great feasts and ordinary entertainments.

CHAPTER III

Of distillations and their virtues, and of perfuming

1   When our English housewife is exact in these rules before rehearsed, and that she is able to adorn· and beautify her table, with all the virtuous illustrations meet for her knowledge; she shall then sort her mind to the understanding of other housewifely secrets, right profitable and meet for her use, such as the want thereof may trouble her when need, or time requires.

2   *Of distillations. Of the nature of waters.*
  Therefore first I would have her furnish herself of very good stills, for the distillation of all kinds of waters, which stills would be either of tin, or sweet earth; and in them she shall distil all sorts of waters meet for the health of her household; as sage water, which is good for all rheums and colics, radish water, which is good for the stone, angelica water good for infection, celandine water for sore eyes, vine water for itchings, rose-water, and eye-bright water for dim sights, rosemary water for fistulas, treacle water for mouth cankers, water of cloves for pain in the stomach, saxifrage water for gravel¹ and hard urine, alum water for old ulcers, and a world of others, any of which will last a full year at the least. Then she shall know that the best waters for the smoothing of the skin, and keeping the face delicate and amiable, are those which are distilled from bean flowers, from strawberries, from vine leaves, from goat's milk, from ass's milk, from the whites of eggs, from the flowers of lilies, from dragons,² from calves' feet, from bran, or from yolks of eggs, any of which will last a year or better.

"The Common furnace that
belongeth to this work." From
Laurence Andrewe, *The Vertuose
Boke of Distillacyon*, sig. A4v.

3   *ADDITIONS to distillations. To distil water of the colour of the herb
or flower you desire.*

First distil your water in a stillatory, then put in a glass of great strength,
and fill it with those flowers again (whose colour you desire) as full as
you can, and stop it and set it in the stillatory again, and let it distil, and
you shall have the colour you distil.

4   *To make aqua vitae.*

Take of rosemary flowers two handfuls, of marjoram, winter savory,
rosemary, rue, unset thyme, germander, ribwort, hart's tongue, mouse-
ear, white wormwood, bugloss, red sage, liverwort;[3] horehound, fine
lavender, hyssop crops, pennyroyal, red fennel, of each of these one
handful; of elecampane roots clean pared and sliced, two handfuls; then
take all these aforesaid and shred them, but not wash them; then take
four gallons and more of strong ale, and one gallon of sack lees, and put
all these aforesaid herbs shred into it, and then put into it one pound of
liquorice bruised, half a pound of aniseeds clean sifted and bruised, and
of mace and nutmegs bruised of each one ounce; then put all together
into your stilling-pot close covered with rye paste, and make a soft fire
under your pot, and as the head of the limbeck[4] heateth, draw out your
hot water and put in cold, keeping the head of your limbeck still with

cold water, but see your fire be not too rash at the first, but let your water come at leisure, and take heed unto your stilling that your water change not white, for it is not so strong as the first draught is; and when the water is distilled, take a gallon glass with a wide mouth, and put therein a pottle of the best water and clearest, and put into it a pottle of *rosa solis*, half a pound of dates bruised, and one ounce of grains,[5] half a pound of sugar, half an ounce of seed pearl beaten, three leaves of fine gold; stir all these together well, then stop your glass and set it in the sun the space of one or two months, and then clarify it and use it at your discretion, for a spoonful or two at a time is sufficient, and the virtues are infinite.

5
Another excellent aqua vitae.

Fill a pot with red wine clean and strong, and put therein the powders of camomile, gillyflowers, ginger, pellitory, nutmeg, galingale, spikenard, quenebits, grains of pure long pepper,[6] black pepper, cumin, fennel seed, smallage, parsley, sage, rue, mint, calamint, and horseshoe, of each of them a like quantity, and beware they differ not the weight of a dram under or above; then put all the powders above said into the wine, and after put them into the distilling pot, and distil it with a soft fire, and look that it be well luted about with rye paste, so that no fume or breath go forth, and look that the fire be temperate; also receive the water out of the limbeck into a glass vial. This water is called the water of life, and it may be likened to balm, for it hath all the virtues and properties which balm hath; this water is clear and lighter than rose-water, for it will fleet above all liquors, for if oil be put above this water, it sinketh to the bottom. This water keepeth flesh and fish, both raw and sodden, in his own kind and state, it is good against aches in the bones, the pox, and such like, neither can anything kept in this water rot or putrify; it doth draw out the sweetness, savour, and virtues of all manner of spices, roots and herbs that are wet or laid therein; it gives sweetness to all manner of water that is mixed with it; it is good for all manner of cold sicknesses, and namely for the palsy or trembling joints, and stretching of the sinews;[7] it is good against the cold gout; and it maketh an old man seem young, using to drink it fasting; and lastly it fretteth away dead flesh in wounds, and killeth the canker.[8]

6
To make aqua composita.[9]

Take rosemary, thyme, hyssop, sage, fennel, nep, roots of elecampane, of each a handful, of marjoram, and pennyroyal of each half a handful; eight slips of red mint, half a pound of liquorice, half a pound of aniseeds, and two gallons of the best ale that can be brewed; wash all these herbs clean, and put the ale, liquorice, aniseeds, and herbs into a clean brass pot, and set your limbeck thereon, and paste it round about that no air come out, then distil the water with a gentle fire, and keep the limbeck cool above, not suffering it to run too fast; and take heed when your water changeth colour to put another glass under, and keep the first water, for it is most precious, and the latter water keep by itself, and put it into your next pot, and that shall make it much better.

7   *A very principal aqua composita.*

Take of balm, of rosemary flowers tops and all, of dried red rose leaves, of pennyroyal, of each of these a handful, of hyssop half a handful, one root of elecampane the whitest that can be got, three quarters of a pound of liquorice, two ounces of cinnamon, two drams of great mace, two drams of galingale, three drams of coriander seed, three drams of caraway seeds, two or three nutmegs cut in four quarters, an ounce of aniseeds, a handful of borage; you must choose a fair sunny day to gather the herbs in; you must not wash them, but cut them in sunder, and not too small; then lay all your herbs in souse all night and a day, with the spices grossly beaten or bruised, and then distil it in order aforesaid; this was made for a learned physician's own drinking.

8   *To make the imperial water.*

Take a gallon of Gascon wine; ginger, galingale, nutmegs, grains, cloves, aniseeds, fennel seeds, caraway seeds, of each one dram, then take sage, mints, red roses, thyme, pellitory, rosemary; wild thyme, camomile, and lavender, of each a handful, then bray the spices small, and the herbs also, and put all together into the wine, and let it stand so twelve hours, stirring it divers times, then distil it with a limbeck, and keep the first water, for it is best: of a gallon of wine you must not take above a quart of water; this water comforteth the vital spirits, and helpeth inward diseases that cometh of cold, as the palsy, the contraction of sinews; also it killeth worms, and comforts the stomach; it cureth the cold dropsy,[10] helps the stone, the stinking breath, and maketh one seem young.[11]

9   *To make cinnamon water.*

Take a pottle of the best sack, and half a pint of rose-water, a quarter and half of a pound of good cinnamon well bruised, but not small beaten; distil all these together in a glass still, but you must carefully look to it that it boil not over hastily, and attend it with cold wet cloths to cool the top of the still if the water should offer to boil too hastily. This water is very sovereign for the stomach, the head, and all the inward parts; it helps digestion, and comforteth the vital spirits.[12]

Six most precious waters, which Hippocrates[13] *made, and sent to a*
queen sometime living in England.

1. Take fennel, rue, vervain, endive, betony, germander, red rose, *capillus veneris*,[14] of each an ounce; stamp them and steep them in white wine a day and a night, and distil water of them, which water will divide[15] in three parts; the first water you shall put in a glass by itself, for it is more precious than gold, the second as silver, and the third as balm, and keep these three parts in glasses: this water you shall give the rich for gold, to meaner for silver, to poor men[16] for balm: this water keepeth the sight in clearness, and purgeth all gross humours.

2. Take *sall gemma* a pound, and lap it in a green dock leaf, and lay it in the fire till it be well roasted, and wax white, and put it in a glass against the air a night, and on the morrow it shall be turned to a white water like unto crystal: keep this water well in a glass, and put a drop into the eye, and it shall cleanse and sharp the sight: it is good for any evil at the heart, for the morphew, and the canker of the mouth, and for divers other evils in the body.

3. Take the roots of fennel, parsley, endive, betony, of each an ounce, and first wash them well in lukewarm water, and bray them well [and steep them] with white wine a day and a night, and then distil them into water: this water is more worthy than balm; it preserveth the sight much, and cleanseth it of all filth, it restraineth tears, and comforteth the head, and avoideth the water that cometh through the pain in the head.

4. Take the seed of parsley, achannes,[17] vervain, caraways and centaury, of each ten drams; beat all these together, and put it in warm water a day and a night, and put it in a vessel to distil: this water is a precious water for all sore eyes, and very good for the health of man or woman's body.

5. Take limail of gold, silver, latten, copper, iron, steel, and lead; and take litharge[18] of gold and silver; take calamint and columbine, and steep all together, the first day in the urine of a man child, that is between a day and a night, the second day in white wine, the third day in the juice of fennel, the fourth day in the whites of eggs, the fifth day in the woman's milk that nourisheth a man child, the sixth day in red wine, the seventh day in the whites of eggs, and upon the eighth day bind[19] all these together, and distil the water of them, and keep this water in a vessel of gold or silver: the virtues of this water are these, first it expelleth all rheums, and doth away all manner of sickness from the eyes, and wears away the pearl, pin, and web;[20] it draweth again into his own kind[21] the eyelids that have been bleared,[22] it easeth the ache of the head, and, if a man drink it, maketh him look young even in old age, besides a world of other most excellent virtues.

The housewife's closet, with her apparatus for distillation. From the title-page of *The Accomplished Lady's Delight in Preserving, Physick, Beautifying and Cookery.*

15   6. Take the goldsmith's stone,[23] and put it into the fire, till it be red hot, and quench it in a pint of white wine, and do so nine times, and after grind it, and beat it small, and cleanse it as clean as you may, and after set it in the sun with the water of fennel distilled, and vervain, roses, celandine, and rue, and a little aqua vitae, and when you have sprinkled it in the water nine times, put it then in a vessel of glass, and yet upon a reversion of the water[24] distil it, till it pass over the touch four or five inches; and when you will use it then stir it all together, and then take up a drop with a feather, and put it on your nail, and if it abide, it is fine and good: then put it in the eye that runneth, or anoint the head with it if it ache, and the temples; and believe it, that of all waters this is the most precious, and helpeth the sight or any pain in the head.

16   *The virtues of several waters.*
The water of chervil is good for a sore mouth.
The water of calamint is good for the stomach.
The water of plantain is good for the flux, and the hot dropsy.[25]
Water of fennel is good to make a fat body small, and also for the eyes.
Water of violets is good for a man that is sore within his body, and for the reins, and for the liver.
Water of endive is good for the dropsy, and for the jaundice, and the stomach.

Water of borage is good for the stomach, and for the *iliaca passio*,[26] and
many other sicknesses in the body.

Water of both sages is good for the palsy.

Water of betony is good for the hearing[27] and all inward sicknesses.

Water of radish drunk twice a day, at each time an ounce, or an ounce
and a half, doth multiply and provoke lust, and also it provoketh the
terms[28] in women.

7   Rosemary water (the face washed therein both morning and night)
causeth a fair and clear countenance: also the head washed therewith, and
let dry of itself, preserveth the falling of the hair, and causeth more to
grow; also two ounces of the same, drunk, driveth venom out of the
body in the same sort as mithridate[29] doth; the same twice or thrice drunk,
at each time half an ounce, rectifieth the mother,[30] and it causeth women
to be fruitful: when one maketh a bath of this decoction, it is called the
bath of life; the same drunk comforteth the heart, the brain, and the
whole body, and cleanseth away the spots of the face; it maketh a man
look young, and causeth women to conceive quickly, and hath all the
virtues of balm.

8   Water of rue drunk in a morning four or five days together, at each
time an ounce, purifieth the flowers in women; the same water, drunk
in the morning fasting, is good against the griping of the bowels, and,
drunk at morning and at night, at each time an ounce, it provoketh the
terms in women.

9   The water of sorrel drunk is good for all burning and pestilent fevers,
and all other hot sicknesses;[31] being mixed with beer, ale, or wine, it
slaketh thirst; it is also good for the yellow jaundice, being taken six or
eight days together; it also expelleth heat from the liver if it be drunk
and a cloth wet in the same and a little wrung out, and so applied to the
right side over against the liver, and when it is dry then wet another, and
apply it; and thus do three or four times together.

o   Lastly the water of angelica is good for the head, for inward infection,
either of the plague or pestilence; it is very sovereign for sore breasts;
also the same water, being drunk of twelve or thirteen days together, is
good to unlade the stomach of gross humours and superfluities, and it
strengtheneth and comforteth all the universal parts of the body: and
lastly, it is a most sovereign medicine for the gout, by bathing the diseased
members much therein.

1   Now to conclude and knit up this chapter, it is meet that our housewife
know that from the eight of the calends of the month of April unto the
eight of the calends of July, all manner of herbs and leaves are in that

time most in strength and of the greatest virtue[32] to be used and put in all manner of medicines; also from the eight of the calends of July unto the eight of the calends of October the stalks, stems, and hard branches of every herb and plant is most in strength to be used in medicines; and from the eight of the calends of October, unto the eight of the calends of April, all manner of roots of herbs and plants are the most of strength and virtue to be used in all manner of medicines.

22   *An excellent water for perfume.*

To make an excellent sweet water for perfume, you shall take of basil, mints, marjoram, corn-flag[33] roots, hyssop, savory, sage, balm, lavender, and rosemary, of each one a handful; of cloves, cinnamon, and nutmegs of each half an ounce, then three or four pomecitrons cut into slices; infuse all these into damask rose-water the space of three days, and then distil it with a gentle fire of charcoal, then when you have put it into a very clean glass, take of fat[34] musk, civet, and ambergris of each the quantity of a scruple,[35] and put into a rag of fine lawn, and then hang it within the water. This, being either burnt upon a hot pan, or else boiled in perfuming pans with cloves, bay leaves, and lemon peels, will make the most delicatest perfume that may be without any offence, and will last the longest of all other sweet perfumes, as hath been found by experience.

23   *To perfume gloves.*

To perfume gloves excellently, take the oil of sweet almonds, oil of nutmegs, oil of benjamin, of each a dram, of ambergris one grain, fat musk two grains: mix them altogether and grind them upon a painter's stone,[36] and then anoint the gloves therewith: yet before you anoint them let them be dampishly moistened with damask rose-water.

24   *To perfume a jerkin.*

To perfume a jerkin well, take the oil of benjamin a pennyworth, oil of spike, and oil of olives half pennyworths of each, and take two sponges and warm one of them against the fire and rub your jerkin therewith; and when the oil is dried, take the other sponge and dip it in the oil and rub your jerkin therewith till it be dry, then lay on the perfume before prescribed for gloves.

25   *To make washing balls.*

To make very good washing balls[37] take storax of both kinds,[38] benjamin, *calamus aromaticus,*[39] *labdanum*[40] of each a like; and bray them to powder with cloves and orris;[41] then beat them all with a sufficient quantity of soap till it be stiff, then with your hand you shall work it like paste, and make round balls thereof.

To make a musk ball.

To make musk balls, take nutmegs, mace, cloves, saffron, and cinnamon, of each the weight of two pence, and beat it to fine powder; of mastic[42] the weight of two pence halfpenny, of storax the weight of six pence; of *labdanum* the weight of ten pence, of ambergris the weight of six pence; and of musk four grains; dissolve and work all these in hard sweet soap till it come to a stiff paste, and then make balls thereof.

A perfume to burn.

To make a good perfume to burn, take benjamin one ounce, storax, calamint two ounces, of mastic, white ambergris, of each one ounce, ireos, *calamus aromaticus*, cypress wood, of each half an ounce, of camphor one scruple, *labdanum* one ounce: beat all these to powder, then take of sallow charcoal six ounces, of liquid storax two ounces, beat them all with aqua vitae, and then shall you roll them into long round rolls.

To make pomanders.

To make pomanders,[43] take two pennyworth of *labdanum*, two pennyworth of storax liquid, one pennyworth of *calamus aromaticus*, as much balm, half a quarter of a pound of fine wax, of cloves and mace two pennyworth, of liquid aloes three pennyworth, of nutmegs eight pennyworth, and of musk four grains; beat all these exceedingly together till they come to a perfect substance, then mould it in any fashion you please and dry it.

To make vinegar.

To make excellent strong vinegar, you shall brew the strongest ale that may be, and having tunned[44] it in a very strong vessel, you shall set it either in your garden or some other safe place abroad, where it may have the whole summer day's sun to shine upon it, and there let it lie till it be extreme sour, then into a hogshead of this vinegar put the leaves of four or five hundred damask roses, and after they have lain for the space of a month therein, house the vinegar and draw it as you need it.

To make dry vinegar.

To make dry vinegar which you may carry in your pocket, you shall take the blades of green corn, either wheat or rye, and beat it in a mortar with the strongest vinegar you can get till it come to a paste; then roll it into little balls, and dry it in the sun till it be very hard; then when you have any occasion to use it, cut a little piece thereof and dissolve it in wine, and it will make a strong vinegar.

A "clotting beetle," or mallet. From *Markhams Farewell to Husbandry*, part v of *A Way to Get Wealth*, p. 12.

31   *To make verjuice.*

To make verjuice,[45] you shall gather your crabs[46] as soon as the kernels turn black, and, having laid them a while in a heap to sweat together, take them and pick them from stalks, blacks, and rottenness: then in long troughs with beetles[47] for the purpose, crush and break them all to mash: then make a bag of coarse haircloth as square as the press, and fill it with the crushed crabs; then put it into the press, and press it while any moisture will drop forth, having a clean vessel underneath to receive the liquor: this done, tun it up into sweet hogsheads, and to every hogshead put half a dozen handfuls of damask rose leaves, and then bung it up, and spend it as you shall have occasion.

32   Many other pretty secrets there are belonging unto curious housewives, but none more necessary than these already rehearsed, except such as shall hereafter follow in their proper places.

33   *ADDITIONS to conceited secrets. To make sweet powder for bags.*

Take of orris six ounces, of damask rose leaves as much, of marjoram and sweet basil, of each an ounce, of cloves two ounces, yellow sanders[48] two ounces, of citron peels seven drams, of lign-aloes[49] one ounce, of benjamin one ounce, of storax one ounce, of musk one dram: bruise all these, and put them into a bag of silk or linen, but silk is the best.

34   *To make sweet bags.*

Take of orris four ounces, of gallaminis[50] one ounce, of ciris half an ounce, of rose leaves dried two handfuls, of dried marjoram one handful, of spike one handful, cloves one ounce, of benjamin and storax of each two ounces, of white sanders and yellow of each one ounce: beat all these into a gross powder, then put to it musk a dram, of civet half a dram,

and of ambergris half a dram; then put them into a taffeta bag and use
it.

How to make sweet water.

Take of bay laves one handful, of red roses two handfuls, of damask
roses three handful, of lavender four handfuls, of basil one handful,
marjoram two handfuls, of camomile one handful, the young tops of
sweet briar two handfuls, of dandelion [and] tansy two handfuls, of
orange peels six or seven ounces, of cloves and mace a groat's worth:[51]
put all these together in a pottle of new ale in corns[52] for the space of
three days, shaking it every day three or four times; then distil it the
fourth day in a still with a continual soft fire, and, after it is distilled,
put into it a grain or two of musk.

A very rare and pleasant damask water.

Take a quart of malmsey[53] lees, or a quart of malmsey simply, one
handful of marjoram, of basil as much, of lavender four handfuls, bay
leaves one good handful, damask rose leaves four handfuls, and as many
of red, the peels of six oranges, or for want of them one handful of the
tender leaves of walnut trees, of benjamin half an ounce, of *calamus
aromaticus* as much, of camphor four drams, of cloves one ounce, of
labdanum half an ounce; then take a pottle of running water, and put in
all these spices bruised into your water and malmsey together in a close
stopped pot, with a good handful of rosemary, and let them stand for
the space of six days; then distil it with a soft fire; then set it in the sun
sixteen days with four grains of musk bruised. This quantity will make
three quarts of water. *Probatum est.*[54]

To make the best vinegar.

Take and brew very strong ale, then take half a dozen gallons of the
first running,[55] and set it abroad to cool, and, when it is cold, put yeast
unto it, and head[56] it very strongly: then put it up in a firkin; and distil
it in the sun; then take four or five handful of beans, and parch them in
a pan till they burst; then put them in as hot as you can into the firkin,
and stop it with a little clay about the bung-hole: then take a handful of
clean rye leaven and put in the firkin; then take a quantity of barberries,
and bruise and strain them into the firkin, and a good handful of salt,
and let them lie and work in the sun from May till August: then, having
the full strength, take rose leaves and clip the white ends off, and let them
dry in the sun; then take elder flowers and pick them, and dry them in
the sun, and, when they are dry, put them in bags, and keep them all

the winter: then take a pottle pot, and draw forth a pottle out of the firkin into the bottle, and put a handful of the red rose leaves, and another of the elder flowers, and put into the bottle, and hang it in the sun, where you may occupy[57] the same, and, when it is empty, take out all the leaves, and fill it again as you did before.

38
To perfume gloves.

Take angelica water and rose-water, and put into them the powder of cloves, ambergris, musk and lign-aloes, benjamin, and *calamus aromaticus*; boil these till half be consumed; then strain it, and put your gloves therein; then hang them in the sun to dry, and turn them often; and thus three times wet them, and dry them again: or otherwise, take rose-water and wet your gloves therein, then hang them up till they be almost dry; then take half an ounce of benjamin, and grind it with the oil of almonds, and rub it on the gloves till it be almost dried in: then take twenty grains of ambergris, and twenty grains of musk, and grind them together with oil of almonds, and so rub it on the gloves, and then hang them up to dry, or else let them dry in your bosom, and so after use them at your pleasure.

CHAPTER IV

The ordering, preserving, and helping of all sorts of wines, and first of the choice of sweet wines[1]

1   I do not assume to myself this knowledge of the vintner's secrets, but ingeniously[2] confess that one professed skilful in the trade, having rudely written, and more rudely disclosed this secret, and preferring it to the stationer, it came to me to be polished, which I have done, knowing that it is necessary, etc.[3]

2   It is necessary that our English housewife be skilful in the election, preservation, and curing of all sorts of wines, because they be usual charges under her hands, and by the least neglect must turn the husband to much loss: therefore to speak first of the election of sweet wines, she must be careful that her malmseys[4] be full[5] wines, pleasant, well hued, and fine: that bastard[6] be fat,[7] and if it be tawny[8] it skills[9] not, for the tawny bastards be always the sweetest. Muscadine[10] must be great, pleasant, and strong, with a sweet scent, and with amber colour. Sack[11] if it be Seres (as it should be) you shall know it by the mark of a cork burned on one side of the bung, and they be ever full gauge, and so are no other sacks, and the longer they lie, the better they be.

3   *To make muscadine,*[12] *and give it a flavour.*
  Take a pleasant butt[13] of malmsey, and draw it out a quarter and more; then fill it up with fat bastard within eight gallons, or thereabouts, and parel[14] it with six eggs, yolks[15] and all, one handful of bay salt, and a pint of conduit water to every parel, and if the wine be high of colour,[16] put in three gallons of new milk,[17] but skim off the cream first, and beat it well: or otherwise if you have a good butt of malmsey, and a good pipe[18] of bastard, you must take some empty butt or pipe, and draw thirty gallons of malmsey, and as many of bastard, and beat them well together;

and when you have so done, take a quarter of a pound of ginger and bruise it, and put it into your vessel; then fill it up with malmsey and bastard: or otherwise thus; if you have a pleasant butt of malmsey, which is called ralt-mow,[19] you may draw out of it forty gallons, and if your bastard be very faint,[20] then thirty gallons of it will serve to make it pleasant; then take four gallons of new milk and beat it, and put it into it when it lacketh twelve gallons of full, and then make your flavour.[21]

4   *How to flavour muscadine.*

Take one ounce of corianders, of bay salt, of cloves, of each as much, one handful of savory; let all these be blended and bruised together, and sew them close in a bag, and take half a pint of damask water and lay your flavour into it, and then put it into your butt, and if it [will not] fine,[22] give it a parel and fill it up, and let it lie till it fine: or else thus; take coriander roots a pennyworth, one pound of aniseeds,[23] one penny-worth in ginger; bruise them together and put them into a bag as before, and make your bag long and small that it may go in and out at the bung hole, and when you do put it in, fasten it with a thread at the bung; then take a pint of the strongest damask water, and warm it lukewarm, then put it into the butt, and then stop it close for two or three days at least, and then if you please you may set it abroach.

5   *To parel muscadine when it comes new in to be fined in twenty-four hours.*

Take seven whites of new laid eggs, two handfuls of bay salt, and beat them well together, and put therein a pint of sack or more, and beat them till they be as short[24] as snow;[25] then overdraw the butt seven or eight gallons, and beat the wine, and stir the lees, and then put in the parel and beat it, and so fill it up, and stop it close, and draw it on the morrow.

6   *To make white bastard.*

Draw out of a pipe of bastard[26] ten gallons, and put to it five gallons of new milk, and skim it as before, and all to beat it with a parel of eight whites of eggs, and a handful of bay salt, and a pint of conduit water, and it will be white and fine in the morning. But if you will make very fine bastard, take a white wine hogshead, and put out the lees, and wash it clean, and fill it half full and half a quarter,[27] and put to it four gallons of new milk and beat it well with the whites of six eggs, and fill it up with white wine and sack, and it will be white and fine.

7   *How to help bastard being eager.*

Take two gallons of the best stoned honey,[28] and two gallons of white wine, and boil them in a fair pan; skim it clean, and strain it through a fair cloth that there be no motes in it: then put to it one ounce of corianders, and one ounce of aniseeds, four or five orange peels dry and beaten to powder, let them lie three days; then draw your bastard into a clean pipe, then put in your honey with the rest, and beat it well; then let it lie a week and touch it not, after draw it at pleasure.

8   *To make bastard white, and to rid away lags.*[29]
If your bastard be fat and good, draw out forty gallons, then may you fill it up with the lags of any kind of white wines or sacks; then take five gallons of new milk, and first take away the cream, then strain it through a clean cloth, and when your pipe is three quarters full, put in your milk; then beat it very well, and fill it so that it may lack fifteen gallons, then parel it thus: take the whites only of ten eggs, and beat them in a fair tray with bay salt and conduit water; then put it into the pipe and beat it well, and so fill it up, and let it stand open all night; and if you will keep it any while, you must on the morrow stop it close; and to make the same drink like osey,[30] give it this flavour: take a pound of aniseeds, two pence in corianders, two pence in ginger, two pence in cloves, two pence in grains, two pence in long pepper, and two pence in liquorice: bruise all these together; then make two bags of linen cloth, long and small, and put your spices into them, and put them into the pipe at the bung, making them fast there with a thread that it may sink into the wine; then stop it close, and in two days you may broach it.

9   *A remedy for bastard if it prick.*[31]
Take and draw him from his lees if he have any, and put the wine into a malmsey butt to the lees of malmsey; then put to the bastard that is in the malmsey butt nigh three gallons of the best wort[32] of a fresh tap, and then fill him up with bastard or malmsey or cuit[33] if you will: then parel it thus; first, parel[34] him, and beat him with a staff, and then take the whites of four new laid eggs, and beat them with a handful of salt till it be short as moss,[35] and then put a pint of running water therein, and so fill the pipe up full, and lay a tile stone on the bung, and set it abroach within four and twenty hours if you will.

10   *To make malmsey.*
If you have a good butt of malmsey,[36] and a butt or two of sack that will not be drunk: for the sack prepare some empty butt or pipe, and draw it more than half full of sack, then fill it up with malmsey, and when your butt is full within a little, put into it three gallons of Spanish cuit, the best that you can get, then beat it well, then take your taster[37] and see that it be deep coloured; then fill it up with sack, and give it a parel, and beat it well: the parel is thus; take the yolks of ten eggs and

beat them in a clean basin with a handful of bay salt, and a quart of conduit water, and beat them together with a little piece of birch, and beat it till it be as short as moss; then draw five or six gallons out of your butt, then beat it again, and then fill it up, and the next day it will be ready to be drawn. This parel will serve both for muscadine, bastard and for sack.

11   *To shift malmsey, and to rid away ill wines.*[38]

If you have two principal butts of malmsey, you may make three good butts with your lags of claret and of sack: if you put two gallons of red wine in a butt, it will save the more cuit; then put two or three gallons of cuit as you see cause; and if it be Spanish cuit, two gallons will go further than five gallons of Candy[39] cuit, but the Candy cuit is more natural for the malmsey: also one butt of good malmsey, and a butt of sack that hath lost his colour, will make two good butts of malmsey with the more cuit; and when you have filled your butts within twelve gallons, then put in your cuit, and beat it half an hour and more; then put in your parel and let it lie.

12   *If sack want his colour.*[40]

First, parel him as you did the bastard, and order him as shall be showed[41] you for the white wine of Gascony[42] with milk, and so set him abroad.

13   *For sack that is tawny.*

If your sack have a strong lee[43] or taste, take a good sweet butt fair washed, and draw your sack into it, and make unto it a parel as you do to the bastard,[44] and beat it very well, and so stop up your butt: and if it be tawny, take three gallons of new milk, and strain it clean, and put it into your sack, then beat it very well, and stop it close.

14   *For sack that doth rope and is brown.*

Take a fair empty butt with the lees in it, and draw your sack into the same from his lees fine;[45] then take a pound of rice flour as fine as you can get, and four grains of camphor, and put it into the sack; and if it will not fine, give it a good parel, and beat it well; then stop it and let it lie.

15   *To colour sack, or any white wine.*

If any of your sacks or white wines have lost their colour, take three gallons of new milk, and take away the cream; then overdraw your wine five or six gallons, then put in your milk and beat it; then lay it aforetake[46] all night, and in the morning lay it up, and the next day if you will you may set it abroad.

16   *If alicant be grown hard.*[47]

Draw him out into fresh lees, and take three or four gallons of stone honey clarified,[48] and, being cool, put it in and parel it with the yolks of four eggs, whites and all, and beat it well, and fill it up, and stop it close, and it will be pleasant and quick[49] as long as it is in drawing.

17   *For alicant that is sour.*

Take three gallons of white honey, and two gallons of red wine, boil them together in a fair pan, and skim it clean, and let it stand till it be fine and cold, then put it into your pipe; yet nothing but the finest; then beat it well, and fill it up, and stop it close, and if your alicant be pleasant and great, it will do much good, for the one pipe will rid away divers.[50]

18   *How to order Rhenish wine.*[51]

There are two sorts of Rhenish wines, that is to say, Elstertune[52] and Brabant: the Elstertune are best, you shall know it by the vat, for it is double barred[53] and double pinned; the Brabant is nothing so good, and there is not so much good to be done with them as with the other. If the wines be good and pleasant, a man may rid away a hogshead or two of white wine, and this is the most vantage a man can have by them: and if it be slender and hard, then take three or four gallons of stone honey and clarify it clean; then put into the honey four or five gallons of the same wine, and then let it seethe a great while, and put into it two pence in cloves bruised; let them seethe together, for it will take away the scent of honey,[54] and when it is sodden take it off, and set it by till it be thorough cold; then take four gallons of milk and order it as before, and then put all into your wine and all to beat it; and (if you can) roll it, for that is the best way; then stop it close and let it lie, and that will make it pleasant.

19   *Of what countries wines are by their names.*

The wines that be made in Bordeaux are called Gascon wines, and you shall know them by their hazel hoops, and the most be full gauge and sound wines.[55]

20   The wines of the high countries, and which is called high country[56] wine, are made some thirty or forty miles beyond Bordeaux, and they come not down so soon as the other; for if they do, they are all forfeited;[57] and you shall know them ever by their hazel hoops, and the length gauge lacks.[58]

21   Then you have wines that be called Gallaway[59] both in pipes and hogsheads, and be long, and lacks two sesters[60] and a half in gauge, and the wines themselves are high coloured. Then there are other whites which is called white wine of Angulle,[61] very good wine, and lacks little of

gauge, and that is also in pipes for the most part, and is quarter bound. Then there are Rochelle[62] wines, which are also in pipes long and slender; they are very small hedge wines,[63] sharp in taste, and of a pallid complexion. Our best sack[64] are of Seres in Spain, your smaller of Galicia[65] and Portugal; your strong sacks are of the islands of the Canaries,[66] and of Malaga;[67] and your muscadines and malmseys are of many parts of Italy, Greece, and some especial islands.

22

Notes of gauging of wines, oils, and liquors.[68]
Every tierce is in depth the middle of the knot in the midst.
The depth of every hogshead is the fourth prick above the knot.
The depth of every puncheon[69] is the fourth prick next to the puncheoner.[70]
The depth of every sack butt is the four pricks next to the puncheon.
The depth of the half hogshead is at the lowest notch, and accounted one.
The depth of the half tierce is at the second notch, and is accounted two.
The depth of the half hogshead and half pipe, is at the third notch, and accounted three.
The depth of the half butt is at the fourth notch, and accounted four.

23

The marks of gauging.

1. The full gauge is marked thus:

2. The half sester lacking, thus:

3. The whole sester lacking, thus:

4. The sester and half lag:

5. The two sesters thus:

6. The two and a half sesters, thus:

24　　*The contents of all manner of Gascon wine, and others.*
　　A butt of malmsey if he be full gauge, is one hundred and twenty-six
　　　gallons.
　　And so the tun is two hundred and fifty-two gallons.
　　Every sester is three[71] gallons.
　　If you sell for twelve pence a gallon, the tun is twelve pound, twelve
　　　shillings.
　　And malmsey and Rhenish wine at ten pence the gallon, is the tun, ten
　　　pound.
　　Eight pence the gallon, is the tun eight pounds.
　　Six pence the gallon, is the tun six pounds.
　　Five pence the gallon, is the tun five pound.
　　Four pence the gallon, is the tun four pound.

25　　Now for Gascon wine there goeth four hogsheads to a tun, and every
　　hogshead is sixty-three gallons; the two hogsheads are one hundred twenty-
　　six gallons, and four hogsheads are two hundred fifty-two gallons; and
　　if you sell for eight pence the gallon, you shall make of the tun eight
　　pounds, and so forth look how many pence the gallons are, and so many
　　pounds the tun is.

26　　Now for bastard it is at the same rate, but it lacketh of gauge two
　　sesters and a half, or three at a pipe, and then you must abate six gallons
　　of the price, and so in all other wines.

27　　　　　　　　　　[*Of Gascon wines.*]
　　See that in your choice of Gascon wines you observe that your claret
　　wines be fair coloured, and bright as a ruby, not deep as an amethyst;
　　for though it may show strength, yet it wants neatness: also let it be
　　sweet as a rose or a violet, and in any case let it be short;[72] for if it be
　　long, then in no wise meddle with it.

28　　For your white wines, see they be sweet and pleasant at the nose, very
　　short, clear and bright and quick in the taste.

29　　Lastly for your red[73] wine, provide that they be deep coloured and
　　pleasant, long, and sweet, and if in them or claret wines be any default
　　of colour, there are remedies enough to amend and repair them.

30　　　　*To remedy claret wine that hath lost his colour.*
　　If your claret wine be faint, and have lost his colour; then take a fresh
　　hogshead with his fresh lees which was very good wine, and draw your
　　wine into the same; then stop it close and tight, and lay it aforetake for
　　two or three days that the lees may run through it, then lay it up till it
　　be fine, and if the colour be not perfect, draw it into a red wine hogshead,

that is new drawn with the lees, and that will colour of himself, and make him strong; or take a pound of turnsole[74] or two, and beat it with a gallon or two of wine, and let it lie a day or two, then put it into your hogshead, draw your wine again, and wash your cloths, then lay it aforetake all night, and roll it on the morrow; then lay it up, and it will have a perfect colour.

31   *A remedy for Gascon wine that hath lost his colour.*
And if your claret wine have lost his colour, take a pennyworth of damsons, or else black bullaces, as you see cause, and stew them with some red wine of the deepest colour, and make thereof a pound[75] or more of syrup, and put it into a clean glass, and after into the hogshead of claret wine; and the same you may likewise do unto red wine if you please.[76]

32   *For white wine that have lost his colour.*
Take three gallons of new milk, and take away the cream off it; then draw five or six gallons of wine, and put your milk into the hogshead, and beat it exceeding well; then fill it up; but before you fill it up, if you can, roll it, and if it be long and small,[77] take half a pound of roche alum[78] finely beaten into powder, and put into the vessel, and let it lie.

33   *A remedy for white wine that hath lost his colour.*
And if your white wine be faint, and have lost his colour, if the wine have any strength in it; take to a hogshead so much as you intend to put in, out of the said milk, and a handful of rice[79] beaten very well, and a little salt, and lay him aforetake all night, and on the morning lay him up again, and set it abroach in any wise the next wine you spend, for it will not last long.

34   *A remedy for claret, or white wine that drinks foul.*
Take and draw it into new lees of the one nature,[80] and then take a dozen of new pippins, and pare them, and take away the cores, and then put them in, and if that will not serve, take a handful of the oak of Jerusalem,[81] and stamp it, then put it into your wine, and beat it exceedingly well, and it will not only take away the foulness, but also make it have a good scent at the nose.[82]

35   *For red wine that drinks faint.*
If your red wine drink faint, then take a hogshead that alicant hath been in with the lees also, and draw your wine into it, and that will refresh it well, and make the wine well coloured; or otherwise draw it

close to fresh lees, and that will recover it again, and put to it three or four gallons of alicant, and turn it on his lees.

36   *For red wine that wants colour.*

If your red wine lack colour, then take out four gallons, and put in four gallons of alicant, and turn him on his lees, and the bung up,[83] and his colour will return, and be fair.

37   *To make Tyre.*[84]

Take a good butt of malmsey, and overdraw it a quarter or more, and fill him up with fat bastard, and with cuit a gallon and more, then parel him as you did your malmsey.

38   *If osey complete, or caprik*[85] *have lost their colour.*

You shall in all points dress him, as you did dress your sack or white wine in the like case, and parel him, and then set him abroach. And thus much touching wines of all sorts, and the true use and ordering of them, so far forth as belongeth to the knowledge, and profit of our English housewife.

CHAPTER V

Of wool, hemp, flax, and cloth, and dyeing of colours, of each several substance, with all the knowledges belonging thereto

1 Our English housewife, after her knowledge of preserving and feeding her family, must learn also how, out of her own endeavours, she ought to clothe them outwardly and inwardly; outwardly for defence from the cold and comeliness to the person; and inwardly, for cleanliness and neatness of the skin, whereby it may be kept from the filth of sweat, or vermin; the first consisting of woollen cloth, the latter of linen.

2 *Of making woollen cloth.*
    To speak then first of the making of woollen cloth, it is the office of the husbandman at the shearing of his sheep to bestow upon the housewife such a competent proportion of wool as shall be convenient for the clothing of his family; which wool, as soon as she hath received it, she shall open, and with a pair of shears (the fleece lying as it were whole before her) she shall cut away all the coarse locks, pitch, brands, tarred locks, and other felterings,[1] and lay them by themselves for coarse cover-lids, or the like:

3 *Of tozing wool.*
then the rest so cleaned she shall break into pieces, and toze it every lock by lock, that is with her hands open, and divide the wool so as not any part thereof may be feltered or close together, but all open and loose; then so much of the wool as she intends to spin white, she shall put by itself, and the rest which she intends to put into colours she shall weigh up, and divide into several quantities, according to the proportion of the web[2] which she intends to make, and put every one of them into particular bags made of netting, with tallies or little pieces of wood fixed unto them,

with privy marks thereon both for the weight, the colour, and the knowledge of the same wool when the first colour is altered:

The dyeing of wool.

4   this done, she shall if she please send them unto the dyers, to be dyed
after her own fancy; yet forasmuch as I would not have our English
housewife ignorant in anything meet for her knowledge, I will show her
here before I proceed any further, how she shall dye her wool herself
into any colour meet for her use.

To dye wool black.

5   First then to dye wool black, you shall take two pound of galls,[3] and
bruise them, then take half so much of the best green copperas, and boil
them both together in two gallons of running water; then shall you put
your wool therein and boil it; so done, take it forth and dry it.

To dye wool of a hair colour.

6   If you will dye your wool of a bright hair colour: first boil your wool
in alum[4] and water; then take it forth, and, when it is cold, take chamber
lye[5] and chimney soot, and, mixing them together well, boil your wool
again therein, and stir it exceeding well about, then take it forth, and lay
it where it may conveniently dry.

To dye wool red.

7   If you would dye your wool into a perfect red colour, set on a pan
full of water; when it is hot put in a peck of wheat bran, and let it boil
a little; then put it into a tub, and put twice as much cold water unto it,
and let it stand until it be a week old: having done so, then shall you put
to ten pounds of wool, a pound of alum, then heat your liquor again,
and put in your alum, and so soon as it is melted, put in your wool, and
let it boil the space of an hour: then take it out again, and then set on
more bran and water:[6] then take a pound of madder,[7] and put in your
madder when the liquor is hot: when the madder is broken, put in the
wool and open it, and when it cometh to be very hot, then stir it with
a staff, and then take it out and wash it with fair water; then set on the
pan again with fair water, and then take a pound of Saradine buck,[8] and
put it therein, and let it boil the space of an egg seething: then put in the
wool, and stir it three or four times about, and open it well; after, dry it.

To dye wool blue.

8   To dye wool blue; take good store of old chamber lye, and set it on
the fire; then take half a pound of blue anil, byse, or indigo[9] and beat it

small in a mortar; and then put it into the lye; and when it seethes put in your wool.

9   *To dye a puke.*

To dye wool of a puke colour,[10] take galls, and beat them very small in a mortar; put them into fair seething water, and boil your wool or your cloth therein, and boil them the space of half an hour: then take them up, and put in your copperas into the same liquor: then put in your wool again, and doing thus once or twice, it will be sufficient.

10   *To dye a cinder colour.*

If you will dye your wool of a cinder colour, which is a very good colour, you shall put your red wool into your puke liquor; and then it will failless be of a cinder colour.

11   *To dye green or yellow.*

If you will dye your wool either green or yellow, then boil your woodward[11] in fair water, then put in your wool or cloth, and the wool which you put in white will be yellow: and that wool which you put in blue will be green, and all this with one liquor; provided that each be first boiled in alum.

12   *Handling of wool after dyeing.*

When you have thus dyed you wool into those several colours meet for your purpose, and have also dried it well: then you shall take it forth, and toze it over again as you did before: for the first tozing was to make it receive the colour or dye: this second is to receive the oil, and make it fit for spinning;

13   *The mixing of colours.*

which as soon as you have done, you shall mix your colours together, wherein you are to note that the best medley is that which is compounded of two colours only; as a light colour, and a dark: for to have more is but confusion, and breeds no pleasure, but distraction to the sight: there-fore for the proportion of your mixtures, you shall ever take two parts of the darker colour, and but a third part of the light. As for example, your web contains twelve pound, and the colours are red and green: you shall then take eight pound of the green wool, and but four pound of the red; and so of any other colours where there is difference in brightness.

14   *Mixing of three colours.*

But if it be so that you will needs have your cloth of three colours, as of two dark and one light, or two light and one dark: as thus, you will have crimson, yellow, and puke; you shall take of the crimson and yellow of each two pound, and of the puke eight pound: for this is two light colours to one dark; but if you will take a puke, a green, and an orange tawny, which is two dark, and one light; then you shall take of the puke and green and the orange tawny of each like quantity; that is to say, of either four pounds. When you have equally divided your proportions, then you shall spread upon the ground a sheet, and upon the same first lay a thin layer or bed of your darker colour, all of one even thickness: then upon the same layer, lay another much thinner of the brighter quantity, being so near as you can guess it hardly half so much as the darker: then cover it over with another layer of the sad[12] colour or colours again, then upon it another of the bright again; and thus lay layer upon layer till all your wool be spread; then, beginning at one end, roll up round and hard together the whole bed of wool; and then, causing one to kneel hard upon the roll that it may not stir nor open, with your hands toze, and pull out all the wool in small pieces: and then taking a pair of stock-cards[13] sharp and large, and bound fast to a form, or such like thing, and, on the same, comb and card over all the wool till you see it perfectly and undistinctly mixed together, and that indeed it is become one entire colour of divers without spots, or undivided locks or knots; in which doing you shall be very careful, and heedful with your eye: and if you find any hard knot, or other felter in the wool which will not open, though it be never so small, yet you shall pick it out and open it, or else being any other fault cast it away: for it is the greatest art in housewifery to mix these wools right, and to make the cloth without blemish.

Of the oiling of wool.

15   Your wool being thus mixed perfectly together, you shall then oil it, or as the plain housewife terms it, grease it: in this manner, being laid in a round flat bed, you shall take of the best rape oil,[14] or for want thereof either well rend[15] red goose grease, or swine's grease, and having melted it, with your hand sprinkle it all over your wool, and work it very well into the same: then turn your wool about, and do as much on the other side, till you have oiled all the wool over, and that there is not a lock which is not moistened with the same.

The quantity of oil.

16   Now forasmuch as if you shall put too much oil upon the wool, you may thereby do great hurt to the web, and make that the thread will not draw, but fall into many pieces, you shall therefore be sure at the first to give it little enough: and, taking some thereof, prove[16] it upon the

wheel; and if you see it draws dry, and breaketh, then you may put more oil unto it; but if it draw well, then to keep it there without any alteration: but because you shall be a little more certain in the truth of your proportions, you shall know that three pound of grease or oil will sufficiently anoint or grease ten pounds of wool: and so according to that proportion you may oil what quantity you will.

<h3 style="text-align:center">17   *Of the tumming of wool.*</h3>

17

Of the tumming of wool.

After your wool is oiled and anointed thus, you shall then tum it[17] which is, you shall put it forth as you did before when you mix it, and card it over again upon your stock-cards: and then those cardings which you strike off are called tummings, which you shall lay by till it come to spinning. There be some housewives which oil it as they mix it, and sprinkle every layer as they lay it, and work the oil well into it: and then, rolling it up as beforesaid, pull it out, and tum it; so that then it goeth but once over the stock-cards, which is not amiss: yet the other is more certain, though somewhat more painful.[18]

18

Of spinning wool.

After your wool is thus mixed, oiled, and tummed, you shall then spin it upon great wool wheels, according to the order of good housewifery; the action whereof must be got by practice, and not relation; only this you shall be careful, to draw your thread according to the nature and goodness of your wool, not according to your particular desire: for if you draw a fine thread from a wool which is of a coarse staple, it will want substance when it comes to the walkmill,[19] and either there beat in pieces, or, not being able to bed,[20] and cover the threads well, be a cloth of a very short lasting. So likewise if you draw a coarse thread from a wool of a fine staple, it will then [be] so much over thick, that you must either take away a great part of the substance of your wool in flocks;[21] or else let the cloth wear coarse, and high, to the disgrace of good housewifery, and loss of much cloth, which else might have been saved.

19

The diversities of spinning.

Now for the diversities of spinning, although our ordinary English housewives make none at all, but spin every thread alike, yet the better experienced make two manner of spinnings, and two sorts of thread; the one they call warp, the other weft, or else woof; the warp is spun close, round and hard twisted, being strong and well smoothed, because it runs through the slays, and also endureth the fretting and beating of the beam;[22] the weft is spun open, loose, hollow, and but half twisted; neither smoothed with the hand, nor made of any great strength, because it but only crosseth the warp, without any violent straining, and by reason of the softness thereof beddeth closer, and covereth the warp so well, that a very little beating in the mill bringeth it to perfect cloth: and though some hold it less substantial than the web, which is all of twisted yarn, yet experience finds they are deceived, and that this open weft keeps the cloth longer from fretting and wearing.

Winding of woollen yarn.

20 After the spinning of your wool, some housewives use to wind it from the broach into round clews for more ease in the warping, but is a labour may very well be saved, and you may as well warp it from the broach as from the clew, as long as you know the certain weight, for by that only you are to be directed in all manner of cloth making.

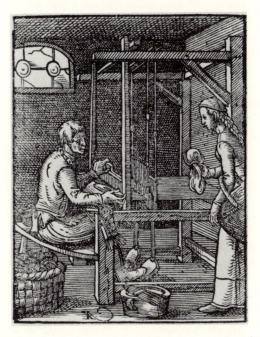

Even Markham, with his concern that the housewife be as self-sufficient as possible, recommends that she take her spun thread to the weaver to be turned into cloth. From Hans Sachs, *Eygentliche Beschreibung aller Stande auf Erden,* sig. Niv.

Of warping cloth.

21 Now as touching the warping of cloth, which is both the skill and

action of the weaver, yet must not our English housewife be ignorant therein, but though the doing of the thing be not proper unto her, yet what is done must not be beyond her knowledge, both to bridle the falsehood of unconscionable workmen,[23] and for her own satisfaction, when she is rid of the doubt of another's evil doing. It is necessary then that she first cast by the weight of her wool, to know how many yards of cloth the web will arise: for if the wool be of a reasonable good staple, and well spun, it will run yard and pound, but if it be coarse, it will not run so much. Now in your warping also, you must look how many pounds you lay in your warp, and so many you must necessarily preserve for your weft; for housewives say the best cloth is made of even and even; for to drive it to greater advantage is hurtful to the cloth. There be other observations in the warping of cloth; as to number your portusses,[24] and know how many goes to a yard; to look to the closeness, and filling of the slay, and such like, which sometimes hold, and sometimes fail, according to the art of the workman; and therefore I will not stand much upon them; but refer the housewife to the instruction of her own experience.

22   *Of weaving cloth, walking and dressing it.*
     Now after your cloth is thus warped, and delivered up into the hands of the weaver; the housewife hath finished her labour: for in the weaving, walking, and dressing thereof she can challenge no property more than to entreat them severally to discharge their duties with a good conscience[25] that is to say, that the weaver weave it close, strong, and true; that the walker or fuller mill it carefully, and look well to his scouring-earth,[26] for fear of beating holes into the cloth; and that the clothworker or shearman[27] burl, and dress it sufficiently, neither cutting the wool too unreasonable high, whereby the cloth may wear rough, nor too low, lest it appear threadbare ere it come out of the hands of the tailor. These things forewarned and performed, the cloth is then to be used at your pleasure.

23   *Of linen cloth.*
     The next thing to this, which our English housewife must be skilful,[28] is in the making of all sorts of linen cloth, whether it be of hemp or flax, for from those two only is the most principal cloth derived, and made both in this, and in other nations.

24   *The ground best to sow hemp on.*
     And first touching the soil fittest to sow hemp upon, it must be a rich mingle earth of clay and sand, or clay and gravel well tempered: and of

these the best [mixed ground] serveth best for the purpose, for the simple clay, or the simple sand are nothing so good; for the first is too tough, too rich, and too heavy, bringeth forth all bun and no rind, the other is too barren, too hot, and too light, and bringeth forth such slender withered increase, that it is nothing near worth the labour: briefly then the best earth is the best mixed ground which husbandmen call the red hazel ground, being well ordered[29] and manured: and of this earth a principal place to sow hemp on is in old stackyards,[30] or other places kept in the winter time for the lair of sheep or cattle, when your ground is either scarce, or formerly not employed to that purpose; but if it be where the ground is plenty, and only used thereunto, as in Holland, in Lincolnshire, the Isle of Axham,[31] and such like places, then the custom of the country will make you expert enough therein: there be some that will preserve the ends of their corn lands which butt upon grass to sow hemp or flax thereon, and for that purpose will manure it well with sheep; for whereas corn which butteth on grass hades, where cattle are tethered, is commonly destroyed, and no profit issuing from a good part thereof; by this means, that which is sown will be more safe and plentiful, and that which was destroyed, will bear a commodity of better value.

The tillage of the ground.

5   Now for the tillage or ordering of the ground where you sow hemp or flax, it would in all points be like unto that where you sow barley,[32] or at the least as often broke up as you do when you sow fallow wheat, which is thrice at least, except it be some very mellow, and ripe mould, as stackyards and usual hemplands be, and then twice breaking up is sufficient; that is to say, about the latter end of February, and the latter end of April, at which time you shall sow it:

Of sowing of hemp or flax.

6   and herein is to be noted, that you must sow it reasonable thick with good, sound, and perfect seed, of which the smoothest, roundest, and brightest with least dust in it is best: you must not lay it too deep in the earth, but you must cover it close, light, and with so fine a mould as you can possibly break with your harrows, clotting beetles, or slighting:[33] then till you see it appear above the earth, you must have it exceedingly carefully tended, especially an hour or two before sunrise, and as much before it set, from birds and other vermin, which will otherwise pick the seed out of the earth, and so deceive you of your profit.

Of weeding of hemp and flax.

7   Now for the weeding of hemp, you may save the labour, because it is

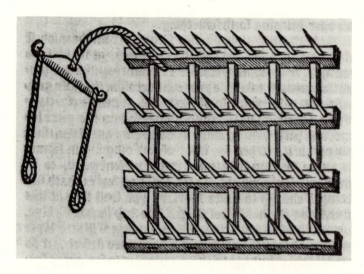

"The harrow." From Gervase Markham, *The English Husbandman*, sig. F2v.

naturally of itself swift of growth, rough, and venomous to anything that grows under it, and will sooner of its own accord destroy those unwholesome weeds than by your labour: but for your flax or line[34] which is a great deal more tender, and of harder increase, you shall as occasion serveth[35] weed it and trim it, especially if the weeds overgrow it, but not otherwise: for if it once get above the weeds, then it will save itself.

28   *The pulling of hemp or flax.*

Touching the pulling of hemp or flax, which is the manner of gathering of the same: you shall understand that it must be pulled up by the roots, and not cut as corn is, either with scythe or hook: and the best time for the pulling of the same is when you see the leaves fall downward, or turn yellow at the tops, for then it is full ripe, and this for the most part will be in July, and about Mary Maudlin's day.[36] I speak now touching the pulling of hemp for cloth: but if you intend to save any for seed, then you shall save the principal buns,[37] and let them stand till it be the latter end of August, or sometimes till mid September following: and then, seeing the seed turned brown and hard, you may gather it, for if it stand longer, it will shed suddenly: as for flax, which ripeneth a little after the hemp, you shall pull it as soon as you see the seed turns brown, and bend the head to the earthward, for it will afterward ripen of itself as the bun drieth.

The ripening of hemp and flax.

Now for the ripening, and seasoning of hemp or flax, you shall, so soon as you have pulled it, lay it all along flat and thin upon the ground, for a night and a day at the most, and no more; and then as housewives call it, tie it up in beats,[38] and rear then upright till you can conveniently carry it to the water, which would be done as speedily as may be. Now there be some which ripen their hemp and flax upon the ground where it grew, by letting it lie thereon to receive dews and rain, and the moistness of the earth, till it be ripe; but this is a vile and naughty[39] way of ripening, it making the hemp or flax black, rough, and often rotten: therefore I would wish none to use it, but such as necessity compelleth thereunto, and then to be careful to the often turning thereof, for it is the ground only which rots it.

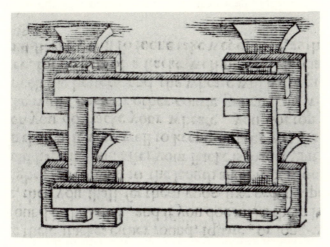

"Overlyers," here designed to be the base of a haystack. From *Markhams Farewell to Husbandry*, part v of *A Way to Get Wealth*, p. 85.

The watering of hemp or flax.

Now for the watering of the hemp or flax, the best water is the running stream,[40] and the worst is the standing pit; yet because hemp is a poisonous thing, and infecteth the water, and destroyeth all kind of fish, it is more fit to employ such pits and ditches as are least subject to annoyance, except you live near some great broad and swift stream, and then in the shallow parts thereof you may water without danger: touching the manner of the watering thereof, you shall, according to the quantity, knock four or six strong stakes into the bottom of the water, and set them square-wise, then lay your round beats or bundles of hemp down under the water, the thick end of one bundle one way, and the thick ends of another bundle another way; and so lay beat upon beat till you have laid in all, and that the water covereth them all over; then you shall take over-lyers[41] of wood, and, binding them overthwart[42] to the stakes, keep the hemp down close, and especially at the four corners; then take great stones, gravel, and other heavy rubbish, and lay it between, and over the overlyers, and so cover the hemp close that it may by no means stir,[43]

31   *The time it shall lie in the water.*

and so let it continue in the water four days and nights, if it be in a running water, but if it be in a standing water, then longer, and then take out one of the uppermost beats and wash it; and if in the washing you see the leaf come off, then you may be assured the hemp is watered enough: as for flax, less time will serve it, and it will shed the leaf in three nights.

32   *Of washing out of hemp or flax.*

When your hemp or flax is thus watered enough, you shall take off the gravel, stones, overlyers of wood, and, unloosing it from the stakes, take and wash out every beat or bundle several[44] by itself, and rub it exceeding clean, leaving not a leaf upon it, nor any filth within it; then set it upon the dry earth upright that the water may drop from it; which done, load it up, and carry it home, and in some open close[45] or piece of ground rear it upright either against hedges, pales, walls, backsides of houses, or such like, where it may have the full strength or reflection of the sun, and, being thoroughly dried, then house it; yet there be some housewives[46] which as soon as their hemp comes from the water will not rear it upright, but lay it upon the ground flat and thin for the space of a fortnight, turning it at the end of every two days; first on the one side, then on the other, and then after rear it upright, dry it, and so house it, and this housewifery is good and orderly.

33   *Special ordering of flax.*

Now although I have hitherto joined hemp and flax together, yet you shall understand that there are some particular differences between them; for whereas your hemp may within a night or two after the pulling be carried to the water, your flax may not, but must be reared up, and dried and withered a week or more to ripen the seed; which done, you must take ripple combs,[47] and ripple your flax over, which is the beating, or breaking off from the stalks the round bells or bobs,[48] which contain the seed, which you must preserve in some dry vessel or place, till the spring of the year, and then beat it, or thresh it for your use, and when your flax or line is rippled, then you must send it to the water as aforesaid.

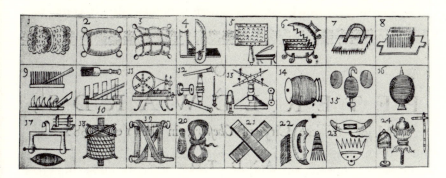

Number 4, a swingle; 5, a wool card; 6, a flax brake; 7, a stock card; 8, a flax comb; 9, a wool comb; 11, a spinning wheel; 19, a reel with a slipping of thread on it; 20, a hank of yarn. From Randle Holme, *The Academy of Armory*, ii, 284.

The braking of hemp or flax.

After your hemp or flax hath been watered, dried, and housed, you may then at your pleasure brake it,[49] which is in a brake of wood (whose proportion is so ordinary, that everyone almost knows them) brake and beat out the dry bun, or kex[50] of the hemp and flax from the rind which covers it, and when you brake either, you shall do it, as near as you can, on a fair dry sunshine day, observing to set forth your hemp and flax, and spread it thin before the sun, that it may be as dry as tinder before it come to the brake; for if either in the lying close together it shall give again or sweat, or through the moistness of the air or place where it lies receives any dampishness, you must necessarily see it dried sufficiently again, or else it will never brake well, nor the bun brake and part from the rind in order as it should:

The drying of hemp or flax.

therefore if the weather be not seasonable, and your need much to use your hemp or flax, you shall then spread it upon your kiln, and, making a soft fire under it, dry it upon the same, and then brake it: yet forasmuch as this is oft times dangerous, and much hurt hath been received thereby through casualty of fire, I would wish you to stick four stakes in the earth at least five foot above ground, and laying over them small overlyers of wood, and open stakes or hurdles[51] upon the same, spread your hemp, and also rear some round about it all, but at one open side; then with straw, small shavings, or other light dry wood make a soft fire under the same, and so dry it, and brake it, and this is without all danger or mistrust of evil; and as you brake it, you shall open and look into it, ever beginning to brake the root ends first;

36   *When it is braked enough.*

and when you see the bun is sufficiently crushed, fallen away, or at the most hangeth but in very small shivers within the hemp or flax, then you shall say it is braked enough, and then terming that which you called a beat or bundle before, now a strike,[52] you shall lay them together and so house them, keeping in your memory, either by score or writing, how many strikes of hemp, and how many strikes of flax you brake up every day.

37   *Diversity of brakes.*

Now, that your hemp or flax may brake so much the better, you must have for each several sort two several brakes, which is an open and wide-toothed, or nicked[53] brake, and a close and strait-toothed[54] brake, the first being to crush the bun, and the latter to beat it forth. Now for flax[55] you must take first that which is the straitest for the hemp, and then after one of purpose, much straiter and sharper; for the bun of it, being more small, tough, and thin, must necessarily be broken into much less pieces.

38   *Of swingling hemp and flax.*

After your hemp and flax is braked, you shall then swingle it,[56] which is upon a swingle tree block made of an half inch board about four foot above ground, and set upon a strong foot or stock that will not easily move and stir, as you may see in any housewife's house whatsoever better than my words can express; and with a piece of wood called the swingle tree dagger, and made in the shape and proportion of an old dagger with a reasonable blunt edge; you shall beat out all the loose buns and shivers[57] that hang in the hemp or flax, opening and turning it from one end to the other, till you have left no bun or shiver to be perceived therein, and then strike a twist and fold in the midst, which is ever the thickest part of the strike; lay them by till you have swingled all; the general profit whereof is not only the beating out of the hard bun, but also an opening, and softening of the tear,[58] whereby it is prepared and made ready for the market.

9

Use of swingle tree first hards.[59]

Now after you have swingled your hemp and flax over once, you shall take and shake up the refuse stuff which you beat from the same, severally, and not only it, but the tops and knots and half braked buns which fall from the brake also, and drying them again cause them to be very well threshed with flails, and then, mixing them with the refuse which fell from the swingle tree, dress them all well with threshing and shaking, till the buns be clean driven out of them; and then lay them in some safe dry place till occasion of use: these are called swingle tree hards, and that which comes from the hemp will make window cloth, and such like coarse stuff, and that which comes from the flax being a little towed again in a pair of wool cards will make a coarse harden.[60]

The second swingling.

0

But to proceed forward in the making of cloth; after your hemp or flax hath been swingled once over, which is sufficient for the market, or for ordinary sale, you shall then for cloth swingle it over the second time, and as the first did beat away the bun, and soften the rind, so this shall break and divide, and prepare it fit for the heckle; and hards which are this second time beaten off you shall also save; for that of the hemp (being tozed in wool cards) will make a good hempen harden and that coming from the flax (used in that manner) a flax harden better than the former.

Of beating hemp.

I

After the second swingling of your hemp, and that the hards thereof have been laid by, you shall take the strikes, and, dividing them into dozens, or half dozens, make them up into great thick rolls, and then as it were broaching[61] them or spitting them upon long sticks, set them in the corner of some chimney, where they may receive the heat of the fire,[62] and there let them abide, till they be dried exceedingly, then take them, and, laying them in a round trough made for the purpose, so many as may conveniently lie therein, and there with beetles beat them exceedingly, till they handle both without and within as soft and pliant as may be, without any hardness or roughness to be felt or perceived; then take them from the trough, and open the rolls, and divide the strikes severally as at the first, and if any be insufficiently beaten,'roll them up, and beat them over as before.

Of heckling hemp.

2

When your hemp hath been twice swingled, dried, and beaten, you shall then bring it to the heckle, which instrument needeth no demonstration, because it is hardly unknown to any woman whatsoever; and the first heckle shall be coarse, open and wide toothed, because it is the first breaker or divider of the same, and the layer of the strikes even and straight: and the hards which come of this heckling you shall mix with those of the latter swingling, and it will make the cloth much better; then you shall heckle it the second time through a good strait heckle made purposely for hemp, and be sure to break it very well and sufficiently thereupon, and save both the hards by themselves, and the strikes by themselves in several places.

43   Now there be some very principal good housewives, which use only but to heckle their hemp once over, affirming that if it be sufficiently dried and beaten, that once going over through a strait heckle will serve without more loss of labour, having been twice swingled before.

44   *Dressing of hemp more fine.*

Now if you intend to have an excellent piece of hempen cloth, which shall equal a piece of very pure linen, then after you have beaten it as before said, and heckled it once over, you shall then roll it up again, dry it as before, and beat it again as much as at the first; then heckle it through a fine flaxen heckle, and the tow which falls from the heckle will make a principal hemping, but the tear itself a cloth as pure as fine housewives' linen, the endurance and lasting whereof is rare and wonderful; thus you see the uttermost art in dressing of hemp for each several purpose in cloth making till it come to the spinning.

45   *Of heckling flax.*

Flax after it hath been twice swingled needeth neither more drying nor beating as hemp doth, but may be brought to the heckle in the same manner as you did hemp; only the heckle must be much finer and straiter; and as you did before the first heckle being much coarser than the latter, holding the strike stiff in your hand, break it very well upon that heckle: then the hards which come thereof, you shall save to make fine harden cloth of, and the strike itself you shall pass through a finer heckle; and the hards which come from thence, you shall save to make fine middling cloth of, and the tear itself for the best linen.

46   *The dressing of flax to the finest use.*

To dress flax for the finest use that may be, as to make fair holland cloth[63] of great price, or thread for the most curious purpose, a secret hitherto almost concealed from the best housewives with us; you shall take your flax after it hath been handled as is before showed, and, laying three strikes together, plait them in a plait of three so hard and close together as it is possible, joining one to the end of another, till you have plaited so much as you think convenient, and then begin another plait, and thus plait as many several plaits as you think will make a roll, like unto one of your hemp rolls before spoke of, and then, wreathing them hard together, make up the roll; and so many rolls more or less, according to the purpose you dress them for: this done, put the rolls into a hemp trough, and beat them soundly, rather more than less than the hemp: and then open and unplait it, and divide every strike from other very carefully; then heckle it through a finer heckle than any formerly used: for of heckles there be ever three sorts, and this must be the finest: and in this heckling you must be exceeding careful to do it gently, lightly, and with good deliberation, lest what you heckle from it should run to knots, or other hardness, as it is apt to do: but, being done artificially[64] as it ought, you shall see it look, and feel it handle like fine soft cotton, or jersey[65] wool; and this which thus looketh and feeleth, and falleth from the heckle, will notwithstanding make a pure linen, and run at least two yards and a half in the pound; but the tear itself will make a perfect, strong, and most fine holland, running at least five yards in the pound.[66]

Spinning: "4. Is the bench of the spinning wheel ... 5. The wheel, which is turned round by the hand without a handle. 6. The stock or nave of the wheel. 7. The spindle on which the thread is wound." From *The Universal Magazine of Knowledge and Pleasure* (London, October 1749), facing p. 180.

Of the spinning of hemp.

7

After your tear is thus dressed, you shall spin it either upon wheel or rock,[67] but the wheel is the swifter way, and the rock maketh the finer thread; you shall draw your thread according to the nature of the tear, and as long as it is even it cannot be too small, but if it be uneven it will never make a durable cloth. Now forasmuch as every housewife is not able to spin[68] her own tear in her own house, you shall make choice of the best spinners you can hear of, and to them put forth your tear to spin, weighing it before it go, and weighing it after it is spun and dry, allowing weight for weight, or an ounce and a half for waste at the most: as for the prices for spinning, they are according to the natures of the country, the fineness of the tear, and the dearness of provisions: some spinning by the pound, some by the lea,[69] and some by day, as the bargain shall be made.

48   *Of reeling yarn.*

After your yarn is spun upon spindles, spools, or such like, you shall then reel it upon reels,[70] of which the reels which are hardly two foot in length, and have but only two contrary cross bars are the best, the most easy and the least to be troubled with ravelling[71] and in the weaving of your fine yarn to keep it the better from ravelling; you shall as you reel it, with a lea band[72] of a big twist, divide the slipping[73] or skein into divers leas, allowing to every lea eighty threads, and twenty leas to every slipping, the yarn being very fine, otherwise less of both kinds: but if you spin by the lea, as at a ob.[74] a lea or so, then the ancient custom hath been to allow to a reel which was eight yards, all above 160 threads to every lea, and twenty-five leas, and sometimes thirty leas to a slipping, which will ordinarily amount to a pound or thereabouts; and so by that you may proportion forth the price for any manner of spinning whatsoever: for if the best thus, then the second so much bated;[75] and so accordingly the worst.

49   *Of the scouring of yarn.*

After thus your yarn is spun and reeled, being in the slipping, you shall scour it. Therefore first to fetch out the spots you shall lay it in lukewarm water, and let it lie so three or four days, each day shifting[76] it once, and wringing it out, and laying it in another water of the same nature; then carry it to a well or brook, and there rinse it, till you see that nothing cometh from it but pure clean water; for whilst there is any filth within it there will never be white cloth:

50   *Bucking of yarn.*

which done take a bucking tub, and cover the bottom thereof with very fine ashen[77] ashes: then, opening your slippings and spreading them, lay them on those ashes; then cover those slippings with ashes again, then

A professional dyer is pictured at work. From Hans Sachs, *Eygentliche Beschreibung aller Stande auf Erden*, sig. Niii.

lay in more slippings, and cover them with ashes as before, and thus lay one upon another, till all your yarn be laid in; then cover the uppermost yarn with a bucking cloth, and lay therein a peck or two (according to the bigness of the tub) of ashes more: then pour into all through the uppermost cloth so much warm water, till the tub can receive no more; and so let it stand all night: the next morning, you shall set a kettle of clean water on the fire, and when it is warm, you shall pull out the spigot of the bucking tub, and let the water therein run into another clean vessel, and as the bucking tub wasteth, so you shall fill it up again with the warm water on the fire, and as the water on the fire wasteth, so you shall fill it up again with the lye[78] which cometh from the bucking tub, ever observing to make the lye hotter and hotter till it seethe; and then when it so seetheth, you shall as before apply it with boiling lye at least four hours together; which is called "the driving[79] of a buck of yarn." All which being done you shall take off the bucking cloth, and then putting the yarn with the lye ashes into large tubs or bowls, with your hands as hot as you can suffer it, to poss and labour the yarn, ashes, and lye a pretty while together;

51   *Whitening of yarn.*

then carry it to a well, river, or other clean scouring water, and there
rinse it as clean as may be from the ashes, then take it, and hang it up
upon poles abroad in the air all day, and at night take the slippings down,
and lay them in water all night, then the next day hang them up again,
and if any part of them dry, then cast water upon them, observing ever
to turn that side outmost which whiteth slowest, and thus do at least
seven days together; then put all the yarn again into a bucking tub without
ashes, and cover it as before with a bucking cloth, and lay thereupon
good store of fresh ashes,[80] and drive that buck as you did before, with
very strong seething lyes, the space of half a day or more, then take it
forth, poss it, rinse it, and hang it up as you did before on the days, and
laying it in water on the nights, another week; and then wash it over in
fair water, and so dry it up. Other ways there are of scouring and whiting
of yarn; as steeping it in bran and warm water, and then boiling it with
osier sticks, wheat straw, water, and ashes, then possing, rinsing, and
bleaching it upon hedges,[81] or bushes; but it is a foul and uncertain way,
and I would not wish any good housewife to use it.

52   *Of winding yarn.*

After your yarn is scoured and whited, you shall then wind it up into
round balls of a reasonable bigness, rather without bottoms[82] than with
any at all, because it may deceive you in the weight, for according to the
pounds will arise your yards and lengths of cloth.

53   *Of warping and weaving.*

After your yarn is wound and weighed, you shall carry it to the weavers,
and warp it as was before showed for woollen cloth, knowing this, that
if your weaver be honest and skilful he will make you good and perfect
cloth of even and even, that is just the same weight in weft that then was
in warp: as for the action of weaving itself, it is the workman's occupation,
and therefore to him I refer it.

54   *The scouring and whiting of cloth.*

After your cloth is woven, and the web or webs come home, you shall
first lay it to steep in all points as you did your yarn, to fetch out the
soiling and other filth which is gathered from the weaver; then rinse it
also as you did your yarn, then buck it also in lye and ashes as beforesaid,
and rinse it, and then having loops fixed to the selvage of the cloth spread
it upon the grass, and stake it down at the uttermost length and breadth,
and as fast as it dries water it again, but take heed you wet it not too
much, for fear you mildew or rot it, neither cast water upon it till you

see it in manner dry, and be sure weekly to turn it first on one side, and then on the other, and at the end of the first week you shall buck it as before in lye and ashes: again then rinse it, spread it, and water it as before; then if you see it whites apace, you need not give it any more bucks with the ashes and the cloth mixed together: but then a couple of clean bucks[83] (as was before showed in the yarn) the next fortnight following; and then being whitened enough, dry up the cloth, and use it as occasion shall require; the best season for the same whitening being in April and May. Now the coarse and worst housewives scour and white their cloth with water and bran, and buck it with lye and green hemlocks: but as before I said, it is not good, neither would I have it put in practice. And thus much for wool, hemp, flax, and cloth of each several substance.

CHAPTER VI

❦

Of dairies, butter, cheese, and the necessary things belonging to that office

1   There followeth now in this place after these knowledges already rehearsed, the ordering and government of dairies, with the profits and commodities belonging to the same.

2   *Of kine.*
    And first touching the stock wherewith to furnish dairies, it is to be understood that they must be kine of the best choice and breed that our English housewife can possibly attain unto; as of big bone, fair shape, right breed, and deep of milk,[1] gentle, and kindly.

3   *Bigness of kine.*
    Touching the bigness of bone, the larger that every cow is, the better she is: for when either age, or mischance shall disable her for the pail, being of large bone she may be fed, and made fit for the shambles, and so no loss but profit, and pay other to the pail as good and sufficient as herself.

4   *Shape of kine.*
    For her shape, it must a little differ from the butcher's rules; for being chose for the dairy, she must have all the signs of plenty of milk, as a crumpled horn, a thin neck, a hairy dewlap, and a very large udder with four teats, long, thick, and sharp at the ends, for the most part either all white, of what colour soever the cow be, or at least the fore part thereof, and if it be well haired before and behind, and smooth in the bottom, it is a good sign also.

5   *The breed of kine.*

As touching the right breed of kine,[2] though our nation generally
affordeth very good ones, yet some countries[3] do far exceed [other] countries; as Cheshire, Lancashire, Yorkshire, and Derbyshire for black kine;
Gloucestershire, Somersetshire, and some part of Wiltshire for red kine,
and Lincolnshire [for] pied kine: and from the breeds of these countries
generally do proceed the breeds of all other, howsoever dispersed over
the whole kingdom. Now for our housewife's direction, she shall choose
her dairy from any of their best breeds before named, according as her
opinion and delight shall govern her, only observing not to mix her breeds
of diverse kinds, but to have all of one entire choice without variation,
because it is unprofitable; neither must you by any means have your bull
a foreigner from your kine, but absolutely either of one country, or of
one shape and colour. Again, in the choice of your kine you must look
diligently to the goodness and fertility of the soil wherein you live, and
by all means buy no kine from a place that is more fruitful than your
own, but rather harder; for the latter will prosper and come on, the other
will decay and fall into disease; as the pissing of blood, and such like,
for which disease and all other you may find assured cures in a litle book
I published, called *Cheape and Good [Husbandry].*[4]

6   *Depth of milk in kine.*

For the depth of milk in kine (which is the giving of most milk) being
the main of a housewife's profit, she shall be very careful to have that
quality in her beasts. Now those kine are said to be deepest of milk which
are new bare[5] that is, which have but lately calved, and have their milk
deep springing in their udders, for at that time she giveth the most milk;
and if the quantity then be not convenient, doubtless the cow cannot be
said to be of deep milch:

7   *Quantity of milk.*

and for the quantity of milk, for a cow to give two gallons at a meal
is rare, and extraordinary; to give a gallon and a half is much, and convenient, and to give but a gallon certain is not to be found fault with:
again those kine are said to be deep of milk which, though they give
not so exceeding much milk as others, yet they give a reasonable
quantity, and give it long as all the year through, whereas other kine
that give more in quantity will go dry, being with calf some three
months, some two, and some one; but these will give their usual measure, even the night before they calve; and therefore are said to be kine
deep of milk.

8 *Of the going dry of kine.*

Now for the retained opinion that the cow which goeth not dry at all, or very little, bringeth not forth so good a calf as the other, because it wanteth much of the nourishment it should enjoy, it is vain and frivolous; for should the substance from whence the milk proceedeth convert to the other intended nourishment, it would be so superabundant that it would convert either to disease, or putrefaction:[6] but letting these secret reasons pass, there be some kine which are so exceedingly full of milk, that they must be milked at least thrice a day, at morning, noon, and evening, or else they will shed their milk, but it is a fault rather than a virtue, and proceedeth more from a laxativeness or looseness of milk, than from any abundance; for I never saw those three meals yet equal the two meals of a good cow, and therefore they are not truly called deep of milk.

9 *Of the gentleness of kine.*

Touching the gentleness of kine, it is a virtue as fit to be expected as any other; for if she be not affable to the maid, gentle, and willing to come to the pail, and patient to have her dugs drawn without skittishness, striking or wildness, she is utterly unfit for the dairy.

10 *Of kindliness in kine.*

As a cow must be gentle to her milker, so she must be kindly[7] in her own nature; that is, apt to conceive and bring forth, fruitful to nourish, and loving to that which springs from her; for so she bringeth forth a double profit; the one for the time present which is in the dairy; the other for the time to come, which is in the maintenance of the stock, and upholding of breed.

11 *The best time to calve in, for the dairy or breed.*

The best time for a cow to calve in, for the dairy, is in the latter end of March, and all April; for then grass beginning to spring to its perfect goodness will occasion the greatest increase of milk that may be: and one good early cow will countervail two later, yet the calves thus calved are not to be reared, but suffered to feed upon their dam's best milk, and then to be sold to the butchers, and surely the profit will equal the charge; but those calves which fall in October, November, or any time of the depth of winter may well be reared up for breed, because the main profit of the dairy is then spent, and such breed will hold up and continue the stock, provided that you rear not up any calves which are calved in the prime days,[8] for they generally are subject to the disease of the sturdy,[9] which is dangerous and mortal.

12   *Rearing of calves.*

The housewife which only hath respect to her dairy, and for whose knowledge this discourse is written (for we have showed the grazier his office in *The English Husbandman*)[10] must rear her calves upon the finger with flotten milk,[11] and not suffer them to run with the dams, the general manner whereof, and the cure of all the diseases incident to them and all other cattle is fully declared in the book called *Cheape and Good [Husbandry]*.[12]

13   *The general use of dairies.*

To proceed then to the general use of dairies, it consisteth first in the cattle (of which we have spoken sufficiently), then in the hours of milking, the ordering of the milk, and the profits arising from the same.

14   *The hours of milking.*

The best and most commended hours for milking are indeed but two in the day; that in the spring and summer time, which is the best season for the dairy, is betwixt five and six in the morning, and six and seven o'clock in the evening: and although nice and curious housewives will have a third hour betwixt them, as between twelve and one in the afternoon, yet the better experienced do not allow it, and say as I believe that two good meals of milk are better ever than three bad ones;

15   *Manner of milking.*

also in the milking of a cow the woman must sit on the near side of the cow; she must gently at the first handle and stretch her dugs, and moisten them with milk that they may yield out the milk the better and with less pain: she shall not settle herself to milk, nor fix her pail firm to the ground till she see the cow stand sure and firm, but be ready upon any motion of the cow to save her pail from overturning; when she seeth all things answerable to her desire, she shall then milk the cow boldly, and not leave stretching and straining of her teats till not one drop of milk more will come from them, for the worst point of housewifery that can be is to leave a cow half milked; for besides the loss of the milk, it is the only way to make a cow dry and utterly unprofitable for the dairy: the milk maid whilst she is in milking, shall do nothing rashly or suddenly about the cow, which may affright or amaze her, but as she came gently, so with all gentleness she shall depart.

16   *The ordering of milk.*

Touching the well ordering of milk after it is come home to the dairy, the main point belonging thereunto is the housewife's cleanliness in the sweet and neat keeping of the dairy house; where not the least mote of any filth may by any means appear, but all things either to the eye or nose so void of sourness or sluttishness, that a prince's bed chamber must not exceed it: to this must be added the sweet and delicate keeping of her milk vessels, whether they be of wood, earth, or lead, the best of which is yet disputable with the best housewives; only this opinion is generally received, that the wooden vessel which is round and shallow is best in cold vaults, the earthen vessels principal for long keeping, and the leaden vessels for yielding of much cream: but howsoever, any and all these must be carefully scalded once a day, and set in the open air to sweeten, lest, getting any taint of sourness into them, they corrupt the milk that shall be put therein.

17 *Siling of milk.*

But to proceed to my purpose, after your milk is come home, you shall as it were strain it from all unclean things through a neat and sweet kept siledish, the form whereof every housewife knows, and the bottom of this sile, through which the milk must pass, shall be covered with a very clean washed fine linen cloth, such an one as will not suffer the least mote or hair to go through it: you shall into every vessel sile a pretty quantity of milk, according to the proportion of the vessel, which the broader it is and the shallower it is the better it is, and yieldeth ever the most cream, and keepeth the milk longest from souring.

18 *Profits arising from milk.*

Now for the profits arising from milk, they are three of especial account, as butter, cheese, and milk, to be eaten either simple or compounded: as for curds, sour milk, or whig,[13] they come from secondary means, and therefore may not be numbered with these.

19 *Of butter.*

For your butter which only proceedeth from the cream, which is the very heart and strength of milk, it must be gathered very carefully, diligently, and painfully: and though cleanliness be such an ornament to a housewife, that if she want any part thereof she loseth both that and all good names else, yet in this action it must be more seriously employed than in any other.

20 *Of fleeting cream.*

To begin then with the fleeting or gathering of your cream from the milk, you shall do it in this manner: the milk which you did milk in the

Churning butter. From Laurence
Andrewe, *The Vertuose Boke of
Distillacyon*, sig. Kiiv.

morning you shall with a fine thin shallow dish made for the purpose
take off the cream about five of the clock in the evening; and the milk
which you did milk in the evening, you shall fleet and take off the cream
about five of the clock the next morning; and the cream so taken off you
shall put into a clean sweet and well leaded earthen pot close covered,
and set in a cool place:

Of keeping cream.

21

and this cream so gathered you shall not keep above two days in the
summer, and not above four in the winter, if you will have the sweetest
and best butter, and that your dairy contain five kine or more; but how
many or few soever you keep, you shall not by any means preserve your
cream above three days in summer, and not above six in the winter.

Of churning butter and the days.

22

Your cream being neatly and sweet kept, you shall churm or churn it
on those usual days which are fittest either for your use in the house, or
the markets adjoining near unto you, according to the purpose for which
you keep your dairy. Now the days most accustomably held amongst
ordinary housewives are Tuesday and Friday: Tuesday in the afternoon, to serve Wednesday morning market, and Friday morning to
serve Saturday market; for Wednesday and Saturday are the most general market days of this kingdom, and Wednesday, Friday, and Saturday the usual fasting days[14] of the week, and so meetest for the use of
butter.

23 *Manner of churning.*

Now for churning, take your cream and through a strong and clean cloth strain it into the churn; and then, covering the churn close, and setting it in a place fit for the action in which you are employed (as in the summer in the coolest place of your dairy; and exceeding early in the morning, or very late in the evening, and in the winter in the warmest place of your dairy, and in the most temperate hours, as about noon, or a little before or after), and so churn it, with swift strokes, marking the noise of the same which will be solid, heavy, and entire, until you hear it alter, and the sound is light, sharp, and more spirity: and then you shall say that your butter breaks, which [is] perceived both by this sound, the lightness of the churn-staff, and the sparks and drops which will appear yellow about the lip of the churn; and cleanse with your hand both the lid and inward sides of the churn, and having put all together you shall cover the churn again, and then with easy strokes round, and not to the bottom, gather the butter together into one entire lump and body, leaving no pieces thereof several or unjoined.

24 *Helps in churning.*

Now forasmuch as there be many mischiefs and inconveniences which may happen to butter in the churning, because it is a body of much tenderness, and neither will endure much heat, nor much cold: for if it be over heated, it will look white, crumble, and be bitter in taste, and if it be over cold it will not come at all, but make you waste much labour in vain; which faults to help if you churn your butter in the heat of summer it shall not be amiss, if during the time of your churning you place your churn in a pail of cold water as deep as your cream riseth in the churn; and in the churning thereof let your strokes go slow, and be sure that your churn be cold when you put in your cream: but if you churn in the coldest time of winter, you shall then put in your cream before the churn be cold after it hath been scalded; and you shall place it within the air of the fire and churn it with as swift strokes, and as fast as may be, for the much labouring thereof will keep it in a continual warmth, and thus you shall have your butter good, sweet, and according to your wish.

25 *The handling of butter.*

After your butter is churned, or churned and gathered well together in your churn, you shall then open your churn, and with both your hands gather it well together, and take it from the buttermilk, and put it into a very clean bowl of wood, or pancheon of earth sweetened for the purpose, and if you intend to spend the butter sweet and fresh, you shall have your bowl or pancheon filled with very clean water, and therein with your hand you shall work the butter, turning and tossing it to and fro till you have by that labour beaten and washed out all the buttermilk, and brought the butter to a firm substance of itself, without any other moisture:

26   *Cleansing of butter.*

which done, you shall take the butter from the water, and with the point of a knife scotch and slash the butter over and over every way so thick as is possible, leaving no part through which your knife must not pass; for this will cleanse and fetch out the smallest hair or mote, or rag of a strainer, and any other thing which by casual means may happen to fall into it.

27   *Seasoning of butter.*

After this you shall spread the butter in a bowl thin, and take so much salt as you shall think convenient, which must by no means be much for sweet butter, and sprinkle it thereupon, then with your hands work the butter and the salt exceedingly well together, and then make it up either into dishes, pounds, or half pounds at your pleasure.

28   *Of May butter.*

If during the month of May before you salt your butter you save a lump thereof, and put it into a vessel, and so set it into the sun the space of that month, you shall find it exceeding sovereign and medicinable for wounds, strains, aches, and such like grievances.

29   *Of powdering up or potting of butter.*

Touching the powdering up or potting of butter, you shall by no means as in fresh butter wash the buttermilk out with water, but only work it clear out with your hands: for water will make the butter rusty, or reese;[15] this done, you shall weigh your butter, and know how many pounds there is thereof: for should you weigh it after it were salted, you would be deceived in the weight: which done, you shall open the butter, and salt it very well and thoroughly, beating it in with your hand till it be generally dispersed through the whole butter; then take clean earthen pots, exceedingly well leaded lest the brine should leak through the same, and cast salt into the bottom of it: then lay in your butter, and press it down hard within the same, and when your pot is filled, then cover the top thereof with salt so as no butter be seen: then closing up the pot let it stand where it may be cold and safe: but if your dairy be so little that you cannot at first fill up the pot, you shall then when you have potted up so much as you have, cover it all over with salt and pot the next quantity upon it till the pot be full.

30 ### *Of great dairies, and their customs.*

Now there be housewives whose dairies, being great, can by no means conveniently have their butter contained in pots; as in Holland, Suffolk, Norfolk, and such like, and therefore are first to take barrels very close and well made, and after they have salted it well, they fill their barrels therewith; then they take a small stick, clean, and sweet, and therewith make divers holes down through the butter, even to the bottom of the barrel: and then make a strong brine of water and salt which will bear an egg,[16] and after it is boiled, well skimmed, and cooled; then pour it upon the top of the butter till it swim above the same, and so let it settle. Some use to boil in this brine a branch or two of rosemary, and it is not amiss, but pleasant and wholesome.

31 ### *When to pot butter.*

Now although you may at any time betwixt May and September pot up butter, observing to do it in the coolest time of the morning: yet the most principal season of all is in the month of May only; for then the air is most temperate, and the butter will take salt the best, and the least subject to reesing.

32 ### *Use of buttermilk.*

The best use of buttermilk for the able housewife is charitably to bestow it on the poor neighbours, whose wants do daily cry out for sustenance: and no doubt but she shall find the profit thereof in a divine place, as well as in her earthly business: but if her own wants command her to use it for her own good, then she shall of her buttermilk make curds in this manner:

33 ### *Of buttermilk curds.*

she shall take her buttermilk and put it into a clean earthen vessel, which is much larger than to receive the buttermilk only; and, looking unto the quantity thereof, she shall take as it were a third part so much new milk and set it on the fire, and when it is ready to rise, take it off and let it cool a little; then pour it into the buttermilk in the same manner as you would make a posset,[17] and having stirred it about let it stand: then with a fine scummer when you will use the curds (for the longer it stands the better the curds will eat), take them up into a colander and let the whey drop well from it: and then eat them either with cream, ale, wine, or beer:

Of whig.

34

as for the whey, you may keep it also in a sweet stone vessel: for it is that which is called whig, and is an excellent cool drink and a wholesome; and may very well be drunk a summer through instead of any other drink,[18] and without doubt will slake the thirst of any labouring man as well, if not better.

Of cheese.

35

The next main profit which ariseth from the dairy is cheese, of which there be divers kinds,[19] as new milk, or morrow milk cheese; nettle cheese; flotten milk cheese; and eddish, or aftermath cheese; all which have their several orderings and compositions as you shall perceive by the discourse following: yet before I do begin to speak of the making of the cheese, I will show you how to order your cheeselip bag[20] or rennet, which is the most principal thing wherewith your cheese is compounded, and giveth the perfect taste unto the same.

Of the cheeselip bag or rennet.

36

The cheeselip bag or rennet, which is the stomach bag of a young suckling calf, which never tasted other food than milk, where the curd lieth undigested. Of these bags you shall in the beginning of the year provide yourself good store, and first open the bag and pour out into a clean vessel the curd and thick substance thereof; but the rest which is not curdled you shall put away: then open the curd and pick out of it all manner of motes, chires of grass, or other filth gotten into the same: then wash the curd in so many cold waters till it be as white and clean from all sorts of motes as is possible; then lay it on a clean cloth that the water may drain from it; which done, lay it in another dry vessel, then take a handful or two of salt[21] and rub the curd therewith exceedingly: then take your bag and wash it also in divers cold waters till it be very clean, and then put the curd and the salt up into the bag, the bag being also well rubbed within with salt: and so put it up, and salt the outside also all over: and then close up the pot close and so keep them a full year before you use them. For touching the hanging of them up in chimney corners[22] (as coarse housewives do) is sluttish, naught, and unwholesome, and the spending of your rennet whilst it is new makes your cheese heave and prove hollow.

37   *Seasoning of the rennet.*

When your rennet or earning is fit to be used, you shall season it after this manner; you shall take the bag you intend to use, and, opening it, put the curd into a stone mortar or a bowl, and with a wooden pestle or a rolling pin beat it exceedingly; then put to it the yolks of two or three eggs, and half a pint of the thickest and sweetest cream you can fleet from your milk, with a pennyworth of saffron finely dried and beaten to powder, together with a little cloves and mace, and stir them all passing well together till they appear but as one substance, and then put it up in the bag again: then you shall make a very strong brine of water and salt, and in the same you shall boil a handful or two of saxifrage, and then when it is cold clear it into a clean earthen vessel; then take out of the bag half a dozen spoonful of the former curd and mix it with the brine, then, closing the bag up again close, hang it within the brine, and in any case also steep in your brine a few walnut tree leaves and so keep your rennet a fortnight after before you use it; and in this manner dress all your bags, so as you may ever have one ready after another, and the youngest a fortnight old ever at the least, for that will make the earning quick and sharp, so that four spoonfuls thereof will suffice for the gathering and seasoning of at least twelve gallons of milk, and this is the choicest and best earning which can possibly be made by any housewife.

38   *To make a new milk cheese compound.*

To make a new milk or morning milk cheese, which is the best cheese made ordinarily in our kingdom; you shall take your milk early in the morning as it comes from the cow, and sile it into a clean tub, then take all the cream also from the milk you milked the evening before, and strain it into your new milk; then take a pretty quantity of clean water, and, having made it scalding hot, pour it into the milk also to scald the cream and it together, then let it stand, and cool it with a dish till it be no more than lukewarm; then go to the pot where your earning bag hangs, and draw from thence so much of the earning, without stirring of the bag, as will serve for your proportion of milk, and strain it therein very carefully; for if the least mote of the curd of the earning fall into the cheese, it will make the cheese rot and mould;[23] when your earning is put in you shall cover the milk, and so let it stand half an hour or thereabouts; for if the earning be good it will come in that space; but if you see it doth not, then you shall put in more: being come, you shall with a dish in your hand break and mash the curd together, possing and turning it about diversely: which done, with the flat palms of your hands very gently press the curd down into the bottom of the tub; then with a thin dish take the whey from it as clean as you can, and so having prepared your cheese-vat answerable to the proportion of your curd, with both your hands joined together put your curd therein and break it and press it down hard into the vat till you have filled it; then lay upon the top of the curd your flat cheese board, and a little small weight thereupon, that the whey may drop from it into the under vessel; when it hath done dropping take a large cheese cloth, and having wet it in cold water lay it on the cheese board, and then turn the cheese upon it; then lay the cloth into the cheese-vat; and so put the cheese therein again, and with a thin slice²⁴ thrust the same down close on every side; then, laying the cloth also over the top, lay on the cheese board, and so carry it to your great press, and there press it under a sufficient weight; after it hath been there pressed half an hour, you shall take it and turn it into a dry cloth, and put it into the press again, and thus you shall turn it into dry cloths at least five or six times in the first day, and ever put it under the press again, not taking it therefrom till the next day in the evening at soonest, and the last time it is turned you shall turn it into the dry vat without any cloth at all.

39   When it is pressed sufficiently and taken from the vat, you shall then lay it in a kimnel,²⁵ and rub it first on the one side and then on the other with salt, and so let it lie all that night, then the next morning you shall do the like again and so turn it upon the brine which comes from the salt two or three days or more, according to the bigness of the cheese, and then lay it upon a fair table or shelf to dry, forgetting not every day once to rub it all over with a clean cloth, and then to turn it till such time that it be thoroughly dry and fit to go into the cheese heck; and in this manner of drying you must observe to lay it first where it may dry hastily, and after where it may dry at more leisure; thus may you make the best and most principal cheese.

Cheese of two meals.

40   Now if you will make cheese of two meals,²⁶ as your morning's new milk, and the evening's cream milk, and all you shall do but the same formerly rehearsed.

Cheese of one meal.

41   And if you will make a simple morrow milk cheese²⁷ which is all of new milk and nothing else; you shall then do as is before declared, only you shall put in your earning so soon as the milk is siled (if it have any warmth in it) and not scald it; but if the warmth be lost you shall put it into a kettle and give it the air of the fire.

42

Of nettle cheese.

If you will have a very dainty nettle cheese,[28] which is the finest summer cheese which can be eaten; you shall do in all things as was formerly taught in the new milk cheese compound; only you shall put the curd into a very thin cheese vat, not above half an inch or a little better deep at the most, and then when you come to dry them, as soon as it is drained from the brine you shall lay it upon fresh nettles and cover it all over with the same; and so lying where they may feel the air, let them ripen therein, observing to renew your nettles once in two days, and every time you renew them, to turn the cheese or cheeses, and to gather your nettles as much without stalks as may be, and to make the bed both under and aloft as smooth as may be, for the more even and fewer wrinkles that your cheese hath, the more dainty is your housewife ever accounted.

43

Of flotten milk cheese.

If you will make flotten milk cheese,[29] which is the coarsest[30] of all cheeses; you shall take some of the milk and heat it upon the fire to warm all the rest; but if it be so sour that you dare not adventure the warming of it for fear of breaking, then you shall heat water, and with it warm it; then put in your earning as before showed, and gather it, press it, salt it, and dry it as you did all other cheeses.

44

Of eddish cheese.

Touching your eddish cheese or winter cheese,[31] there is not any difference betwixt it and your summer cheese touching the making thereof, only, because the season of the year denieth a kindly drying or hardening thereof, it differeth much in taste, and will be soft always; and of these eddish cheeses you may make as many kinds as of summer cheeses, as of one meal, two meals, or of milk that is flotten.

45

Of whey and the profits.

When you have made your cheese, you shall then have care of the whey, whose general use differeth not from that of buttermilk, for either you shall preserve it to bestow on the poor, because it is a good drink for the labouring man, or keep it to make curds[32] out of it, or lastly to nourish and bring up your swine.

46

Of whey curds.

If you will make curds of your best whey, you shall set it upon the fire, and, being ready to boil, you shall put into it a pretty quantity of buttermilk, and then as you see the curds arising up to the top of the whey, with a scummer skim them off, and put them into a colander, and then put in more buttermilk, and thus do whilst you can see any curds arise; then, the whey being drained clean from them, put them into a clean vessel, and so serve them forth as occasion shall serve.

CHAPTER VII

The office of the maltster, and the several secrets and knowledges belonging to the making of malt

1   It is most requisite and fit that our housewife be experienced and well practised in the well making of malt, both for the necessary and continual use thereof, as also for the general profit which accrueth and ariseth to the husband, housewife, and the whole family: for as from it is made the drink, by which the household is nourished and sustained, so to the fruitful husbandman (who is the master of rich ground, and much tillage) it is an excellent merchandise, and a commodity of so great trade, that not alone especial towns and counties are maintained thereby, but also the whole kingdom, and divers others of our neighbouring nations. This office or place of knowledge belongeth particularly to the housewife; and though we have many excellent men maltsters, yet it is properly the work and care of the woman, for it is a house work, and done altogether within doors, where generally lieth her charge; the man only ought to bring in, and to provide the grain, and excuse her from portage of too heavy burdens; but for the art of making the malt, and the several labours appertaining to the same, even from the vat to the kiln, it is only the work of the housewife and the maid-servants to her appertaining.

2   *Election of corn for malt.*
To begin then with the first knowledge of our maltster, it consisteth in the election and choice of grain fit to make malt on, of which there are indeed truly but two kinds, that is to say, barley, which is of all other the most excellent for this purpose; and oats, which when barley is scant or wanting maketh also a good and sufficient malt; and though the drink which is drawn from it be neither so much in the quantity, so strong in the substance, nor yet so pleasant in the taste, yet is the drink very good

and tolerable, and nourishing enough for any reasonable creature. Now
I do not deny, but there may be made malt of wheat, pease, lupins,[1]
vetches, and such like, yet it is with us of no retained custom, nor is the
drink simply drawn or extracted from those grains either wholesome or
pleasant, but strong and fulsome; therefore I think it not fit to spend any
time in treating of the same.

3

[*The election of barley.*]

To speak then of the election of barley, you shall understand that there
be divers kinds thereof, according to the alteration of soils, some being
big, some little, some full, some empty, some white, some brown, and
some yellow: but I will reduce all these into three kinds, that is, into the
clay barley, the sand barley, and the barley which groweth on the mixed
soil. Now the best barley to make malt on, both for yielding the greatest
quantity of matter, and making the strongest, best, and most wholesome
drink, is the clay barley well dressed, being clean corn of itself, without
weed or oats, white of colour, full in substance, and sweet in taste: that
which groweth on the mixed grounds is the next; for though it be subject
to some oats and some weeds; yet being painfully and carefully dressed,
it is a fair and a bold corn, great and full; and though somewhat browner
than the former, yet it is of a fair and clean complexion. The last and
worst grain for this purpose is the sand barley, for although it be seldom
or never mixed with oats, yet if the tillage be not painfully and cunningly
handled, it is much subject to weeds of divers kinds, as tares,[2] vetches,
and such like, which drink up the liquor in the brewing, and make the
yield or quantity thereof very little and unprofitable; besides, the grain
naturally of itself hath a yellow, withered, empty husk, thick and un-
furnished of meal, so that the drink drawn from it can neither be so much,
so strong, so good, nor so pleasant; so that, to conclude, the clean clay
barley is best for profit in the sale, drink for strength, and long lasting.

4   The barley on the mixed grounds will serve well for households and
families: and the sand barley for the poor,[3] and in such places where
better is not to be gotten. And these are to be known of every husband
or housewife; the first by his whiteness, greatness, and fulness: the second
by his brownness, and the third by his yellowness, with a dark brown
nether end, and the emptiness and thickness of the husk, and in this
election of barley you shall note that if you find in it any wild oats, it is
a sign of a rich clay ground, but ill husbanded, yet the malt made thereof
is not much amiss, for both the wild oat and the perfect oat give a pleasant
sharp relish to the drink, if the quantity be not too much, which is
evermore to be respected. And to conclude this matter of election, great
care must be had of both husband and housewife that the barley chosen

for malt be exceeding sweet, both in smell and taste, and very clean dressed: for any corruption maketh the malt loathsome, and the foul dressing affordeth much loss.

5 *Of the malt-house, and the situation.*

After the skilful election of grain for malt, the housewife is to look to the situation, goodness, and apt accommodation of the malt-house; for in that consisteth both much of the skill, and much of the profit: for the general situation of the house, it would (as near as can be) stand upon firm dry ground, having prospect[4] every way, with open windows and lights to let in the wind, sun, and air which way the maltster pleaseth, both to cool and comfort the grain at pleasure, and also close-shuts[5] or draw-windows to keep out the frosts and storms, which are the only lets and hindrances for making the malt good and perfect; for the model or form of these houses, some are made round, with a court on the middle, some long, and some square, but the round is the best and the least laborious, for the cisterns or vats being placed (as it were) at the head, or beginning of the circle, and the pump or well (but the pump is best) being close adjoining, or at least by conveyance of troughs made as useful as if it were near adjoining, the corn, being steeped, may with one person's labour and a shovel, be cast from the vat or cistern to the floor and there couched;[6] then when the couch is broken it may in the turning either with the hand or the shovel be carried in such a circular house round about from one floor to another, till it come to the kiln, which would also be placed next over against the pump and cisterns, and all contained under one roof; and thus you may empty steeping after steeping, and carry them with one person's labour from floor to floor, till all the floors be filled: in which circular motion you shall find that ever that which was first steeped shall first come to the kiln, and so consequently one after another in such sort as they were steeped, and your work may evermore be constant, and your floors at no time empty but at your own pleasure, and all the labour done only with the hand and shovel, without carrying or recarrying, or lifting heavy burdens, which is both troublesome and offensive, and not without much loss, because in such cases ever some grain scattereth.

6 Now over against the kiln-hole or furnace (which is evermore intended to be on the ground) should a convenient place be made to pile the fuel for the kiln, whether it be straw, bracken, furze, wood, coal, or other fuel; but sweet straw is of all other the best and neatest. Now it is intended that this malt house may be made two storeys in height, but no higher: over your cisterns shall be made the garners[7] wherein to keep your barley before it be steeped; in the bottoms of these garners, standing directly

over the cisterns shall be convenient holes made to open and shut at pleasure, through which shall run down the barley into the cistern. Over the bed of the kiln can be nothing but the place for the hair-cloth,[8] and a spacious roof open every way, that the smoke may have free passage, and with the least air be carried from the kiln, which maketh the malt sweet and pleasant. Over that place where the fuel is piled, and is next of all to the bed of the kiln, would likewise be other spacious garners made, some to receive the malt as soon as it is dried with the come[9] and kiln dust, in which it may lie to mellow and ripen; and others to receive the malt after it is screened and dressed up;[10] for to let it be too long in the come, as above three months at longest, will make it both corrupt, and breed weevils and other worms, which are the greatest destroyers of malt that may be. And these garners should be so conveniently placed before the front of the kiln bed that either with the shovel or small scuttle you may cast or carry the malt once dried into the garners. For the other part of the floors, they may be employed as the ground floors are for the receiving of the malt when it comes from the cistern: and in this manner, and with these accommodations you may fashion any malt-house either round, long, square, or of what proportion soever, as either your estate, or the convenience of the ground you have to build on shall administer.

Of malt floors.

7

Next to the site or proportion of the ground, you shall have a principal care for the making of your malt floors (in which all be custom, and the nature of the soil binds many times a man to sundry inconveniences, and that a man must necessarily build according to the matter he hath to build withal, from whence ariseth the many diversities of malt floors) yet you shall understand that the general best malt floor, both for summer and winter, and all seasons,[11] is the cave or vaulted arch[12] which is hewed out of a dry and main gritty rock,[13] for it is both warm in winter, cool in summer, and generally comfortable in all seasons of the year whatsoever. For it is to be noted, that albeit housewives do give over the making of malt in the extreme heat of summer, it is not because the malt is worse that is made in summer than that which is made in winter, but because the floors are more unseasonable, and that the sun, getting a power into such open places, maketh the grain which is steeped to sprout and come so swiftly that it cannot endure to take time on the floor, and get the right seasoning which belongeth to the same: whereas these kind of vaults being dry, and as it were couched under the ground, not only keepeth out the sun in summer, which maketh the malt come much too fast, but also defendeth it from frosts and cold bitter blasts in sharp winters, which will not suffer it to come, or sprout at all; or if part do come and sprout, as that which lieth in the heart of the bed; yet the upper parts and outside by means of extreme cold cannot sprout; but, being again dried, hath his first hardness, and is one and the same with raw barley; for every house-wife must know, that if malt do not come as it were all together, and at an instant, and not one come more than another, the malt must needs be very much imperfect. The next floor to the cave, or dry sandy rock, is the floor which is made of earth, or a stiff strong binding clay well watered, and mixed with horse dung, and soap ashes, beaten and wrought together, till it come to one solid firmness; this floor is a very warm comfortable floor in the winter season, and will help the grain to come and sprout exceedingly, and with the help of windows to let in the cold air, and to shut out the violent reflection of the sun, will serve very conveniently for the making of malt for nine months in the year, that is to say, from September till the end of May; but for June, July, and August, to employ it to that purpose will breed both loss, and encumbrance.

8   The next floor to this of earth, is that which is made of plaster, or plaster of paris, being burned in a seasonable time, and kept from wet, till the time of shooting, and then smoothly laid, and well levelled; the imperfection of the plaster floor is only the extreme coldness thereof, which in frosty and cold seasons so bindeth in the heart of the grain that it cannot sprout, for which cause it behoveth every maltster that is com-pelled to these floors to look well into the seasons of the year, and when he findeth either the frosts, northern blasts, or other nipping storms to rage too violently, then to make his first couches or beds, when the grain cometh newly out of the cistern, much thicker and rounder than otherwise he would do; and as the cold abateth, or the corn increaseth in sprouting so to make the couches or beds thinner and thinner; for the thicker and closer the grain is couched and laid together, the warmer it lieth; and so catching heat, the sooner it sprouteth, and the thinner it lieth the cooler it is; and so much the floor in sprouting. This floor, if the windows be close, and guard of the sun sufficiently, will (if necessity compel) serve for the making of malt ten months in the year, only in July and August which contain the dog days[14] it would not be employed, nor in the time of any frost, without great care and circumspection. Again, there is in this floor another fault, which is a natural casting out of dust, which much sullieth the grain, and being dried makes it look dun and foul, which is much disparagement to the maltster; therefore she must have great care that when the malt is taken away, to sweep and keep her floors as clean and neat as may be.

9   The last and worst is the boarded floor, of what kind soever it be, by

reason of the too much heat thereof, and yet of boarded floors the oaken boarded is the coolest and longest lasting; the elm or beech is next; then the ash, and the worst (though it be the fairest to the eye) is the fir, for it hath in itself (by reason of the frankincense[15] and turpentine which it holdeth) a natural heat, which, mixed with the violence of the sun in the summertime, forceth the grain not only to sprout, but to grow in the couch, which is much loss, and a foul imputation.[16] Now these boarded floors can hardly be in use for above five months at the most, that is to say, October, November, December, January, and February; for the rest, the sun hath too much strength, and these boarded floors too much warmth; and therefore [even] in the coolest times it is good to observe to make the couches thin, whereby the air may pass through the corn, and so cool it, that it may sprout at leisure.

Imperfect floors.

Now for any other floor besides these already named, there is not any good to malt upon; for the common floor which is of natural earth, whether it be clay, sand or gravel, if it have no mixture at all with it more than its own nature, by oft treading upon it, groweth to gather the nature of saltness or saltpetre[17] into it, which not only giveth an ill taste to the grain that is laid upon the same, but also his moisture and mouldiness, which in the moist times of the year arise from the ground, it often corrupteth and putrifieth the corn. The rough paved floor, by reason of the unevenness is unfit to malt on, because the grain getting into the crannies doth there lie, and are not removed or turned up and down as they should be with the hand, but many times is so fixed[18] to the ground, it sprouteth and groweth up into a green blade, affording much loss and hindrance to the owner.

The smooth paved floor, or any floor of stone whatsoever, is full as ill; for every one of them naturally, against much wet or change of weather, will sweat and distil forth such abundant moisture, that the malt lying upon the same can neither dry kindly and expel the former moisture received in the cistern, but also by that overmuch moisture many times rotteth, and comes to be altogether useless. Lastly, for the floor made of lime and hair, it is as ill as any formerly spoken of, both in respect of the nature of the lime, whose heat and sharpness is a main enemy to malt, or any moist corn, as also in respect of the weakness and brittleness of the substance thereof, being apt to moulder and fall in pieces with the lightest treading on the same, and that lime and dust once mixing with the corn, it doth so poison and suffocate it that it can neither sprout, nor turn serviceable for any use.

12   *Of the kiln and the building thereof.*

Next unto the malt floors, our maltster shall have a great care in the framing and fashioning of the kiln, of which there are sundry sorts of models, as the ancient from which was in times past used of our forefathers, being only made in a square proportion at the top with small splints or rafters, joined within four inches one of another, going from a main beam crossing the mid part of that great square: then is this great square from the top with good and sufficient studs to be drawn slopewise narrower and narrower, till it come to the ground, so that the hearth or lowest part thereof may be not above a sixth part to the great square above on which the malt is laid to be dried, and this hearth shall be made hollow and descending,[19] and not level nor ascending: and these kilns do not hold any certain quantity in the upper square, but may ever be according to the frame of the house, some being thirty foot each way, some twenty, and some eighteen. There be other kilns which are made after this manner open and slope, but they are round of proportion; but both these kind of kilns have one fault, which is danger of fire; for lying every way open and apt for the blaze, if the maltster be anything negligent either in the keeping of the blaze low and forward, or not sweeping every part about the hearth anything may take fire, or foreseeing that no straws which do belong to the bedding of the kiln do hang down, or are loose, whereby the fire may take hold of them, it is very possible that the kiln may be set on fire, to the great loss and often undoing of the owner.[20]

13   *The perfect kiln.*

Which to prevent, and that the maltster may have better assurance and comfort in her labour, there is a kiln now of general use in this kingdom, which is called a French kiln, being framed of brick, ashlar, or other fire stone, according to the nature of the soil in which husbands and housewives live: and this French kiln is ever safe and secure from fire, and whether the maltster wake or sleep, without extreme wilful negligence, there can no danger come to the kiln; and in these kilns may be burned any kind of fuel whatsoever, and neither shall the smoke offend or breed ill taste in the malt, nor yet discolour it, as many times it doth in open kilns, where the malt is as it were covered all over, and even parboiled in smoke: so that of all sorts of kilns whatsoever, this which is called the French kiln is to be preferred and only embraced. Of the form or model whereof, I will not here stand to entreat, because they are now so generally frequent amongst us, that not a mason or carpenter in the whole kingdom but can build the same; so that to use more words thereof were tediousness to little purpose.

14   Now there is another kind of kiln[21] which I have seen (and but in the

West Country only) which for the profitable quaintness thereof, I took some especial note of, and that was a kiln made at the end of a kitchen range or chimney, being in shape round, and made of brick, with a little hollowness narrowed by degrees, into which came from the bottom and midst of the kitchen chimney a hollow tunnel or vault, like the tunnel of a chimney, and ran directly on the backside, the hood, or back of the kitchen chimney; then in the midst of the chimney, where the greatest strength of the fire was made, was a square hole made of about a foot and a half every way, with an iron thick plate to draw to and fro, opening and closing the hole at pleasure; and this hole doth open only into that tunnel which went to the kiln, so that the malt being once laid, and spread upon the kiln, draw away the iron plate, and the ordinary fire with which you dress your meat, and perform other necessary businesses, is sucked up into this tunnel, and so conveyeth the heat to the kiln, where it drieth the malt with as great perfection as any kiln that ever I saw in my life, and needeth neither attendance or other ceremony more than once in five or six hours to turn the malt, and take it away when it is dried sufficiently: for it is here to be noted that how great or violent soever the fire be which is in the chimney, yet by reason of the passage, and the quantity thereof, it carrieth no more but a moderate heat to the kiln; and for the smoke, it is so carried away in other loop holes which run from the hollowness between the tunnel and the malt bed, that no malt in the world can possibly be sweeter, or more delicately coloured: only the fault of these kilns are that they are but little in compass, and so cannot dry much at a time, as not above a quarter or ten strike[22] at the most in one drying, and therefore are no more but for a man's own particular use, and for the furnishing of one settled family; but so applied, they exceed all the kilns that I have seen whatsoever.

Bedding of the kiln.

5

When our maltster hath thus perfected the malt house and kiln, then next look to the well bedding of the kiln,[23] which is diversely done according to men's divers opinions; for some use one thing, and some another, as the necessity of the place, or men's particular profits draw them. But first to show you what the bedding of a kiln is, you shall understand that it is a thin covering laid upon the open rafters, which are next unto the heat of the fire, being made either so thin or so open that the smallest heat may pass through it and come to the corn: this bed must be laid so even and level as may be, and not thicker in one place than another, lest the malt dry too fast where it is thinnest, and too slowly where it is thick, and so in the taste seem to be of two several dryings: it must also be made of such stuff as, having received heat, it will long continue the same, and be an assistant to the fire in drying the corn: it should also have in it no moist or dankish property, lest at the first receiving of the fire, it send out a stinking smoke, and so taint the malt: nor should it be of any rough or sharp substance, because upon this bed or bedding is laid the hair-cloth, and on the hair-cloth the malt, so that with the turning the malt, and treading upon the cloth, should the bed be of any such roughness, it would soon wear out the hair-cloth, which would be both loss and ill housewifery, which is carefully to be eschewed.

16   But now for the matter or substance whereof this bedding should be made, the best, neatest, and sweetest, is clean long rye straw, with the ears only cut off, and the ends laid even together, not one longer than another, and so spread upon the rafter of the kiln as even and thin as may be, and laid as it were straw by straw in a just proportion, where skill and industry may make it thin or thick at pleasure, as but the thickness of one straw, or of two, three, four, or five, as shall seem to your judgement most convenient; and than this, there can be nothing more even, more dry, sweet, or open to let in the heat at your pleasure: and although in the old open kilns it be subject to danger of fire, by reason of the quickness to receive the flame, yet in the French kilns (before mentioned) it is a most safe bedding, for not any fire can come near unto it. There be others which bed the kiln with mat; and it is not much to be misliked, if the mat be made of rye straw sewed and woven together according to the manner of the Indian mats, or those usual thin bent-mats,[24] which you shall commonly see in the summertime standing in husbandmen's chimneys, where one bent or straw is laid by another, and so woven together with a good strong pack-thread: but these mats accord to the old proverb ("more cost more worship")[25] for they are chargeable to be bought, and very troublesome in the making, and in the wearing will not outlast one of the former loose beddings; for if one thread or stitch break, immediately most in that row will follow: only it is most certain that during the time it lasteth it is both good, necessary, and handsome. But if the mat be made either of bullrushes, flags,[26] or any other thick substance (as for the most part they are) then it is not so good a bedding, both because the thickness keepeth out the heat, and is long before it can be warmed; as also in that it ever being cold naturally of itself draweth into it a certain moisture, which with the first heat being expelled in smoke doth much offend and breed ill taste in the malt.

17   There be others that bed the kiln with a kind of mat made of broad thin splints of wood wrought checkerise one into another, and it hath the same faults which the thick mat hath; for it is long in catching the heat, and will ever smoke at the first warming, and that smoke will the

malt smell on ever after; for the smoke of wood is ever more sharp and piercing than any other smoke whatsoever. Besides, this wooden mat, after it hath once bedded the kiln, it can hardly afterward be taken up or removed; for by continual heat, being brought to such an extreme dryness, if upon any occasion either to mend the kiln, or cleanse the kiln, or do other necessary labour underneath the bedding, you should take up the wooden mat, it would presently crack and fall to pieces, and be no more serviceable. There be others which bed the kiln with a bedding made all of wickers,[27] or small wands folded one into another like a hurdle, or such like wand work; but it is made very open, every wand at least two or three fingers one from another: and this kind of bedding is a very strong kind of bedding, and will last long, and catcheth the heat at the first springing, only the smoke is offensive, and the roughness, without great care used, will soon wear out your hair-cloth: yet in such places where straw is not to be got or spared, and that you are compelled only to use wood for your fuel in drying your malt, I allow this bedding before any other, for it is very good, strong and long-lasting: besides, it may be taken up and set by at pleasure, so that you may sweep and cleanse your kiln as oft as occasion shall serve; and in the neat and fine keeping of the kiln doth consist much of the housewife's art, for to be choked either with dust, dirt, soot, or ashes, as it shows sluttishness and sloth, the only great imputations hanging over a housewife, so they likewise hinder the labour, and make the malt dry a great deal worse, and more unkindly.

Of fuel for the drying of malt.

Next the bedding of the kiln, our maltster by all means must have an especial care with what fuel she drieth the malt[28] for commonly according to that, it ever receiveth and keepeth the taste, if by some especial art in the kiln that annoyance be not taken away. To speak then of fuels in general, they are of divers kinds according to the natures of soils and the accommodation of places in which men live; yet the best and most principal fuel for the kilns (both for sweetness, gentle heat, and perfect drying) is either good wheat straw, rye straw, barley straw, or oaten straw; and of these the wheat straw is the best, because it is most substantial, longest lasting, makes the sharpest fire, and yields the least flame: the next is rye straw, then oaten straw, and last barley straw, which, by reason it is shortest, lightest, least lasting, and giveth more blaze than heat, it is last of these white straws to be chosen; and where any of these fail, or are scarce, you may take the stubble or after-crop of them, when the upper part is shorn away; which, being well dried and housed, is as good as any of the rest already spoken of and less chargeable, because it is not fit for any better purpose as to make fodder, manure, or such like, of more than ordinary thatching, and so fittest for this purpose.

19   Next to these white straws, your long fen rushes, being very exceedingly well withered and dried, and all the sappy moisture gotten out of them, and so either safely housed or stacked, are the best fuel; for they make a very substantial fire, and much lasting, neither are apt to much blazing, nor the smoke so sharp or violent but may very well be endured: where all these are wanting, you may take the straw of pease, vetches, lupins, or tares, any of which will serve; yet the smoke is apt to taint, and the fire without prevention drieth too suddenly and swiftly. Next to these is clean bean straw, or straw mixed of beans and pease together; but this must be handled with great discretion, for the substance containeth so much heat, that it will rather burn than dry if it be not moderated, and the smoke is also much offensive. Next to this bean straw is your furze, gorse, whins,[29] or small brushwood, which differeth not much from bean straw; only the smoke is much sharper, and tainteth the malt with a much stronger savour. To these I may add bracken or bracks, ling, heath, or broom, all which may serve in time of necessity, but each one of them have this fault, that they add to the malt an ill taste or savour. After these I place wood of all sorts, for each is alike noisome, and if the smoke which cometh from it touch the malt the infection cannot be recovered; from whence amongst the best husbands have sprung this opinion, that when at anytime drink is ill tasted, they say straight it was made of wood-dried malt.[30] And thus you see the generality of fuels, their virtues, faults, and how they are to be employed. Now for coal of all kinds, turf or peat, they are not by any means to be used under kilns, except where the furnaces are so subtly made, that the smoke is conveyed a quite contrary way, and never cometh near the malt; in that case it skilleth not what fuel you use, so it be durable and cheap it is fit for the purpose, only great regard must be had to the gentleness of the fire; for as the old proverb is ("soft fire makes sweet malt")[31] so too rash and hasty a fire scorcheth and burneth it, which is called amongst maltsters "firefanged"; and such malt is good for little or no purpose: therefore to keep a temperate and true fire is the only art of a most skilful maltster.

20   *The making of the garners.*

When the kiln is thus made and furnished of all necessaries duly belonging to the same, our maltster's next care shall be to the fashioning and making of the garners, hutches, or holds in which both the malt after it is dried, and the barley before it be steeped is to be kept and preserved[32] and these garners or safes for corn are made of divers fashions, and divers matters, as some of boards, some of bricks, some of stone, some of lime and hair, and some of mud, clay, or loam: but all of these have their several faults; for wood of all kinds breedeth weevils and worms which destroy the grain, and is indeed much too hot: for although malt would ever be kept passing dry, yet never so little over-plus of heat withers it, and takes away the virtue; for as moisture rots and corrupts it, so heat takes it away and decayeth the substance. Brick, because it is laid with lime, is altogether unwholesome, for the lime, being apt at change of weather to sweat, moisteneth the grain and so tainteth it, and in the driest seasons with the sharp hot taste doth fully as much offend it: those which are made of stone are much more noisome, both in respect of the reasons before rehearsed, as also in that all stone of itself will sweat, and so more and more corrupteth the grain which is harboured in it. Lime and hair, being of the same nature, carrieth the same offences, and is in the like sort to be eschewed. Now for mud, clay, or loam, inasmuch as they must necessarily be mixed with wood, because otherwise of themselves they cannot knit or bind together, and besides that the clay or loam must be mixed either with chopped hay, chopped straw, or chopped litter, they are as great breeders of worms and vermin as wood is, nor are they defences against mice, but easy to be wrought through, and so very unprofitable for any husband or housewife to use. Besides, they are much too hot, and being either in a close house near the kiln, or the back or face of any other chimney, they dry the corn too sore, and make it dwindle and wither, so that it neither filleth the bushel, nor enricheth the liquor, but turns to loss every way.

[*The best garner.*]

The best garner then that can be made both for safety and profit, is to made either of broken tile-shard,[33] or broken bricks, cunningly and even laid, and bound together with plaster of paris, or our ordinary English plaster, or burnt alabaster, and then covered all over both within and without, in the bottom and on every side, at least three fingers thick with the same plaster, so as no brick or tile-shard may by any means be seen, or come near to touch the corn; and these garners you may make as big, or as little as you please, according to the frame of your house, or places of most convenience for the purpose, which indeed would ever be as near the kiln as may be that the air of the fire in the days of drying may come unto the same, or else near the backs or sides of chimneys, where the air thereof may correct the extreme coldness of the plaster which of all things that are bred in the earth is the coldest thing that may be, and yet most dry, and not apt to sweat, or take moisture but by some violent extremity, neither will any worm or vermin come near it, because the great coldness thereof is a mortal enemy to their natures; and so the safest and longest these garners of plaster keep all kind of grain and pulse in the best perfection.

22 *The making of cisterns.*

After these garners, hutches, or large keeps for corn are perfected and made, and fitly adjoined to the kiln, the next thing that our maltster hath to look unto is the framing of the vats or cisterns, in which the corn is to be steeped; and they are of two sorts, that is either of coopers' work, being great vats of wood, or else of mason's work, being cisterns made of stone; but the cistern of stone is much the better, for besides that these great vats of wood are very chargeable and costly (as a vat to contain four quarters of grain, which is but two and thirty bushels, cannot be afforded under twenty shillings), so likewise they are very casual and apt to mischance and spilling; for besides their ordinary wearing, if in the heat of summer they be never so little neglected without water, and suffered to be overdry, it is ten to one but in the winter they will be ready to fall in pieces; and if they be kept moist, yet if the water be not oft shifted and preserved sweet, the vat will soon taint, and being once grown faulty it is not only irrecoverable, but also whatsoever cometh to be steeped in it after will be sure to have the same savour: besides the wearing and breaking of garths and plugs, the binding, cleansing, sweetening, and a whole world of other troubles and charges do so daily attend them that the benefit is a great deal short of the encumbrance; whereas the stone cistern is ever ready and useful, without any vexation at all, and, being once well and sufficiently made, will not need trouble or reparation (more than ordinary washing) scarce in an hundred years.

23 Now the best way of making these malt cisterns, is to make the bottoms and sides of good tile-shards, fixed together with the best lime and sand, and the bottom shall be raised at least a foot and a half higher than the ground, and at one corner in the bottom a fine artificial round hole must be made, which being outwardly stopped the maltster may through it drain the cistern dry when she pleaseth, and the bottom must be so artificially levelled and contrived, that the water may have a true descent to that hole, and not any remain behind when it is opened.

24 Now when the model is thus made of tile-shard, which you may do great or little at your pleasure, then with lime, hair, and beasts' blood mixed together you shall cover the bottom at least two inches thick, laying it level and plain as is before showed: which done, you shall also cover all the sides and top, both within and without with the same matter, at least a good finger's thickness, and the main wall of the whole cistern shall be a full foot in thickness as well for strength and durableness as other private reasons for the holding the grain and water, whose poise

and weight might otherwise endanger a weaker substance. And thus much concerning the malt-house, and those several accommodations which do belong unto the same.

The manner how to make malt.

I will now speak a little in general as touching the art, skill, and knowledge of malt making, which I have referred to the conclusion of this chapter, because whosoever is ignorant in any of the things before spoken of cannot by any means ever attain to the perfection of most true and most thrifty malt-making. To begin then with this art of making, or (as some term it) melting of malt, you shall first (having proportioned the quantity you mean to steep, which should ever be answerable to the continent[34] of your cistern, and your cistern to your floors) let it either run down from your upper garner into the cistern, or otherwise be carried into your cistern, as you shall please, or your occasions desire; and this barley would by all means be very clean, and neatly dressed; then when your cistern is filled, you shall from your pump or well convey the water into the cistern, till all the corn be drenched, and that the water float above it: if there be any corn that will not sink, you shall with your hand stir it about, and wet it, and so let it rest and cover the cistern; and for the space of three nights[35] you shall let the corn steep in the water. After the third night is expired, the next morning you shall come to the cistern, and pluck out the plug or bung-stick which stoppeth the hole in the bottom of the cistern, and so drain the water clean from the corn, and this water you shall by all means save, for much light corn and others will come forth with this drain water, which is very good swine's meat, and may not be lost by any good housewife. Then, having drained it, you shall let the cistern drop all that day, and in the evening with your shovel you shall empty the corn from the cistern unto the malt floor, and when all is out, and the cistern cleansed, you shall lay all the wet corn on a great heap round or long, and flat on the top; and the thickness of this heap shall be answerable to the season of the year; for if the weather be extreme cold, then the heap shall be made very thick, as three or four foot, or more, according to the quantity of the grain: but if the weather be temperate and warm, then shall the heap be made thinner, as two foot, a foot and a half, or one foot, according to the quantity of the grain. And this heap is called of maltsters a couch or bed of raw malt.

[Of the couch.]

In this couch you shall let the corn lie three nights more without stirring, and after the expiration of the three nights you shall look upon it, and if you find that it beginneth but to sprout (which is called coming of malt) though it be never so little, as but the very white end of the sprout peeping out (so it be in the outward part of the heap or couch) you shall then break open the couch, and in the midst (where the corn lay nearest) you shall find the sprout or come of a greater largeness; then with your shovel you shall turn all the outward part of the couch inward, and the inward outward, and make it at least three or four times as big[36] as it was at the first, and so let it lie all that day and night, and the next day you shall with your shovel turn the whole heap over again, increasing the largeness, and making it of one indifferent[37] thickness over all the floor; that is to say not above a handful thick at the most, not failing after for the space of fourteen days, which doth make up full in all three weeks, to turn it all over twice or thrice a day according in the season of the weather; for if it be warm, the malt must be turned oftener; if cool, then it may lie closer, thicker, and longer together:[38]

27 *The drying of malt.*

and when the three weeks is fully accomplished, then you shall (having bedded your kiln, and spread a clean hair-cloth thereon) lay the malt as thin as may be (as about three fingers' thickness) upon the hair-cloth, and so dry it with a gentle and soft fire, ever and anon turning the malt (as it drieth on the kiln) over and over with your hand, till you find it sufficiently well dried, which you shall know both by the taste when you bite it in your mouth, and also by the falling off of the come or sprout when it is thoroughly dried. Now as soon as you see the come begin to shed, you shall in the turning of the malt rub it well between your hands, and scour it, to make the come fall away; then finding it all sufficiently dried; first put out your fire, then let the malt cool upon the kiln for four or five hours, and after raising up the four corners of the hair cloth, and gathering the malt together on a heap, empty it with the come and all into your garners, and there let it lie (if you have not present occasion to use it) for a month or two or three to ripen, but no longer, for as the come or dust of the kiln for such a space melloweth and ripeneth the malt, making it better both for sale or expense,[39] so to lie too long in it doth engender weevils, worms and vermin which do destroy the grain.

28 *The dressing of malt.*

Now for the dressing and cleansing of malt at such time as it is either to be spent in the house, or sold in the market, you shall first winnow it with a good wind either from the air, or from the fan; and before the winnowing you shall rub it exceeding well between your hands to get the come or sproutings clean away: for the beauty and goodness of malt is when it is most smug, clean, bright, and likest to barley in the view, for then there is least waste and greatest profit: for come and dust drinketh up the liquor,[40] and gives an ill taste to the drink. After it is well rubbed and winnowed, you shall then ree[41] it over in a fine sieve, and if any of the malt be uncleansed, then rub it again in the sieve till all be pure, and the rubbings will arise on the top of the sieve, which you may cast off at pleasure, and both those rubbings from the sieve and the chaff and dust which cometh from the winnowings should be safe kept, for they are very good swine's meat, and feed well mixed either with whey or swillings: and thus after the malt is reed, you shall either sack it up for especial use, or put it into a well cleansed garner, where it may lie till there be occasion for expense.

Observation in the making of malt.

Now there be certain observations in the making of malt which I may by no means omit: for though divers opinions do diversely argue them, yet as near as I can I will reconcile them to that truth which is most consonant to reason, and the rule of honesty and equality.

[The mellowing of malt.]

First, there is a difference in men's opinions as touching the constant time for the mellowing and making of the malt; that is, from the first steeping to the time of drying; for some will allow both vat and floor hardly a fortnight, some a fortnight and two or three days, and do give this reason: first, they say it makes the corn look whiter and brighter, and doth not get so much the sullying and foulness of the floor as that which lieth three weeks,[42] which makes it a great deal more beautiful and so more saleable: next, it doth not come or shoot out so much sprout, as that which lieth a longer time, and so preserveth more heart in the grain, makes it bold and fuller, and so consequently more full of substance, and able to make more of a little, than the other much of more; and these reasons are good in show, but not in substantial truth: for (although I confess that corn which lieth least time of the floor must be the whitest and brightest) yet that which wanteth any of the due time can neither ripen, mellow, nor come to true perfection, and less than three weeks cannot ripen barley: for look what time it hath to dwell and sprout, it must have full that time to flourish, and as much time to decay: now in less than a week it cannot do the first, and so in a week the second, and in another week the third; so that in less than three weeks a man cannot make perfect malt. Again, I confess, that malt which hath the least come, must have the greatest kernel, and so be most substantial; yet the malt which putteth not out his full sprout, but hath that moisture (with too much haste) driven in which should be expelled, can never be malt of any long lasting, or profitable for endurance, because it hath so much moist substance as doth make it both apt to corrupt and breed worms in most great abundance: it is most true, that this hasty made malt is fairest to the eye, and will soonest be vented in the market; and being spent as soon as it is bought, little or no loss is to be perceived, yet if it be kept three or four months, or longer (unless the place where it is kept be like a hot-house) it will so dank and give again, that it will be little better than raw malt, and so good for no service without a second drying: besides, malt that is not suffered to sprout to the full kindly, but is stopped as soon as it begins to peep, much of that malt cannot come at all, for the moistest grains do sprout first, and the hardest are longer in breaking the husk; now if you stop the grain on the first sprouts, and not give all leisure to come one after another, you shall have half malt and half barley, and that is good for nothing but hens' and hogs' trough. So that to conclude, less than three weeks you cannot have to make good and perfect malt.

31
[*The turning of malt.*]
Next there is a difference in the turning of the malt, for some (and those be the most men maltsters whatsoever) turn all their malt with the shovel, and say it is most easy, most speedy, and dispatcheth more in an hour than any other way doth in three; and it is very true, yet it scattereth much, leaveth much behind unturned, and commonly that which was undermost it leaveth undermost still, and so by some coming too much, and others not coming at all, the malt is oft much imperfect, and the old saying made good, that "too much haste, maketh waste." Now there are others (and they are for the most part women maltsters) which turn all with the hand, and that is the best, safest, and most certain way; for there is not a grain which the hand doth not remove and turn over and over, and lays every several heap or row of such an even and just thickness, that the malt both equally cometh, and equally seasoneth together without defect or alteration: and though he that hath much malt to make will be willing to hearken to the swiftest course in making, yet he that will make the best malt, must take such convenient leisure, and employ that labour which cometh nearest to perfection.

32
[*The sprouting of malt.*]
Then there is another especial care to be had in the coming or sprouting of malt, which is that as it must not come too little, so it must not by any means come too much, for that is the grossest abuse that may be: and that which we call comed or sprouted too much is when, either by

negligence for want of looking to the couch and not opening of it, or for want of turning when the malt is spread on the floor, it come or sprout at both ends, which husbands call akerspyerd;[43] such corn, by reason the whole heart or substance is driven out of it, can be good for no purpose but the swine trough, and therefore you must have an especial care both to the well tending of the couch, and the turning the malt on the floor, and be sure (as near as you can by the ordering of the couch, and happing[44] the hardest grain inward and warmest) to make it all come very indifferently together. Now if it so fall out that you buy your barley, and happen to light on mixed grain, some being old corn, some new corn, some of the heart of the stack, and some of the staddle,[45] which is an ordinary deceit with husbandmen in the market, then you may be well assured that this grain can never come or sprout equally together; for the new corn will sprout before the old, and the staddle before that in the heart of the stack, by reason the one exceedeth the other in moistness: therefore in this case you shall mark well which cometh first, which will be still in the heart of the couch, and with your hand gather it by itself into a separate place, and then heap the other together again; and thus as it cometh and sprouteth, so gather it from the heap with your hand, and spread it on the floor, and keep the other still in a thick heap till all be sprouted. Now lastly observe, that if your malt be hard to sprout or come, and that the fault consist more in the bitter coldness of the season than any defect of the corn, that then (besides the thick and close making of the heap or couch) you fail not to cover it over with some thick woollen cloths, as coarse coverlids, or such like stuff, the warmth whereof will make it come presently: which once perceived, then forthwith uncloth it, and order it as aforesaid in all points. And thus much for the art, order, skill and cunning belonging to malt making.

Of oatmalt.

Now as touching the making of oats into malt, which is a thing of general use in many parts of this kingdom where barley is scarce, as in Cheshire, Lancashire, much of Derbyshire, Devonshire, Cornwall, and the like, the art and skill is all one with that of barley, nor is there any variation or change of work, but one and the same order still to be observed, only, by reason that oats are more swift in sprouting, and apter to clutter, ball and hang together by the length of the sprout than barley is, therefore you must not fail but turn them oftener than barley, and in the turning be careful to turn all, and not leave any unmoved. Lastly, they will need less of the floor than barley will, for in a full fortnight, or a fortnight and two or three days you may make very good and perfect oatmalt. But because I have a great deal more to speak particularly of oats in the next chapter, I will here conclude this, and advise every skilful housewife to join with mine observations her own tried experience, and no doubt but she shall find both profit and satisfaction.

CHAPTER VIII

Of the excellency of oats, and the many singular virtues and uses of them in a family

1 Oats, although they are of all manner of grain the cheapest because of their generality, being a grain of that goodness and hardness that it will grow in any soil whatsoever, be it never so rich or never so poor, as if nature had made it the only loving companion and true friend to mankind, yet is it a grain of that singularity for the multiplicity of virtues, and necessary uses for the sustenance and support of the family, that not any other grain is to be compared with it; for if any other have equal virtue, yet it hath not equal value, and if equal value, then it wants many degrees of equal virtue: so that joining virtue and value together, no husband, housewife, or house-keeper whatsoever hath so true and worthy a friend as his oats are.

Virtue of oats to cattle.

2 To speak then first of the virtues of oats, as they accrue to cattle and creatures without door, and first to begin with the horse; there is not any food whatsoever that is so good, wholesome, and agreeable with the nature of a horse as oats are, being a provender in which he taketh such delight, that with it he feedeth, travaileth and doth any violent labour whatsoever with more courage and comfort than with any other food that can be invented, as all men know that have either use of it, or horses; neither doth the horse ever take surfeit of oats (if they be sweet and dry), for albeit he may well be glutted or stalled upon them (with indiscreet feeding) and so refuse them for a little time, yet he never surfeiteth, or any present sickness followeth after; whereas no other grain but glut a horse therewith, and instantly sickness will follow, which shows surfeit, and the danger is oft incurable: for we read in Italy, at the seige of Naples,[1]

of many hundred horses that died on the surfeit of wheat; at Rome also died many hundred horses of the plague, which by due proof was found to proceed from a surfeit taken of pease and vetches; and so I could run over all other grains, but it is needless, and far from the purpose I have to handle: suffice it, oats for horses are the best of all foods whatsoever, whether they be but only clean threshed from the straw, and so dried, or converted to oatmeal, and so ground and made into bread; oats boiled and given to a horse whilst they are cool and sweet are an excellent food for any horse in the time of disease, poverty, or sickness, for they scour[2] and fat exceedingly.

3   In the same nature that oats are for horses, so are they for the ass, mule, camel, or any other beast of burden.

4   If you will feed either ox, bull, cow, or any neat whatsoever to an extraordinary height of fatness, there is no food doth it so soon as oats doth, whether you give them in the straw, or clean threshed from the sheaf, and well winnowed; but the winnowed oat is the best, for by them I have seen an ox fed to twenty pound,[3] to twenty-four pound, and thirty pounds, which is a most unreasonable reckoning for any beast, only fame and the tallow hath been precious.

5

[*For sheep, goats, and hounds.*]

Sheep or goats may likewise be fed with oats, to as great price and profit as with pease, and swine are fed with oats, either in raw malt, or otherwise, to as great thickness as with any grain whatsoever; only they must have a few pease after the oats to harden the fat, or else it will waste, and consume in boiling. Now for holding swine, which are only to be preserved in good flesh, nothing is better than a thin mange[4] made of ground oats, whey, buttermilk, or other ordinary wash or swillings which either the dairy or kitchen affordeth; nor is there any more sovereign or excellent meat for swine in the time of sickness, than a mange made of ground oats and sweet whey, warmed lukewarm on the fire and mixed with the powder of raddle, or red ochre. Nay, if you will go to the matter of pleasure, there is not any meat so excellent for the feeding and wholesome keeping of a kennel of hounds, as the mange made of ground oats and scalding water, or of beef broth, or any other broth in which flesh hath been sodden;[5] if it be for the feeding, strengthening, and comforting of greyhounds, spaniels, or any other sort of tenderer dogs, there is no meat better than sheep's heads, hair and all, or other entrails of sheep chopped and well sodden, with good store of oatmeal.

6

[*For poultry.*]

Now for all manner of poultry, as cocks, capons, chickens of great size, turkeys, geese, ducks, swans, and such like, there is no food feedeth them better than oats, and if it be the young breed of any of those kinds, even from the first hatching or disclosing, till they be able to shift for themselves, there is no food better whatsoever than oatmeal grits,[6] or fine oatmeal, either simple of itself, or else mixed with milk, drink, or else new made urine.

Virtue of oats.

7

Thus much touching the virtues and quality of oats or oatmeal, as they are serviceable for the use of cattle and poultry. Now for the most necessary use thereof for man,[7] and the general support of the family, there is no grain in our knowledge answerable unto it; first, for the simple oat itself (excepting some particular physic helps, as frying them with sweet butter, and putting them in a bag, and very hot applied to the belly or stomach to avoid colic or windiness, and such like experiments) the most especial use which is made of them is for malt to make beer or ale of which it doth exceeding well, and maintaineth many towns and countries; but the oatmeal which is drawn from them, being the heart and kernel of the oat, is a thing of much rarer price and estimation; for to speak troth, it is, like salt, of such a general use that without it hardly can any family be maintained:

Making of oatmeal.

8

therefore I think it not much amiss to speak a word or two touching the making of oatmeal: you shall understand then that to make good and perfect oatmeal you shall first dry your oats exceeding well, and then put them on the mill, which may either be water-mill, wind-mill, or horse-mill (but the horse-mill is best) and no more but crush or hull them; that is, to carry the stones so large[8] that they may no more but crush the husk from the kernel: then you shall winnow the hulls from the kernels either with the wind or a fan, and finding them of an indifferent cleanness (for it is impossible to hull them all clean at the first) you shall then put them on again, and, making the mill go a little closer, run them through the mill again, and then winnow them over again, and such grits or kernels as are clean hulled and well cut you may lay by, and the rest you shall run through the mill again the third time, and so winnow them again, in which time all will be perfect, and the grits or full kernels will separate from the smaller oatmeal; for you shall understand that at this first making of oatmeal you shall ever have two sorts of oatmeals; that is, the full whole grit or kernel, and the small dust oatmeal: as for the coarse hulls or chaff that cometh from them, that also is worthy saving, for it is an excellent good horse provender for any plow or labouring horses, being mixed with either beans, pease, or any other pulse whatsoever.

9   *The virtues of oatmeal.*

Now for the use and virtues of these two several kinds of oatmeals in
maintaining the family, they are so many (according to the many customs
of many nations) that it is almost impossible to reckon all; yet (as near
as I can) I will impart my knowledge, and what I have ta'en from relation:[9]
first, for the small dust or meal oatmeal, it is that with which all pottage
is made and thickened, whether they be meat pottage, milk pottage, or
any thick or else thin gruel whatsoever, of whose goodness and wholesomeness it is needless to speak, in that it is frequent with every experience: also with this small oatmeal is made in divers countries six several
kinds of very good and wholesome bread, every one finer than other, as
your anacks, janacks,[10] and such like. Also there is made of it both thick
and thin oaten cakes, which are very pleasant in taste, and much esteemed:
but if it be mixed with fine wheat meal, then it maketh a most delicate
and dainty oatcake,[11] either thick or thin, such as no prince in the world
but may have them served to his table; also this small oatmeal mixed with
blood, and the liver of either sheep, calf or swine, maketh that pudding
which is called the haggas or haggus,[12] of whose goodness it is in vain to
boast, because there is hardly to be found a man that doth not affect
them. And lastly from this small oatmeal, by oft steeping it in water and
cleansing it, and then boiling it to a thick and stiff jelly, is made that
excellent dish of meat, which is so esteemed in the west parts of this
kingdom, which they call washbrew,[13] and in Cheshire and Lancashire
they call it flammery or flummery,[14] the wholesomeness and rare goodness, nay the very physic helps thereof being such and so many that I
myself have heard a very reverend and worthily renowned physician speak
more in the commendation of that meat than of any other food whatsoever: and certain it is that you shall not hear of any that ever did surfeit
of this washbrew or flummery; and yet I have seen them of very dainty
and sickly stomachs which have eaten great quantities thereof, beyond
the proportion of ordinary meats. Now for the manner of eating this
meat, it is of divers diversely used; for some eat it with honey, which is
reputed the best sauce; some with wine, either sack, claret or white; some
with strong beer or strong ale, and some with milk, as your ability, or
the accommodations of the place will administer. Now there is derived
from this washbrew another coarser meat, which is as it were the dregs
or grosser substance of the washbrew, which is called girtbrew,[15] which
is a well filling and sufficient meat, fit for servants and men of labour;
of the commendations whereof, I will not much stand, in that it is a meat
of harder digestion, and fit indeed but for strong able stomachs, and such
whose toil and much sweat both liberally spendeth evil humours, and
also preserveth men from the offence of fullness and surfeits.

10   *[Of oatmeal grits.]*

Now for the bigger kind of oatmeal, which is called grits, or corn oatmeal, it is of no less use than the former, nor are there fewer meats compounded thereof: for first, of these grits are made all sorts of puddings,[16] or pots (as the West Country terms them) whether they be black, as those which are made of the blood of beasts, swine, sheep, geese, red or fallow deer, or the like, mixed with whole grits, suet, and wholesome herbs: or else white, as when the grits are mixed with good cream, eggs, bread crumbs, suet, currants, and other wholesome spices. Also of these grits are made the Good Friday pudding, which is mixed with eggs, milk, suet, pennyroyal, and boiled first in a linen bag, and then stripped and buttered with sweet butter. Again, if you roast a goose, and stop her belly with whole grits, beaten together with eggs, and after mixed with the gravy, there cannot be a better or more pleasanter sauce: nay, if a man be at sea in any long travel, he cannot eat a more wholesome and pleasant meat than these whole grits boiled in water till they burst, and then mixed with butter, and so eaten with spoons; which although seamen call simply by the name of loblolly, yet there is not any meat how significant soever the name be, that is more toothsome or wholesome. And to conclude, there is no way or purpose whatsoever to which a man can use or employ rice, but with the same seasoning and order you may employ the whole grits of oatmeal, and have full as good and wholesome meat, and as well tasted: so that I may well knit up this chapter with this approbation of oatmeal, that the little charge and great benefit considered, it is the very crown of the housewife's garland, and doth more grace her table and her knowledge, than all grains whatsoever; neither indeed can any family or household be well and thriftily maintained, where this is either scant or wanting. And thus much touching the nature, worth, virtues, and great necessity of oats and oatmeal.

CHAPTER IX

Of the office of the brew-house, and the bake-house, and the necessary things belonging to the same

1

Of bread and drink.

When our English housewife knows how to preserve health by wholesome physic; to nourish by good meat, and to clothe the body with warm garments, she must not then by any means be ignorant in the provision of bread and drink; she must know both the proportions and compositions of the same. And forasmuch as drink is in every house more generally spent[1] than bread, being indeed (but how well I know not) made the very substance of all entertainment, I will first begin with it;

2

Diversities of drinks.

and therefore you shall know that generally our kingdom hath but two kinds of drinks, that is to say, beer and ale, but particularly four, as beer, ale, perry, and cider; and to these we may add two more, mead and metheglin,[2] two compound drinks of honey and herbs, which in the places where they are made, as in Wales and the Marches,[3] are reckoned for exceeding wholesome and cordial.

3

Strong beer.

To speak then of beer, although there be divers kinds of tastes and strength thereof, according to the allowance of malt, hops, and age given unto the same; yet indeed there can be truly said to be but two kinds thereof; namely, ordinary beer and March beer,[4] all other beers being derived from them.

4

Of ordinary beer.

Touching ordinary beer, which is that wherewith either nobleman,

Although the illustration is of brewing as a trade, not of the housewife's more modest establishment, it gives some idea of her equipment, and of the effective use of differing levels that Markham recommends. From Hans Sachs, *Eygentliche Beschreibung aller Stande auf Erden*, sig. Miii.

gentleman, yeoman, or husbandman shall maintain his family the whole year; it is meet first that our English housewife respect the proportion or allowance of malt due to the same, which amongst the best husbands is thought most convenient, and it is held that to draw from one quarter of good malt three hogsheads of beer is the best ordinary proportion that can be allowed, and having age and good cask to lie in, it will be strong enough for any goodman's drinking.[5]

Of brewing ordinary beer.

Now for the brewing of ordinary beer, your malt being well ground and put in your mash vat, and your liquor in your lead[6] ready to boil, you shall then by little and little with scoops or pails put the boiling liquor to the malt, and then stir it even to the bottom exceedingly well together (which is called the mashing of the malt) then, the liquor swimming in the top, cover all over with more malt, and so let it stand an hour and more in the mash vat, during which space you may if you please heat more liquor in your lead for your second or small drink; this done, pluck up your mashing strom,[7] and let the first liquor run gently from the malt, either in a clean trough or other vessels prepared for the purpose, and then stopping the mash vat again, put the second liquor to the malt and stir it well together; then your lead being emptied put your first liquor or wort therein, and then to every quarter of malt put a pound and a half of the best hops you can get, and boil them an hour together, till taking up a dishful thereof you see the hops shrink into the bottom of the dish; this done, put the wort through a straight sieve, which may drain the hops from it, into your cooler,[8] which, standing over the gyle vat,[9] you shall in the bottom thereof set a great bowl with your barm and some of the first wort (before the hops come into it) mixed together, that it may rise therein, and then let your wort drop or run gently into the dish with the barm which stands in the gyle vat; and this you shall do the first day of your brewing, letting your cooler drop all the night following, and some part of the next morning, and as it droppeth if you find that a black scum or mother riseth upon the barm, you shall with your hand take it off and cast it away; then nothing being left in the cooler, and the beer well risen, with your hand stir it about and so let it stand an hour after, and then, beating it and the barm exceeding well together, tun it up into the hogsheads being clean washed and scalded, and so let it purge:[10] and herein you shall observe not to tun your vessels too full, for fear thereby it purge too much of the barm away: when it hath purged a day and a night, you shall close up the bung holes with clay, and only for a day or two after keep a vent-hole in it, and after close it up as close as may be.

6   *[Of small beer.]*
Now for your second or small drink[11] which are left upon the grains, you shall suffer it there to stay but an hour or a little better and then drain it off also; which done, put it into the lead with the former hops and boil the other also, then clear it from the hops and cover it very close till your first beer be tunned, and then as before put it also to barm and so tun it up also in smaller vessels, and of this second beer you shall not draw above one hogshead to three of the better.[12] Now there be divers other ways and observations for the brewing of ordinary beer, but none so good, so easy, so ready, and quickly performed as this before showed: neither will any beer last longer or ripen sooner, for it may be drunk at a fortnight's age, and will last as long and lively.

7   *Of brewing the best March beer.*
Now for the brewing of the best March beer you shall allow to a hogshead thereof a quarter of the best malt well ground: then you shall

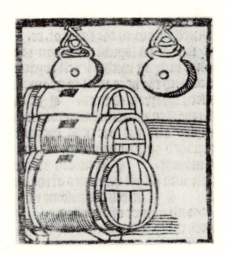

Barrels for beer, wine, or aqua vitae;
leather containers hang from the wall.
From Laurence Andrewe, *The
Vertuose Boke of Distillacyon*, sig. Xi.

take a peck of pease, half a peck of wheat, and half a peck of oats and
grind them all very well together, and then mix them with your malt:
which done, you shall in all points brew this beer as you did the former
ordinary beer; only you shall allow a pound and a half of hops to this
one hogshead: and whereas before you drew but two sorts of beer, so
now you shall draw three; that is a hogshead of the best, and a hogshead
of the second, and half a hogshead of small beer without any augmentation
of hops or malt.

8   This March beer would be brewed in the months of March or April,
and should (if it have right) lie a whole year to ripen: it will last two,
three and four years if it lie cool and close, and endure the drawing to
the last drop, though with never so much leisure.

9
Brewing of strong ale.
Now for the brewing of strong ale, because it is drink of no such long
lasting as beer is,[13] therefore you shall brew less quantity at a time thereof,
as two bushels of northern measure (which is four bushels or half a quarter
in the south) at a brewing, and not above, which will make fourteen
gallons of the best ale. Now for the mashing and ordering of it in the
mash vat, it will not differ anything from that of beer; as for hops,
although some use not to put in any, yet the best brewers thereof will
allow to fourteen gallons of ale a good espen[14] full of hops, and no more;
yet before you put in your hops, as soon as you take it from the grains
you shall put it into a vessel and change it, or blink[15] it in this manner:
put into the wort a handful of oak boughs and a pewter dish, and let
them lie therein till the wort look a little paler than it did at the first, and

then presently take out the dish and the leaf, and then boil it a full hour with the hops as aforesaid, and then cleanse it, and set it in vessels to cool; when it is no more but milk warm, having set your barm to rise with some sweet wort, then put all into the gyle vat, and as soon as it riseth, with a dish or bowl beat it in, and so keep it with continual beating a day and a night at least, and after tun it. From this ale you may also draw half so much very good middle ale, and a third part very good small ale.

10

Brewing of bottle ale.

Touching the brewing of bottle ale, it differeth nothing at all from the brewing of strong ale, only it must be drawn in a larger proportion, as at least twenty gallons of half a quarter;[16] and when it comes to be changed you shall blink it (as was before showed) more by much than was the strong ale, for it must be pretty and sharp, which giveth the life and quickness to the ale: and when you tun it,[17] you shall put it into round bottles with narrow mouths, and then stopping them close with cork, set them in a cold cellar up to the waist in sand, and be sure that the corks be fast tied in with strong pack-thread, for fear of rising out, or taking vent, which is the utter spoil of the ale. Now for the small drink arising from this bottle ale, or any other beer or ale whatsoever, if you keep it after it is blinked and boiled in a close vessel, and then put it to barm every morning as you have occasion to use it, the drink will drink a great deal the fresher, and be much more lively in taste.

A cider-mill (left) and a press for verjuice. From *The Universal Magazine of Knowledge and Pleasure* (London, September 1747), facing p. 178.

11

Of making perry or cider.

As for the making of perry and cider, which are drinks much used in the west parts, and other countries well stored with fruit in this kingdom;

you shall know that your perry is made of pears only, and your cider of apples; and for the manner of making thereof, it is done after one fashion; that is to say, after your pears or apples are well picked from the stalks, rottenness, and all manner of other filth, you shall put them in the press mill which is made with a millstone running round in a circle, under which you shall crush your pears or apples, and then, straining them through a bag of haircloth, tun up the same, after it hath been a little settled, into hogsheads, barrels, and other close vessels.[18]

12   Now after you have pressed all, you shall save that which is within the haircloth bag, and, putting it into several vessels, put a pretty quantity of water thereunto, and after it hath stood a day or two, and hath been well stirred together, press it over also again, for this will make a small perry or cider, and must be spent first. Now of your best cider, that which you make of your summer or sweet fruit, you shall call summer or sweet cider or perry, and that you shall spend first also; and that which you make of the winter and hard fruit you shall call winter and sour cider, or perry; and that you shall spend last, for it will endure the longest.

13

Of baking.

Thus after our English housewife is experienced in the brewing of these several drinks, she shall then look into her bakehouse, and to the baking of all sorts of bread, either for masters, servants, or hinds, and to the ordering and compounding of the meal for each several use.

14

Ordering of meal.

To speak then first of meals for bread, they are either simple or compound; simple as wheat and rye, or compound, as rye and wheat mixed together, or rye, wheat, and barley mixed together; and of these the oldest meal is ever the best, and yieldeth most so it be sweet and untainted; for the preservation whereof, it is meet that you cleanse your meal well from the bran, and then keep it in sweet vessels.

15

Of baking manchets.

Now for the baking of bread of your simple meals, your best and principal bread is manchet,[19] which you shall bake in this manner; first your meal, being ground upon the black stones if it be possible, which makes the whitest flour, and bolted through the finest bolting cloth, you shall put it into a clean kimnel,[20] and, opening the flour hollow in the midst, put into it of the best ale barm the quantity of three pints to a bushel of meal, with some salt to season it with: then put in your liquor reasonable warm and knead it very well together both with your hands and through the brake;[21] or for want thereof, fold it in a cloth, and with your feet tread it a good space together, then, letting it lie an hour or thereabouts to swell, take it forth and mould[22] it into manchets, round, and flat; scotch about the waist to give it leave to rise, and prick it with your knife in the top, and so put it into the oven, and bake it with a gentle heat.

16   *Of baking cheat bread.*[23]

To bake the best cheat bread, which is also simply of wheat only, you shall, after your meal is dressed and bolted through a more coarse bolter than was used for your manchets, and put also into a clean tub, trough, or kimnel, take a sour leaven, that is a piece of such like leaven saved from a former batch, and well filled with salt, and so laid up to sour, and this sour leaven you shall break in small pieces into warm water, and then strain it; which done, make a deep hollow hole, as was before said, in the midst of your flour, and therein pour your strained liquor; then with your hand mix some part of the flour therewith, till the liquor be as thick as pancake batter, then cover it all over with meal, and so let it lie all that night; the next morning stir it, and all the rest of the meal well together, and with a little more warm water, barm, and salt to season it with, bring it to a perfect leaven, stiff, and firm; then knead it, break it, and tread it, as was before said in the manchets, and so mould it up in reasonable big loaves, and then bake it with an indifferent good heat: and thus according to these two examples before showed, you may bake any bread leavened or unleavened whatsoever, whether it be simple corn,[24] as wheat or rye of itself, or compound grain as wheat and rye, or wheat, rye, and barley, or rye and barley, or any other mixed white corn; only, because rye is a little stronger grain than wheat, it shall be good for you to put to your water a little hotter than you did to your wheat.

17   *Baking of brown bread.*

For your brown bread, or bread for your hind servants, which is the coarsest bread for man's use,[25] you shall take of barley two bushels, of pease two pecks, of wheat or rye a peck, a peck of malt; these you shall grind all together and dress it through a meal sieve, then putting it into a sour trough set liquor on the fire, and when it boils let one put on the water, and another with a mash-rudder[26] stir some of the flour with it after it hath been seasoned with salt, and so let it be till the next day, and then, putting to the rest of the flour, work it up into a stiff leaven, then mould it and bake it into great loaves with a very strong heat: now if your trough be not sour enough to sour your leaven, then you shall either let it lie longer in the trough, or else take the help of a sour leaven with your boiling water: for you must understand, that the hotter your liquor is, the less will the smell or rankness of the pease be received. And thus much for the baking of any kind of bread, which our English housewife shall have occasion to use for the maintenance of her family.

18   *General observations in the brew-house and bake-house.*

As for the general observations to be respected in the brew-house or bake-house, they be these: first, that your brew-house be seated in so convenient a part of the house, that the smoke may not annoy your other more private rooms; then that your furnace be made close and hollow for saving fuel, and with a vent for the passage of smoke lest it taint your liquor; then that you prefer a copper before a lead, next that your mash vat be ever nearest to your lead, your cooler nearest your mash vat, and your gyle vat under your cooler, and adjoining to them all several clean tubs to receive your worts and liquors: then in your bake-house you shall have a fair bolting house with large pipes[27] to bolt meal in, fair troughs to lay leaven in, and sweet safes to receive your bran: you shall have bolters, searces, ranges, and meal sieves of all sorts both fine and coarse; you shall have fair tables to mould on, large ovens to bake in, the soles thereof rather of one or two entire stones than of many bricks, and the mouth made narrow, square, and easy to be close covered: as for your peels,[28] coal-rakes, malkins,[29] and such like, though they be necessary yet
they are of such general use they need no further relation. And thus
much for a full satisfaction to all husbands and housewives
of this kingdom touching brewing, baking,
and all what else appertaineth
to either of their offices.

FINIS

Appendix

"The Husbandman's House"

From Markham's *The English Husbandman* (1613)

Here you behold the model of a plain country man's house, without plaster or imbosture [ornamentation], because it is to be intended that it is as well to be built of stud and plaster, as of lime and stone, or if timber be not plentiful it be built of coarser wood, and covered with lime and hair; yet if a man would bestow cost in this model, the four inward corners of the hall would be convenient for four turrets, and the four gavel [gable] ends, being thrust out with bay windows might be formed in any curious manner: and where I place a gate and a plain pale [paling fence], might be either a terrace, or a gatehouse, of any fashion whatsoever; besides all those windows which I make plain might be made bay windows, either with battlements, or without: but the scope of my book tendeth only to the use of the honest husbandman, and not to instruct men of dignity, who in architecture are able wonderfully to control me; therefore that the husbandman may know the use of this facsimile, he shall understand it by this which followeth.

A. Signifieth the great hall.
B. The dining parlour for entertainment of strangers [visitors].
C. An inward closet within the parlour for the mistress' use, for necessaries.
D. A stranger's lodging within the parlour.
E. A staircase into the rooms over the parlour.
F. A staircase into the goodman's rooms over the kitchen and buttery.
G. The screen in the hall.
H. An inward cellar within the buttery, which may serve for a larder.
I. The buttery.
K. The kitchen, in whose range may be placed a brewing lead, and convenient ovens, the brewing vessels adjoining.

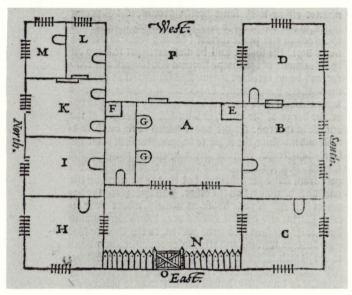

L. The dairy house for necessary business.
M. The milkhouse.
N. A fair sawn pale before the foremost court.
P. A place where a pump would be placed to serve the offices of the house.

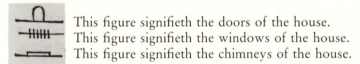 This figure signifieth the doors of the house.
This figure signifieth the windows of the house.
This figure signifieth the chimneys of the house.

Now you shall further understand that on the South side of your house, you shall plant your garden and orchard, as well for the prospect thereof to all your best rooms, as also your house will be a defence against the northern coldness, whereby your fruits will much better prosper. You shall on the west side of your house, within your inward dairy and kitchen court, fence in a large base court, in the midst whereof would be a fair large pond, well stoned and gravelled in the bottom, in which your cattle may drink, and horses when necessity shall urge be washed; for I do by no means allow washing of horses after instant labour. Near to this pond you shall build your dovecote, for pigeons delight much in the water; and you shall by no means make your dove house too high, for pigeons cannot endure a high mount, but you shall build it moderately, clean, neat, and close, with water pentisses [over-hanging eaves] to keep away vermin. On the north side of your base court you shall build your stables, ox-house, cow-house, and swinecotes, the doors and windows opening all on the south. On the south side of the base court, you shall build your hay barns, corn barns, pullen-houses for hens, capons, ducks, geese; your French kiln, and malting floors, with such like necessaries: and over cross betwixt both these sides you shall build your bound hovels [connected sheds], to carry your pease, of good and sufficient timber, under which you shall place when they are out of use your carts, wains, tumbrels [dung carts], ploughs, harrows, and such like, together with plough timber and axletrees [frames and axles], all which should very carefully be kept from wet, which of all things doth soonest rot and consume them. And thus much of the husandman's house, and the necessaries thereto belonging. (Sigs. A4v–B1v.)

Collation

1: Edition of 1615 (Poynter 23.1)
2: Edition of 1623 (Poynter 34.1)
3: Edition of 1631 (Poynter 34.5)

For textual history, see Introduction, p. liv. Only substantive variants involving a significant shift in meaning are recorded. Readings of the copy-text (*3*) are followed by a square bracket. References are to paragraph numbers.

[CHAPTER I]

(*The paragraphs in this chapter were reorganized between editions 1 and 2; this edition follows the latter order as in 2 and 3.*)

[Heading] And first … purposes.] *om. 1*

[2] they ought *ed.*: only they ought *1, 2, 3*

[4] adversities *1*: adversaries *2, 3*

[5] cleanly *1*: *om. 2, 3*

[7] in the ensuing discourse] *om. 1, 2*

[8] art] science *1, 2*

    load her mind *1653*: lead her minde *1, 2, 3*

    by two excellent … knowledge] *om. 1, 2*

    common experience *1, 2*: common and ordinary experience *3*

[15] incivilly *ed.*: insiuelly *1, 2*; infinitely *3*

    as hereafter said *ed.*: as beforesaid *1, 2*; as hereafter *3*

[17] To cure … endure it. *1*: *om. 2, 3*

[18] ague] again *1*

    because many times *1, 2*: *om. 3*

    laid to the soles … cloths *1, 2*: *om. 3*

[19] and manifest] *om. 1, 2*

[20] dewition *1, 2*: decoction *3*

    pour it into water *ed.*: power it into water *1*; pouder it in water *2*; put it in water *3*

[21] as on a nosegay, to the *1*: on a nose-gay to the *2*; on a nose-gay made of the *3*

[22] your feet ... keep him *1*: your feet, after you ... the sicke person ... keepe him *2*; your feet, after you ... compel your selfe to sweat, which if you do, keep your selfe *3*

    live pigeon *1*: little pigeon *2, 3*

[23-8] *om. 1*

[23] at once *2*: *om. 3*

[25] briar leaves or] Bryer leaves, of *2*

[29] woman's] worme *1, 2*

[33] mix it *1*: mixt *2, 3*

[34] dewition *1, 2*: decoction *3*

[36] skirret *ed.*: Sheruit *1, 2, 3*

    an ounce, of liquorice *ed.*: an ounce of Licoras *1, 2, 3*

    offendeth *1, 2*: taketh *3*

[42] digestion] discretion *1*

    coarse marjoram *1, 2*: Maioram *3*

[46] siled] stll'd *1, 2*; syled *3*; filled *1653*

[52] quinancy *ed.*: Quiuarie *1*; Quinarie *2*; Quinacy *3*

[56-88] *om. 1*

[65] of the green] *om. 2*

[77] very well] *om. 2*

[79] tutia *2*: Tussia *3*

[80] euphrasy *ed.*: Eusaace *2, 3*

[85] skim] slyme *2*

[88] little] *om. 2*

    every] *om. 2*

    good handfull] handfull *2*

[94-7] *om. 1*

[97] quick *2*: hot *3*

[102] Another ... whatsoever *1*: *om. 2, 3*

[104] caudle *1*: *om. 2, 3*

[110-16] *om. 1*

[111] upper] ouer *2*

[112] garlic] Garbycke *2*; Garcicke *3*; Garlick *1653*

[113] and mix it with] *om. 2*

[114] list,] lyst, two or three, *2*

[117] dauke, *ed. following Banckes*: darke *1, 2, 3*

[118] half a handful *1*: a handfull *2, 3*

[121–6] *om. 1*
[127] take nutmegs *2*: take large Nutmegs *1*; take a Nutmeg *3*
[132] so is the jaw bones ... whatsoever] *om. 1, 2*
[133] rule *1, 2*: cure *3*
  them distilled *1, 2*: the hearbes distil'd *3*
[134] fenugreek *ed.*: Fenicreete *1, 2, 3*
[135] navel and] navel or *1, 2*
[136–44] *om. 1*
[142, 143] *For the wind colic ... For the stopping of the womb*
  Headings reversed in *2*
[142] milk with alum] allom milke *2*
[143] taken] an enemy *2*
[144] polypody of the oak *ed.*: Polipode, of the oake *2, 3*
  heal] breake *2*
[145] diffuse or *1*: *om. 2, 3*
[148] every one of them a like *1*: each one of them a little *2, 3*
[158] *strangury ed.*: Strangullion *1, 2, 3*
[160] in a morning] *om. 1, 2*
[161–5] *om. 1*
[165] and stamp ... strain them *2*: *om. 3*
[168] above *1*: about *2, 3*
[169] *om. 1*
[175] dittander *Banckes, 1653*: vitander *1, 2, 3*
[177–85] *om. 1*
[178] the flowers witholden in women *2*: womens Termes *3*
[179] to drink up] drink *2*
  dewition *2*: decoction *3*
[188] thin pieces *1*: peeces *2, 3*
[189] worn *1*: warme *2, 3*
[190] For the hot gout ... ease. *1*: *om. 2, 3*
[194] There be divers others which] Others *1, 2*
  very clean] *om. 1, 2*
[195] bathe *ed.*: hath *1*; *om. 2*; wash *3*
[200] *Privy parts burned ... it will cure it. 1: follows paragraph 198 in
  2, 3*
[201] thick *1, 2*: good *3*
[205] red lead] white lead *1, 2*
[208–48] *om. 1*
[208] good quarter of a pound] quarter of a pound *2*
  ground ivy] ground, iuye *2*
[210] germanders] Germaunders dyrte *2*
[221] *tetter or serpigo ed.: or tetter serpego 2, 3*

[227] opoponax] Apponaxe *2*; Apopanax *3*
ammoniacum ed.: Ammonianum *2, 3*
clarified clean *2*: clarified *3*
[230] made] mayden *2*
[240] *joints] bones 2*
[241] wine] *om. 2*
[246] mix it *ed.*: mixt *2, 3*
[253] all summer *1, 2: om. 3*
[254] after distil it through a limbeck, then] *om. 1, 2*
beer] Bread *1*
[255–8] *om. 1*
[CHAPTER II]
[Heading] as sallats ... feasts *2 continues* Also Distillations, Perfumes,
conceited Secrets, and preserving Wine of all sorts.
[2] true labour] labour *2*
[4] (and later) cabbage–lettuce *ed.*: Cabadge, Lettice *1, 2, 3*
[5] In the month of April ... parsnips *ed., following Surflet: wrongly
placed by all eds. in paragraph 8*
[7] holy] *om. 1, 2*
[9] quarter] *om. 1, 2*
[19] *Sallats ... only 1: om. 2, 3*
[24] walnut tree] Wall-nut *1, 2*
dissolved or] *om. 1, 2* or relish] *om. 1, 2*
[25] very sweet seam] sweete seame *1, 2*
consume or decay] decay *1, 2*
[29] and cover it with sugar *1, 2: om. 3*
[31–9] *om. 1*
[32] very sweet and] *om. 2*
[34] a dozen or fourteen] ten or twelue *2*
very well] well *2*
white grated bread] grated bread *2*
very small shred] small shred *2*
plenty] store *2*
and stirred] *om. 2*
[38] bread-grater] great bread-grater *2*
[37] sorrel *ed.*: Sollell *2*; Sarnell *3*
pieces *1653*: peyres *2, 3*
[39] very self same] same *2*
sharp] *om. 2* broiled *ed.*: boiled *2, 3*
[40] endive *1: om. 2, 3*
[43] washed *ed.*: wash *1, 2, 3*
whole endive, whole succory *1*: endiue, succory *2, 3*

[47] (twice) olla podrida *ed.*: Olepotrige *1, 2, 3*
  whole boiled herbs *ed.*: wholeboiled hearbes, and the hearbes *1, 2, 3*
[48] very dainty sippets] sippets *1, 2*
  to the table] *om. 1, 2*
[49] walm *1, 2*: boil *3*
[50] in which it lay to the gravy *1, 2*: in, and put in likewise the
  grauie *3*
[53] spices.] spices: and thus much for broths & boild meats. *1, 2 (see
  paragraph 58)*
[54–8] *om. 1*
[54] summer] some *2*
  edges *ed.*: Egges *2*; edge *3*
[55] barberries *ed.*: Barberberries *2*; Barbery-berries *3*
[58] And thus... meats *1, 2*: *om. 3 (see paragraph 53)*
[59] (twice) meats.] *meates and carbonadoes 1, 2*
[65] rareness *1, 2*: rawnes *3*
  smoke] stroke *1, 2*
  ascendeth] offendeth *1, 2*
  then is the meat enough] *om. 1, 2*
[66] a loin *1*: a lone *2*
  alone *3*
  edges *ed.*: egges *1, 2*; edge *3*
[74] good soaking *1, 2*: soaking *3*
[75] first stop it all over *1, 2*: stop it *3*
[77–8] *om. 1*
[77] cow's] Calues *2*
[85] pulers *1, 2*: Puets *3*
[87] The sauce] The same *1, 2*
[88] (twice) *A galantine or*] *om. 1, 2*
[91–4] *om. 1*
[96] Inns] skinne *1, 2*
[97] much] most *1*
[99–107] *om. 1*
[101] chevin *ed.*: cheain *2, 3*
  slit *2*: *om. 3*
[102] sole *ed.*: soale *2, 3*
[113] pricked *1*: pickt *3*
  To prevent ... be firm] *om. 1, 2*
[117–45] *om. 1*
[122] *Norfolk*] *om. 2*
[126] mere *2*: meat *3*
[128] of the flesh *ed.*: of the best flesh *2*; of flesh *3*

[131] range or] raunger *2*
[134] cover all] cover all well *2*
[137] and rolled ... the dish *2*: *om. 3*
[140] and cinnamon] cinamon *2*
[142] and as this ... pure] *om. 2*
[154] steam] teane *1*
[156] off the veil *ed.*: of the veill *1, 2*; off the froth *3*
[157] Coriander seedes] *om. 1, 2*
    a little cream] a little cream and a few coriander seeds clean rubbed
    1, 2
[158] and also coriander seed.] *om. 1, 2*
[167] knops *1, 2*: tops *3*
[170] hips *ed.*: heapps *1, 2*; Hepps *3*
[172] good barm *2*: barm *3*
[179–89] *om. 1*
[179] butter, a pound of *2*: butter *3*
    a little mace and good store of water to] one ounce of Mace, and so
    much Rose-water as will *2*
[183] be preserued] keep *2*
[184] high coloured] ill coloured *2*
[189] *To candy any root* ... stand till they candy.] *om. 1, 2*
[191–3] *om. 1*
[192] [*near end*] all fish baked *2*: *om. 3*
[193] [*near end*] entertainments *2*: contentments *3*
[CHAPTER III]
[Heading] *CHAPTER* ... *perfuming.*] *Of divers conceited secrets. 1*;
    om. 2
[2] *distillations 1, 2*: *om. 3*
[3–21] *om. 1*
[6] put the ale *ed.*: put into the Ale *2, 3*
[7] of hyssop half a handful *2*: *om. 3*
[10] *sometime ed.*: sometimes *2, 3*
    steep *2*: keep *3*
[11] lap] lay *2*
[16] hearing *ed.*: hearynge *Banckes*; the heary ago *2*; old age *3*
[33–8] *om. 1*
[35] dandelion [and] tansy *ed.*: Mandelion-tansey *2, 3*
[36] labdanum *ed.*: Baldamum *2, 3*
[CHAPTER IV]
[Entire chapter] *om. 1*
[Heading] *CHAPTER IV* ... it is necessary, etc.] *om. 2*
[3] beat them well together] beate them together *2*
[4] will not *Sloane 3692*: *om. 2, 3*

[21] and a half in gauge *ed.*: in gadge and a half *2, 3*
[24] Gascon] Gaswine *2*
[32] *For white wine ... lie ed.: follows paragraph 31 in 2*
[CHAPTER V]
[Heading] CHAPTER V] CHAP. III *1, 2 and dying of colours*] *om.* *1*
   with all ... thereto] *om.* *1*
[1] outwardly for defence *1, 2*: for defence *3*
[7] after, dry it] *om.* *1, 2*
[10] which is a very good colour] *om.* *1, 2*
[12] your wool] your worke *1, 2*
[21] filling] fulling *1, 2*
24] Axham] Apham *1, 2*
[38] market *1*: maker *2, 3*
[39] harden *ed.*: harding *1, 2, 3*
[41] open the rolls *1*: open the roler *2, 3*
[45] middling *ed.*: midlen *1, 2, 3*
[48] ob. *1, 12*: pound *3*
[CHAPTER VI]
[Heading] CHAPTER VI] CHAP. III *1, 2*
[3] pay *ed.*: ay *1*; any *2, 3*
[5] though our nation *ed.*: through our nation *1, 2*; through our nation,
   it *3*
   a little book *1, 2*: the former booke *3*
[7] not to be found fault with] much, and not to be found fault with
   1, 2
[11] and continue ... rear not up *1, 2*: *om.* *3*
[17] siledish] syle *1, 2*
   most cream] best creame *1, 2*
[27] shred *1, 2*: spread *3*
[29] and pot the next ... full] *om.* *1, 2*
[30] barrel] larraill *1, 2*
[35] aftermath] after much *1, 2*
[38] [*near end*] lay on the cheese board *ed.*: to lay on the cheese-board
   1, 2, 3
[39] cheese heck] presse *1, 2*
[41] siled *ed.*: fil'd *1, 2, 3*
[CHAPTER VII]
[Entire chapter] *om.* *1*
[Heading] CHAPTER VII] CHAP. V. *2*
[5] receiving of the malt] flourishing of the Malt *2*
[6] [*end*] in the time of any frost] in the time of any violent frost *2*
[12] frame of the house] frame of *2*
[13] whole kingdom] Kingdome *2*

[16] accord to the old proverb *ed.*: according to the old Prouerbe *2, 3*
[19] Next to these is] Next to *2*
[22] stone cistern] *om. 2*
[26] closer *2*: looser *3*
[28] reed] red *2*
   sack] stack *2*
[33] *oatmalt ed.*: *oatmeal 2, 3*
[CHAPTER VIII]
[Entire chapter] *om. 1*
[Heading] CHAPTER VIII *ed.*: CHAP. VI. *2, 3*
[5] no meat better] no meat *2*
[9] [*near end*] girtbrew *2*: *Gird brew 3*
[CHAPTER IX]
[Heading] CHAPTER IX *ed.*: CHAP. V. *1*; CHAP. VII *2*; Chap. 8. *3*
[1] *Of bread and drink 1*: *om. 2, 3*
[2] reckoned] renowned *1, 2*
[7] if it have right lie *1*: (if it have rightlie *2*; –(if it haue right) haue *3*
   the drawing] then dropping *1, 2*
[8] no more but milkwarm *1, 2*: milke-warme *3*
[12] baking *1, 2*: making *3*
[14] scotch] scorcht *1*
[15] wheat, rye and barley *1*: wheat and barley *2, 3*

Notes

1 Markham's own phrase; see the letter to Thomas Markham quoted below.
2 F.N.L. Poynter, *A Bibliography of Gervase Markham, 1568?–1637* (Oxford: Oxford Bibliographical Society, 1962), p. 8. The summary of Markham's life which follows is indebted to Poynter's work; see also his article "Gervase Markham," *Essays and Studies*, xv (1962), 27–39, and his PH.D. thesis, "The Life and Work of Gervase Markham, 1568(?)–1637" (University of London, 1955), p. 3. A more general study, providing insight into the background to the decline of such families as the Markhams, is found in Lawrence Stone's *The Crisis of the Aristocracy, 1558–1641* (Oxford: Clarendon Press, 1965; abridged edition, 1967).
3 "Francis Markham, second son of Robert Markham of Cotham, born 7[th year] of Elizabeth [i.e. 1565] on a Wednesday at afternoon between 10 and 11, July 25. First brought up at my Lord of Pembroke's ... Brought up after 10 years with Bilson, school-master of Winchester ... After, I was put to Hadrian de Saravia at Southampton, a schoolmaster ... then my Lord put me to one Malin, a lewd fellow, schoolmaster of Paul's. Then, 1582, my Lord put me to Trinity College in Cambridge ... My tutor dying, left me with Dr Gray. I contemned him and went to seas. Whereat my Lord was angry and cut off my pension." *Markham Memorials*, pp. 58–9. The quotation in the text which follows is from the same source.
4 *Markhams Farewell to Husbandry* (1620), p. 3.
5 *Devoreux* (1597), *Rodomonths Infernall* (1607), and *The Most Famous Historie of Mervine* (1612).
6 From his suit to the Court of Requests concerning the debt owed him by "thirty-nine defendants, chiefly actors"; the complete document is recorded by C.W. Wallace, *Jahrbuch der Deutschen Shakespeare Gesellschaft*, xlvi (Berline-Schoneberg, 1910), 345–50.

7 See Poynter, p. 14 and note; the comment is made in a letter from Sir Robert Sidney to Gervase's cousin, Sir John Harington.

8 Quoted Poynter, p. 16; the letter was replying to Thomas Markham.

9 The long, unpublished narrative poem *The Newe Metamorphosis* was written between 1600 and 1614 or 1615; *The Famous Whore* was published in 1609 (*Rodomonths Infernall*, though published in 1607, was written earlier).

10 On the general subject of literature and puritanism in domestic life, see Levin L. Schucking, *The Puritan Family: A Social Study from the Literary Sources*, trans. Brian Battershaw (London: Routledge and Kegan Paul, 1969). Puritan distrust of literature was notorious; a recent study is Russell Fraser, *The War Against Poetry* (Princeton: Princeton University Press, 1970).

11 Quoted by Poynter, p. 23.

12 From the records in the Court of Requests (see n. 6 above).

13 See Don Cameron Allen, *Francis Meres' Treatise "Poetrie": A Critical Edition* (Urbana, Ill.: University of Illinois Press, 1933), p. 92: "As *Nonnus Panapolyta* writ the Gospel of Saint *John* in Greek Hexameters, *Iervis Markham* hath written *Salomons Canticles* in English Verse" (i.e. *The Poem of Poems*, 1595).

14 *Hobsons Horseload of Letters*, a work midway between instruction and fiction, was reissued in a second, substantially enlarged edition.

15 See Robert S. Gittings, *Shakespeare's Rival* (London: Heinemann, 1960).

16 Details are found in Poynter, p. 38; a summary of the positive criticism on these lines is found on pp. 43–4 of Poynter's work.

17 See Poynter for the complete list of Markham's works.

18 One article on Markham, Charles F. Mullet, "Gervase Markham, Scientific Amateur," *Isis*, xxxv (1944), 106–18, is almost wholly given over to quotations of Markham's title-pages.

19 Those relatively few words from *The English Housewife* which are not recorded in the *OED*, or which have some significance so far as date is concerned, are marked with an asterisk in the glossary. The *OED* quotes *The English Housewife* with remarkable frequency. See also the *Dictionary of Early English*, ed. Joseph T. Shipley (London: Peter Owen, 1957).

20 See vii, 16; vii, 19; vii, 21 and notes, for example.

21 A prime example is Sir Frederick Smith, *The Early History of Veterinary Literature* (London: Baillière, Tindall & Cox, 1913–33); see vol. i. Smith castigates Markham for his "superstition," at the same time revealing a remarkable ignorance of seventeenth-century medical practice (see the note to "cat's tails," i, 208), and, in the same "irresponsible manner" (Poynter, p. 1), accuses Markham of plagiarism and opportunism.

22 The final edition of *The English Housewife* in which Markham had a hand (1631) contains two passages added to acknowledge his debt to the manuscripts of others in the chapters on medicine and wine (i, 8 and iv, 1 of this edition).

23 A fuller discussion of the manuscript tradition which lies behind this chapter is found in my article, "The Mystery of Vintners," *Agricultural History*, l (1976), 362–76.

24 *Here begynneth a new matter, the which sheweth and treateth of ye vertues and proprytes of herbes, the which is called an Herball* (London:

R. Banckes, 1525). A full discussion of the use made by Markham of this herbal is found in my article "Medical Use of a Sixteenth-Century Herbal," *Bulletin of the History of Medicine*, liii (1979), 449–58.

25 See i, 30, 47, 48, 117, and the accompanying notes. Detailed demonstration of this method of compilation is provided in "Medical Use of a Sixteenth-Century Herbal."

26 *Cavelarice*, bk. 7, p. 74.

27 A good example of his scepticism is found in the remedy "For the falling sickness," taken from the Banckes herbal, i, 37.

28 The study of women in the Renaissance has recently become both more active and more sceptical of received opinion. A useful bibliographical summary of works relevant to women in the period is the chapter "Women in an Age of Transition, 1485–1714" by Rosemary Musek in *The Women of England from Anglo-Saxon Times to the Present*, ed. Barbara Kanner (Hamden, Conn.: Archon Books, 1979); see also Michael Macdonald, *Bibliography on the Family from the Fields of Theology and Philosophy* (Ottawa: Vanier Institute of the Family, 1964), and *Chaste, Silent & Obedient: English Books for Women, 1475–1640* (San Marino, Calif.: Huntington Library, 1982), by Suzanne W. Hull. Perhaps the best introduction to the subject is through studies of the literature. The most thorough and most readable of the recent works is *Women and the English Renaissance: Literature and the Nature of Womankind, 1540–1620* by Linda Woodbridge (Urbana and Chicago: University of Illinois Press, 1984). Several other recent works deal with the image of women found in Renaissance literature: Katharine Rogers, *The Troublesome Helpmeet: A History of Misogyny in Literature* (Seattle and London: University of Washington Press, 1966), and Catherine M. Dunn, "The Changing Image of Woman in Renaissance Society and Literature," in *What Manner of Woman: Essays in English and American Society and Literature*, ed. Marlene Springer (New York: New York University Press, 1977), pp. 15–38. Studies specifically concerned with Shakespeare are Juliet Duisenberre, *Shakespeare and the Nature of Women* (London: Macmillan, 1975); Linda Bamber, *Comic Women, Tragic Men: A Study in Gender and Genre in Shakespeare* (Stanford: Stanford University Press, 1982); Ann Jennalie Cook, "Wooing and Wedding: Shakespeare's Dramatic Distortion of the Customs of His Time," in *Shakespeare's Art from a Comparative Aspect*, ed. Wendell M. Aycock (Lubbock: Texas Tech Press, 1981); Marilyn French, *Shakespeare's Division of Experience* (New York: Summit Books, 1981); Lisa Jardine, *Still Harping on Daughters* (Totowa, N.J.: Barnes and Noble, 1983); Coppelia Kahn, *Man's Estate: Masculine Identity in Shakespeare* (Berkeley: University of California Press, 1981); Marianne Novy, *Love's Argument: Gender Relations in Shakespeare* (Chapel Hill: University of North Carolina Press, 1984); and the collection *The Woman's Part: Feminist Criticism of Shakespeare*, ed. Carolyn R.S. Lenz and others (Urbana: University of Illinois Press, 1980), which also includes an extensive bibliography. Joan M. Ferrante, *Woman as Image in Medieval Literature* (New York: Columbia University Press, 1975), and Andrée Kahn Blumstein, *Misogyny and Idealization in the Courtly Romance* (Bonn: Herbert Grundmann, 1977), throw light on the attitudes that prevailed in literature before the Renaissance. A study of

a more general nature is Natalie Zemon Davis, "Women on Top: Symbolic Sexual inversion and Political Disorder in Early Modern Europe," in *The Reversible World* ed. Barbara A. Babcock, (Ithaca, N.Y.: Cornell University Press, 1978). Two recent works argue that women did not effectively participate in the Renaissance: "Did Women Have a Renaissance," by Joan Kelly-Gadol, in *Becoming Visible: Women in European History*, ed. Renate Bridenthal and Claudia Koonz (Boston: Houghton Mifflin, 1977), pp. 137–64; and *The Underside of History: A View of Women Through Time*, by Elise Boulding (Boulder, Col.: Westview Press, 1976), chapter x.

The best of the earlier studies is Carroll Camden, *The Elizabethan Woman* (London: Cleavery-Hume, 1952); see, for similar studies, Barbara Winchester, *Tudor Family Portrait* (London: Jonathan Cape, 1955), two books by Christina Hole, *English Home Life*, 1500–1800 (London: Batsford, 1947), and *The English Housewife in the Seventeenth Century* (London: Chatto & Windus, 1953); and Lu Emily Pearson, *Elizabethans at Home* (Stanford, Calif.: Stanford University Press, 1957). Alice Clark, *Working Life of Women in the Seventeenth Century* (New York: Harcourt, Brace and Rowe, 1920), offers insight into the economic value of the work performed by women; see also Louise A. Tilly and Joan W. Scott, *Women, Work, and Family* (New York: Holt, Rinehart and Winston, 1978), Mary R. Beard, *Women as a Force in History* (New York: Macmillan, 1946), particularly ch. x, and Hannelore Sachs, *The Renaissance Woman* (New York: McGraw-Hill, 1971), trans. Marianne Herzfield.

Information about the life of an English housewife in the sixteenth and early seventeenth centuries can be found in such comprehensive studies of popular culture as Louis B. Wright, *Middle Class Culture in Elizabethan England* (Chapel Hill: University of North Carolina Press, 1935); Peter Laslett, *The World We Have Lost* (London: Methuen, 1971), Muriel St. Clare Byrne, *Elizabethan Life in Town and Country* (London: Methuen, 1961); and the still useful *Shakespeare's England*, 2 vols., ed. C.T. Onions (Oxford: Clarendon Press, 1917). The various writings of G.E. and K.R. Fussell deal with rural history as it touches the housewife, particularly *The English Countrywoman* (New York: Benjamin Blom, 1971; reprint of 1953 ed.). Biographical accounts of representative Tudor women are provided by Pearl Hogrefe in *Tudor Women: Commoners and Queens* (Ames, Iowa: Iowa University Press, 1975), and *Women of Action in Tudor England* (Ames, Iowa: Iowa University Press, 1975). The life of aristocratic women is dealt with in Ruth Kelso, *Doctrine for the Lady of the Renaissance* (Urbana: University of Illinois Press, 1956).

Specialized studies of pamphlets and advice books are Christine W. Sizemore, "Early Seventeenth-Century Advice Books: The Female Viewpoint," *South Atlantic Bulletin*, xli (1976), 41–8; W. Lee Ustick, "Advice to a Son: A Type of Seventeenth-Century Conduct Book," *Studies in Philology*, xxix (1932), 409–41; see also G.E. Noyes, *Bibliography of Courtesy and Conduct Books in Seventeenth-Century England* (New Haven, Conn.: Tuttle, Morehouse and Taylor Co., 1937), and John C. Bean, "Passion Versus Friendship in the Tudor Matrimonial Handbooks and Some Shakespearian Implications," *Wascana Review*, ix (1974), 231–40.

There is a summary of the controversy both attacking and defending women, begun by Joseph Swetnam in 1622, in *Swetnam the Woman-hater: The Controversy and the Play*, ed. Coryll Crandall (Lafayette, Ind.: Purdue University Studies, 1969); see also Woodbridge, *Women of the English Renaissance*. A discussion of those activities by women which did not follow convention is found in S.C. Shapiro, "Feminists in Elizabethan England," *History Today*, xxvii (1977), 703–11.

A survey of attitudes towards marriage in the period is provided by Chilton Latham Powell, *English Domestic Relations, 1487–1653* (New York: Columbia University Press, 1917): see also Lawrence Stone, *The Family, Sex and Marriage in England, 1500–1800* (London: Weidenfeld and Nicolson, 1977); the contributions by Peter Laslett to the volume edited by him, *Household and Family in Past Time* (Cambridge: Cambridge University Press, 1972); the same author's *Family Life and Illicit Love in Earlier Generations* (Cambridge: Cambridge University Press, 1977); Allan Mc-Farlane *The Family Life of Ralph Josselin* (Cambridge: Cambridge University Press, 1970); Edward Shorter, *The Making of the Modern Family* (London: Collins, 1976); Edmund S. Morgan, *The Puritan Family: Religious and Domestic Relations in Seventeenth-Century New England*, Boston, 1966 (rev. ed.); and A.L. Rowse, *Simon Forman: Sex and Society in Shakespeare's Age* (London: Weidenfeld and Nicolson, 1974).

Beliefs held about women in Renaissance theological, medical, philosophical, and legal texts are explored in *The Renaissance Notion of Women* by Ian Maclean (Cambridge: Cambridge University Press, 1980). A glimpse of the persistence of human nature in the face of official doctrine is provided by F.G. Emmison in his summary of the Essex archidiaconal records, *Elizabethan Life: Morals and the Church Courts* (Chelmsford: Essex County Council, 1973).

29 See Roland M. Frye, "The Teachings of Classical Puritanism on Conjugal Love," *Studies in the Renaissance*, ii (1955), 148–59, and the article by Bean cited in note 28.

30 See Ivy Pinchbeck and Margaret Hewitt, *Children in English Society from Tudor Times to the Eighteenth-Century* (London: Routledge and Kegan Paul, 1969), vol. 1; see also Ariès, Phillipe, *Centuries of Childhood*, trans. Robert Baldrick (London: Jonathan Cape, 1962); Lloyd de Mause (ed.), *The History of Childhood* (New York: Harper and Row, 1975); and Boyd M. Berry, "The First English Pediatricians and Tudor Attitudes Toward Childhood," *Journal of the History of Ideas*, xxxv (1974), 561–77.

31 The housewife's status is discussed below.

32 *Diary of Lady Margaret Hoby, 1599–1605*, ed. Dorothy M. Meads (London: Routledge and Sons, 1930).

33 Christopher Hill, in *Society and Puritanism in Pre-Revolutionary England* (London: Secker and Warburg, 1964), gives other examples of this belief; see ch. xiii, "The Spiritualization of the Household," particularly p. 451.

34 The poor are mentioned again in vi, 3, where Markham indicates that inferior barley grown on sandy soil is suitable only "for the poor and in such places where better is not to be gotten."

35 See ii, 13, 18, 47, 67, 73, and 146 ff., for example.

36 A more detailed discussion is found on p. xxxvi below.

37 *The Works of George Herbert*, ed. F.E. Hutchinson (Oxford: Clarendon Press, 1953), p. 239.

38 Title-page, *The Husbandmans Recreations.*

39 The *Book of Common Prayer* directs the priest to read, to the newly married pair, a homily which quotes the well-known passage of St. Paul (Ephesians 5: 22–5): "Ye women, submit your selves unto your own husbands, as unto the Lord. For the husband is the wife's head, even as Christ is the head of the Church, and he is the saviour of the whole body. Therefore as the Church in congregation is subject unto Christ: so likewise let the wives be in subjection unto their own husbands in all things." In addition to the works cited in notes 28 and 29, see William and Malleville Haller, "The Puritan Art of Love," *Huntington Library Quarterly*, v (1942), 235–72, and James T. Johnson, "The Covenant Idea and the Puritan View of Marriage," *Journal of the History of Ideas*, xxxii (1971), 107–18.

40 David Cressy, *Literacy and the Social Order* (Cambridge: Cambridge University Press, 1980) concludes that the literacy of women in Markham's time would have been low, estimating from the evidence of signatures and marks that in the early seventeenth century only about 10% of women in London and East Anglia could read. Less objective, but nonetheless illuminating evidence is discussed by Louis B. Wright, p. 103 ff.; Peter Laslett *The World We Have Lost*, p. 195; and Duisenberre, ch. iv (see note 28).

41 Markham would have found the distinction in his most immediate source, Estienne and Liebault's *The Countrie Farme*: "the woman ... is tied to matters within the house and base court[yard] (the horses excepted) as the husband is tied to do what concerneth him, even all the business of the field" (Surflet, ed. Markham, p. 38); see also the quotation from William Whately, p. liii below.

42 John Fitzherbert, *Boke of Husbandry* (London, 1525), sigs. I3–I3v.

43 This point is made by Alice Clark (see note 28 above).

44 The ideal history of Renaissance medicine has not yet been written; see Rudolph S. Klein, "The History of Medicine in Tudor Times: An Historiographical Survey," *The Historian*, xxxiii, 3 (May 1971), 365–84. A general, but somewhat dated introduction is *A Short History of Medicine* by Charles Singer and E.A. Underwood (Oxford: Oxford University Press, 1962). Studies concentrating on early and Renaissance medicine include *Leechdoms, Wortcunning and Starcraft of Early England*, trans. Rev. Oswald Cockayne (London: Holland Press, 1961; a re-issue, with an introduction by Charles Singer, of the original edition 1864–6), *The Medical Background of Anglo-Saxon England* by Wilfrid Bonser (London: Wellcome Historical Medical Library, 1963); "Anglo-Saxon Plant Remedies and the Anglo-Saxons," by Linda E. Voigts, *Isis*, lxx, 252 (June 1979), 250–68; *Medieval English Medicine* by Stanley Rubin (New York: Harper & Row, 1974), pp. 128, 131–7; *Medicine in Medieval England* (London: Oldbourne, 1967) by Charles H. Talbot; *Medieval and Renaissance Medicine* by Benjamin Lee Gordon (London: Peter Owen, 1959); "Theory and Practice in Medieval Medicine" by John Riddle, *Viator*, 5 (1974), 157–84; and *Doctors and Disease in Tudor Times* by W.S.C. Copeman (London: Dawson, 1960). Problems of disease and death in the period are discussed by Thomas R. Forbes in *Chronicle from Aldgate* (New Haven and London: Yale University Press, 1971).

On the role of women in medicine see Muriel Joy Hughes, *Woman Healers in Medieval Life and Literature* (1943; reprinted, New York: Books for Libraries Press, 1968); Thomas R. Forbes, *The Midwife and the Witch* (New Haven: Yale University Press, 1966); a pamphlet by Barbara Ehrenreich and Deirdre English, *Witches, Midwives and Nurses: A History of Women Healers* (Old Westbury, New York: Feminist Press, 1973); and "The Compleat Housewife" by John B. Blake, *Bulletin of the History of Medicine*, xlix (1975), 30–42.

It is still difficult to separate belief from proven effect in the use of herbal remedies of the kind used by the housewife. One balanced and thorough study is *Medical Botany: Plants Affecting Man's Health* (New York: John Wiley and Sons, 1977), by Walter F. Lewis and Memory P.F. Elvin-Lewis. The herbs the housewife used are best understood by reference to the herbals: Agnes Arber, *Herbals, Their Origin and Evolution* (Cambridge: Cambridge University Press, 1938) remains the authoritative study; there is also Frank J. Anderson, *An Illustrated History of the Herbals* (New York: Columbia University Press, 1977); and Charles E. Raven, *English Naturalists from Neckham to Ray* (Cambridge: Cambridge University Press, 1947). See also the herbals referred to in the notes, and recorded in the Bibliography: Banckes, Gerarde, Lyte, and Turner.

The beliefs held about the nature of women by medical philosophers of the time are recorded by Ian Maclean, *The Renaissance Notion of Women* (see note 28); the same author's *The Great Instauration* (London: Duckworth, 1975) is a history of medicine in the period which followed Markham's death. The extent to which physicians were available to members of the general public is explored in *A Directory of English Country Physicians* 1603–43 by J.H. Raach (London: Dawson, 1962) and two articles by R.S. Roberts, "The Personnel and Practice of Medicine in Tudor and Stuart England, Part I: The Provinces," *Medical History*, vi (1962), 363–82, and "Part II: London," *Medical History*, viii (1964), 217–34; these studies do not, however, attempt to assess the importance of the housewife's role. There are also a number of specialized works which convey an accurate picture of the learned (as distinct from the popular) medicine of the time: *Selected Writings of William Clowes* 1544–1604, ed. F.N.L. Poynter; a discussion by Poynter based largely on this material, "Patients and Their Ills in Vicary's Time," *Annals of the Royal College of Surgeons*, lvi (1975), 141–52; and "William Bullein and the 'Lively Fashions' in Tudor Medical Literature" by Catherine Cole Mambretti, *Clio Medica*, ix (1974), 285–97.

The development of pharmacy and *materia medica* are dealt with in *Four Thousand Years of Pharmacy* by Charles H. La Wall (Philadelphia: Lippincott, 1927); *The Art and Mystery of the Apothecary* by Charles J.S. Thompson (London: John Lane, 1929); and *Pharmacies Anciennes* by Gunther Kallinich, translated from the German (*Schone Alte Apotheken*) by Gerda Bouvier and Pierre Champendal (Fribourg: Office du Livre, 1976). *The Evolution of Pharmacy in Britain*, ed. F.N.L. Poynter (London: Pitman, 1965), includes a study by R.S. Roberts, "The Early History of the Import of Drugs into Britain" (pp. 165–86); two brief articles are "Pharmacy in the 16th and 18th Centuries" by J.M. Rawson, *Pharmaceutical Journal*, clxxiii (1954), 515–17, and "Pharmacy and Therapeutics in the Age of Elizabeth I" by F. Ashworth Underwood, *Pharmaceutical Journal*, clxx (1953), 406–7, 411–15. The development of interest in chemical treatments for disease was largely the result of the influence of Paracelsus; see Allen G. Debus, *The English Paracelsians* (London: Osborne, 1965).

45 Several plants were called "wormseed" because they were believed to expel worms from the body. Markham (i, 135) recommends the powerful purgative, aloes.

46 *A Quippe for an Vpstart Courtier* (London, 1592; reprinted Scolar Press, 1971), see sigs. D4–D4v.

47 Knight, esquire, gentleman, priest, printer, grocer, skinner, dyer, pewterer, sadler, joiner, bricklayer, cutler, plasterer, sailor, ropemaker, smith, glover, husbandman, shepherd, waterman, water-bearer, bellows-mender, and (chosen somewhat reluctantly in preference to a player) a poet.

48 Markham's belief in household medicine was shared by George Herbert; see his *Works* (note 37 above), pp. 261–2.

49 Markham may well have found this principle of organization in one of the manuscripts he was using in revising the first edition, for the arrangement is traditional; see, though not one of Markham's sources, the *Liber de Diversis Medicinis*, an early fifteenth-century medical manuscript edited by Margaret Sinclair Ogden (Early English Text Society, orig. ser. no. 207; Oxford: Oxford University Press, revised reprint 1969).

50 See the compilations, listed in the Bibliography, edited by Dawson and Henslowe, and the *Liber de Diversis Medicinis*, which contains an admirable history of the tradition, pp. xviii–xxiv; some parallel passages are listed in the "Summary of Sources and Close Parallels." I have no doubt that further investigation into the manuscript tradition would unearth more. That such recipes continued in use in the medical profession is shown in the diary of John Symcotts; see *A Seventeenth Century Doctor and His Patients: John Symcotts, 1592?–1662*, ed. F.N.L. Poynter and W.J. Bishop (Streatley: Bedfordshire Historical Record Society, 1951).

51 See M.B. Donald, "Burchard Kranich (c. 1515–1578), Miner and Queen's Physician," *Annals of Science*, vi (1950), 308–22, and the same author's "A Further Note on Burchard Kranich," *Annals of Science*, vii (1951), 107–8. Poynter, *Bibliography*, identifies Bomelius, but says of "Burket" that he is "unknown" (p. 128); there can be little doubt, however, that Burcot is intended.

52 F.E. Halliday, "Queen Elizabeth and Dr Burcot," *History Today*, v (1955), 542–4; Dr Burcot certainly received a gift of 100 marks from Elizabeth, and Halliday quotes an extensive account of the circumstances leading up to the cure reported at second hand in the early seventeenth century. Unfortunately, Markham records no remedies for the smallpox.

53 Catherine Mambretti, "William Bullein and the 'Lively Fashions' in Tudor Medical Literature" (see note 44). This article records a further unflattering mention of Burcot by Gabriel Harvey as a physician "none of the learnedest or expertest ... but one that ... hath grown to much wealth and some reputation." See Gabriel Harvey's *Marginalis*, ed. G.C. Moore Smith (Stratford-upon-Avon: Shakespeare Head Press, 1913), p. 158.

54 *A Prooued Practise for All Young Chirugians* (London, 1588), sig. Piiiiii3; see also *Selected Writings of William Clowes, 1544–1604*, p. 115; Poynter summarizes Bomelius' life on p. 174.

55 F.E. Halliday, "Queen Elizabeth and Dr Burcot" and Catherine Mambretti,

"William Bullein"; Mambretti draws attention to a reference to Burcot by
Reginald Scot in his courageous work *The Discovery of Witchcraft* (London,
1548); Scot speaks of Burcot as a sorcerer and alchemist.

56 For the relationship between magic and medicine see Paul H. Kocher, *Science
and Religion in Elizabethan England* (San Marino, Calif.: Huntington
Library, 1953); Frances A. Yates, *Giordano Bruno and the
Hermetic Tradition* (London: Routledge and Kegan Paul, 1964); Richard S.
Westfall, *Science and Religion in Seventeenth Century England* (London:
Oldbourne, 1967); Keith V. Thomas, *Religion and the Decline of Magic*
(London: Weidenfeld and Nicolson, 1971); Peter J. French, *John Dee: The
World of an Elizabethan Magus* (London: Routledge and Kegan Paul,
1972); and the introduction by Allen G. Debus to his edition of John Dee's
*The Mathematical Praeface to the Elements of Geometrie of Euclid of
Megara (1570)* (New York: Science History Publications, 1975).

57 *The Household Account Book of Sarah Fell of Swarthmoor Hall*, ed. N.
Penney (Cambridge: Cambridge University Press, 1920), records on several
occasions the purchase of "blooding leeches" (pp. 113, 117, 339), but it
is not clear whether these were to be used on humans or livestock. An article
by Peter H. Niebyl describes the career of a pioneer who argued against
the practice: "Galen, Van Helmont and Blood Letting," *Science, Medicine
and Society in the Renaissance: Essays to Honour Walter Pagel*, ed. Allen G.
Debus (New York: Science History Publications, 1972), vol. i, 13–25;
J.B. van Helmont was active almost a century after Markham. A sixteenth-
century textbook on blood letting is *The English Phlebotomy* by Nicholas
Gyer (London, 1592).

58 The best known and most widely followed was Nicholas Culpeper who was
influential in the generation which followed Markham's, and whose writings
on herbs continue to be reprinted today. His popular translation (with
comments) of the *Pharmacopoeia Londinensis, A Physicall Directory* (1651),
and *Culpeper's School of Physick* (1659) are his best known works.

59 Affecting and harrowing evidence of the continuing battle is provided by *The
Autobiography of Mrs. Alice Thornton* (Surtees Society, lxii, 1875) reprinted
in extract in *By a Woman Writt*, ed. Joan Goulianos (Baltimore: Penguin
Books, 1974). Alice Thornton describes without sentiment the physical ex-
haustion caused by bearing a child a year, with the untimely deaths of
her daughter Elizabeth (from rickets) and her first son and fifth child. After a
difficult birth, in August 1659, she wrote:

> It was the good pleasure of God to continue me most wonderfully,
> though in much weakness, after the excessive loss of blood and spirits in
> childbed, with the continuance of lameness above twenty weeks after,
> and the loss of blood and strength by the bleeding of the haemorrhoids,
> which ... was caused by my last travail and torment in childbirth, which
> brought me so low and weak that I fainted almost every day upon such
> occasions ... (p. 97)

It was her chief worry that her weakness would cause her to become
barren.

60 The historical relationship between food and medicine is examined in
"Foods or Medicines? A Study in the Relationship between Foodstuffs

and *Materia Medica* from the Sixteenth to the Nineteenth Century"
by Jane O'Hara-May, *Transactions of the British Society for the History of
Pharmacy*, i (1971), 61–99. The first section of this article summarizes
sixteenth-century theories about diet.

61 Thomas Tusser writes of November's husbandry (p. 49): "At Hallowmass,
slaughter time soon cometh in, / And then doth the husbandman's feasting
begin." See also *The Englishman's Food* by J.C. Drummond and Anne
Wilbraham (London: Jonathan Cape, 1957), p. 97, and *Famine in Tudor
and Stuart England* by Andrew B. Appleby (Stanford: Stanford University
Press, 1978).

62 *Paston Letters and Papers of the Fifteenth Century*, ed. Norman Davis
(Part i, Oxford: Clarendon Press, 1971), p. 251; letter no. 148, written in
about 1453.

63 C. Anne Wilson, *Food and Drink in Britain* (London: Constable, 1973),
p. 38.

64 William Harrison, *Description*, pp. 125–6. See also *A Briefe Discovery of
the Damages that Happen to this Realme by Disordered and Unlawful
Diet* (London, 1590), by Edward Jeninges; Jeninges complains that fish-
days are not properly observed, with the result that the navy has degener-
ated and many fishermen are out of work. Colin Clark, *Kitchen and
Table* (see note 82), discusses compulsory fish days, pp. 78–9.

65 Markham includes instructions on such ponds in *The English Husbandman*; see also John Taverner, *Certaine Experiments Concerning Fish
and Fruit* (London, 1600).

66 Venner, p. 111; see Wilson, *Food and Drink in Britain*, p. 348. Fruit
would certainly have been eaten more than orthodox medical opinion
recommended, however, particularly by the less wealthy; in addition
to the abundance of fruit from the orchard (care of which was explained
by Markham in *The English Husbandman*), there was a flourishing
fruit trade, one interesting indication of which is the publication of *The
Fruiterers Secrets* (London, 1604), a practical handbook on the gathering,
picking, sorting, and storing of various fruits.

67 Drummond and Wilbraham, pp. 106 ff.

68 Paul Hentzner, writing of 1598; see William B. Rye, *England as Seen by
Foreigners in the Days of Elizabeth and James the First* (New York:
Benjamin Blom, 1965; a reprint of the edition of 1865).

69 Drummond and Wilbraham have a chapter on scurvy, pp. 133 ff.

70 Hentzner, in Rye, p. 104.

71 Drummond and Wilbraham, p. 112; Wilson, pp. 297 ff. According to
Muffett, the best sugar was to be "hard, solid, exceeding light and sweet,
glistening like snow, close [dense] and not spongy, melting (as salt
doth) very speedily in any liquor. Such cometh from Madiera in little
loaves of three or four pound weight apiece; from whence also we have a
coarser sort of sugar-loaves ... not fully so good for candying fruits,
but better for syrups and kitchen uses" (p. 250).

72 See Wilson, *Food and Drink in Britain*, pp. 280–92.

73 The point is made by Constance B. Hieatt and Sharon Butler, *Pleyn Delit*
(Toronto: University of Toronto Press, 1976), p. ix.

74 F.G. Emmison, *Tudor Food and Pastimes* (London: Ernest Benn, 1964),
p. 45.

75 A reaction against excessively spiced foods is already evident in 1652, when George Herbert admonished the country parson: "As for spices, he doth not only prefer house-bred things before them, but condemns them for vanities, and so shuts them out of his family, esteeming that there is no spice comparable, for herbs, to rosemary, thyme, savoury, mints; and for seeds, to fennel and caraway seeds [both of which could be grown in England]" (*Works*, pp. 261–2).

76 *Description of England*, p. 130.

77 Hentzner, in Rye, p. 110.

78 See *The Complete Works of John Lyly*, ed. R.W. Bond (Oxford: Oxford University Press, 1902), vol. i, pp. 448–9.

79 Modern treatments of early cookery all too often emphasize the quaint at the expense of the scholarly. Exceptions are *Pleyn Delit* by Constance B. Hieatt and Sharon Butler (see note 73), and two books by Lorna Sass: *To the King's Taste* and *To the Queen's Taste* (London: John Murray, 1976 and 1977 respectively). See also *Dining with William Shakespeare* by Madge Lorwin (New York: Atheneum, 1976); *The Cookery of England* by Elizabeth Ayrton (London: A. Deutsch, 1974); *Seven Centuries of English Cooking* by Maxime McKendry, ed. Arabella Boxer (London: Weidenfeld and Nicolson, 1973); *Sallets, Humbles, and Shrewsbery Cakes* by Ruth Anne Beebe (Boston, Mass.: David R. Godine, 1976); and *The Compleat Cook* by Rebecca Price (1660–1740), ed. Madeline Masson (London: Routledge and Kegan Paul, 1974). More general works relevant to cookery are *Early English Meals and Manners*, ed. Frederick J. Furnivall (London: Early English Text Society, orig. ser. no. 32, 1868); Emmison's *Tudor Food and Pastimes* (see note 74); and Colin Clair, *Kitchen and Table* (London: Abelard-Schuman, 1964). On cookery books contemporary with Markham's, there is a bibliography by Arnold W. Oxford, *English Cookery Books to the Year* 1850 (London: Henry Frowde, 1913), supplemented by a note in *Notes and Queries* (22 November 1934). See also *The Gastronomic Bibliography* by Katherine Bitting (San Francisco, 1939) and *Bibliographie Gastronomique* by Georges Vicaire (London: Derek Verschoyle, 1954; a reprint of the edition of 1890).

80 A brilliant and eccentric figure, George Digby was related to Sir Kenelm Digby, who was an experimenter in many areas, from the scientific to the magical and alchemical (see the notes to ii, 24 and vi, 42).

81 Reprinted in Dodsley's *Old English Plays* (edition of 1876; vol. xv, pp. 65–6, 75).

82 Tusser, pp. 103, 108.

83 See *A Short History of the Art of Distillation* by R.J. Forbes (Leiden: E.J. Brill, 1970): Forbes makes no mention of the role played by women in popularizing techniques of distillation.

84 Emmison, p. 58.

85 Fell pp. 303, 315.

86 See my article, "The Mystery of Vintners," *Agricultural History*, l (1976), 362–76.

87 See pp. 307, 309. *Mrs. Beeton's Book of Household Management* (London: Ward Lock, 1906) also gives recipes for fruit wines, and instructs the butler in the art of fining, recommending, like Markham, "eggs, isinglass,

gelatine, and gum arabic," and giving directions very similar to Markham's "parel" (p. 1790; see Markham iv, 3, etc.).

88 Alice Clark, *Working Life*, ch. iv.

89 See Clark for demonstration of the poverty of those employed in spinning. Sarah Fell records many payments for spinning; there are also several payments to weavers (pp. 93, 99, for example).

90 *An Essay Towards the Improving of the Hempen and Flaxen Manufacturers in the Kingdom of Ireland*, by Louis Crommelin (Dublin, 1705), p. 16.

91 Slator, pp. 47–8.

92 "The Wright's Chaste Wife" by "Adam of Cobham" (c. 1462), ed. Frederick J. Furnivall (London: Early English Text Society, orig. ser. no. 12, 1865).

93 Bk. 1, ch. 7, "The Dairy."

94 *The English Dairy Farmer, 1500–1900*, by G.E. Fussell (London: Frank Cass, 1966), pp. 11–15.

95 Alice Clark, *Working Life*, pp. 54–5. The number of fast days varied. Christina Hole, *English Home Life* (see note 30), points out that the prohibition on eating flesh was unenforceable. In Middleton's comedy *A Chaste Maid in Cheapside* there is an amusing sequence (II, ii) in which two "promoters," professional informers, waylay various passers-by on a fast day in order to search them for illegal joints of meat (which they plan to eat); inevitably they are tricked themselves.

96 Most recently reprinted in *Drama of the English Renaissance,* i: The Tudor Period, ed. Russell A. Fraser and Norman Rabkin (London: Macmillan, 1976); see I.iii.91–5.

97 Alice Clark, *Working Life*, pp. 22 ff.

98 See vii, 25.

99 Quoted in *In Praise of Ale* by W.T. Marchant (London, 1888, reprinted by Singing Tree Press [Detroit, 1968]), pp. 320–4. There is also a version by Robert Burns, "John Barley Corn."

100 *John Skelton's Complete Poems, 1460–1529,* ed. Philip Henderson (London: Dent, 1964), p. 117. See "The Alehouse and the Alternative Society" by Peter Clark, in *Puritans and Revolutionaries: Essays in Seventeenth Century History Presented to Christopher Hill*, ed. Donald Pennington.

101 In an article, "An English Gentlewoman: The Journal of Lady Mildmay, circa 1570–1617" by Rachel Weigall, *Quarterly Review*, ccxv (1911), 119–38, we are told that "A prescription for a child of three suffering from its teeth has a special direction that the medicine is to 'be given at night in its posset of beer'."

102 Wilbraham and Drummond, p. 114.

103 From the comedy *Gammer Gurton's Needle* (published 1576), II.i.1–41.

104 Not all writers on Markham have found an opportunity to make this remark.

105 See ii, 3 and note.

106 Estienne and Liebault (Surflet, ed. Markham, p. 38); and Markham's co-author in *A Way to Get Wealth*, William Lawson, in *A New Orchard and Garden*: "I will not account her any of my good housewives, that wanteth [lacketh] either bees, or skilfulness about them" (1631 edition, published as the sixth part of the 1632 edition of *A Way to Get Wealth*,

p. 98); see also *The Office of the Good Housewife* by B.F. (London, 1672), pp. 10–20.

107 The point is made eloquently in Peter Laslett's *The World We Have Lost* (see note 28); see particularly ch. v, "Did the Peasants Starve?"

108 See, for example, evidence collected by Pearl Hogrefe in her accounts of the lives of various Tudor women (cited in note 28 above); Alice Clark, *Working Lives*, pp. 21 ff.; and the impressive competence in business affairs demonstrated by the women in the Paston family, whose letters are most readily available in the selection edited by Norman Davis (Oxford: Clarendon Press, Medieval and Tudor series, 1958).

109 See the 1623 edition, pp. 83–5. Whately is not advocating equality in the modern sense, though he does argue for all goods to be held in common between the married pair (p. 82). Elsewhere he affirms emphatically the wife's subservience to her husband: "O thou wife, let thy best under-standing be to understand ... that thine husband is by God made thy gov-ernor and ruler, and thou his inferior, to be ruled by him. Though he be of meaner birth and of lesser wit, though he were of no wealth, nor account in the world, before thou didst marry him; yet, after the tying of this knot, God will have thee subject" (p. 192).

110 See in particular chapter v on wool, flax, and hemp. Thomas Tusser is an honourable exception to my generalization; he wrote before Markham, and he wrote on the whole approvingly of the woman in the dairy.

111 An example of the problems posed by reciprocal borrowings is discussed in my article, "A Lost Sixteenth Century Cookery Book," *The Library*, xxxii (1977), 156–60.

112 If Poynter's conjecture about the relationships between the Earl of Rutland and Markham is correct, the Countess of Rutland is a possible candidate.

DEDICATION

1 Thomas Cecil, son of Elizabeth's counsellor, William Cecil, was created Earl of Exeter in 1605; he married his second wife, Frances, in 1610, at which time he was 68 years old, his wife 30: "A youthful widow she had been, virtuous, and so became bedfellow to this aged, gouty and diseased, but noble Earl" (quoted in Debrett's *Peerage* [London, 1926], v, 217). Frances' husband died in 1622, just before this dedication appeared in the second edition of *The English Housewife*. She survived until 1663.

CHAPTER I

1 *The English Housewife* was originally published as the second part of a larger work, *Countrey Contentments*, the first part of which was called *The Husbandmans Recreations*: "containing the whole art of riding great horses in very short time, with the breeding, breaking, dieting and ordering of them, and of running, hunting, and ambling horses ... likewise in two treatises the arts of hunting, hawking, coursing of greyhounds with the laws of the leash, shooting, bowling, tennis, balloon [a game played with an inflated ball] etc." (Title page).

2 See the discussion of the status of the housewife in the Introduction.

3 Though Markham's religious beliefs inclined towards the puritan he shows here that he was opposed to the growing zeal of the puritan move-

ment; his comment is an early reference to the existence of women preachers.

4 Qualified preachers or theologians.

5 Narrow.

6 Relating to physic, or medicine.

7 Here a synonym of "symptoms."

8 See Introduction pp. xxx–xxxi.

9 Fevers which come at regular intervals (quotidian, tertian, and quartan) were usually the results of malarial diseases; the pestilent fever was the plague, and the "accidental," or symptomatic was a by-product of other injury.

10 A consumption is "a disease, wherein, the lungs being exulcerated, there followeth a leanness in all the body" (Bullokar); usually tuberculosis.

11 Distilled spirits, flavoured by infusion with herbs. See the recipes for its preparation iii, 4, 7, and 8.

12 Spiced milk curd made by pouring hot milk into ale; see for example the recipe "How to make good posset curd" in *The Good Huswifes Handmaide*, fol. 47. In the next recipe only the whey is used.

13 Sweating is a symptom of the passing of fever; here the attempt is made to induce the symptom in the belief that it is a cause of the cure rather than an effect. See also i, 18–19, 22, etc.

14 Potent ointments.

15 Water distilled from an infusion of gum dragon (tragacanth gum; see ii, 164).

16 See the recipes for its preparation, ii, 167 and iii, 36.

17 One of the most popular of medical compounds, "so called from Mithridates vi, king of Ponius (died c. 63 B.C.), who was said to have rendered himself proof against poison by the constant use of antidotes" (*OED*). *The London Dispensatory* (pp. 145–6) has the long list of ingredients, and says that it "provokes sweat."

18 The meaning may be that the blood is rebelling (unnaturally) against the body; the 1631 edition, however, substitutes "infinitely" for the earlier "inciuelly."

19 Herbs, like everything else, were categorized in terms of the four basic "qualities," hot, cold, dry, and moist; all the herbs mentioned here were said by Turner and Gerarde to be cold – sorrel cold and dry in the first degree, purslane cold and moist in the third degree, etc. By the principle of antagonism, cold herbs were thought to counteract the heat of a fever:

> Good housewives provide, ere an sickness do come,
> Of sundry good things in her house to have some.
> Good *aqua composita*, vinegar tart,
> Rose-water and treacle, to comfort the heart.
>
> Cold herbs in her garden for agues that burn,
> That over-strong heat to good temper may turn
> While endive and succory, with spinach enough,
> All such with good pot-herbs should follow the plough.
> (Thomas Tusser, p. 179.)

20 John Evelyn wrote of lettuce that it "is indeed of nature more cold and moist than any [other vegetable]; yet less astringent, and so harmless that it may safely be eaten raw in fevers; for it allays heat, bridles choler, extinguishes thirst, excites appetite, kindly nourishes, and above all, represses vapours, conciliates sleep, mitigates pain; besides the effect it has upon morals, temperance and chastity" (see pp. 30–5).

21 "A physical [medicinal] clear drink made of distilled waters and sugar" (Bullokar); see vii, 26.

22 An infected sore or pustule.

23 "the colour [of jaundice in old people] is more inclinable to a deep green, which often turns to a black jaundice ... which never fails to put an end to their lives." Nicholas Robinson, *A New Theory of Physick and Diseases, Founded on the Principles of the Newtonian Philosophy* (London, 1725), p. 162.

24 The plague.

25 See Introduction, pp. xxxii–xxxiii.

26 *Cichorium intybus*, closely related to the endive *C. endivia*, which Turner (*Names*) called "garden succory." Both herbs were considered cold and dry "almost in the third degree" (Lyte, p. 563).

27 Distillation; the 1631 text substitutes the more usual "decoction." "Dewition" does not appear in the *OED*; the word may have been an invention of Markham's, derived from the dew-like drops of moisture which form during the process of distillation.

28 Gerarde mentions the use of French mallows, *Lavatera olbia*, as a potherb, and says that "it is not to be found wild" (p. 786).

29 See ii, 189.

30 Similar recipes are found in Dawson, *Leechbook*, pp. 71 and 277.

31 Following Banckes, Markham ("Hard Words") wrongly identified *aristolochia longa* with "red madder," *Rubia tinctorum*. See i, 181.

32 The power of angelica (*Angelica archangelica*) against the plague was widely accepted: Turner (III *Herbal*, p. 5) described it as "good against poison, pestilent airs, and the pestilence itself," and William Taswell used it when he was required to take a trip to London during the plague of 1665 (*Autobiography*, p. 9).

33 "I do hope nobody is so simple as to eat plasters. The general way of application is to the grieved place ... Plasters are so called from sticking, cleaving and being smeared upon leather or cloth, as the plaster is spread upon a wall" (*The London Dispensatory*, p. 196).

34 Rue (*Ruta graveolens*); "it is singular good against the stinging of serpents: for the very weasels when they prepare themselves to combat with them, use to eat this herb beforehand, for to be secured from their venom" (Pliny, trans. Holland, 20, xiii); see i, 216.

35 The recipes for melilot plasters, simple and compound, are given in *The London Dispensatory*, p. 201; made from the yellow melilot (*Melilotus officinalis*), the plasters were used for "all sores and putrefactions."

36 Probably a misreading of "matfelon," a name that Turner (*Names*) gives for scabious, *Centaurea scabiosa*. The reading would then be "matfelon or scabious." Scabious was "thought to be forceable ... against all pestilent fevers" (Gerarde, p. 586), and as the name suggests it was also thought to be effective in the treatment of skin diseases, here no doubt plague-sores.

37 See note, i, 176.
38 *Achillea millefolium*, confused by Markham with "a herb called the water-violet" ("Hard Words"); *Hottonia palustris* is similar to yarrow in appearance, as Gerarde explains: "Water violet hath long and great jagged leaves, very finely cut or rent like yarrow, but smaller" (p. 678).
39 Possibly wild mallow (*Malva sylvestris*) or the vervain mallow (*M. alcea*); see note to i, 100.
40 *Langue de boeuf*, or "oxtongue," a name related to bugloss, here probably referring to *Picris echioides*: "The physicians or our time do affirm, that these herbs ... comfort and assuage the heaviness of the heart" (Lyte, p. 9).
41 Rose petals pressed into a cake.
42 "If the juice [of beet] be put in the nostrils of a man, it cleanseth a man's head" (Banckes, 14); many of the following recipes were taken from the Banckes herbal, first published in 1525. See the Introduction and the article "Medical Use of a Sixteenth Century Herbal: Gervase Markham and the Banckes Herbal," *Bulletin of the History of Medicine*, liii (1979), 449–58, by Michael R. Best.
43 For a horse suffering from this complaint, Markham recommends similarly that it be "kept waking with noises and affrights whether he will or no" but adds further that the horse should be bled "in the neck vein," and treated with various herbs including the "powder of strong tobacco well dried" (*Cavelarice* bk. 7, pp. 23–44). See also note to paragraph 34 below.
44 The "chaste tree" *Vitex agnus-castus*; but Markham ("Hard Words") believed it to be tutsan (see i, 179), an identification roundly criticized by Turner (*Names*, p. 223).
45 All editions record this otherwise unknown herb, but the Banckes herbal, the origin of the recipe, records "brownwort," a name for water betony (*Scrophularia aquatica*); Markham cannot have known the herb himself, for in the "Table of Hard Words" he repeats *verbatim* the description given in the herbal.
46 A dram is one-sixteenth part of an ounce, or approximately 1.8 gm.
47 See i, 254.
48 Wirsung describes five degrees of palsy: *lethargus* or sleeping sickness; *tremor*, which is quaking (trembling); *paralysis*, the true or dead palsy; *epilepsia*, the falling sickness; the fifth and most severe, *apoplexia*, stroke (p. 134).
49 In a healthy body the four humours (melancholic, choleric, phlegmatic, and sanguine) were held in balance; the excessive concentration of any humour was thought to lead to disease. Here hot and dry remedies are suggested to counteract the excess of the phlegmatic (cold and moist) humour.
50 "Any medicine taken inwardly, made of divers powders mixed together, and by tempering with some syrups, or honey brought to a soft liquid form" (Bullokar).
51 Powder. The term is also used in cookery; see ii, 64.
52 A plant of doubtful identity. Markham, in "Hard Words," transcribes the description given in his source, the Banckes herbal: "Asterion, is an herb growing amongst stones, as on walls ... It hath yellow flowers like foxgloves, and the leaves are round and bluish."

53 During the mating season.
54 Alive.
55 Decomposing dung was often used by alchemists as a steady source of low heat.
56 Any disease which caused running nose and eyes; usually the common cold.
57 "The kinds of mineral salts used at tables and for seasoning meats are to be esteemed three in number: one kind is the bay or sea salt, dried merely from salt sea-water by the heat of the sun. The second sort is ... made by decoction. The third is the salt that groweth ... in the bowels of the earth." John Woodall, *The Surgions Mate* (London, 1617), p. 272. Celia Fiennes has a detailed description of the "salterns" at Lymington where bay salt was made: "The sea water they draw into trenches and so into several ponds ... and it stands in the sun to exhale the watery fresh part of it ... when they think it's fit to boil, they draw off the water from the ponds by pipes which conveys it into a house full of large square iron and copper pans; they are shallow, but they are a yard or two if not more square ... under which is the furnace that burns fiercely to keep these pans boiling apace, and as it candies about the bottom, so they shovel it up and fill it in great baskets ... and as fast as they shovel out the boiling salt out of the pond, they do replenish it with more of the salt water" (see *The Journeys of Celia Fiennes*, p. 49).
58 "A white stone found in silver mines" (Bullokar); antimony trisulphide, which, in its naturally occurring form, is a lead grey.
59 "Like unto wild marjoram, but it is neither so hot, neither so well smelling. It may be called in English unsavoury marjoram (Turner, *Names*, p. 219); *Prunella vulgaris*, self-heal.
60 Probably a misreading of *calamus aromaticus*, "sweet reed," usually in England referring to the sweet flag, *Acorus calamus* (*OED*); in the "Table of Hard Words," however, Markham refers to "carthamus" – "an herb in taste like saffron ... called bastard saffron or mock saffron" – which is safflower, *Carthamus tinctorius*. See iii, 25.
61 Probably Turner's "stinking may-weed" (*Names*), *Anthemis cotula*.
62 This recipe from the Banckes herbal was sufficiently trusted by Markham for him to recommend it for use with horses (*Cheape and Good Husbandry*, p. 25).
63 Cf. *Cavelarice* bk. 7, p. 37, and *Markhams Maister-peece* (1610) p. 233.
64 Either potash alum or ammonia alum. The *Pharmaceutical Codex* for 1968 describes alum as "a powerful astringent," and adds, "It is now seldom given by mouth."
65 The Banckes herbal specifies that the leaves of skirret rather than the root (which was used as a vegetable) should be used.
66 Inflammation of the throat, in its mild form probably tonsilitis; Wirsung writes of the severe form (diphtheria) that it is "a strong perilous sickness that ariseth about the throat, in the mouth, and about the throatball, and very quickly stoppeth the breath ... in greatest extremity is wont to be made a vent in the patient's throat between the two gristles, that he through the same vent may take air and breath" (pp. 190–4).
67 A name applied to any plant of the cabbage family.
68 "The hard swelling of the glandules or kernels commonly about the neck:

they be called also scrophules [scrofula]" (Pliny, trans. Holland, "The explanation of the words of art"). The last English sovereign to put to the test the belief that the reigning monarch could cure the disease by touching the afflicted person was Queen Anne; as a child, Dr Johnson was taken to her, though, as Boswell remarks, "This touch, however, was without any effect" (*Life*, Everyman Library, 1949, p. 17).

69 Sympathetic magic associated with its colour (blood) made red dock (*Rumex sanguineus*) widely used in medicine.

70 See note to "olibanum," i, 258.

71 Marble would be expected to give some relief through its association with cold.

72 *Agrimonia eupatoria*, a member of the rose family, contains a certain amount of tannin, which could be beneficial to cuts or wounds.

73 "Top or dome of the head" (*OED*).

74 Quinsy; see note above, i, 52.

75 Rock alum; see note to i, 50.

76 This recipe is found in Dawson, *Leechbook*, p. 281. Several recipes here come from the same tradition of English medicine: paragraphs 67 and 68 are found in Henslow (pp. 112 and 93), while Moulton (E4) and Dawson, (p. 239) suggest different juices – henbane and elder – for 68; and 69 appears in both Dawson (p. 265) and Moulton, sig. E6.

77 Powdered or calcined hart's horn; sympathetic magic associates ivory or horn with teeth.

78 "Cumin scattereth and breaketh all the windiness of the stomach" (Lyte, p. 275).

79 Like red dock (i, 55) the colour of this plant is the reason for the belief in its power; the association is clearer in this recipe from Gerarde: "Being stamped, and the juice put up into the nostrils, it stoppeth the bleeding of the nose" (p. 571).

80 Liquid (live) honey; cf. "stone" honey, i, 225, and "stoned" honey, iv, 7.

81 Here the reference is to "dyer's grains," the dried bodies of the coccus insect, earlier thought to be a berry; they are gathered from the evergreen oak in Southern Europe and used to make a red dye. Elsewhere "grains of paradise" or cardamom is meant (See i, 136 and iii, 8 for example).

82 This appears to have been a popular recipe, for it appears in Moulton (E4) with black snails recommended, and twice in Dawson, *Leechbook* (pp. 156 and 159). Dawson comments: "A reddish brown slug is evidently meant, *Arion hortensis* or *Agriolimax laevis*. The [oil] is the copious discharge of mucus which the animal would discharge under the irritation of salt" (p. 156n).

83 The "helm" or upper part of a still in which the vapour condensed.

84 *Plantago major*; "Plantain is a flat leaf and sinewy, growing close to the ground, and is called waybread leaf" (Markham, "Hard Words").

85 A disease of the eye with a film or opacity spreading from a central point.

86 "Dragon's blood": "Cinnabar, or *sanguis draconis*, or as we call it, vermillion, is a certain metal drawn from quicksulphur, and quicksilver" (*Markhams Maister-peece* [1610], p. 488).

87 Found also in Henslow, p. 94; similar recipes will be found in iii, 10 and 12.

88 The earlier editions all have "eusaace," a misreading of "eufrace," euphrasy

or eyebright (*Euphrasia officinalis*). Euphrasy is recommended universally in the early herbals for treatment of the eyes, by the doctrine of signatures; a black spot in the middle of the flower was taken to resemble the pupil.

89 According to Gerarde, hillwort is "puliol mountaine" ("Supplement unto the generall table"); most probably wild thyme (*Thymus serpyllum*), speedwell (*Veronica montana*) or pennyroyal (*Mentha pulegium*) is the herb intended.

90 Affected by sauce-fleume ("salt phlegm"), a condition of acute pimples and inflammation, thought to be brought about by an excess of salt humours.

91 Hyssop is a pungently aromatic herb, and the treatment described might indeed give some relief from a head cold.

92 A quarter; here probably a quarter ounce.

93 "A kind of consumption accompanied with an ulceration and cough of the lungs" (Bullokar).

94 The liquor, made by an infusion of malt in water, from which beer and ale are fermented; see ix, 5ff. "Barm" is yeast.

95 Turner reports also that "The dry leaves of horehound sodden in water with the seed or the juice of the green leaves is good to be given with honey ... for the cough and the phthisic" (II *Herbal* fol. 51v).

96 The wild mint *Mentha sylvestris*, or, since Banckes refers to "horse-mint or water-mint or brook-mint," *Mentha aquatica*.

97 A waxy substance found in the whale; Markham described it as "the seed of the whale, excellent for inward bruises, and to be bought at the Pothecaries" ("Hard Words").

98 Brooklime (see i, 95); the recipe comes from Banckes (p. 30), and is recommended by Markham for use with horses (*Cheape and Good Husbandry*, [1614], p. 56).

99 Since a plaster is involved, clearly the navel is intended; see also i, 135 where the phrase "the navel or mouth of the stomach" is used. Venner, however, is using it in a different, internal sense in the passage quoted in the note to "warden," ii, 130.

100 The Banckes herbal records the emetic effect of stonecrop (*Sedum acre*), but the very sensible caution Markham adds may have been the result of his own experience, or may have been added from some other written source; William Langham's *Garden of Health* (1597) has a similar warning (p. 673), though there is no evidence that Markham used it as a source.

101 "Gripings or stitches in the uppermost small guts, which be caused of some obstruction or swellings of the guts ... whereby such great intolerable pain, sickness, and griping do ensue, that the guts seem to be bored through with a bodkin [dagger]" (Wirsung, p. 421).

102 The purgative effect of the fern *Polypodium vulgare* was recorded by Dioscorides (ed. Gunther, p. 589; see note to i, 118 below).

103 Literally the uterus, but extended to mean diseases thought to arise from excessive humours in the womb; specifically the "passion of the mother" was hysteria, and the pungent aromatics mentioned in the recipe would have much the same shock effect as the traditional burning of feathers.

104 Ammi (*Ammi majus*), an aromatic herb which was known by several other names, as Markham explains: "amees or cumin-royal is a herb of some called bullwort, bishop's-weed or herb-william" ("Hard Words").

105 Turner said that the greater centaury (*Centaurea rhaponticum*) grew "only in gardens, I never saw it saving only in Italy and Germany" (*Names*, p. 166), but Gerarde reported with pride that "It groweth very plentifully … in Lycia, Pelaponnesus, Arcadia … and likewise in my garden" (p. 436).

106 As of a bell-ringer.

107 Markham is careful not to suggest that the housewife do the bloodletting herself.

108 The Banckes herbal says of "Althea" that it "is called hollyhock or the wild mallow"; *Althea officinalis* is marsh mallow, hollyhock is *Althea rosea*, and wild mallow is *Malva sylvestris* – a typical case of confused identity. The original recipe in Banckes is not specifically for pleurisy, but for "wicked gatherings that be engendered in a man's body" (p. 9).

109 Doves were noted for their sexual heat; hence, in this instance, the use of their dung would be thought to increase the effectiveness of the heat treatment

110 "Cordial" originally meant "that which comforteth the heart" (Bullokar), generalized here to mean "restorative"; a caudle was a warm gruel mixed with wine, herbs, and spices, in the manner described by the following recipe. Later editions omitted the word "caudle," presumably because it was wrongly thought to be redundant.

111 An example of the use of the doctrine of signatures: a yellow substance is thought to be effective against a disease which makes the skin yellow.

112 The original recipe in Banckes (p. 57) is said to be good against the "black choler."

113 "Saint Mary" may be a variant of costmary – the *OED* records that costmary was known as *herbe Sainte Marie* in fifteenth-century France. Costmary is also known as alecost (see note, paragraph 249 below); garlic, because of its powerful smell, was frequently used medicinally.

114 A fulling mill in which cloth is cleansed and thickened by being beaten with wooden mallets.

115 Strip of cloth; the technique described is the effective one of applying a tourniquet.

116 "The dropsy is a sickness which is caused of a cold humour that doth penetrate throutgout all the members, in such manner that they thereby are all puffed up and swollen … The common signs … are … swelling or puffing up of the feet and the legs, afterwards of the face (in men of the cods) and a little over all the whole body: secondly, the alteration of the colour of the body into a white colour" (Wirsung, p. 400).

117 The original reads "darke Wallwoorte," but this is clearly a misreading of the plant names "dauke" (*Daucus carota*) and "wallwort." The recipe was compiled from Banckes, which records, under *Daucus*: "This herb is called dauke. Its virtue is to heal the dropsy" (p. 25).

118 A leguminous plant grown for fodder, not the modern flower, which is of American origin.

119 Turner was one of the first to recognize the difference between these two flowers: "I could never see this herb [affodil] in England but once, for the herb that the people calleth here affodil or daffodil is a kind of narcissus. The right affodil hath a long stalk … and many white flowers in the top, and not one alone, as the kinds of narcissus have" (1 *Herbal*,

p. 24). Affodil or asphodel is *Asphodelus ramosus*; the daffodil *Narcissus pseudo-narcissus*.

120 "The milt of man or beast, which is like a long narrow tongue lying under the short ribs on the left side, and hath this office of nature to purge the liver of superfluous melancholic blood" (Bullokar).

121 Gerarde (p. 1195) follows Dioscorides, who wrote of tamarisk that "the decoction of the leaves, being drunk with wine, doth melt the spleen." *The Greek Herbal of Dioscorides*, trans. John Goodyer (1655), ed. Robert J. Gunther (New York: Haffner Publishing Co., 1959), p. 62.

122 Usually known as bole (clay) armeniac, it was an astringent earth imported from Armenia. Wirsung says that it has "especial virtue to purge melancholy" (p. 9); the seat of the melancholy humour was supposed to be the spleen. See i, 193.

123 Nutmeg is still listed in the *Pharmaceutical Codex* as a carminative, for use in relieving flatulence. The Banckes herbal recommends it "for coldness or feebleness of digestion in the stomach" (p. 52).

124 The fruit of *Prunus spinosa*; Gerarde believed that "wild plums do stay and bind the belly, and so do unripe plums" (p. 1314).

125 The liquor of a tan vat, rich in tannin and mucilage.

126 Penis; Culpeper's translation of *The London Dispensatory* also recorded that "The yard of a stag helps fluxes" (p. 20).

127 Void, evacuate.

128 Markham also recommends fenugreek for constipation in cattle (*Cheape and Good Husbandry*, p. 51); he says that the herb can be "sown in gardens, but easiest to be had at the Pothecary's" ("Hard Words"). The original texts have "fennicreete," apparently a misreading of Markham's spelling elsewhere, "fennegreeke."

129 The socotrine aloe, so-called because of its origin on the island of Socotra, is a strong purgative, still listed in the *Pharmaceutical Codex*.

130 A fruity, sweet wine; see below, iv, 3.

131 Markham is probably, once again, combining different recipes. Gerarde notes the belief that "the leaves [of savin] boiled in oil olive, and kept therein, killeth the worms in children if you anoint their bellies therewith" (p. 1194). Savin is a powerful and poisonous drug derived from the shrub *Juniperus sabina*.

132 A variety of pepper, not now in general use, derived from the fruit of *Piper longum* and related plants; case pepper was a similarly pungent spice obtained from the dried fruit of one of many varieties of *Capsicum*. The informative pamphlet, *A Short Discourse of the Three Kindes of Peppers in Common Use* (London, 1588) discusses black, white, and long pepper, but not case pepper.

133 Here probably the pot-herb allgood (*Chenopodium Bonus-Henricus*); the name is also applied to a number of poisonous plants.

134 Turner says that cinquefoil (*Potentilla reptans*) is "good against the flux" (ii *Herbal* fol. 110v).

135 See i, 136, note on long pepper.

136 *Symphytum officinale*, a member of the borage family. Turner specifies that it is the roots which are "good if they be broken and drunken for them that ... are bursten [ruptured]" (ii *Herbal* fol. 150v).

137 The original reads "polypody, of the oak and avens..." but polypody (see

i, 93) was often described as "of the oak," "of the wall," etc. according to the place of growth (see below, i, 158, for example).

138 *Geum urbanum* is also known as herb bennet (see i, 220); according to Lyte, the root decocted and drunk in wine "cureth all inward wounds and hurts" (p. 919).

139 Nightshade; see i, 240.

140 "The cause of the stone either in the kidneys or bladder, is the heat of either part which hardeneth the gross filmy substance into stone" (Culpeper, *School*, p. 236).

141 The winged seeds of the ash.

142 The name saxifrage comes from the Latin "rock-breaking"; it grows in the clefts of rocks. Its use in recipes for the "stone" is another example of the doctrine of signatures

143 The leaves and fruit of *Cassia senna* are a strong purgative. Turner adds a sensible warning note: "I can witness by experience in ... weak persons that senna in working maketh a great rumbling, gnawing and pain in the belly, and that in other[s] that be strong it maketh no such business" (III *Herbal*, p. 71).

144 Wine from the region of the Rhine; see iv. 18.

145 The Banckes herbal gives this as the English name for "*centonodium*"; Lyte (p. 98) translates *centumnodia* as "knot grass," an identification re-inforced by Gerarde, who says that knotgrass is known as "bird's tongue in the north of England" (p. 452; the "table" of Gerarde's herbal records "sparrow's-tongue, that is knotgrass"). Knotgrass is *Polygonum aviculare*.

146 *Parietaria officinalis*, often known as "pellitory of the wall," was recommended by Gerarde (p. 261) to be drunk for the gravel or stone. See the next paragraph (154) also.

147 The zodiac sign *scorpio*, the scorpion, was held to have influence over the genitals, hence the use of the oil of scorpions for a disease of the bladder. Wirsung makes the same recommendation: "This oil breaketh the stone of the bladder, and of the reins [kidneys] ... if it be anointed upon the reins, and upon the privities, or if it be injected into the bladder" (p. 750); *The London Dispensatory* tells how to make it: "Oil of scorpions, is made of thirty live scorpions, caught when the sun is in Leo; oil of bitter almonds 2 lb.; let them be set in the sun, and after forty days, strained" (p. 180).

148 "In the strangury the urine comes away by drops with much pain; with a great desire to piss" (Culpeper, *School*, p. 239. Culpeper goes on to propose a remedy more unpleasant than Markham's: "The best remedy in the world against the strangury, is this; to save all the water the diseased party maketh, and let the diseased party drink it down back again, and that in a very few days will cure him" (p. 241).

149 It is not clear what specific disease this recipe is for; goat's blood (thought from the time of Pliny to be capable of splitting a diamond) was recommended as a cure for the stone by the compiler of the fourteenth century manuscript edited by Henslow (p. 98) and by Culpeper (*School*, p. 236).

150 A strong-smelling substance obtained from a gland in the beaver; the glands were thought to be the animal's testicles, hence the use of castoreum for diseases of the genitals. Culpeper was even more optimistic of its effect, for he maintained that "it incites to generation [intercourse] being

anointed upon the cods" (*The London Dispensatory*, p. 177). A popular fable was that the beaver voluntarily castrated itself when being hunted, preferring that fate to death.

151 A sweet desert wine; see iv, 10.

152 Unidentified. Culpeper records an *unguentum pectorale*, used to "assuage the pains of any part of the body, as well as of the breast" (*The London Dispensatory*, p. 192).

153 Catmint, *Nepeta cataria*. See also the note to "wild nep," i, 188.

154 A sherry-type wine; see iv, 2.

155 Normally refers to *Peucedanum ostruthium*, but the original recipe in Banckes uses "pellitory of Spain" as a translation of "elleborus albus," white hellebore (*Veratrum album*).

156 "The cause of falling out of the fundament [anus], is weakness, or relaxation of the sphincter muscles; and therefore the cure must be by such medicines as dry and bind" (Culpeper, *School*, p. 229).

157 Coddled, partially cooked.

158 *Toute sain*, "all sound," a "healing" herb, properly *Hypericum androsaemum*; but Markham, in common with many others, thought it a synonym for *agnus castus* – see above i, 33. In "Hard Words," Markham described it as "an herb with reddish leaves, and sinewy like plantain."

159 An aromatic plant of doubtful identity; Turner gives a detailed description of one plant he saw in Cologne, brought from Jerusalem, but goes on to say that "for lack of the true amomum we may use the common *calamus aromaticus*" (1 *Herbal*, p. 40).

160 This recipe is not a purge but a "protein meal" still recommended for women in the early stages of labour.

161 Culpeper called *Aristolochia rotunda* "birthwort"; its magic is of long standing, for the name is derived from the same source as "aristocrat," and, as Turner explains, it "is so called because it is very good for women that labour of child" (1 *Herbal*, p. 57). Markham, following the Banckes herbal, wrongly identified it with galingale ("Hard Words").

162 Turner records a very similar recipe; "the juice of the fruit [of bryony] draweth milk to the breast, if it be taken with frumenty made of sodden [boiled] wheat" (11 *Herbal*, p. 167).

163 Swooneth.

164 See note to "mugwort," i, 176.

165 Hyoscine, which is present in henbane (*Hyoscyamus niger*) is a narcotic, but its effect as a plaster would be the sympathetic magic of a plant which is "cold" (see note to i, 32).

166 A skin disease, "the signs: the skin to be spotted like a snake [scaly]," Pope John xxi, *The Treasurie of Healthe* sig. F7.

167 "The foam that riseth from lead or silver when it is tried [refined]" (Bullokar); impure lead oxide. Culpeper gives directions on its preparation (*The London Dispensatory*, p. 213) and records a similar recipe for "deformities of the skin" (p. 186).

168 *Artemisia abrotanum*, a plant related to wormwood. Banckes and Lyte give similar accounts of its effect on hair: "This herb burnt and the ashes meddled with oil, it restoreth where any man lacketh hair" (Banckes, p. 7, the probable source); "The ashes ... mingled with the oils of Palma Christi, rapes, or old oil olive, restoreth the hair fallen from the head,

if the head be rubbed therewith, twice a day in the sun, or against a fire"
(Lyte).

169 Turner (*Names*, p. 163) says that "wild neppe" is another name for
bryony; the plant intended may also be the ground ivy, *Nepeta glechoma*
(*Glechoma hederacea L*) which is also called nep. The recipe is from
the Banckes herbal, which refers to the "wild nep or woodbind," but
woodbine is a different plant, honeysuckle, *Lonicera periclymenum*.
See also the note on nep, i, 165.

170 "The produce of an unspotted (immaculate) animal was naturally more
connected with both purity and perfection than that of a spotted one."
Wilfrid Bonser, *The Medical Background of Anglo-Saxon England*
(London: Wellcome Historical Medical Library, 1963), p. 217.

171 Oxycrate is a mixture of vinegar and water, but it is more likely here to
be a reference to the *emplastrum oxycroceum*, described by Culpeper (*The
London Dispensatory*, p. 202); of its properties he says: "It is of notable
softening and discussing [dispersing] quality, helps broken bones, and any
parts molested with cold, old aches."

172 Severe; involving considerable inflammation.

173 Dwarf mallow, *Malva borealis* (*M. rotundifolia L*), said by Gerarde to be
"good against the stinging of scorpions, bees, wasps and such like" (p.
784).

174 A fine clay imported from Armenia, used for its ability to reduce bleeding.
See i, 123.

175 The juice of sour crab-apples; see the instructions for making it, iii, 31.

176 This recipe, minus the *de minio* plaster, appeared earlier in *Markhams
Maister-peece* (1610), p. 451, and also in *Markhams Methode or Epitome*
(London, 1616; Poynter No. 26.1), p. 16.

177 "Royal ointment"; Culpeper says that it "bring[s] the filth or corrupted
blood from green fresh wounds," and gives directions for making it
(*The London Dispensatory*, p. 185).

178 A plaster containing red lead (*minium*); there were two kinds, a simple
and a compound, both said to be healing and drying when applied to
sores (*The London Dispensatory*, p. 201).

179 Ointment of poplar-buds, said by Culpeper to be "exceeding good in
burnings and scaldings, and inflammations" (*The London Dispensatory*,
p. 170, where the instructions for making it are also given).

180 See *The London Dispensatory*, "Unguentum nervinum. The nerve or
sinew-ointment" (p. 192).

181 When mercury is mixed vigorously with certain materials (oil, sugar,
chalk, etc.) it becomes dispersed into very finely divided globules which
have the appearance of a white powder. The mercury thus "killed"
(no longer "quick," or alive) is not changed chemically, but it is more
easily assimilated into an ointment.

182 In the first part of *Countrey Contentments* (1615), Markham suggests that
this recipe be used for hounds troubled with the itch; the hound, however, should be anointed "before a good fire" (p. 22).

183 "To rip up any thing that is sewed" (*Dialect Dictionary*).

184 Lichen; the modern term did not become general in use until the eighteenth
century, hence the seeming circumlocution.

185 Possibly dialect for a herb, but more likely a misprint for or misreading of "fine," influenced by the word "fire" earlier in the sentence.
186 "Wort" is a general word for any plant; it is Markham's generalization of "red dock," as the word is an addition to the original recipe in Banckes (p. 8).
187 "The name of a corrosive powder called red mercury [mercuric oxide] used by surgeons to eat corrupted flesh" (Bullokar).
188 Unidentified. There is an "ivy-wort" recorded in the *Middle English Dictionary* (ed. S.M. Kuhn).
189 "Ointment of gold," but the name comes from the colour – yellow wax and saffron are two of the ingredients – not from the metal.
190 A healing ointment for the head; Culpeper mentions an *emplastrum* ["plaster"] *cephalicum* (*Directory*, p. 197).
191 "Green" means "fresh"; for the melilot plaster, see i, 22.
192 Scraps of soft leather.
193 The flowers of the plant *Typha latifolia*. A fine example of the absurdity of Sir Frederick Smith's judgement of Markham is his comment on this recipe: "There is also a prescription for injuries due to burns and scalds, which among other ingredients contains 'half a bushel of the downs of catts tayles.' ... Was he serious? At times it would seem that he deliberately wrote nonsense. My own belief is that the inclusion of these outrageous prescriptions was deliberate and intentional" (*The Early History of Veterinary Literature*, vol. i, London, 1919, p. 274). How "outrageous" Markham was may be measured by Lyte's comment that "the down of [the herb cats' tails] mingled with swine's grease, well washed, healeth burnings and scaldings" (p. 513).
194 The name given by "herbaries and pothecaries" to honeysuckle or woodbine (see Turner, *Names*, p. 60).
195 The same combination of mucilage and tannin is recommended by Thomas Moulton in *The Myrour or Glasse of Helth*: "For burning with fire. Take the rind of an elm tree and seethe it half a day and let it cool, and gather of the thick that thou findest upon the water with a feather, and every day anoint with the feather" (Sigs. 7–7v).
196 "It is recommended by the later physicians to be good for green wounds, and old filthy ulcers" (Gerarde, p. 219).
197 "This ointment being acknowledged to be the invention of Avicenna ... is called the Apostles' ointment because of the twelve ingredients, as if the Apostles had consulted to make a rare ointment, and every one had put in his ingredient" (*The London Dispensatory*, p. 189; the ingredients are given, and the mixture is said to "consume corrupt and dead flesh"). The recipe for "A salve for a green wound," i, 227 is a version of *unguentum apostolorum*.
198 "Ointment of Egypt"; "a reddish unguent to be bought at the Pothecary's, and is sovereign for fistulas" (Markham, "Hard Words"). According to Culpeper: "It cleanseth filthy ulcers and fistulas forcibly, and not without pain. It takes away dead and proud flesh ... the surgeons of our days use it commonly instead of *Apostolorum* to cleanse wounds" (*The London Dispensatory*, p. 184). William Clowes (see Introduction p. xxxi) tells an amusing story of a patient who was given *unguentum Aegyptiacum* for an ulcer, and a purgative to be taken at the same time; she applied the

purgative to the ulcer and swallowed the ointment, but was cured in any case (*Selected Writings*, ed. Poynter, pp. 56–8).

199 The *Dialect Dictionary* records a "slake-trough" as the container for water in a smith's forge, where the steel is slaked or tempered by rapid cooling.

200 *Rubia tinctorum*, used as a source of red dye; the colour suggests its use as a vulnerary (see the note on red dock, i, 55). "It staucheth bleeding, mitigateth inflammations ... For these causes they be mixed with potions, which the later physicians call 'wound drinks'" (Gerarde, p. 962).

201 The plaster described is very similar to the *de minio* (simple version) described in *The London Dispensatory*, p. 201; Dawson's *Leechbook* also contains a similar recipe (p. 115).

202 Pliny said that salvia was "very effectual against scorpions and sea-dragons. Also an inunction [ointment] made therewith and oil together, is commended much for the sting of serpents" (trans. Holland, 26, VI, p. 246).

203 While the dew is still on, thus adding further power to the herb.

204 Oil from bay leaves; the technique for extracting it is described in Henslow, p. 105, and in *The London Dispensatory*, p. 176.

205 A skin disease in which the skin becomes scaly and covered with scabs: scabies, tinea, ringworm, etc.

206 Avens; see i, 144.

207 "A tetter is a filthy kind of ulcer like unto a canker, only it is somewhat more knotty, and doth not spread ... and many times it will remain between the skin and the flesh ... and will not break" (*Markhams Maisterpeece*, p. 472). Serpigo is a creeping skin disease; both the tetter and the serpigo are mentioned by Thersites in *Troilus and Cressida* (v.i.27 and II.3.81).

208 "Sublimed mercury is called by the vulgar speech ... white mercury ... This corrosive medicine is made of quicksilver, salt, and the calcother of vitriol [calcium sulphate] only by sublimation, or distilling them together" (John Woodall, *The Surgions Mate*, 1617, p. 299). The result of this reaction would be the formation of calomel, a white powder formerly used in many medicines, including purges.

209 Syphilis, probably brought from the New World by the Spanish, spread from Spain through France to England.

210 "A green substance made of the rust of brass or copper, which hath been hanged certain days over strong vinegar; it is of a fretting [corrosive] nature, and therefore to be used with great discretion" (Bullokar). The substance thus formed would be copper acetate.

211 A mucilageneous gum obtained from the tree *Acacia senegal*, native to north Africa.

212 "A strong corrosive powder called white mercury [see i, 221], used by surgeons to consume corrupted flesh" (Bullokar on "*sublimatum*").

213 Candied or solid honey; see note to "stoned" honey, iv, 7, and cf. "life" honey, i, 71.

214 This recipe is for the "ointment of the apostles," *unguentum apostolorum* (see i, 212).

215 "A sap or liquor flowing in some hot countries out of a plant *panax* [*Opopanax chironium*]. It is brought hither dry, being of a yellow colour on the outside, and white within, if it be not over-stale" (Bullokar).

216 "A gum or liquor drawn forth of a plant in Syria ... called *ferula*. It is of

a strange savour and very pure, close and firm, neither too moist, nor too dry" (Bullokar).

217 "A kind of gum almost like to frankincense, so-called because it groweth in Lybia, near the place where the temple of Ammon was" (Bullokar).

218 A mistake for *bdellium*, one of the ingredients for *unguentum apostolorum*; bdellium is another gum, taken from plants of the genus *Balsamodendron*.

219 Calamine, zinc carbonate or zinc silicate; other recipes for *unguentum apostolorum* recommend verdigris or white copperas (zinc sulphate).

220 *Aristolochia longa*, according to other recipes for *unguentum apostolorum*.

221 True; genuine.

222 See above, i, 226.

223 An oil made from the hooves of cattle.

224 Near.

225 Coarse soap; see iii, 25 and note.

226 Literally a winding-sheet for a body; here a plaster.

227 Oil from *Lavendula spica*, French lavender.

228 Boiled.

229 The context suggests that this is the morello cherry, described by Cotgrave (1611) as "late-ripe cherries, dried for winter provision." "Petty" morel is black nightshade.

230 Wild marjoram, *Origanum vulgare*: "It healeth scabs, itchings, and scurfiness being used in baths" (Gerarde, p. 242).

231 Usually another name for comfrey; the mention of comfrey itself later in the recipe may be the result of Markham's technique of editing recipes together under the same topic.

232 A recipe for almond milk is given by A.W., fol. 34.

233 Here, *Ranunculus aquatilis*.

234 Or pomewater, a cooking apple; Murrell (1617) recommends them for making apple fritters (p. 50). Drayton mentions the pomewater in *Poly-Olbion* (song 18), and Shakespeare in *Love's Labour's Lost* (iv.ii.4).

235 Costmary, *Chrysanthemum balsamita*, also called alecost from its use in flavouring ale before the introduction of hops into England.

236 It is not clear whether this refers to a particular variety of sage, or whether it means a sage of "strength" or "power."

237 A plant introduced from North America, *Ambrosia artemisifolia*.

238 *The London Dispensatory* records a less complicated recipe for oil of swallows, p. 182.

239 The same recipe is recorded by Culpeper in *The London Dispensatory*, p. 177.

240 "The camomile, especially the white, is hot and dry in the first degree" (Lyte, p. 184).

241 A popular panacea of the period, the ingredients of which varied considerably; see Peter Levens (or Levins), *The Pathway to Health* (1582), pp. 219–20, for a more elaborate version; also Sir Hugh Platt, *Delightes*; and *The London Dispensatory*, pp. 108–9. Thomas Cogan gives us a glimpse of the process which led to so many variations of popular recipes of this kind: "I for my part, having made [Dr Stevens' water] right according to the prescription, found the water so weak of the wine, so strong of the herbs, so unpleasant in taste, that I was fain to make it after another manner. So taking double the spices ... and of every herb but half a

handful, and not Gascon wine but sack or very strong ale, I made a water very strong in taste ... and let no man condemn me until he have proved [it]" (*The Haven of Health* [London, 1584], pp. 231–2).

242 Wines from the old province of Gascony, now roughly equivalent to the Bordeaux wine-growing area; the dry red table wines in particular are referred to. See iv, 31.

243 Both origanum and wild marjoram are usually identified with *Origanum vulgare*, much used in the kitchen today; the mention of them both in this recipe may again be an indication that more than one source was used.

244 More properly *ros solis*, sundew (not "sunrose"), *Drosera rotundifolia*. "Our Englishmen nowadays set very much by it and hold that it is good for consumptions, swooning and faintness of heart, but I have no sure experience of this, neither have I read of any old writer what virtues it hath, wherefore I promise nothing of it" (Turner, iii *Herbal*, p. 79). A plant which has what appears to be dew on it even in the heat of the sun was naturally thought to be particularly powerful.

245 See vi, 28.

246 "A small round thing, as small as the hoar frost on the ground ... it was like coriander-seed, white; and the taste of it was like wafers made with honey" (Exodus 16:14, 31).

247 Mastic is the gum or resin from the tree *Pistacia lentiscus* (see iii, 26).

248 Olibanum is "The right frankincense, which is a gum growing in Arabia, whereof there are two kinds; the female or smaller frankincense, and the male, the greater, whiter, and stronger" (Bullokar). The "smaller" frankincense would have been resin from the fir tree, which was often called frankincense because of a similarity in appearance (see vii, 9).

CHAPTER II

1 "Wilt thou have this man to thy wedded husband, to live together after God's ordinance, in the holy estate of Matrimony; wilt thou obey him, and serve him, love, honour, and keep him in sickness and in health; and forsaking all other, keep thee only unto him, so long as you both shall live?" (*The Book of Common Prayer*). The first chapter described how the housewife was to care for her husband "in sickness"; the chapter which follows demonstrates how she is to keep him "in health."

2 The section which follows (paragraphs 3–9) is taken from the table introducing *Maison Rustique, or, The Countrie Farme* by Charles Estienne and John Liebault, translated by Richard Surflet and first published in English in 1600 (see Introduction). The advice which follows is thus more appropriate to the French housewife and the French climate. More reliable information on English habits can be gathered from William Lawson's *A New Orchard and Garden ... with The Countrie Housewifes Garden for Herbs* (London, 1617), later incorporated with *The English Housewife* as part of *A Way to Get Wealth*; and John Parkinson's *Paradisi in Sole, Paradisus Terrestris* (London, 1629), "The Ordering of The Kitchen Garden," pp. 461–553. Markham himself, in *The English Husbandman* (pt. ii, 1615, pp. 17–30) has several far more thoroughly thought out chapters on the kitchen garden.

3 Surflet's text reads "coleworts of all sorts." Parkinson commented on the

use of plants of the cabbage family in salads: "Coleworts are of divers kinds, and although some of them are wholly spent among the poorer sort of people, yet some of them may be dressed and ordered as may delight a curious palate" (p. 469).

4 Of borage, John Evelyn wrote: "The tender leaves, and flowers especially, may be eaten in composition [a 'compound sallat' – see paragraph 12 below]" (p. 13). Garden bugloss was *Anchusa officinalis*, common bugloss *Lycopsis arvensis* (see also the note on langdebeef, i, 27).

5 According to Parkinson the common chervil was much used "both with French and Dutch who do much more delight in herbs of stronger taste than the English do ... It is used as a pot-herb with us. Sweet chervil, gathered while it is young, and put among other herbs for a sallat, addeth a marvellous good relish to the rest" (pp. 469, 495).

6 Here probably the castor-oil plant, *Ricinus communis*; the housewife grew herbs for medicinal as well as culinary purposes.

7 Not grown merely for ornament, as Parkinson explains: "The flowers of marigold, picked clean from the heads, and pickled up against winter, make an excellent sallat" (p. 470). See also the list of herbs used in soup, ii, 40.

8 Surflet's translation of the French *anise muscat*, probably to be understood as "aniseeds, muscatel grapes," though, like several plants mentioned here, the muscatel vine is not an annual.

9 Blites, or wild spinach, a plant similar to orach (*Atriplex hortensis*) mentioned below, paragraph 6. Markham, in *The English Husbandman*, remarks that there are two kinds of blite, red and white, and continues, "This herb never needeth weeding, and if he be suffered to shed his seed it will hardly ever to be got out of the garden." Comments on it as a salad herb are uncomplimentary: "the leaves of blite are unsavoury and are of no quality" (Turner, 1 *Herbal*, p. 85); "it is counted but a weed, or unprofitable herb" (Lyte, p. 547); "the tops may be eaten as asparagus, or sodden boiled in pottage ... but...'tis insipid enough" (Evelyn, p. 12).

10 Gerarde says that skirrets are planted in March or April rather than February, and that "at this time the roots which be gathered are eaten raw" (p. 871).

11 White succory is endive; Evelyn says that "The largest, whitest, and tenderest leaves [are] best boiled ... the ampler leaves by many preferred before lettuce" (pp. 24–5).

12 Originally "cabbage" meant "head"; cole was the general name for what is now the cabbage family (cf. "kale").

13 A name given to several wild plants, most commonly *Plantago coronopus*, hartshorn plantain; the mystery as to why such a plant should be cultivated in the housewife's garden is solved by reference to Markham's source. In *Maison Rustique* the plant is "corne de boeuf"; hartshorn is given by Cotgrave (1611) as the translation of "corne de cerf." "Corne boeuf" is translated as the more probable "herb fenugreek."

14 The reading in Surflet; Markham has "cabbage, lettuce" in all editions. Cabbage-lettuces are explained by Parkinson as lettuces that "grow very great, and close their heads" (p. 468), i.e. head lettuce.

15 The garden burnet, *Poterium sanguisorba*, used to flavour claret (Parkinson, p. 483), and much admired by John Evelyn, who said it was "of

so cheering and exhilarating a quality, and so generally commended, as [gives] it admittance unto all salads" (pp. 54–5).

16 The chicory, closely related to endive or white succory; see i, 16. According to Parkinson, succory was sometimes used in salads, "but because it is more bitter than endive, it is not so generally used" (p. 469).

17 Tomatoes, so named because (like potatoes) when first introduced they were thought to have aphrodisiac qualities.

18 The balsam apple, a plant related to the gourd, cucumber etc., introduced from the West Indies.

19 The natural habitat of samphire (*Crithmum maritimum*) is on rocks by the sea, but Lyte mentions that "The herbarists of this country do plant it in their gardens" (p. 578).

20 Surflet's translation of the French *muguets*, which now means lily of the valley; Lyte, however, gives *muguet* as the French equivalent of "wood-row" (woodruff, *Asperula odorata*), and says that "In this country [England] they plant it in all gardens" (p. 540).

21 From Surflet, omitted by Markham.

22 Garden orach or mountain spinach, *Atriplex hortensis*. Parkinson says that "there are many dishes of meat made with them while they are young, for being almost without savour of themselves, they are the more convertible into what relish anyone will make them, with sugar, spice etc." (p. 488).

23 From Surflet which reads "preserve from the cold."

24 A Welsh onion (*Allium fistulosum*) midway in strength of flavour between an onion and a leek. John Evelyn, writing of chibols and leeks, remarks that "The Welsh, who eat them much, are observed to be very fruitful" (Evelyn, p. 30).

25 Fastidious, sensitive.

26 See below, ii, 20.

27 See below, ii, 95.

28 Elaborate and unusual dishes.

29 The original spelling is retained because Markham and his contemporaries used the term for cooked vegetables as well as raw. Markham was the first published writer on English cookery to devote any significant space to vegetables, brief though his treatment is.

30 Gerarde says that skirrets "be eaten boiled, with vinegar, salt, and a little oil, after the manner of a salad, and sometimes they be fried in oil and butter" (p. 872; for "boiled sallats" see below, ii, 14); he adds that they are supposed to provoke lust (sympathetic magic associated with a "hot" plant).

31 Markham thought highly enough of purslane as an "excellent sallat herb" that he added a paragraph on it to his editions of Heresbach, *The Whole Art of Husbandry* (p. 111).

32 "An honest laborious country-man, with good bread, salt, and a little parsley, will make a contented meal with a roasted onion" (Evelyn, p. 48).

33 "We have seen how necessary it is, that in the composure of a [compound] sallat, every plant should come in to bear its part, without being over-power'd by some herb of a stronger taste, so as to endanger the native *sapor* and virtue of the rest; but fall into their places, like the notes in music, in which there should be nothing harsh or grating: and though

admitting some discords (to distinguish and illustrate the rest) striking in the more sprightly and sometimes gentler notes, reconcile all dissonancies and melt them into an agreeable composition"; sound advice from John Evelyn (pp. 91–2), not always followed by Markham's contemporaries, judging by the rather overpowering salad in paragraph 13.

34 Probably a red broccoli; its presence in this recipe is to be explained by its rarity: "Cauliflowers are to be had in this country but very seldom, for that it is hard to meet with good seed" (Parkinson, p. 469).

35 Particularly noteworthy in this recipe is the number of ingredients which must have been imported; almonds, raisins, figs, capers, olives, currants, sugar, oranges, and lemons. Murrell's *Two Books* has a similarly extravagant recipe, pp. 116–17.

36 A similar recipe is given by John Murrell (1617, pp. 52–3). Murrell adds: "Then cut hard eggs into quarters to garnish it withal, and serve it upon sippets. So may you serve borage, bugloss, endive, succory, cauliflowers, sorrell, marigold leaves, water cresses, leeks boiled, onions, asparagus, rocket, alexanders ... Eggs are necessary, or at least very good for all boiled sallats."

37 In 1568 Turner wrote "spinach ... is an herb lately found and not long in use ... I know not wherefore it is good saving to fill the belly and loose it a little" (III *Herbal*, p. 71). Henry Buttes, writing in 1599, was more informative; as well as recommending a method of preparation similar to Markham's ("Fried with its own juice, without water, then condite [seasoned] with oil, sorrel-juice [see i, 15], and raisins of the sun"), he describes amongst its medicinal qualities the following: "[It] doth enlarge the breast; cure the cough; moderately cool the lungs" (*Dyets Dry Dinner*, sig. F5v).

38 The staple starch served with most meals: small slices of bread, toasted or fried, then used to soak up the gravy or broth.

39 "Broom buds [are] hot and dry, retaining the virtue of capers ... and, being pickled, are sprinkled among the sallats, or eaten by themselves" (Evelyn, p. 14).

40 According to Parkinson (p. 470), "Clove gillyflowers ... preserved or pickled ... make a sallat nowadays in the highest esteem with Gentles and Ladies of the greatest note."

41 The particular example given seems to be quite edible, particularly since it is to be seasoned with "vinegar, oil, and a little pepper."

42 Henry Buttes agrees that carrots should be boiled "thoroughly" but suggests a more adventurous seasoning: "Vinegar, oil, mustard and coriander" (*Dyets Dry Dinner*, sig. H2).

43 Shields and coats of arms.

44 Fricassee is a term still used for dishes of stewed and spiced meat; Markham uses the term more generally for dishes with several ingredients mixed, and the result either fried or stewed. "Quelquechoses" are literally "somethings": the word became corrupted to "kickshaw," a worthless trifle; Murrell (1617) has a recipe "To make Kicks-Hawes" (p. 67).

45 The fish, a staple Lenten dish, often preserved by salting. See paragraph 121 below.

46 Rind.

47 See the following recipe.

48 An egg dish mid-way between an omelette and a pancake, so called because (as the recipe shows) it was often flavoured with the herb tansy: "In the spring time are made, with the leaves [of tansy] newly sprung up and with eggs, cakes or tansies, which are pleasant in taste, and good for the stomach" (Gerarde, p. 526).

49 *The French Pastry-cooke* gives alternative recipes for flesh days and fish days: cream or milk is to be used only on fish days, for the preference is for "good fresh broth which hath been made without herbs" to be added (pp. 247–8).

50 Sir Kenelm Digby preferred his tansy both rich and heavy: "Take three pints of cream, fourteen new-laid eggs (seven whites put away), one pint of juice of spinach, six or seven spoonfuls of juice of tansy, a nutmeg (or two) sliced small, half a pound of sugar, and a little salt. Beat all these well together, then fry it in a pan with no more butter than is necessary." *The Closet of Sir Kenelm Digby, Knight, Opened* (1669), p. 218.

51 A recipe calling for the use of tansy is in *The Good Huswifes Handmaide*, fols. 50v–51, but *The Good Hous-wiues Treasurie*, like Markham, recommends "walnut tree leaves or lettuce alone, or all other good herbs" (B4v). Tansy is a rather rank flavoured herb.

52 "Water is not wholesome, sole by itself, for an Englishman ... water is cold, slow, and slack of digestion. The best water is rain-water, so be it that it be clean and purely taken. Next to it is running water, the which doth swiftly run from the east unto the west upon stones or pebbles. The third water to be praised is river or brook water, the which is clear, running on pebbles and gravel. Standing waters, the which be refreshed with a fresh spring, is commendable; but standing waters and well-waters, to which the sun hath no reflection, although they be nigher than other running waters be, yet they be not so commendable. And let every man beware of all waters the which be standing, and be putrified with froth ... The water the which every man ought to dress his meat withal, or shall use baking or brewing, let it be running; and put it in vessels that it may stand there two or three hours ere it be occupied; then strain the upper part through a thick linen cloth, and cast the inferial part away." Andrew Boorde, *A Dyetary of Helth* (1542), pp. 252–3.

53 *The Good Huswifes Handmaide* is one book which recommends cream, but it also provides further information on the method of cooking: "Take a frying pan, and put in it a little piece of butter, as big as your thumb, and when it is molten brown, cast it out of your pan, and with a ladle put to the further side of your pan some of your stuff [batter], and hold your pan aslope so that your stuffing may run abroad over all the pan as thin as may be: then set it to the fire, and let the fire be very soft [gentle], and when the one side is baked, then turn the other, and bake them as dry as ye can without burning" (fol. 49v).

54 A less detailed recipe in *The Good Huswifes Handmaide* (fol. 43) recommends a "soft fire"; *The Ladies Cabinet Enlarged and Opened* (London, 1654) omits the toast, and instructs the cook to stir the ingredients "well together, and make them into the form of little pasties, and fry them in a pan with sweet butter" (p. 202).

55 "Pain perdu," hidden bread, a variety of the modern French toast. The

French origin of the term is not in this case evidence of "strangeness and rarity ... from other countries" (see i, 6) for similar, though simpler recipes are found in *Two Fifteenth Century Cookery Books* (bk. i, p. 42; bk. ii, p. 83). See "Vocabulary of Cooking in the Fifteenth Century" by M.S. Sergeantson, *Essays and Studies*, xxxiii (1937), 25–37. A modern version, "Smothered Bread" is given in *Pleyn Delit* by Constance B. Hieatt and Sharon Butler.

56 The edition of 1631, which was revised by Markham (see Introduction, pp. liv–lvi) omits this passage; it may have been a simple printer's error, or Markham may have decided against the extra sweetness (but see Introduction, p. xxxvi, on the use of sugar).

57 The earlier name for these was "ising puddings" (see *The Good Huswifes Handmaide*, fol. 50, and II Dawson, p. 54). Joseph Cooper (1654) gives more detailed quantities: 3 pints oatmeal, 2 lb. beef suet minced, 8–10 egg yolks and half the number of whites, 1/4 oz. nutmeg, 1/4 oz. sugar, 1 quart cream, a little mace and salt (p. 146).

58 The coarse hulled grain: see chapter viii, in particular viii, 10, for Markham's own recipes for puddings.

59 The cleaned intestines, which were stuffed to make sausages. The *OED*, quoting this one occurrence of the word, defines it as a "shape" for a pudding, but the context clearly indicates otherwise (see also ii, 39, etc.). Compare Joseph Cooper's recipe for white puddings: "mix [the ingredients] well together and fill them into guts, being clean."

60 It seems that an ingredient, grated bread, has been omitted; Dawson (II, p. 9) has a similar recipe, but adds the information that "the quantity of a farthing loaf grated" should be added. The result is similar to a haggis; see II Dawson, pp. 53–4 and viii, 9 below.

61 "And so boil it with a little mutton broth and wine, lettuce and spinach whole in the same broth" (II Dawson, p. 9).

62 A "link" in a chain of sausages; the recipe again misses out bread crumbs; cf. *The Good Hous-wiues Treasurie*: "How to make sausages. Take the fillets of a hog, and half as much of the suet of the hog, and chop them both very small, then take grated bread, two or three yolks of eggs, a spoonful of gross pepper, as much salt, temper them with a little cream, and so put them into the skins and broil them on a gridiron" (Sig. B4).

63 A chine is the backbone and adjoining flesh left after the bacon has been cut off.

64 The flank; this passage is the only example of this usage recorded in the *OED*.

65 A castrated fowl. Venner writes: "Their flesh is of all fowls the best and wholesomest for students, and such as live delicately, or are by nature weak and sickly, for it is very easily digested" (p. 61).

66 The way food was used as a status symbol is satirized by Philip Massinger in *The City Madam*; when questioned by Lady Frugal on the nature of his purchases, the steward Holdfast replies that he has

> The cream of the market, provision enough
> To serve a garrison. I weep to think on't.
> When my master got his wealth, his family fed
> On roots and livers, and necks of beef on Sundays

> But now I fear it will be spent on poultry.
> Butcher's meat will not go down. (1.i.144–9)

67 Markham was proud of the husbandman's right to this title: "[The] husbandman is he whom God in the scriptures giveth many blessings, for his labours of all other are most excellent, and therefore to be a husbandman is to be a goodman; whence ... we even to this day do seriously observe to call every husbandman ... Goodman Such-a-one, a title (if we rightly observe it) of more honour and virtuous note than many which precede it at feasts and in gaudy places" (*The English Husbandman*, p. 3).

68 Sour crab-apple juice; see iii, 31 below. The nearest modern equivalent would be apple vinegar.

69 *Chrozophoria tinctoria*. "With the seed of the small turnsole (being yet green) they dye and stain old linen clouts and rags into a purple colour ... wherewithal in this country men use to colour jellies, wines, fine confections and comfits" (Lyte, p. 61).

70 Red sandalwood, used as a dye; see note to yellow sanders, iii, 33.

71 The same basic technique is used in *The Good Huswifes Handmaide* (fols. 5–5v), but the mallard is stuffed with whole onions, and the broth seasoned with verjuice (two spoonsful) and salt.

72 Literally "all rotten"; the name might be taken to suggest that the herbs and spices are added to conceal an "off" flavour in the meat, but it is more an indication that the meat was to be stewed until extremely soft and, as it were, decomposed (see in *OED* the entry under 1622). The earlier texts have the form "olepotrige" (not recorded in *OED*), which suggests a connection by analogy with "porridge," plausible enough if the meat is to be cooked until it disintegrates.

73 Venison from the large red deer and the smaller fallow deer: "fallow" refers to the colour, a pale brown.

74 According to Muffett, rails "deserve to be placed next the partridge, for their flesh is as sweet as their feeding good, and they are not without cause preferred to noblemen's tables" (p. 95).

75 Robert May gives more precise directions on the number of "fowls" to be added: "A goose or turkey, two capons, two ducks, two pheasants, two widgeons, four partridges, four stockdoves, four teals, eight snipes, twenty four quails, forty eight larks" (pp. 1–2).

76 A popular dish: similar recipes (with no evidence of verbal borrowings) can be found in *The Good Huswifes Handmaide*, fols. 3v and 4 (two recipes); 1 Dawson, fols. 5v–6; A.W., fol. 5v; *The Good Hous-wiues Treasurie*, A3 and A4; Platt, *Delightes*, F2v (no. 5); and Murrell (1617), pp. 28–9.

77 Like the teal and the mallard, the widgeon is a wild duck; "Widgeon and curlew are of hard digestion ... they are good for them that live near to moors, and that have no better meat" (Venner, p. 68). See also ii, 85.

78 Platt suggests, with more imagination, that the cook should "put into the belly of the fowl a few sweet herbs and a litle mace, stick half a dozen of cloves in his breast..." (*Delightes* F2v, no. 6).

79 An early work on carving is the *Boke of Keruynge* (1513), often pillaged by later writers for its quaint vocabulary. Giles Rose, in *A Perfect School*

of *Instructions for the Officers of the Mouth* (1682) gives diagrams of the various ways fowl, fish and joints should be carved.

80 Later editions substitute the synonym "boil."

81 Platt recommends that the sippet should be "a toast of bread steeped in verjuice" (*Delightes*, F2v. no. 6).

82 Take from the spit when it begins to drip fat.

83 Here refers to the guinea fowl, often called the turkey-cock or -hen (see Venner, p. 61, who refers in the margin to "Guineas or Turkeys," and cf. 191 below, where turkeys are included amongst the "lesser land fowl").

84 A fresh-water fish often, like carp, raised in ponds in Markham's day.

85 A large freshwater fish, related to the carp; Muffett writes: "It is most likely that this is the fish dedicated to Diana, the goddess of chastity, for it is a very cold, moist, and gelid fish ... quenching lust, and greatly troubling both head and belly, if it be usually and much eaten of; so we eat it cold laid in jelly" (p. 175).

86 Simmered or braised in a closed vessel. The technique and the word are still used in Nova Scotia; there is a recipe for "smoored pullets" in *The Canadian Cookbook* by Jehane Benoit (Toronto, 1974), p. 94.

87 The red gurnard. Henry Buttes suggests a simpler method of preparation: "Fry and condite [season] it with orange juice and pepper; or eat it hot with vinegar" (sig. M7v); Muffett agrees, suggesting that they are best "fried with onions, butter, and vinegar," and explaining that "they are so little, that seething would soak out their best nourishing substance" (p. 166).

88 "Sheeps' pummices [purtenance], is the head, heart, lights, liver and wind-pipe of a sheep, all hanging together" (Holme II, iii, p. 88). *Mrs. Beeton's Book of Household Management* (London: Ward Lock, 1906) has a modernized version for "Lamb's head and pluck" (p. 569).

89 For a similar dish, carrots replacing parsnips, *The Good Huswifes Hand-maide* (fol. 7v) suggests thyme, savoury, and hyssop.

90 A.W. tells more of this first part of the cooking process: "First let your neat's foot be scalded and made clean. Then take onions, slice them and boil [blanch] them in fair water. Then take half water and half wine, so much as need to serve for the boiling of the neat's foot ... and put it in a pipkin; put therein some cloves, and a little whole pepper, and take the onions out of the water they were sodden [boiled] in, and put them into the same pipkin, and the neat's foot with them till it be almost enough" (fol. 10).

91 Usually a pickling-fluid; here the water in which the foot was boiled.

92 The next few paragraphs of sensible general comments are almost certainly by Markham. From early times the English were highly regarded for their roast meats; in 1617 Fynes Moryson commented that "the English cooks in comparison with other nations are most commended for roasted meat." *An Itinerary (1617)* (Glasgow: James Mackehose and Sons, 1907–8), vol. iii, p. 150.

93 To render swan palatable, Markham recommends: "For the feeding and fatting of the swan, which is a noble and prime dish at any great feast, you are to understand that they be the cygnets which are to be fed, and not the old swan ... you shall put them into a close [fenced] pond out of which they cannot get ... near to the verge of this pond you shall place

three tubs; in the one you shall put good old dry oats, in another some maslin [mash] of wheat and barley mixed together and swimming in water, and in the third some old dried malt ... and three weeks or a month in this manner is a sufficient time to fat any swan thoroughly and cleanly" (addition to Heresbach, p. 344).

94 "The flesh is neither good, delicate nor wholesome, but only a bird for state and show ... being a bird that delighteth to eat newts, toads, frogs, adders and snakes, whence it comes that he is called the scavenger of the husbandman's yards; and more than his beauty to look upon, and the ornament of his feathers for sundry purpose, I hardly know any other virtue in him" (Markham, in addition to Heresbach, p. 331).

95 Compare "soaking fire," i, 211, and ii, 24. The term is still used by potters when a kiln is kept at a steady temperature for an extended period.

96 See paragraph 69 below.

97 See below, paragraph 71.

98 The dredging is sprinkled on the roast towards the end of the cooking period, and forms a crisp crust on the outside of the joint.

99 John Murrell suggests that the oysters should be used in the sauce, not as stuffing (*Two Books*, pp. 129–30).

100 This seems to have been a popular trick, though some other recipes require the meat which has been cut off the bone to be minced and added to the pudding. The leg is then boiled or baked rather than roasted. See *The Good Huswifes Handmaide*, fol. 2; Platt, *Delights*, sig. F3 (no. 7); Murrell (1617), pp. 25–6 and 71. See also Introduction, p. xxxv.

101 Or indeed the whole animal: Prince Hal describes Falstaff as "that roasted Manningtree ox with the pudding in his belly" (1 Henry IV, II.iv.451).

102 An ancient and popular dish, though the olives were more often baked (see paragraph ii, 14 and note). The word was earlier spelt "allows" or "aloes," and the derivation can be seen in the definition of "Aloyau de boeuf" in Randle Cotgrave's French-English dictionary (1611): "A short rib of beef, or the fleshy end of the rib, divided from the rest and roasted." The association with olives may be a result of the shape of the stuffed slices.

103 Dawson has a similar recipe, but adds the following stuffing: "Take the liver, parboil it and strain it with a little cream and yolks of eggs, and put thereto grated bread, marrow, small raisins, nutmegs in powder, mace, sugar and salt, and stir all these together, and put into the pig's belly, and sew the pig, then spit it with the hair on" (II, p. "49," i.e. 65).

104 Pluck, disembowel; as in the execution of a criminal "hanged, drawn and quartered."

105 This curious dish was probably devised to provide some variety on fast days.

106 See ii, 67.

107 The turner would be on the cooler side of the fire.

108 A.W. recommends that the venison be parboiled first (fol. 25v; the same recipe appears in *The Good Huswifes Handmaide*, fol. 33v).

109 According to Venner, "Some judge [woodcocks] to approach somewhat near unto the nature of the partridge, and therefore is of them called 'rustic partridge'" (p. 66).

110 Spoonbills: "Shovellers feed most commonly upon the sea coast upon

cockles and shell-fish; being taken home and dieted with new garbage [scraps] and good meat, they are nothing inferior to fatted gulls" (Muffett, p. 109; see ii, 85 below).

111 Large waterfowl related to the heron. Muffett also offers advice on the preparation of these birds, in a passage that describes their flesh as of a fishy and strong savour. He suggests that young birds be chosen, and that they be marinated and cooked with "much spice, salt, or onions" (p. 93).

112 The flesh, or muscle, in this case probably of the wings.

113 Describing the birds in England that "make fine spirits and blood" Michael Drayton lists the following:

> The corn-land-loving quail, the daintiest of our birds,
> The rail, which seldom comes, but upon rich man's spits,
> The puet, godwit, stint, the palate that allure
> The miser, and do make a wasteful epicure:
> The knot that called was Canutus bird of old,
> Of that great King of Danes, his name that still doth hold.
> (*Poly-Olbion*, song xxv, 337–42.)

114 Further evidence of the range of birds used in early cookery comes from *A Proper New Booke of Cookery* (1575): "A mallard is good after a frost, till Candlemass, so is a teal and other wild fowl that swimmeth. A woodcock is best from October to Lent, and so be all other birds, as ousels, and thrushes, robins and such other; herons, curlews, crane, bittern, bustard, be at all times good, but best in winter; pheasants, partridge and rail be ever good, but best when they be taken with a hawk. Quail and larks be ever in season" (Sigs. A2–A2v). See also Venner, pp. 61–70.

115 Young birds or fledgelings. The edition of 1631 substitutes "puets," pewits.

116 "The seagull is to be rejected as all other birds of flesh of fishy savour: for he is of a very ill juice, and is not only unpleasant, but also very offensive to the stomach" Venner, p. 68). Muffett may have had Venner in mind when he commented: "[gulls] are rejected of everyone as a filthy meat; nevertheless being fed at home with new curds and good corn till they be fat, you shall seldom taste of a lighter or better meat" (p. 108).

117 "A goose is worst at midsummer moon, and best in stubble time [see paragraph 87], but when they be young green geese then they be best." *A Proper New Booke of Cookery* (1575), sig. A2.

118 The northern dialect word for gooseberries (see Gerarde, p. 1143); despite the sugar the sauce would be tart, as sorrel, gooseberries and verjuice are all sour. There is a similar recipe in A.W., fol. 6.

119 A goose fed on stubble; see the note to "green geese," note 117 above.

120 Usually, as here, a sauce made from blood, but Dawson (II, p. 15) and *Two Fifteenth Century Cookery Books* (pp. 77 and 108) have recipes without blood.

121 Heron; according to Venner, the heron "is of very hard and fibrous substance, it is fardly digested ... Moreover the flesh is of a fishy savour,

which in flesh is a note of greatest pravity [depravity, corruption]"
(p. 67).

122 A chawdron or chaudron usually includes not only the blood of the
animal, but the minced gizzards as well. See *Two Fifteenth Century
Cookery Books*, pp. 76 and 95.

123 Large sippets: slices of bread or toast soaked in a sauce. A similar recipe
in A.W. specifies that the bread be toasted (fol. 6).

124 The name still given to the four legal societies in London which train
students in the law. The students, often the younger sons of noblemen,
were noted for their extravagance; there is a hint in Markham's phrase that
the dish may have been thought mildly aphrodisiac; see the "marrow
bone pie," and note 147 below.

125 The Elizabethans went to great length to avoid a "barbecue" taste on their
meat; Sir Hugh Platt explains how to avoid smoke when carbonadoing:
"Make little dripping pans of paper, pasting up the corners with starch or
paste, wet them a little in water ... lay them on your gridiron and place
therein your slices of bacon, turning them as you see cause ... You must
be careful that your fire under the gridiron flame not, lest you happen
to burn your dripping pans" (*Delightes*, F12–12v, no. 26).

126 "To make carbonadoes of mutton. Cut a leg of mutton in thin fillets, and
to make it tender, chop it on both the sides with the back of a knife,
so that they be not chopped through, then salt them well, and lay them
on a gridiron, and broil them till they be enough, and with vinegar
and minced onions serve them forth" (A.W., fol. 30).

127 The seven paragraphs added here are taken, with modifications, from
Murrell (1617).

128 The roach and dace are small fresh-water fish.

129 The bottom crust (cf. the phrase "the heel of the loaf"); the original reads
"soale," which could also mean "soul," perhaps for the centre.

130 Pie-crust made in the shape of a coffin.

131 Murrell, from whom this recipe comes, advises that you should "put your
butter uppermost, to keep the rest moist" (1617, p. 41).

132 "Two or three new-laid eggs" (Murrell, 1617, p. 42).

133 "Pudding" (Murrell, 1617, p. 42).

134 Markham omitted a useful passage from Murrell here: "if you have no
wine, take fair water, and one spoonful of vinegar, and a little sugar, and
let these stew a quarter of an hour, then mince the yolk of an hard
egg..." (Murrell, *Two Books*, pp. 96–7).

135 Most friable, more like modern pastry (see the following paragraph).

136 The pies were baked on a flat tray rather than in a pie-dish, so the crust
had to be self-supporting.

137 *The Good Huswifes Handmaide* gives further advice: "To make paste, and
to raise coffins. Take fine flour, and lay it on a board, and take a certain
[quantity] of butter and water, and boil them together, but you must
take heed you put not too many yolks of eggs, for if you do, it will make
it dry and not pleasant in eating; and you must take heed you put not
in too much butter, for if you do, it will make it so fine and so short that
you cannot raise [it]: and this paste is good to raise all manner of coffins"
(fols. 17–17v).

138 Joseph Cooper gives more precise quantities: half a peck of flour, one

pound of butter, the whites only of nine or ten eggs and a very little salt (pp. 87–8); *The Ladies Companion* (1654) suggests that some rose-water should be added (pp. 71–2); and Sir Hugh Platt recommends a technique still used: "Drive [the paste] with a rolling-pin abroad, then put on small pieces of butter as big as nuts upon it, then fold it over, then drive it abroad again ... do this ten times" (*Delightes*, sig. B11v, no. 24).

139 A pie or tart baked in a dish with a cover of pastry; see paragraph 137 below.

140 Marinade.

141 Mild ale or beer; see below, ix, 6.

142 As the recipe shows, a spiced custard pie; the word is derived from the French "doucette," a diminutive of "douce," sweet.

143 *The Good Hous-wiues Treasurie* gives these instructions for the paste: "How to make doucets. Take a pint of flour, wet it with water, butter, and an egg, white and all and make not your paste too lithe [soft]; when they be raised, prick them with a pin on the bottom, then harden them either on the hearth or in the oven" (sig. B1).

144 See above, paragraph 69, and note. Other versions of this popular recipe are found in *Two Fifteenth Century Cookery Books* (pp. 40, 83); *A Proper New Book of Cookery* (1575, sig. B2v); *The Good Huswifes Handmaide* (fol. 32v); II Dawson (fols. 13, 15); and Murrell's *Two Books* (pp. 122–3).

145 Markham elsewhere remarks of strawberries that their "leaves are an excellent pot-herb and the fruit the most wholesome berry" (addition to Heresbach, p. 111).

146 Slices.

147 Eryngo is the candied root of the sea holly, *Eryngium maritimum*. Both the potato, newly introduced from America, and the eryngo were thought to have aphrodisiac qualities. At the moment when Falstaff, in *The Merry Wives of Windsor*, believes his amours to be on the point of con-summation, he cries: "Let the sky rain potatoes; let it thunder to the tune of Greensleeves, hail kissing-comfits and snow eringoes; let there come a tempest of provocation" (v.v.23). Marrow was also thought to give strength. Other cookery books of the period record similar recipes; "A tart to provoke courage either in man or woman" adds a further ingredient guaranteed to increase the power of the sympathetic magic, the "brains of three or four cock sparrows" (see I Dawson, fols. 20v–21 and *The Good Huswifes Handmaide*, fol. 32).

148 This recipe, and the one which follows, may be expanded from Murrell (1617, p. 48).

149 A pie made with minced meat; see paragraph 127 below.

150 Salt fish were soaked in fresh water before use.

151 Served cold during Lent. "Ling perhaps looks for great extolling, being counted the beef of the sea, and standing every fish day (as a cold supporter) at my Lord Mayor's table, yet is it nothing but a long cod" (Muffett, pp. 154–5). The ling would be salted rather than fresh, hence the reference to its "watering," or soaking in water to reduce saltiness.

152 A dessert of spiced clotted cream, as the recipe indicates. Holme describes the fool as "a kind of custard, but more crudelly [curdled], being made of cream, yolks or eggs, cinnamon, [and] mace, boiled, and served on

sippets, with sliced dates, sugar, and white and red comfits strewed thereon" (II, iii, 82).

153 See i, 40.

154 See ii, 111.

155 Recipes from other early books all recommend chewet pies made of veal: *Two Fifteenth Century Cookery Books*, p. 48; *The Good Huswifes Handmaide*, fols. 18–18v; Murrell (1617), pp. 39–40, and *Two Books*, p. 134.

156 May is more specific: 2 lb. currants, 2 lb. raisins, 2 lb. prunes, 1 oz. cloves and mace, 6 oz. salt.

157 *The Good Hous-wiues Treasurie* recommends a cooking time of 2–2 1/2 hours, and says that the pie "is good when the quince is out of season" (A7).

158 "Pear-wardens, in regard of the solidness of their substance, may be longest kept; they are of all sorts of pears the best and wholesomest. They are not to be eaten raw, because ... they are hardly digested ... yet they may be to a hot and choleric stomach well liking and agreeable, especially after the drinking of much strong wine or beer, because by sigillating [sealing]the mouth of the stomach ... they repress and infrigidate [cool] the hot fumes that vaporate to the head. But being baked or roasted, they are a delicate meat" (Venner, p. 115).

159 Sir Hugh Platt says that quinces can be kept in "penny ale" (small ale, see ix, 6) if the ale is renewed every 10 or 12 days, and maintains that "these quinces being baked at Whitsuntide did taste more daintily than any of those which are kept in our usual decoctions or pickles" (*Delightes*, D10v–11v). Other techniques for preserving are described in paragraphs 149, 181, 183, and 185 below.

160 The liquor obtained by infusing malt in water in preparation for making beer; see chapter ix.

161 A codling is a variety of cooking apple; to coddle is to stew, to simmer.

162 A general term for a pie made in a pastry-lined dish rather than a "coffin" of pastry; it could be a meat pie (as here), a vegetable pie or a fruit pie. Similar recipes are found in 1 Dawson (fol. 31v), A.W. (fol. 21), *The Good Hous-wiues Treasurie* (A7) and *The Good Huswifes Handmaide* (fol. 24); there is also a collection of recipes in Raffald, pp. 35–6.

163 Dawson suggests the use of "red wine [port] or claret wine" (1, 17).

164 In anticipation of.

165 The sense seems to be that tarts made with white blanched almonds will also have a pure white colour.

166 Coats of arms. The terms which follow are heraldic: "field," background; "charge," the device upon the "escutcheon" or shield; "mantles," ornamental scrolls and curves; "trails," trailing wreaths and sprays.

167 Codiniacs or quiddany; sweet meats made from quinces. Recipes for "paste of quinces" and "quince cakes" are given in paragraphs 147, 148, and 163 below. The *OED* records only the form used in late editions (1668), "cotiniates."

168 Heraldic devices used to unite the badges of two families.

169 May gives these quantities: 1 quart cream, 2 oz. rice, 8 egg yolks, 2 egg whites, 2 oz. currants (p. 282). The whitepot was a dish particularly associated with Devon.

170 The quince sweetmeats described here are what Markham calls "goodi-nyakes" or codiniacs (see paragraph 142 above).

171 "then set them in a box by the fire, with the lid of the box open, some two days, that they may dry" (Cooper, p. 185).

172 So called because the wine was strained through a conical cloth strainer, the invention of which was attributed to Hippocrates. Another recipe is found in paragraph 182 below; the spiced wine thus made can be very pleasant, though modern taste would dictate that less sugar be used.

173 Change the water; cf. Murrell (1617), "To make crystal jelly ... wash [calves' feet] in two or three warm waters, and lay them all night in fair water..." (p. 98).

174 Egg-white is still added to soup to clarify it; compare the "parel" used to clarify wine, iv, 3.

175 Randle Cotgrave's French-English dictionary (1611) defines "lesche" as "a long slice"; a leach was a dish which could be sliced. It was made of jellied meats or sweets (as here); a "dry" leach (see paragraph 159), was gingerbread or an uncooked sweetmeat. Platt gives these proportions for Markham's leach: 1/2 lb. almonds, 1 pint milk, 2 tsp. rose-water, 2 oz. sugar, and "the weight of three whole shillings" of isinglass (*Delightes*, B12v).

176 Platt gives the following proportions in a similar recipe: 3 stale manchets, 1 oz. ginger, 1 oz. cinnamon, 1 oz. liquorice and aniseeds beaten to-gether, 1/2 lb. sugar, 1 quart claret; "This is your gingerbread used at the Court, and at all gentlemen's houses at festival times" (*Delightes*, B10v). See also paragraphs 162 and 188 below.

177 "Box" was a general term for a container.

178 Probably the membrane, the "film" referred to in paragraphs 55, 122, and 141 above; the original reads "take of the viell," and this was amended in the 1631 edition to "take off the froth." The *OED* does not record "veil" as meaning "membrane" before 1760.

179 John Murrell in *A Delightful Daily Exercise* (London, 1621) has more precise measurements: 2 egg whites, 8 oz. flour, 4 oz. sugar, and 1 oz. aniseeds. He recommends rose-water instead of milk to make the paste, and directs that it be baked in an oven "as hot as for a manchet" for a quarter of an hour, with the proviso that they should "not be brown in any case" (No. 6, sig. A7).

180 Probably an error for "but"; i.e. eight whites and four yolks.

181 In Sir Thomas Platt's recipe, ale yeast is added (*Delightes*, B9v); since the cakes are expected to rise, it seems a necessary addition.

182 The jumbles would then be baked; see above, paragraph 156, and Platt *Delightes*, sig. B8.

183 Tragacanth gum, "obtained from several species of *Astragalus* ... (only partially soluble in water)" (*OED*).

184 The upper part of a still, in which the distilled vapour condensed.

185 The buds or seed vessels of a flower, usually rich in essential oils.

186 Orris; an aromatic powder made from the root of the Florentine iris.

187 A name used for many reeds; here probably *calamus aromaticus*. See iii, 25.

188 Benzoin, "A sweet smelling gum, good against hoarseness and the cough

... the tree upon which it groweth is not with us certainly known" (Bullokar). The gum from *Styrax benzoin* is still officinal; like storax, a resin which comes from the tree *Liquidambar orientalis*, it is used in inhalations designed to give relief to congestion.

189 The fruit of the wild rose.

190 A variable measure equivalent to 1/4 bushel or 2 gallons.

191 Yeast.

192 A town in Oxfordshire still noted for its cakes.

193 Murrell (1617): "It must be extremely much beaten before it will be a perfect paste, at least an hour" (no. 73).

194 The proportion of sugar to almonds varies: *A Closet for Ladies and Gentlewomen* (London, 1608) suggests 2 lb. almonds to 1 lb. sugar (pp. 37–8), *The French Pastry-cooke* a similar proportion of 1/2–3/4 lb. sugar to 1 lb. of almonds.

195 See Markham's recipe for wafers, paragraph 177 below. *The French Pastry-cooke* gives detailed instructions on making marchpane wafers – almond-flavoured yeast biscuits – pp. 102–6.

196 Other writers advise a gentle heat: "you must put [the wafers] into an oven which is above half cold, to dry your said marchpane almost half dry, but not to burn it" (*The French Pastry-cooke*, p. 228).

197 Platt's recipe calls for 1/2 lb. sugar for every pound of "quince pap," *The Ladies Companion* recommends equal weight, as does Markham in the next recipe.

198 *The Ladies Companion* describes the technique: "Set your [paste spread on a] pie plate in a warm oven or stove (upon two billets of wood for to keep it from the bottom of the oven) all night; then on the morrow turn it, and so do it every day until it be dry" (p. 46).

199 Adequate degree of viscosity; see below, ii, 189, and note 205.

200 A wooden mill, varieties of which were used for crushing hops, kneading bread, or separating the fibres of flax and hemp (see v, 34 and ix, 15 below).

201 See iii, 31.

202 See also paragraph 150 above.

203 Egg whites were used to clarify wine as well as water; see iv, 5, for example.

204 *The Ladies Cabinet Enlarged and Opened* (1654) continues "lay them on the bottom of a sieve and dry them before the fire" (pp. 15–16).

205 "To boil sugar to a candy height, you must boil it till it will draw as a thread betwixt your finger and your thumb" (*The Ladies Companion*, pp. 9–10).

206 This recipe seems to be a condensed and rather confused version of one recorded by Sir Hugh Platt: "Dissolve refined, or double-refined sugar, or sugar-candy itself, in a little rose-water, boil it to a reasonable height, put in your roots or flowers when your syrup is either fully cold or almost cold, let them rest therein till the syrup have pierced them sufficiently, then take out your flowers with a skimmer, suffering the loose syrup to run from them as long as it will; boil that syrup a little more, and put in more flowers as before; divide [drain] them also, then boil all the syrup which remaineth [i.e. the third time] ... to the height ... putting in more sugar if you see cause, but no more rose-

water; put your flowers therein when your syrup is cold, or almost cold, and let them stand till they candy" (*Delightes*, 1, p. 9).

207 Fruit in syrup (see paragraph 187 above); "dried suckets" are pieces of candied fruit prepared the same way.

208 See above, paragraph 142.

209 In his "model of a plain countryman's house," published in *The English Husbandman* (London, 1613), Markham describes this room as "An inward closet within the parlor for the mistress's use." In the diagram it is shown adjoining the "dining parlor for entertainment of strangers." See Appendix.

210 "In number of dishes and charge of meat, the nobility of England (whose cooks are for the most part musical-headed Frenchmen and strangers [foreigners]) do most exceed, sith there is no day ... wherein they have not only beef, mutton, veal, lamb, kid, pork, cony, capon, pig, or so many of these as the season yieldeth, but also some portion of the red or fallow deer, besides great variety of fish and wild fowl, and thereto sundry other delicates" (Harrison, p. 126).

211 Markham is more likely to intend the older meaning of the phrase "in order" than the more modern sense "disorderly retreat." Markham's choice of image reveals his interest in military affairs; he not only served as a soldier, but wrote several books on military matters.

212 "The clerk of the kitchen is to see into all inferior offices in the house at the least once a week ... he is to keep a ledger or journal book, for the noting therein weekly the particular expense of every office ... He is to receive all provisions of spice ... He is to see into the ewery ... the cellar ... the pantry ... the buttery ... the wet and dry larders ... He is to see the cooks dress the meat cleanly and well, and to see they keep those under them in good order; the kitchen sweet and cleanly, and that there be no waste made therein ... He is to see into the baker and brewer their offices ... He is to see into the slaughterman's charge, that ox skins and sheepskins be looked into, and the tallow and suet safely laid ... He is to see into the scullery, that the vessels be well and cleanly kept ... He is to attend at the surveying place, or dresser, every meal, and to see good order be kept and the Lord from thence to be honourably served, for that place belongeth only to him and the government thereof." Quoted from "A Breviate Touching the Order and Government of a Nobleman's House," a MS. of 1605, ed. Joseph Banks, in *Archaeologia*, xiii (1800), 328–31.

213 Server. "[The Gentleman Usher] is to appoint before dinner and supper, cup-bearer, carver, and sewer, and to go with them to the ewery, and there to wash their hands together ... the sewer is to go from the ewery through the hall ... to the surveying place or dresser, where the clerk of the kitchen is to attend him ... and from thence to countenance the meat to the lord's table" ("A Breviate," pp. 323–4).

214 The various dishes mentioned in the following section can be found earlier in this chapter; Markham's organization of the chapter is based on the order of serving to the table. (The one exception is the section on carbonadoes, which are discussed before baked meats, whereas Markham here advises that they be served after.)

215 "The bustard, if he be lean, is in ... evilness of juice very like unto the

crane. But, being fat, and kept a day or two before he be killed to expulse his ordure and afterwards baked, well seasoned with pepper, cloves and salt, is for them that have strong stomachs, a good, fit, and well nourishing meat" (Venner, p. 67; see also Cogan, p. 137).

216 William Harrison gives an idea of a normal day's fare: "The gentleman and merchants keep much about one rate, and each of them contenteth himself with four, five or six dishes when they have but small resort [company], or peradventure with one or two or three at the most when they have no strangers to accompany them at their tables" (pp. 128–9).

217 "A company of persons eating together" (*OED*).

218 The skin of a boar's shoulder filled with meat, cooked, marinated, then cooled in a mould; Harrison gives a long and enthusiastic report of it (pp. 312–14).

219 Somewhat after Markham's time, Samuel Pepys described with satisfaction a dinner he offered to six guests: "So my poor wife rose by 5 a-clock in the morning, before day, and went to market and bought fowl and many other things for dinner – with which I was highly pleased ... I had for them, after oysters – at first course, a hash of rabbits and lamb, and a rare chine of beef – next, a great dish of roasted fowl, cost me about 30s, and a tart; and then fruit and cheese. My dinner was noble and enough ... At night to supper; had a good sack-posset and cold meat and sent my guests away about 10 a-clock at night, both them and myself highly pleased with our management of this day. So weary to bed." (Entry for 13 January 1663.)

CHAPTER III

1 A collection of "stones" in the bladder.

2 The herb *Dracunculus vulgaris*, said by Markham to be "common in every garden" ("Hard Words").

3 Identified by Turner (*Names*) as the common liverwort *Marchantia polymorpha*, though then as now the name was more generally applied.

4 The "helm" or upper part of the still where the distillate condenses; the stilling pot is the lower container to which heat is applied. See Introduction, pp. xli–xlii.

5 Grains of paradise (cardamom).

6 See i, 136.

7 A pulled muscle or ligament.

8 A persistent sore or ulcer. Many of the properties listed above could be attributed to the effects of alcohol applied externally or internally.

9 A "compound water" as distinct from the simple waters of a single herb or spice. This recipe is the same as one found in *The Pathway to Health* by Peter Levens (1582), p. 222, where it is described as "*Aqua composita* for a surfeit."

10 "Dropsy" was a general term for diseases which were characterized by swelling and accumulations of fluid; cold dropsy would have meant that there was no accompanying fever.

11 This recipe appears as "Steven's *aqua composita*" in Platt's *Delightes* (ii, 8).

12 "Spirit is any substance subtle, stirring the powers of the body to perform

their operations, which is divided into: *natural*, which taketh his beginning of the liver, and by the veins which have no pulse, spreadeth into all the whole body; *vital*, which proceedeth from the heart, and by the arteries or pulses is sent into all the body; *animal*, which is engendered in the brain, and is sent by the sinews [nerves] throughout the body, and maketh sense or feeling." Sir Thomas Elyot, *Castel of Helth* (1539), fol. 10v.

13 The famous Greek physician (5th century B.C.), considered to be the father of medicine; the attribution is undoubtedly spurious, not only because of the patriotic but improbable reference to an English Queen, but because none of Hippocrates' writings is known to survive.

14 *Adiantum capillus-veneris*, said by Turner (*Names*, p. 151) not to grow in England, was often confused with maidenhair (spp. *Asplenium*).

15 Will form liquids of differing density; the distillate collected at the beginning will have a higher proportion of alcohol and volatile oils.

16 This somewhat mercenary statement may be evidence that Markham's source intended the advice for physicians rather than housewives.

17 Probably an error for "acharnes," acorns.

18 See i, 186.

19 So in all editions consulted; the sense would suggest "bray" (grind).

20 Names for various opacities or cataracts forming in the eye.

21 Normal form.

22 "Blear eyes ... is when the underlid of the eye is subverted [everted, the inner side turned outward]." Andrew Boorde, *The Breuiary of Healthe* (1552), fol. 60v.

23 Touchstone, shortened to "touch" later in the recipe; a smooth, dark stone used by the goldsmith to test the quality of gold.

24 I.e. when the powdered touchstone has settled out again.

25 See note to "cold dropsy," paragraph 8 above.

26 See i, 93.

27 Originally the text read "the heary ago," emended in later editions to "old age"; the source (a late edition of the Banckes herbal), however, solves the puzzle, for it reads "the hearynge."

28 Menstruation; the effects are gained by sympathetic magic, since radish is a "hot" vegetable.

29 See i, 14, and note.

30 The womb; but see i, 97, and note.

31 See the note on "cold" herbs, i, 15.

32 Power.

33 Normally a species of gladiolus, but see note to *calamus aromaticus*, note 39 below.

34 "The richest or most nourishing part of anything" (*OED*).

35 20 grains, 1/3 drachm, 1/24 oz., or a little more than a gramme.

36 The stone on which a painter ground his pigments, hence capable of producing a particularly fine powder.

37 Many recipes of a similar kind are found in *The Secrets of ... Alexis of Piemont* (1558) pt. 1, bk. 2, fol. 63 ff.

38 Storax, the resin obtained from the tree *Liquidambar orientalis*, was sold in both dry and liquid forms.

39 Originally an eastern aromatic reed or grass, but in 1578 Lyte wrote:

"That which they use to sell for *calamus aromaticus* is no reed nor root of a reed, but is the root of a certain herb like unto the yellow flag, or bastard *acorus* [*Acorus calamus*]" (p. 514).

40 Ladanum: "a yellowish gum, as some write; notwithstanding, others affirm it to be made of a dew which falleth upon a certain herb in Greece. Avicenna saith it is taken hanging on the hair of goats' beards that have fed upon that plant" (Bullokar).

41 The aromatic root of the Florentine iris, referred to elsewhere by Markham as "ireos."

42 "A white and clear gum, of a sweet savour. This gum groweth on the lentisk tree [i.e. *Pistacia lentiscus*]" (Bullokar).

43 Perfumed balls, carried in the belief that they provided protection from disease.

44 Put in a tun, or barrel.

45 Sour crab-apple vinegar, used widely in cookery. The word is derived from the French, meaning "green (or unripe) juice"; in France it was made from unripe grapes.

46 Crab-apples.

47 Wooden mallets.

48 A variety of sandalwood: "The yellow [sanders] is best smelling, next unto that is the white, and last of all is the red" (iii Turner, p. 67).

49 The drug (extracted from the aloe) in a solid form; see also i, 135.

50 Evidently misreadings of the manuscript source; "gallaminis" could be calamint (the aromatic herb) or *calamus aromaticus* (see paragraph 25 above), and "ciris" could be cistis (the name of the ladanum tree) or cypre (the henna-shrub, the flowers of which were used for their perfume). The second possibility in each case is perhaps more likely, for elsewhere, in a very similar recipe also headed "To make sweet bags," the ingredients are identical except that spike and sanders are omitted while coriander seed is added, and the two aromatics equivalent to "gallaminis" and "ciris" are "calamus" and "ciprus." See *A Closet for Ladies and Gentlewomen*, p. 42.

51 A groat was equal to four pence.

52 Drunken Alice is revived with a "cup/ Of newe ale in cornes" in "The Tunning of Elinour Rumming" (See *John Skelton's Complete Poems*, ed. Philip Henderson [London, 1964] p. 122). The *OED* suggests that it means ale newly drawn from the malt, hence perhaps only partly fermented.

53 A sweet, fruity wine; see iv, 10.

54 "It is proven."

55 The strongest brew; see ix, 5, where it is referred to as the "first liquor."

56 "To close (a barrel or cask) by fitting the head on; to enclose (something) in a barrel or cask by this means" (*OED*).

57 Use.

CHAPTER IV

1 The chapter which follows is the first printed version of a manuscript dealing with the care and adulteration of wine which was reprinted in many forms up to the early nineteenth century. A manuscript version

(c. 1600) is preserved as Sloane 3692 in the British Library. Markham edited and rearranged the material in his manuscript, but changed less than his claim that it was "rudely written" suggests, for he follows it almost word for word. A full history of the manuscript tradition can be found in "The Mystery of Vintners," *Agricultural History*, l (1976), 362–76 by Michael R. Best. See also Introduction, pp. xviii–xix.

2 Ingenuously, frankly.

3 Clear evidence of revision between the 1623 and 1631 editions; Markham obviously intended that the following paragraph should follow without interruption.

4 See paragraph 10 below, and note.

5 Sloane 3692 (fol. 28v) has "great," i.e. full-bodied.

6 See paragraph 6 below, and note.

7 "A big, soft wine without the hardness to give it body" (*Alex Lichine's Dictionary of Wines and Spirits*, London, 1967); a character ("rancio") often found in old, sweet wines.

8 Older wines tend to become tawny, whether originally red or white; for a comment on the general attitude of seventeenth-century Englishmen towards colour in wines, see note 16.

9 Matters.

10 See following paragraph.

11 "A general name for a class of white wines formerly imported from Spain and the Canaries" (*OED*); here definitely sherry, as the mention of Seres (Jeres, the town in Spain from which sherry takes its name) indicates.

12 Also known as muscadel, muscadine is a fruity, sweet wine, made from the muscat grape. It was obviously more popular and more expensive than other similar wines, since the recipes which follow (paragraphs 5 and 6 below) describe ways of adulterating cheaper wines in order to sell them as muscadine. Thomas Venner rated malmsey, muscadel, and bastard thus: "Bastard is in virtue somewhat like to muscadel ... It is in goodness so much inferior to muscadel as the same is to malmsey" (p. 28).

13 A butt or a pipe was a barrel of variable size, containing from about 100 to 140 gallons; Sloane 3692 defines a butt of malmsey as 126 wine-gallons (fol. 29v), equivalent to 105 imperial gallons, or 475 litres.

14 A term for the process of "fining" or clarifying wine. Newly fermented wine, particularly after transportation, is apt to have a cloudy appearance; the active ingredient in this parel is the albumen in egg-white, which precipitates and absorbs the cloudy colloidal matter. Salt is added because it "dissolves the globulin and helps to give a more rapid fining" (Lionel Frumkin, *The Science and Technique of Wine* [London, 1965], p. 109). Egg albumen is still used for fining wines, though bentonite (a clay) is generally preferred, as it imparts less flavour to the wine.

15 The addition of yolks would add more flavour to the wine than the whites alone, but would cause the wine to go "off" more quickly.

16 Dark, tawny coloured; a defect in the eyes of the English wine-drinking public. Sir Hugh Platt, who must have had some contact with a copy of the MS. Markham used, in *A Jewell House of Art and Nature* commented on the English preference for light wines: "We are grown so nice in taste, that almost no wines, unless they be more pleasant than they can be of the grape, will content us, nay no colour unless it be perfect, fine

and bright, will satisfy our wanton eyes" (p. 65). For recipes for improving the colour of red wine see paragraphs 28 and 29 below.

17 The cassein in milk is still used for the decolouration of wine, though tannin is sometimes added to assist precipitation and to preserve the balance of the wine.

18 A barrel of the same capacity as a butt; see note to paragraph 2 above.

19 Obscure; the word appears in the same recipe in Sloane 3692 as "Rate-mowe" (fol. 26) and in the British Library's Add. MS. 22565 as "Ratemue" (fols. 3 and 4).

20 Without character.

21 An artificial "bouquet" explained in the following recipe; the modern vermouth is a similarly "flavoured" wine.

22 Refine, clarify.

23 The Sloane MS. adds at this point "iid in collanders," i.e. two pennyworth of coriander [seeds].

24 Stiff, frothy. This sense of the word is not recorded in *OED*; see also paragraph 9 below.

25 Whipped white of eggs alone or with cream is still called "neige" in French; this, together with the use of "moss" (paragraph 9 below) is evidence of the French origin of the manuscript.

26 Bastard is another sweet wine, probably made from the *bastardo* grape, though there were other theories of the origin of the name: "Such wines are called mongrel or bastard wines which ... have neither manifest sweetness nor manifest astriction, but indeed participate and contain in them both the qualities"; "so called because they are oftentimes adulterated and falsified with honey." Both comments are translated from Estienne and Liebault (Surflet, ed. Markham, pp. 635 and 642). Compare also paragraph 8 below which, like the second recipe in this paragraph, goes beyond fining and decolouration of the wine to actual adulteration.

27 The sense seems to be $1/2 + (1/2 \times 1/4) = 5/8$ full, but the Sloane MS. has "half full / or half and quarter" $= 3/4$. In any case it is probable that one is to fill the hogshead between half and three quarters full of real bastard wine, then fine it and "stretch" it with inferior (less sweet) white wine or sherry.

28 "The nectar or liquid honey is of two sorts; one hard and white even like unto sugar, which is therefore called stone honey, or corn honey; the other so soft that it will run, which therefore is called live-honey." Charles Butler, *The Feminine Monarchy*, vi, 27. The effect of the honey and spices is to mask any "off" flavour in the wine.

29 To purify, or to rid of rubbish, i.e. to extract the drinkable portion; "lags" are lees. The recipe is openly advocating the adulteration of good wine by the addition of left-overs and the masking of any resulting unpleasant flavour. According to Platt, writing in 1594, this was a recent development: he speaks of a man "that within this few years taught divers of the [vintner's] company how to draw out of a hogshead of wine lees, 10 gallons of clear wine at the least, which being tricked or compassed, or at the least mingled with other wines, hath ever since by divers vintners been retailed for wine, whereas before it was wholly sold to the aqua vitae men" (*A Jewell House*, pp. 64–5).

30 Probably a version of "Azoia," a town near Lisbon in Portugal which

produced another sweet, fortified wine; see Roger Dion, *Histoire de la vigne et du vin en France des origines au xixe siècle* (Paris: Sevin et Cie, 1959), pp. 321–2, and André Simon, *History*, vol. i, pp. 287–9. Less likely is Alexander Henderson's conjecture that the name is a corruption of "Auxois," a town in Alsace known for its sweet "straw wine," an "auslese," or wine made from grapes picked late then laid on straw to sweeten further (*History of Ancient and Modern Wines* [London, 1824] p. 289). Osey is also mentioned in Wynkyn de Worde's *Boke of Keruynge* (1513), sig. A2v.

31 "All perfect wines have some acidity, and when this acidity prevails too much, the wine is said to be pricked, which is really the wine's tending to vinegar" (*The Vintner's ... Guide*, p. 230). The remedy proposed would mask the acidity by adding sweeteners, then fining the wine and providing a moderate aeration, all of which might induce a beneficial secondary fermentation.

32 Wort newly drawn from the malt; see ix, 5.

33 New must – unfermented grape juice – concentrated by boiling.

34 The repetition here is the result of inattentive editing. The Sloane MS. reads: "[heading] Parrell for ye same Bastarde / [main text] first parrell hym ... " (fol. 27v).

35 Mousse; the writer or translator of Markham's original text was apparently unable to find an English equivalent of the French term, reintroduced in the late nineteenth century and now in common use. The *OED* records no use before 1892; the whole phrase is repeated in the next paragraph.

36 A sweet dessert wine made from the malvasia grape; Candia (formerly a name for the island of Crete) was the main area of its cultivation, so that it was often called "candy" wine. See also note to muscadine, paragraph 2 above.

37 "A small shallow cup of silver, often with an embossed or corrugated bottom which reflects the light through the liquor, for tasting wines" (*OED*).

38 To shift is "To employ shifts ... evasions ... or frauds" (*OED*). Markham's "ill" replaces "Evil" in Sloane 3692.

39 Candia, formerly a name for the island of Crete, famous for its malmsey.

40 Become "tawny" or dark coloured, see note on "high coloured," paragraph 3 above; "want" means "lack," the ideal colour for sherry being pale (cf. "lost their colour," paragraph 15 below).

41 See paragraphs 30 and 31 below.

42 A region, formerly a province, in south-west France, roughly equivalent to the region of the modern Bordeaux wines (see paragraph 19 below). André Simon (*History*, vol. i, p. 269) lists all the vineyards associated with the name.

43 Sloane 3692 heads this passage "For sack that hath [a flying lee] and is tawny"; the first part of the recipe is thus to clarify the wine, the second to improve the colour. Donald D. Couche, *Modern Detection and Treatment of Wine Diseases and Defects* (London: The Author, 1935) describes the "lee" taste as resulting from the wine's being put in a cask containing dry lees, and suggests a similar treatment: "draw the wine off into a perfectly sound ... cask and apply a fairly heavy fining" (p. 80).

44 See paragraph 6 above, and note.

45 Finely, carefully.

46 The meaning is clear: the cask is to be placed upside down so that the lees will settle through the wine, in the process giving it some colour, and possibly some character. The word is not recorded in the *OED*, but appears several times in Markham's text (also as "aforetarke"), in Sloane 3692, and in another MS. on wine in the British Library, Add. MS. 22565.

47 Alicant is a dark, sweet red wine: "[Some] Spanish wines are composed ... of an infusion of dry grapes in weak must [grape juice before fermentation] ... as the *Alicant*, which is a thick, strong, very sweet, and almost nauseous wine" (*The Vintner's ... Guide*, p. 61). Here "hard" means acetic, or vinegary (the modern meaning is "with excessive tannin," meaning that the wine must age before use); Sloane 3692 adds "or faint" – lacking in flavour. If there is a distinction between the terms "prick" and "hard," it is probable that pricking is the process of a secondary (acetic) fermentation, and hardness the result. See paragraph 9 above.

48 "Clarify it over the fire and take it off and skim it cleane and let it be thoroughly cold" (Sloane 3692, fol. 30).

49 Lively in flavour; the effect again is to mask the acetic quality of the wine by adding sweetening.

50 "An ill hogshead or two" (Sloane 3692, fol. 28v); the sense seems to be that one can "rid away" – use by disguising the ill taste – a poor hogshead by incorporating it in a pipe of good wine in the way suggested (a hogshead is 1/4 of a pipe).

51 To "order" is to manage; here, however, it is a euphemism for "adulterate" (note the use of "rid away" and "vantage" later in the recipe).

52 Probably "Esterling," a name given to Hanse merchants; the Hanseatic League included Rhenish towns above Cologne. Merchants from the Flemish Duchy of Brabant, now North Brabant in The Netherlands, would have dealt in wine coming from closer to the mouth of the Rhine, and would have shipped their goods from Antwerp. According to André Simon, Antwerp became more important as a source of wine towards the end of the sixteenth century (*History*, vol. ii, p. 202).

53 The bars were pieces of wood, fastened by pins, holding the head of the cask in place.

54 Sir Hugh Platt must have had this passage in mind as he wrote: "The vintners ... trick or compass all their natural wines ... if they prick a little, they have a decoction of honey with a few cloves to deceive the taste" (*A Jewell House*, p. 66).

55 Part of the passage which follows is recorded, though not taken from Markham or Sloane 3692, in *The Art and Mystery of Vintners*, book IV nos. 31–2, "A Note for Wines and What Country."

56 Wine from the "haut pays," the vineyards on the upper Garonne and its tributaries, the Lot, the Tarn and the Baïse. On the medieval wine-trade with this area, see *Studies in the Medieval Wine Trade* by Margery Kirkbride James, ed. E.M. Veale (Oxford: Clarendon Press, 1971), pp. 2–3. In Ben Jonson's play, *The Alchemist*, Sir Epicure Mammon considered high-country wines to be a gourmet delight worthy his attention; in one of the fantasies describing what he would do on possession of the philosopher's stone, he plans this exotic meal:

> ... we will eat our mullets
> Sous'd in high-country wine, sup pheasant's eggs,
> And have our cockles boil'd in silver shells,
> Our shrimps to swim again, as when they liv'd,
> In a rare butter, made of dolphin's milk,
> Whose cream does look like opals ...
> (iv.i.156–61)

57 Given up, worthless.

58 The London merchants had much trouble with the suppliers of wine, who made the tuns well short of measure. Many laws were passed to control this problem (see André Simon, *History*. vol. ii, pp. 62–7).

59 *The Art and Mystery of Vintners* (book iv no. 32) has the more probable "Galliack"; Gaillac, a commercial centre in southern France is known today particularly for its sparkling wines.

60 Small measures of wine, containing three or four gallons (see paragraph 24 below).

61 Probably Angoulême, a region (formerly a province) of western France, close to Bordeaux; wine grapes are grown particularly along the Charente River.

62 Wine exported from the sea port of western France, La Rochelle; like Angoulême it is in the general area of Bordeaux.

63 Probably wines made from wild grapes grown in hedgerows, which would be low in sugar content, and hence acid tasting.

64 See paragraph 2 above. The passage that follows shows clearly that "sack" referred to several different wines, not merely sherry; they were all full-bodied, sweet, and probably fortified wines.

65 "The wines of Galicia, chiefly from the banks of the Minho, were abundant, but held in no great estimation in England, where they appear to have been brought only when they happened to be included in the cargo of a captured Spanish vessel" (Simon, *History*, vol. ii, p. 212). Galicia was the north-west corner of Spain.

66 Viticulture was introduced to the Canary Islands by the Spaniards in the sixteenth century; the wine exported was another of the full-bodied sweet wines, probably fortified, which were so popular in England during the sixteenth and seventeenth centuries.

67 A modern opinion notes malaga as "one of the best sweet wines made in Spain. It comes from the Province of Eastern Andalucia and is shipped from the port of Malaga" (André Simon, *A Dictionary of Wines, Spirits and Liqueurs* [London, 1958], p. 106); like malmsey, malaga is made from the muscatel grape.

68 Gauging or measurement of wine was carried out by means of a gauging-rod; the references which follow to "pricks" and "knots" are evidently to marks and reference points on the rod.

69 A tierce was one-third of a pipe, usually 42 gallons, a puncheon was a cask which varied in content from 72 (beer) to 120 (whiskey) gallons.

70 A puncheon (modern "punch"), a tool for piercing holes; the puncheoner may have been part of the gauging-rod, used perhaps to force out the bung. Though their connection here is suggestive, the two words "puncheon," a punch and a cask, are not known to be etymologically related.

71 *The Art and Mystery of Vintners*, in an incomplete quotation of a similar passage, gives the volume of a sester as four gallons (p. 15).

72 By contrast with "long," which means "heavy" or "viscous"; a sweet, fortified wine may be "long," but in a table wine it would mean that some kind of bacteriological spoilage had occurred.

73 "Red wine" was not the modern generic term, as its distinction from claret in this passage indicates. It was probably a term for a port-type wine, since it is desirable that it be "long" (viscous) and sweet. William Turner, in *A New Boke of the Natures of All Wines* (London, 1568) says that "red" wine is dark in colour, and should be called "black": he writes of "red wine, which here in England is commonly called clared [claret] wine, and ... black wine which is called commonly in England red wine" (sig. C5v).

74 See ii, 44; a red dye imported in impregnated linen cloths: "A common way with the wine-coopers is, to infuse the rags, cold, for a night or two, and then wring them out with their hands; but the inconveniency of this method is, that it gives the wine a disagreeable taste" (*The Vintner's ... Guide* [1826], p. 63).

75 Sloane 3692 has "pottle," half a gallon.

76 The popularity of this technique of deepening the colour of red wine must have been considerable, for similar recipes were reprinted for 200 years: "Take as many as you please of damsons or black sloes, and stew them with some of the deepest coloured wine you can get and as much sugar as will make it into a syrup. A pint of this will colour a hogshead of claret. It is also good for red Port wines, and may be kept ready for use in glass bottles" (*The Vintner's ... Guide*, p. 238). Several recipes warn that this will make the wine rougher in taste.

77 Like "slender" (paragraph 18 above), a wine lacking in character.

78 The effect of alum is that of rather drastic fining, suitable perhaps to rescue wine (temporarily) which has suffered bacteriological spoilage; recipes in *The Art and Mystery of Vintners* that call for alum describe the wine as "long," "lumpish," or "louring" (looking dark?).

79 Any finely powdered starch will have a fining effect on wine.

80 Of the same kind.

81 An aromatic herb, *Chenopodium botrys*: "This herb groweth in many places of France ... but it groweth not of himself in this country" (Lyte, p. 242).

82 Striking evidence of the continuity of the vintner's recipes is found in *The Vintner's ... Guide* (1826), which records a recipe identical with Markham's, apart from a slight modernization of the style (p. 239).

83 Both Markham and Sloane 3692 are corrupt here. The intention of the recipe is made clear in *The Art and Mystery of Vintners* in a closely related passage: "If red wine be faint, draw it out into fresh lees and put into him 4 or 5 gallons of alicant; then turn twice in the lees, *and let him lie upright* 7 days before you broach him, and it will have a good colour and taste" (p. 17 – italics supplied). See also *The Vintner's ... Guide*, p. 238.

84 Tyre was another sweet wine, but opinion as to its origin varies; according to André Simon it was "shipped from some of the islands off the coast in Italy, in the Tyrrhenean Sea, such as Capri and Isdria" (*History*, vol. ii,

pp. 240–1); but Alexander Henderson maintains that " 'Tire,' if not of Syrian growth, was probably a Calabrian or Sicilian wine, manufactured from the species of grape called tirio." (*History of Ancient and Modern Wines* [1824], p. 297.)

85 An unidentified sweet wine, judging from this context, white; also listed by Wynkyn de Worde in his *Boke of Keruynge* (1513), sig. Aiiv. Alexander Henderson makes the obvious guess that it "may have been from the islands of Capri or Cyprus" (*History of Ancient and Modern Wines*, p. 297).

CHAPTER V

1 Imperfections, tangles (a felter is a tangle). The only use of the word recorded in the *OED* is quoted from this passage.

2 "A whole piece of cloth in process of being woven or after it comes from the loom" (*OED*).

3 "Oak apples" or galls are the protuberances on oaks caused by insect parasites. Galls are particularly rich in tannin, which reacts with iron (copperas is iron sulphate) to form ink. William Harrison remarked on the similar property of the bark of alder, which was "therefore much used by our country wives in colouring their knit hosen" (p. 280).

4 The alum is used as a mordant, a fixing agent.

5 Urine.

6 *The Whole Art of Dyeing* (London, 1705) recommends at this point that one should "cool [the wool] very well, and hang it out for one night" (p. 38).

7 The root of the madder plant, *Rubia tinctorum*, formerly used widely as a dye.

8 Alum, an essential mordant (fixing agent) in madder dyes on wool, was mined in Sardinia. See Charles J. Singer, *The Earliest Chemical Industry* (London: Folio Society, 1948), pp. 237 ff.

9 Different shades of blue dye: anil is, like indigo, a dye extracted from the plant species *Indigofera*; "byse" is bice, a pigment obtained from pulverizing glass that has been coloured blue by the presence of cobalt.

10 A deep purplish brown. The modern meaning (to vomit) first appeared at the very end of the sixteenth century; its appearance no doubt caused the older word to disappear abruptly (the only entry in the *OED* after Markham is in a passage from a dictionary which in fact quotes paragraph 14 below; the first recorded use of puke meaning "to vomit" is in Shakespeare's famous passage in the "seven ages of man" speech from *As You Like It*, c. 1600).

11 (I.e. "woodweed"?) The plant known as woodwaxen, greenweed, dyer's broom or dyer's weed (see Gerarde, 1134), *Genista tinctoria*. This variant is not recorded in the *OED*.

12 Dark, sombre.

13 Large coarse combs fastened to a stock, or support. The word "card" is derived from *carduus*, thistle, as the first cards were teasels, dry thistle-heads.

14 Rape seed oil (now often called Canola oil).

15 Rendered; melted and clarified.

16 Test; a meaning preserved in the phrase "the exception which proves the rule."

17 As Markham explains, tumming is the first or second carding (combing) of the wool, in preparation for finer cards.

18 Painstaking.

19 A fulling mill; see paragraph 22 below.

20 "To form a compact layer" (*OED*).

21 Scraps of wool, here the by-product of "shearing" the cloth to bring it to an even thickness.

22 Refers both to the cylinder on which the warp is first wound, and also to that onto which the woven cloth is rolled as it is completed.

23 Speaking of the deceits of weavers, Robert Greene wrote: "[your] woof and warp is so cunningly drawn out that you plague the poor country Huswives for their yarn, and ... you make it seem both well wrought and to bear weight, when it is slenderly woven, and you have stolen a quarter of it from the poor wife" (*A Quippe for an Vpstart Courtier*; see Greene's *Works* ed. A.B. Grosart [London, 1881–6], xi, 281).

24 Probably a misreading of "pullaces," pulleys: "The pulleys or pullaces are those turning things on the top of the frame by which with the help of the treadles the springstaves are raised up and down" (Holme, II, iii, p. 107).

25 The cloth is treated in a walkmill or fulling mill to settle the fibres and to clean it; it is then trimmed, sheared, or dressed, to give it uniform thickness. Celia Fiennes described the whole process towards the end of the seventeenth century: "the mill does draw out and gather in the serges, it's a pretty diversion to see it, a sort of huge notched timber like great teeth; one would think it should injure the serges but it does not; the mill draws in with such great violence that if one stands near it, and it catch a bit of your garments it would be ready to draw in the person even in a trice; when they are thus scoured they dry them in racks ... then when dry they burl them, picking out all knots" (*The Journeys of Celia Fiennes*, p. 246).

26 Fuller's earth, "a hydrous silicate of alumina used in cleansing cloth" (*OED*).

27 One who "shears" woollen cloth by cutting off the superfluous nap, and removing burls, or lumps from the cloth.

28 See the adverse remarks of Louis Crommelin, Introduction, p. xliv.

29 Managed; specifically, tilled (see paragraph 25).

30 (Hay)stack yards.

31 Axholme, a district in Lindsey, Lincolnshire, between Hatfield Moors and the River Trent.

32 Markham describes the characteristics of good ground for barley in *The English Husbandman*, sigs. F4v and I1v.

33 Instruments for levelling and smoothing the soil: "if ... there remain any clots or lumps of earth unbroken, you shall let them rest till after the next shower of rain, at which time you shall either with a heavy roller, or the backside of your harrows, run over your lands, which is called slighting of ground." " ... smooth and slight your land, and look what clots they fail to break, you shall with clotting beetles [mallets] beat them

asunder" (*The English Husbandman*, sigs. B2v, I1v; for illustrations of
the roller and harrow, see sigs. D4 and F2v).

34 Flax; it is from "line" that the products "linseed" and "linen" are derived.
35 Lionel Slator is more specific: "Flax must be weeded when it is about
four inches high, the weeds must be cut with a sharp knife, as near the
root as you please, but the roots must not be pulled, beause that loosens
and abuses the flax" (see p. 11). Sarah Fell records several occasions
when women were paid for "weeding line."
36 "Now for the best time of gathering your hemp, it is, according to the
common custom of housewives, about Saint Margaret's day, being toward
the latter end of July" (Surflet, ed. Markham, p. 567). Mary Magdalen's
day is celebrated on 22 July; the day of St Margaret, Virgin and Martyr, is
20 July. Tusser also admonishes the housewife to harvest hemp and flax
in July; under that month's husbandry he writes (p. 116):

> Wife, pluck fro thy seed hemp the fiemble [female] hemp clean,
> This looketh more yellow, the other more green:
> Use t'one for thy spinning, leave Mikel the t'other,
> For shoe thread and halter, for rope and such other.
> Now pluck up thy flax, for the maidens to spin,
> First see it dried, and timely got in.

37 Here used generally: "plants" or "stalks."
38 Bundles (similar instructions are found in Surflet, ed. Markham, p. 567).
39 Evil; Slator (1724) agrees: "In England ... when they grass [flax] ...
without watering it, they call it 'dew-rating' it; I have often tried to dew-
rate flax, without success ... and I have likewise observed many counties
in England to practise it, but they fail both with respect to colour and
goodness" (p. 26).
40 Richard Hall, *Observations ... on the Method Used in Holland, in Cultivating or Raising of Hemp or Flax* (Dublin, 1724), has a chapter on
"Reasons why flax ought not to be rated [soaked] in running waters"
(pp. 78–80); Tusser, writing in 1580, commented similarly (p. 35):

> Now pluck up thy hemp and go beat out the seed,
> And afterward water it as ye see need:
> But not in the river where cattle should drink,
> For poisoning them and the people with stink.

41 Cf. Slator: "Then must the head of the flax be covered with fern, two or
three inches thick, and over the fern weight of stones be laid to keep
the flax and all under water if possible" (p. 30). Markham provides diagrams of similar "overlyers" in *Markhams Farewell to Husbandry*, published as the fifth part of *A Way to Get Wealth* (1631), p. 85.
42 Crosswise.
43 "As soon as the flax has been laid four and twenty hours in the rating
[watering] pond, it will ferment so strongly as to require 'all hands at
work' to keep it down" (Slator, p. 30).
44 Separate[ly].
45 Field or paddock.

46 This latter is the method recommended by both Crommelin (see paragraph 23) and Slator (pp. 13–14 and 36–40 respectively).

47 "The manner of rippling of flax is thus: a rippling-comb, made of iron, is fixed in a long form, which form is placed over a winnowing-sheet, to receive the boughs [bobs, or seed-vessels] of the flax; thro' this comb the flax is gently drawn, to sever the leaves and boughs from the stalk" (Slator, p. 13).

48 The seed-vessels, so called for their shape.

49 The action of beating the hemp on a brake to separate the fibres from the rest of the stalk. The brake is described in detail by Holme: "A flax or hemp brake is a log of wood, cut along with teeth like a saw; having a like piece of wood cut into teeth, which falls into the under teeth, being fastened at the end with a hinge; it hath liberty to rise and fall at one end, between which teeth the flax being put, the teeth bruise and break the hard husk of the stalk all into shivers" (II, vi, p. 285). The process of braking is recorded by Marcandier, Magistrate of Bourges, in *A Treatise on Hemp* (1764): "One need see hemp braked but once, to be immediately master of the whole art. The man or woman who brakes (for in many places it is the work of women) takes in the left hand a handful of hemp, and in the other the upper jaw of the brake. The hemp is put between the two jaws, and by raising and letting fall several times with all his force, the jaw he has in his right hand breaks the dry stems under the bark that lies around them ... A woman may brake from twenty to thirty pounds of hemp in a day, and this is a very great advantage to those who cultivate this plant" (pp. 43–5).

50 The pith of the stalk, which contains the fibres.

51 Wooden frames, of a size suitable to be used as a temporary fence.

52 A bundle of coarse fibres. Chaucer may have been using the word "smooth" ironically in the General Prologue to the *Canterbury Tales* when he described the Pardoner's hair: "Smothe it heng as dooth a strike of flex" (II.675–6).

53 Notched.

54 Narrow-toothed.

55 Louis Crommelin (see paragraph 23 above) wrote critically of the use of a brake in the preparation of flax: "They also in the cleaning of their flax make use of things which they call brakes, which I can no way approve of ... such things are never used beyond seas to flax, but to hemp only" (p. 17).

56 "To sever the harl or skin of the flax from the bun or straw of it" (Slator, p. 46). Holme provides a diagram of the swingle tree dagger, II, plate 4, opposite p. 285.

57 Fragments of the broken stalk.

58 Fibre of the quality fine enough for spinning.

59 "That part [of the flax] which is utmost and next to the peel or rind, is called tow or hards, and it is the worst of the line or flax, good for little or nothing but to make lamp-match or candlewick ... the good flax indeed ... is the tear, or marrow as it were, within the line" (Pliny, trans. Holland, ii, xix).

60 Harding; a coarse cloth, often made, as here, with leftover fibres.

61 The term is usually associated with cookery; see ii, 60 above.

62 Louis Crommelin (see paragraph 23 above) considered this the worst of many sins committed by Irish women in the preparation of hemp and flax: "and what is yet worse than all this, they constantly dry their flax by the fire, which makes it impossible to bleach cloth made of their yarn" (p. 16).

63 Linen of the finest grade, so called because the best came from the province of Holland in The Netherlands.

64 With artifice or skill.

65 High-quality wool, named after the Channel Island famous for its woollen goods.

66 Markham thought this process of sufficient importance that he added a similar passage to his edition of *The Countrie Farme* (p. 568). The identical passage from *The English Housewife* is recorded much later by Nathaniel Whittock in *The Complete Book of Trades* (London, 1837), pp. 238–9.

67 Distaff; a cleft staff on which the raw yarn was held while it was being spun by hand. The wheel was a later and more efficient invention.

68 For the generally low wages earned by those who spun, see Alice Clark, *Working Life of Women in the Seventeenth Century* (New York: Harcourt Brace and Rowe, 1920), chap. iv.

69 A variable measure of thread (see next paragraph).

70 As Markham's explanation shows, the measures for quantities of yarn were variable. The thread was wound on a simple rectangular reel; the "slipping" or skein, enough yarn to weigh a pound, was divided into "leas" weighing between half an ounce and an ounce, varying in number of threads according to the size of the reel and the coarseness of the thread (see also Holme, ii, iii, p. 107).

71 Unravelling; compare *Macbeth*, "Sleep, that knits up the ravell'd sleeve of care" (ii.ii.36).

72 "A lay-band is an inkle [tape] or packthread as tieth the hank in the middle, by which it is hung up" (Holme, iii, iii, p. 107). A "big twist" would mean coarse and thick, making it easier to separate from the linen thread it was holding.

73 A skein weighing about a pound.

74 Abbreviation of obolus, halfpenny. *OED* quotes a passage of 1442: "xvi skeins of great packthread at ob. a piece, in all viii pence."

75 Abated, reduced.

76 Changing (the water).

77 Of the ash tree.

78 Here, the strong alkaline solution which is the bleaching agent.

79 A pun on hunting terminology.

80 This time the ashes and the yarn are separated by the "bucking cloth," making it a "clean buck" (see paragraph 54 below).

81 Falstaff (1 Henry iv, iv.ii.48) and Autolycus (*The Winter's Tale*, iv.iii.24) both profit by the fact that housewives left cloth to bleach upon hedges.

82 The pegs on which the yarn is wound.

83 I.e. with the ashes separated from the cloth by the bucking cloth (see paragraph 51 above).

CHAPTER VI

1 See below, paragraph 6.
2 Markham treats this subject with more detail in *Cheape and Good Husbandry*, pp. 40–1.
3 Counties.
4 *Cheape and Good Husbandry* (London, 1614) has a section (pp. 41–63) on the diseases of cattle, including some cures which he also recommends for humans in the first chapter of this book (see Introduction, pp. xix–xx). The book also contains chapters on horses, sheep, goats, swine, conies (rabbits), poultry, bees, and the art of fishing.
5 This meaning of the word, which as usual Markham is careful to explain, is not recorded in the *OED*.
6 Markham is referring to the accepted medical theory that excess vitality or nourishment would lead to decay and disease, a belief which was behind the widespread practice of letting blood regularly, both in humans and animals, to reduce the possibility of dangerously good health.
7 Used in earlier sense of "kind," true to one's breeding or nature; compare the origin of "gentle" as in the phrase "of gentle birth."
8 In the prime of the summer.
9 "This disease of the sturdy is known by a continual turning about of the beast in one place" (*Cheape and Good Husbandry*, p. 47). Markham goes on to recommend a cure for this brain disease that involves cutting a hole in the animal's skull to relieve pressure on the brain.
10 Published in two parts, in 1613–14, *The English Husbandman* was Markham's first book on husbandry. Markham discusses methods of ploughing and seeding; planting, grafting, and care of fruit trees; the planning and use of a hop-field; the laying out of ornamental gardens; (in book ii) the kitchen garden, in terms more useful to the English experience than the passages in *The English Housewife* (see ii, 3–9 and notes); care and maintenance of woodlands and pastures; a section on disease in horses derived from similar passages in his other books on horses; and a further section which deals with angling and the sport of cock-fighting.
11 The calf is taught to drink from the pail by being encouraged to suck a finger wetted with milk; "flotten milk" is skim milk.
12 The section on rearing calves is found on p. 44.
13 Whey; see below, paragraph 34.
14 See Introduction p. xxxv.
15 Become reasty, or rancid. The form "reese" is not recorded in *OED* before 1784.
16 Cause the egg to float.
17 See i, 10.
18 Markham is no doubt thinking of ale.
19 For these different varieties of cheese, see the recipes below, paragraphs 38–44.
20 Explained in the next paragraph; a calf's stomach was the usual source of the cheese-making enzyme.
21 Estienne recommends seasoning the rennet with "cloves, mace and a little nutmeg" as well as salt (Surflet, ed. Markham, p. 65).
22 "I saw the way of making rennet as they do in Cheshire: they take the

reed bag and curd and having washed it clean, salt it and break the curd small about the bag, so dry them being stretched out with sticks like a glove, and so hang them in a chimney till you need it" (Celia Fiennes, in *The Journeys of Celia Fiennes*, p. 112). Josiah Twamley provides an explanation for Markham's censure: "Don't let [the bags] in drying be too near a fire; if heated too much, [it] renders them liable to reeze [become rancid]" (p. 42).

23 Thomas Tusser describes in detail the faults that dairy maid Cicely must avoid. The cheese must not be white and dry, too salt, full of eyes, "hoven" (with "puffed up cheeks"), tough, full of spots, full of hairs, full of whey, full of "gentils" (maggots), or made from burnt milk (pp. 100–1).

24 The cooking utensil.

25 A tub used in the preparation of bread, salt meat, brewing, and, as here, the making of cheese.

26 "What is generally known by the name of two-meal cheese, is ... made from one meal of new milk and one of old, or skimmed milk, having the cream taken away" (Twamley, p. 56).

27 Cheese made from fresh milk with no cream or water added.

28 As the recipe indicates, a thin cheese, drained on nettles rather than cheesecloth; the effect would be both to give a flavour to the cheese and to retain more moisture, while giving adequate ventilation (see Valerie Cheke, *The Story of Cheesemaking in Britain* [London, 1959], p. 105). The cheese thus made is similar to the "slip-coat" or cream cheese of Sir Kenelm Digby, though he recommends green rushes in preference to nettles or grass; see *The Closet of Sir Kenelm Digby, Knight, Opened*, p. 268.

29 Cheese made with skim milk; "flotten" is the past participle of the verb "to fleet," or skim.

30 Though coarser in texture and ranker in flavour, skim milk cheese had its uses: "Skimmed cheese, or flet-milk cheese is ... much used on shipboard, not being so much affected by the heat of the ship as richer cheese, or so subject to decay in long voyages, and being bought at a low price, makes it much called for" (Twamley, p. 56).

31 Cheese made from the milk of cows fed on the eddish or aftermath – the late grass which grows after the harvest.

32 In his edition of Heresbach's *The Whole Art of Husbandry*, Markham added a similar passage: "They put the whey into a brass kettle or pan and sit it over a soft fire, heating it till the fatness of the cheese swim aloft upon the whey; which with a skimmer you shall take and put into a clean vessel ... and thus do till the strength of the whey is spent" (p. 282).

CHAPTER VII

1 Here the lupin is a leguminous plant grown for fodder, not the modern flower, which is of American origin.

2 The tare is a variety of vetch, particularly common as a weed in fields of grain; see the parable of the sower, Matthew 13: 24.

3 For those who could not even afford "sand barley" William Vaughan has some advice: "[Q.] *What shall poor men drink when malt is extreme*

dear? [A.] They must gather the tops of heath, whereof the usual brushes are made, and dry them, and keep them from moulding. Then they may at all times brew a cheap drink for themselves therewith. Which kind of drink is very wholesome as well for the liver as the spleen, but much the more pleasant if they put a little liquorice unto it. There is another sort of drink of water and vinegar proportionately mingled together, which in summer they may use." William Vaughan, *Naturall and Artificial Directions for Health* (1600), pp. 8–9.

4 An open view.

5 Hinged windows or casements which can be opened or closed to regulate the temperature inside.

6 The couch is the heap of sprouting grain; see paragraph 19 below.

7 Containers, both for grain and the finished malt; see paragraph 15 below.

8 See paragraph 12 below.

9 The sprouting root, which later becomes withered and separated from the grain.

10 Sifted and cleaned; see paragraph 23 below.

11 "Our malt is made all the year long in some great towns; but in gentlemen's and yeoman's houses, who commonly make sufficient for their own expenses only, the winter half is thought most meet for that commodity" (Harrison, p. 135).

12 I.e. concave.

13 A one-piece, sandy rock.

14 The hottest days in summer, so called because Sirius, the dog star, is visible.

15 Gum from fir or pine was often called frankincense; see note to "olibanum," i, 258.

16 I.e. on the reputation of the maltster.

17 Salt, specifically potassium nitrate.

18 The grain is; Markham confuses singular and plural subjects.

19 I.e. concave.

20 Thomas Tusser (p. 170) suggests that Gillet (the maid in charge of the kiln) take care to avoid fire:

> *Take heed to the kell [kiln]*
> *Sing out as a bell.*
> Be sure no chances to fire can draw,
> The wood, or the furze, the bracks or the straw.
>
> Let Gillet be singing, it doth very well,
> To keep her from sleeping and burning the kell.

21 The principle of drying malt in hot air was energetically espoused by John Busby in his *Proposals for Drying Malt with Hot Air* (London, 1725?).

22 A variable measure, here, as was usually the case, equal to a bushel.

23 As Markham explains, the bedding is a mat which goes above the rafters of the kiln, over which a cloth is laid before the malt is put on it to dry.

24 "Bent" (earlier "bennet") was a general term for rushlike grasses; not, however the same as the "herb bennet" used medicinally by Markham (see note on "avens," i, 144).

25 "The more it costs the more you praise it (whatever its real value)";
recorded by Morris P. Tilley, *A Dictionary of the Proverbs in England in
the Sixteenth and Seventeenth Centuries* (Ann Arbor, Mich.: University
of Michigan Press, 1950) as no. C670 (p. 120).

26 Now refers to irises, but is here applied to reeds or rushes.

27 Thin, long twigs, usually of the willow, as used in the making of baskets,
etc.

28 The history of fuels in industrial malting is summarized in *The Brewing
Industry in England* 1700–1830 by Peter Mathias (Cambridge: Cambridge
University Press, 1959), pp. 412–13; later coke became popular.

29 Prickly plants (gorse, for example) or heather.

30 "In some places [malt] is dried at leisure with wood alone, or straw alone,
in other with wood and straw together, but, of all, the straw-dried is
the most excellent. For the wood-dried malt, when it is brewed, beside that
the drink is higher [darker] of colour, it doth hurt and annoy the head
of him that is not used thereto, because of the smoke" (Harrison, p. 136).
Tusser also criticizes the drying of malt with wood:

> Some drieth with straw, and some drieth with wood,
> Wood asketh more charge, and nothing so good. (p. 170.)

31 A popular saying recorded by Tilley (see note 25 above) as no. F280
(p. 216).

32 Similar advice on storage containers is given in *Markham's Farewell to
Husbandry* (1631 ed., pp. 107–9).

33 Fragments of tile.

34 Content, volume.

35 "The ... barley ... is steeped in a cistern, in greater or less quantity, by
the space of three days and three nights" (Harrison, p. 135). See also
"John Barleycorn" (Introduction, p. xlviii).

36 I.e. in area.

37 Consistent, not differing.

38 Harrison's description of the making of malt is, though less detailed, very
similar. The soaked grain is laid "upon the clean floor on a round heap;
it resteth so until it be ready to sprout at the root end, which maltsters call
'coming.' When it beginneth, therefore, to shoot in this manner, they
say it is come, and then forthwith they spread it abroad, first thick, and
afterward thinner and thinner, upon the said floor" (p. 136).

39 Use.

40 The water to be added to malt to make beer.

41 "To clean or sift ... by giving a circular motion to the contents of the
sieve so that the chaff etc. collects in the centre" (*OED*). Sarah Fell paid
Pegg Dodgson four pence for three days' work "scaling [spreading]
manure and reeing" (p. 419; see Introduction, note 45).

42 Harrison says that maltsters allow "one-and-twenty days at the least"
(p. 136).

43 Acrospired, a term for corn which had sprouted not only the root, which
appears first, but the leaf. In Markham's addition to Surflet's translation
of *The Countrie Farme* the form "aker-spire" appears; only this second
form of the word is recorded in the *OED*. Harrison remarks on the

care taken by the workman, "not suffering [the malt] in any wise to take any heat, whereby the bud end should spire ... by which drought or hurt of the stuff itself the malt would be spoiled and turn small commodity to the brewer" (p. 136).

44 Covering over.

45 The base of a stack (cf. staddle stones, on which the stack rests).

CHAPTER VIII

1 Markham's source has not been traced; Charles VIII of France attacked Naples in 1494.

2 Cleanse (the stomach).

3 In value, not in weight.

4 Food (cf. Fr. *manger*); Markham is the only writer quoted in the *OED* to use the word in this sense.

5 Boiled.

6 Oats husked but not ground or rolled.

7 Markham would have deprecated Dr Johnson's well-known definition: "Oats, a grain, which in England is generally given to horses, but in Scotland supports the people" (*Dictionary*, 1755). See also note 10 below.

8 Far apart.

9 For a discussion of Markham's stout defence of oats and oatmeal against the opinions of Estienne and Liebault, see Introduction p. xxi.

10 Jannocks: "A jannock, is bread made of oats, leavened very sour and made round but not very thick, with a cop [mound] on the top, for it can be made no otherwise; by reason it is ovened very soft, the sides will fall thinner than the middle" (Holme, II, vi, p. 293). Muffett is as anxious as Markham to defend oatmeal from the scorn of foreigners, however eminent: "Had Galen seen the oaten cakes of the north, the Jannocks of Lancashire and the grues of Cheshire, he would have confessed that oats and oatmeal are not only meat for beasts, but also for tall, fair and strong men and women of all callings and complexions; but we pardon the Grecian's delicacy, or else ascribe it to the badness of their soil, which could bring forth no oats for nourishment" (pp. 232–3).

11 Celia Fiennes, visiting a village near Lancaster, was more impartial in her description of oatcakes: "Here it was I was first presented with the clap bread which is much talked of and made all of oats: I was surprised when the cloth was laid and they brought a great basket ... and set [it] on the table, full of thin wafers as big as pancakes and dry that they easily break into shivers; but coming to dinner found it to be the only thing I must eat for bread. The taste of oat bread is pleasant enough, and where it's well made is very acceptable, but for the most part is scarce baked, and full of dry flour on the outside" (p. 188).

12 Variants of haggis.

13 Elsewhere, Markham explains that washbrew is "nothing but the very heart of the oatmeal boiled and drained ... having neither hull nor bran in it, but the pure meal and water; and it is to be eaten either with wine, strong beer, or ale, or with clarified honey, according to men's stomachs or abilities" (*Markham's Farewell to Husbandry*, 1631 ed., p. 132).

14 Flummery; a food made from grain boiled to a jelly; the modern use refers to a sweet custard or jelly.
15 Gruel made from oatmeal grits, "somewhat more coarse, and less pleasant than washbrew, having both the bran and hulls in it" (*Markham's Farewell to Husbandry*, 1631 ed., p. 131).
16 See the specific recipes above, ii, 32ff.

CHAPTER IX

1 Expended, used.
2 "Metheglin is a very strong kind of drink, made of two parts of water, and one of honey, boiled together and scummed very clean, and if rosemary, hyssop, thyme, organy and sage be first well boiled in the water whereof you make the metheglin, it will be the better. And afterwards, when you boil the same water with honey, if you also boil in it a quantity of ginger (as to every gallon of water, one ounce of ginger scraped clean and sliced) ... it will be much the better ... Mead is like to metheglin ... for mead is made of one part of honey and four times so much of pure water, or more" (Venner, pp. 44–5). Harrison comments approvingly of metheglin that of it "the Welshmen make no less account (and not without cause if it be well handled) than the Greeks did of their ambrosia or nectar, which for the pleasantness thereof was supposed to be such as the gods themselves did delight in" (pp. 139–40).
3 The border country adjoining Wales and Scotland.
4 See the recipe, paragraph 6 below. Paul Hentzner, travelling in England in 1598, must have sampled March beer: "The general drink is ale, which is prepared from barley, and is excellently well tasted, but strong and intoxicating." Quoted from William B. Rye, *England as Seen by Foreigners in the Days of Elizabeth and James the First* (1865; reissued New York: Benjamin Blom, 1967), p. 109.
5 William Harrison was just such a good man; his wife also derived three hogsheads of beer ("tenscore [200] gallons of beer or more") from a quarter of malt (eight bushels). Harrison's wife followed the same steps in making beer as Markham recommends, with some slightly more complex variations. Harrison's description of the process (too long to quote) is both detailed and informative (see Harrison, pp. 137–8).
6 Cauldron or large kettle; use of leaden vessels for brewing could lead to lead poisoning, though it was not realized in Markham's day that this was possible. Poynter conjectures that Markham may himself have been a victim of such poisoning (p. 21, n. 2).
7 "An oblong basket of wickerwork placed over the bung-hole within the wash-tub to prevent the grain and hops passing through when the liquor is drawn off" (*OED*).
8 "When the hops and liquor shall have thus boiled twelve hours, they empty the copper again, and put the wort to cool at leisure into other vessels called floats or coolers, and they be broad like unto the vats, but only one foot deep" (Surflet, ed. Markham, p. 587).
9 "The gyle tins, or squares, in which the liquor is first put to ferment" (*The Vintner's ... Guide*, p. 122); "gyle" is the name given to fermenting wort.

10 Clarify; this use of the word is not recorded in *OED* before 1681.

11 In his addition to the section on beer in Estienne's *The Countrie Farme*, Markham explains the use "small beer" was put to: "They have March beer, household beer, and small beer: the first is for strangers [visitors], the second for the Master, Mistress and better sort of the family, and the last is for ploughmen or hind [lower] servants" (Surflet, ed. Markham p. 588). Compare Iago's ironical suggestion that the ideal woman is fit only "To suckle fools and chronicle small beer" – to be a poor housewife who must keep track even of the most trivial expenses (*Othello*, II.i.161).

12 Uncharacteristically, Markham does not tell us what is to be done with the "grains" remaining; the omission is remedied by Thomas Tusser, who writes (p. 167):

> *Brew somewhat for thine,*
> *Else bring up no swine ...*
> In buying of drink, by the firkin or pot,
> The tally [cost] ariseth, but hog amends not.

13 The difference between ale and beer is explained by Markham in his addition to Estienne's comments on beer: "The general use is by no means to put hops into ale, making that the difference betwixt it and beer, that the one hath hops, the other none: but the wiser housewives do find an error in that opinion, and say the utter want of hops is the reason why ale lasteth so little a time, but either dyeth or soureth, and therefore they will to every barrel of the best ale allow half a pound of good hops ∴ also blinked [soured] a little to give it a quick and sharp taste" (Surflet, ed. Markham, p. 189). Not everyone was in favour of the recent introduction of hops: "Beer is a Dutch boorish liquor, a thing not known in England, till of late days, an alien to our nation, till such times as hops and heresies came amongst us; it is a saucy intruder into this land." "In this island the old drink was ale ... but since beer hath *hopp'd* in amongst us, ale is thought to be adulterated, and nothing so good as Sir John Oldcastle, and Smug the smith used to drink." See John Taylor, *Ale, Ale-vated into the Ale-titude* (1651) and James Howell, *Epistolae Ho-Elianae* (1645), II, iv; p. 65.

14 Obscure; since the amount would be a small one, perhaps it is a misreading of "spoon" ("speen" is a dialect variation of "spoon").

15 Turn the taste slightly more astringent, here by the addition of tannin.

16 I.e. from half a quarter (the measure) of malt.

17 According to the previous recipe, this would be "after a day and a night at the least," which would be much sooner than modern practice. Platt criticizes the early bottling of beer: "This is the reason why bottle ale is both so windy and muddy, thundering and smoking upon the opening of the bottle, because it is commonly bottled the same day that it is laid into the cellar." He recommends that it not be bottled till "the beer is ten or twelve days old" (*Delightes*, iii, 27).

18 Markham mentions in similar terms the making of cider and perry in two other works, *The English Husbandman* (pt. ii, p. 87) and his edition of Conrad Heresbach's *The Whole Art of Husbandry* (1631); in the latter work he adds a comment that suggests he experimented with some of

the recipes in chapter iv above, on wine: "you may also if you please make a small long bag of fine linen cloth, and filling it full of the powder of cloves, mace, cinnamon, ginger and lemon peels, hang it with a string at the bunghole down into the vessel, and it will give the cider an excellent flavour" (p. 172, cf. iv, 4).

19 White loaves; white flour, however, was simply whole wheat flour finely sifted, so would have been very pale brown rather than white by modern standards. See Jack C. Drummond and Anne Wilbraham, *The Englishman's Food* (London: J. Cape, 1958), p. 43.

20 A tub; see vi, 39.

21 Here, a device to assist in kneading; see the note on the similar tool used in the preparation of hemp, vi, 34 above.

22 "The manner of moulding must be first with strong kneading, then with rolling to and fro, and last of all with wheeling or turning it round about, that it may sit the closer [i.e. more compactly]" (Muffett, p. 241).

23 Bread of middle grade, here made with a sour dough.

24 A single type of grain.

25 Harrison puts it more bluntly: "[brown bread] is not only the worst and weakest of all the other sorts but also appointed in old time for servants, slaves, and the inferior kind of people to feed upon."

26 A paddle, most often used for mixing malt and water in brewing.

27 Here, a general term for a large cask.

28 "The peel is that which puts the batch into, and takes it out of the oven when baked" (Holme, ii, vi, p. 293).

29 "The Maukin is a foul and dirty cloth hung at the end of a long pole, which being wet, the baker sweeps all the ashes together therewith, which the fire or fuel in the heating of the oven hath scattered all about within it" (Holme, ii, vi, p. 293).

Picture Credits

The following institutions have given permission for reproducing illustrations:

Bibliography

Only works written before 1800 and works referred to by abbreviated titles are recorded here. For more recent books and articles, see the notes to the Introduction, where they are gathered by subject.

A.W. See W., A.

Alexis Piemontese. *The Secrets of ... Alexis of Piemont*. London, 1558–69.

Amman, Jost. *Kunnst vnd Lehrbüchlein*. Franckfurt am Mayn, 1578.

"*Art and Mystery of Vintners*." *Art and Mystery of Vintners and Wine-Coopers, The*. London, 1682.

"Banckes." *An Herball (1525)*, ed. Sanford V. Larkey and Thomas Pyles. New York: Scholar's Facsimiles and Reprints, 1941.

Book of Soveraigne Approved Medicines and Remedies, A. London, 1577.

Boorde, Andrew. *The Breviary of Healthe*. London, 1552.

– *A Compendyous Regyment, or a Dyetary of Helth*. London, 1542; ed. F.J. Furnivall, Early English Text Society Extra Series No. 10, 1870.

Bonnefons, Nicholas de. *The French Gardiner*. Trans. John Evelyn. London, 1691.

Brathwait, Richard. *The English Gentlewoman*. London, 1631.

Braun, Georgius, and Hohenberg, Franz. *Civitates Orbis Terrarum*. Cologne, 1597.

Braunschweig (Brunschwig, Brunschwygk), Hieronymous von. *Liber de Arte Distillandi*. 1500, 1512. Trans. Laurence Andrewe, *The Virtuose Booke of Distillacyoun*. London, 1527.

"A Breviate Touching the Order and Government of a Nobleman's House," ed. Joseph Banks. In *Archaeologia*, xiii (1800), 328–31.

Bullein, William. *Dialogue Against the Fever Pestilence*. London, second ed., 1573.

Bullokar, John. *An English Expositor*. London, 1656. Edition of 1616 reprinted. Menston: Scolar Press, 1967.

Busby, John. *Proposals for Drying Malt with Hot Air*. London, 1725?

Butler, Charles. *The Feminine Monarchy*. London, 1609

Buttes, Henry. *Dyets Dry Dinner*. [London, 1599].

Closet for Ladies and Gentlewomen, A. London, 1608.

Cervio, Vincenzo. *Il Trinciante.* Rome, 1593.

Clowes, William. *A Prooued Practise for All Young Chirugians.* London, 1588. See also *Selected Writings of William Clowes, 1544–1604,* ed. F.N.L. Poynter. London: Harvey and Blythe, 1948.

Cogan, Thomas. *The Haven of Health.* [London, 1584].

Cooper, Joseph (Chief Cook to Charles I). *The Art of Cookery Refin'd and Augmented.* London, 1654.

Cotgrave, Randle. *A Dictionary of the French and English Tongues.* London, 1611. Reprinted, Amsterdam: Da Capo Press, 1971.

Crommelin, Louis. *An Essay Towards the Improving of the Hempen and Flaxen Manufacturers in the Kingdom of Ireland.* Dublin, 1705.

Culpeper, Nicholas. *The London Dispensatory: A Physical Directory, or a Translation of the London Dispensatory ... By N. Culpeper.* London, 1651. A popular translation of the *Pharmacopoeia Londinensis* with Culpeper's comments added.

– "School." *Culpeper's School of Physick.* London, 1659.

"I Dawson." Dawson, Thomas. *The Good Huswifes Iewell,* "Newly set foorth with additions." London, 1596. Reprinted, Amsterdam: Da Capo Press, 1977.

"II Dawson." Dawson, Thomas. *The Second Part of the Good Hus-wiues Iewell.* London, 1597. There is an earlier edition of 1585.

"Dawson, Leechbook." Dawson, Warren R. *A Leechbook, or Collection of Medieval Recipes of the Fifteenth Century.* London: Royal Society of Literature of the U.K., 1934.

de Worde, Wynkyn. *Boke of Keruynge.* London, 1513.

Dee, John. *Praeface to the Elements of Geometrie of Euclid of Megara (1570),* ed. Allen G. Debus. New York: Science History Publications, 1975.

Digby, Sir Kenelm. *The Closet of Sir Kenelm Digby, Knight, Opened.* London, 1669.

Elyot, Sir Thomas. *Castel of Helth.* London, 1539.

Erasmus, Desiderius. *A Modest Means to Marriage.* Trans. Nicholas Leigh. London, 1568.

"Estienne and Liebault." Estienne, Charles and Liebault, Jean. *L'agriculture et maison rustique,* 2 pt. Paris, 1569–70; also refers to those parts of Markham's edition (see Surflet, ed. Markham) which are translated from the original French.

Evelyn, John. *Aceteria: A Discourse of Sallats.* London, 1699.

F., B. *The Office of the Good Housewife.* London, 1672.

Fairfax Family. *Arcana Fairfaxiana,* ed. George Weddell. Newcastle-on-Tyne, 1890.

Fell, Sarah. *The Household Account Book of Sarah Fell of Swarthmoor Hall,* ed. N. Penney. Cambridge: Cambridge University Press, 1920.

Fiennes, Celia. *The Journeys of Celia Fiennes,* ed. Christopher Morris. London: Cresset Press, 1949.

Fitzherbert, John. *Boke of Husbandry.* London, 1525.

"French Pastry-cooke, The." La Varenne, François P. *The French Pastry-cooke.* London, 1653.

Fruiterers Secrets, The. London, 1604.

Gerarde, John. *The Herball, or Generall Historie of Plantes.* London, 1597.

Good Hous-wiues Treasurie, The. London, 1588.

Good Huswifes Handmaide for the Kitchin. London, 1594.

Goodyer, John, trans. *The Greek Herbal of Dioscorides*. London, 1655; ed. Robert J. Gunther. New York: Haffner Publishing Co., 1959.

Greene, Robert. *A Quippe for an Vpstart Courtier*. London, 1592. Reprinted, Scolar Press, 1971.

Gyer, Nicholas. *The English Phlebotomy*. London, 1592.

Hall, Richard. *Observations ... on the Method Used in Holland, in Cultivating or Raising of Hemp or Flax*. Dublin, 1724.

"Hard Words." See Markham, Gervase, "Hard Words."

Harrison, William. *The Description of England*, ed. Georges Edelen. Ithaca, New York: Cornell University Press, 1968.

Harvey, Gabriel. *Marginalia*, ed. G.C. Moore Smith. Stratford-upon-Avon: Shakespeare Head Press, 1913.

Henslow, George. *Medical Works of the Fourteenth Century*. London: Chapman and Hall, 1899.

Herbert, George. *A Priest to the Temple*. In *The Works of George Herbert*, ed. F.E. Hutchinson. Oxford: Clarendon Press, 1953.

Heresbach, Conrad. *The Whole Art of Husbandry*, trans. Barnabe Googe, ed. Gervase Markham. London, 1631. Googe's translation was first published in 1577.

Heywood, Thomas. *A Curtaine Lecture*. London, 1637.

Hill [Hyll], Thomas. *A Most Briefe and Pleasaunt Treatyse, Teaching Howe to Dress, Sowe, and Set a Garden*. London, 1563.

Holme, Randle. *The Academy of Armory*. [Vol. i] Chester, 1688. Vol. ii, ed. I.H. Jeayes. London: Roxburghe Club, 1905. Vol. i. reprinted, Menston: Scolar Press, 1972.

Howell, James. *Epistolae Ho-Elianae*. London, 1645.

Jeninges, Edward. *A Briefe Discovery of the Damages that Happen to this Realme by Disordered and Unlawful Diet*. London, 1590.

John XXI, Pope. (Petrus Hispanus) *The Treasurie of Healthe*. Trans. Humphrey Lloyd. [London], c. 1550.

La Varenne, François P. See *French Pastry-cooke, The*.

Ladies Cabinet Enlarged and Opened, The. London, 1654.

Ladies Companion, The. "By Persons of Quality." London, 1654.

Langham, William. *Garden of Health*. London, "1579" i.e. 1597.

Lawson, William. *A New Orchard and Garden*. London, 1631. (Published as the sixth part of the 1632 edition of *A Way to Get Wealth*).

Levens (Levins), Peter. *The Pathway to Health*. London, 1582.

Liber de Diversis Medicinis, ed. Margaret Sinclair Ogden. Early English Text Society, orig. ser. no. 207; Oxford: Oxford University Press, revised reprint 1969.

London Dispensatory, The. See Culpeper.

Lyte, Henry. *A Niewe Herball*. London, 1578. (A translation of Rembert Dodoens' *Cruydeboeck*, 1554.)

Marcandier (Magistrate of Bourges). *A Treatise on Hemp*. London, 1764.

Markham, Gervase.

(The numbers refer to the texts used for this edition, as recorded in the bibliography of Markham's works compiled by F.N.L. Poynter – see Introduction, note 2).

- *Cavelarice, or The English Horseman*. London, 1607; Poynter 19.1.
- *Cheape and Good Husbandry, or the Well-ordering of All Beastes and Fowles*. London, 1614; Poynter 22.1. Reprinted. Amsterdam: Da Capo Press, 1969.
- "*The Country Farme.*" See Surflet, ed. Markham.
- *The English Housewife*. For a description of the texts on which this edition is based, see Introduction, "The Text."
- *The English Husbandman*. London, 1613–15; Poynter 21.1 (i) and 21.1 (ii).
- *Markham's Far[e]well to Husbandry*. London, 1620; Poynter 24.1, 34.1, etc.
- "Hard Words." "A short table expounding all the hard words in this booke." In *Cheape and Good Husbandry* (q.v.), sigs. A5-A8; appears also in *A Way to Get Wealth* (q.v.).
- *Markham's Maister-peece*. London, 1610; Poynter 20.1.
- *A Way to Get Wealth*. London, 1631, Poynter 34.5.
May, Robert. *The Accomplisht Cooke*. London, 1660.
Marnette, M. *The Perfect Cook*. London, 1656.
Moryson, Fynes. *An Itinerary* (1617). Glasgow: James Mackehose and Sons, 1907–8.
Moulton, Thomas. *The Myrour or Glasse of Helth*. London, 1539.
Muffett (Moffet, Moufet), Thomas. *Health's Improvement*. [London, 1655].
Murrell, John. *A Delightful Daily Exercise*. London, 1621.
"Murrell (1617)." Murrell, John. *A New Booke of Cookerie*. London, 1617.
- "Two Books." Murrells *Two Books of Cookerie and Carving*, "the fifth time printed." London, 1638.
"OED." *The Oxford English Dictionary*, ed. James A.H. Murray and others. Compact Edition, Oxford: Oxford University Press, 1971.
Parkinson, John. *Paradisi in Sole, Paradisus Terrestris*. London, 1629. Reprinted. Amsterdam: Da Capo Press, 1975.
Paston Family. *Paston Letters and Papers of the Fifteenth Century*, ed. Norman Davis. Oxford: Clarendon Press, 1971.
Patissier François, Le. Amsterdam, 1655.
Pharmacopoeia Londinenis, A Physicall Directory, trans. Nicholas Culpeper. London, 1651.
Platt, Sir Hugh. *Delightes for Ladies*. London, 1602. Reprinted with an introduction by G.E. and K.R. Fussell. London: Crosby, Lockwood and Son, 1948.
- *A Jewell House of Art and Nature*. London, 1594.
"Pliny (trans. Holland)." Plinius Secundus. *The Historie of the World, Commonly Called the Natural Historie*, trans. Philemon Holland. London, 1601.
Poynter, F.N.L. *A Bibliography of Gervase Markham, 1568?-1637*. Oxford: Oxford Bibliographical Society Publications, new series, vol. xi, 1962.
Proper New Booke of Cookery, A. London, 1575.
Raffald, Elizabeth. *The Experienced Housekeeper*. London, 1769.
Robinson, Nicholas. *A New Theory of Physick and Diseases Founded on the Principles of the Newtonian Philosophy*. London, 1725.
Rose, Giles. *A Perfect School of Instructions for the Officers of the Mouth*. London, 1682.
Rumpolt, Marx. *Ein new Kochbuch*. Franckfort am Mayn, 1604.
Rye, William B., ed. *England As Seen by Foreigners in the Days of Elizabeth*

and James the First. New York: Benjamin Blom, 1965; a reprint of the edition of 1865.

Sachs, Hans. *Eygentliche Beschreibung aller Stande auf Erden*. Franckfurt am Mayn, 1568.

Scot, Reginald. *The Discovery of Witchcraft*. London, 1548.

Short Discourse of the Three Kindes of Peppers in Common Use, A. London, 1588.

Simon, André L. *The History of the Wine Trade in England*. 3 vols. London: Wyman and Sons, 1906–7.

Slator, Lionel. *Instructions for the Cultivating and Raising of Flax and Hemp*. Dublin, 1724.

"Sloane 3692." The manuscript thus catalogued at the British Library, fols. 26–30v.

"Surflet." Charles Estienne and Jean Liebault (q.v.). *Maison Rustique, or The Countrie Farme*, trans. Richard Surflet. London, 1600.

– "ed. Markham." Estienne and Liebault (q.v.). *Maison Rustique, or the Countrey Farme*, trans. R. Surflet (q.v.), ed. Gervase Markham. London, 1616; Poynter 31.1.

Symcotts, John. *Diary*. In *A Seventeenth Century Doctor and His Patients: John Symcotts, 1592?-1662*, ed. F.N.L. Poynter and W.J. Bishop. Streatley: Bedfordshire Historical Record Society, 1951.

Taswell, William. *Autobiography*, ed. G.P. Elliot, Camden Society *Miscellany* vol. ii, 1853.

Taverner, John. *Certaine Experiments Concerning Fish and Fruit*. London, 1600.

Taylor, John. *Ale, Ale-vated into the Ale-titude*. London, 1651.

Thornton, Alice. *The Autobiography of Mrs. Alice Thornton*. Surtees Society, lxii, 1875. Reprinted in extract in *By a Woman Writt*, ed. Joan Goulianos. Baltimore: Penguin Books, 1974.

Turner, William. *A New Boke of the Natures of All Wines*. London, 1568.

"Turner, I *Herbal*." Turner, William. *A New Herball*. London, 1551.

– "II *Herbal*." *The Second Parte of William Turners Herball*. Cologne, 1562.

– "III *Herbal*." *The First and Seconde Partes of the Herbal of William Turner ... Enlarged with the Third Parte*. Cologne, 1568.

– "*Names*." *Libellus de Re Herbaria (1538); The Names of Herbes (1548)*, ed. James Britten and others. London: The Ray Society, 1965.

Tusser, Thomas. *Five Hundred Points of Good Husbandry*, ed. E.V. Lucas. London: James Tregaskis and Son, 1931. A reprint of the edition of 1580.

Twamley, Josiah. *Dairying Exemplified, or the Business of Cheesemaking*. Warwick, 1784.

Two Fifteenth Century Cookery Books, ed. Austin Thomas. London, Early English Text Society Original Series No. 91, 1888.

Universal Magazine of Knowledge and Pleasure, The. London. September, October 1747.

Vaughan, William. *Naturall and Artificial Directions for Health*. London, 1600.

Venner, Thomas (Tobias). *Via Recta ad Vitam Longam*. London, 1620.

"*The Vintner's ... Guide*." *Vintner's, Brewer's, Spirit Merchant's and Licensed Victualler's Guide, The*, by "A Practical Man." London, 1826.

W., A. *A Book of Cookrye*. London, 1584. Reprinted. Amsterdam: Da Capo Press, 1976.

Whately, William. *A Bride-bush*. London, 1619.

Whittock, Nathaniel, and others. *The Complete Book of Trades*. London, 1837.

Wirsung, Christoph. *Praxis Medicinae Universalis, or a Generall of Physicke*, trans. Jacob Mosan. London, 1598.

Whole Art of Dyeing, The. London, 1705.

Woodall, John. *The Surgions Mate*. London, 1617.

Glossary

Numbers in bold type indicate that fuller information is contained either in the text or in its accompanying note; references are to chapter and paragraph of the text. At least one occurrence of each is recorded. Plant binomials conform with those in H.L. Gerth van Wijk, *A Dictionary of Plant Names* (2 vols., Vaals-Amsterdam: A. Asher & Co., 1971). *The English Housewife* is quoted extensively in the *OED*; those few words that were passed over are indicated by *.

abate (of egg yolks), hold back; ii, 24.
abroach, open for use; iv, 4.
*****acrospired** (ackerspyerd), used of grain which has sprouted not only the root, which appears first, but the leaf, or acrospire; **vii, 22.** Pre-dates *OED* entries.
affodil, properly asphodel (*Asphodelus ramosus*), but often used for daffodil; **i, 117.**
*****aforetake,** placed upon the bung, upside down; **iv, 15.** Not in *OED.*
agnus castus, Vitex agnus-castus, the "chaste tree," but identified by Markham with the plant tutsan; **i, 33.**
agrimony, *Agrimonia eupatoria,* a member of the rose family; i, 60.
ague, fever; i, 16.
akerspyerd, see acrospired.
alexanders, *Smyrnium olustratum,* horse-parsley, formerly eaten like celery; i, 17.
alicant, a dark, sweet, red wine; iv, 16.
aloe socotrine, a variety of aloe named from the island of Socotra; **i, 135.**
*****althea,** hollyhock or marshmallow (Latin *althaea*); **i, 100.** Pre-dates *OED* entries.
amee, *Ammi majus,* ammi, an aromatic herb, **i, 11.**
amomum, an aromatic plant of doubtful identity (now refers to the *Zingiberaceae*); **i, 179.**

anack, jannock; an oatcake; **viii, 9.**

angelica, *Angelica archangelica,* a herb believed effective against the plague; **i, 21.**

anil, blue, a vegetable dye; **v, 8.**

anise, *Pimpinella anisum;* aniseed oil is carminative and is a mild expectorant; i, 77.

apple, marvellous, the balsam apple, related to the gourd and cucumber; ii, 5.

apple of love, the tomato, so named because it was originally thought to have aphrodisiac qualities; ii, 5.

aqua vitae, "water of life"; distilled spirits flavoured by herbs. Recipes are given in iii, 4ff.

arabic, a mucilageneous gum; **i, 223.**

aristolochia longa, a variety of the genus *Aristolochia* (birthwort), characterized by long leaves; wrongly identified by Markham as red madder, *Rubia tinctorum;* i, 21.

aristolochia rotunda, "round-leaved" *Aristolochia;* Markham believed that it referred to galingale; **i, 181.**

armeniac, see bole armeniac.

artificially, with artifice or skill; v, 46.

ashlar, a square hewn stone; vii, 22.

asterion, a herb of doubtful identity (the name is derived from the Greek word for star); **i, 37.**

avens, *Geum urbanum,* also known as herb bennet; i, 144.

avoid, void, get rid of; iii, 12.

bag, stomach (of an animal); ii, 37.

balm, balsam, an aromatic resin; **iii, 5.**

barbel, a large fresh-water fish related to the carp; **ii, 52.**

barberry, *Barberea vulgaris,* an edible berry; **i, 20.**

*****bare** (of cows), newly calved; vi, 6. Not recorded in *OED.*

barm, yeast; i, 88.

barrow, a castrated boar; i, 208.

bastard, a sweet wine; **iv, 6.**

bay, *oil de,* oil from bay leaves; i, 219.

bay salt, the salt that crystallizes when sea-water is evaporated; i, 40.

beam, one of the rollers on a loom; **v, 19.**

beat, a bundle; v, 29.

beer, small, beer made from a second infusion of the malt; **ix, 6,** "small drink" and note.

beetle, a wooden mallet; iii, 31.

benjamin, a resin from the tree *Liquidambar orientalis;* ii, 168.

bennet, see avens; i, 220.

bent, bennet; a rush-like grass; vii, 16.

betony (of the wood), *Betonia officinalis,* a member of the mint family; i, 165.

Bittern, a wading bird similar to but smaller than a heron; ii, 76.

blink, to make the taste slightly more astringent; **ix, 9.**

bole armeniac, a fine clay imported from Armenia, used medicinally; i, 193.

bolt,to sift; i, 144.

bolter, a sieve; ix, 18.

borage, *Borago officinalis;* a herb once used frequently as a cordial; i, 27.

botch, an eruption or boil; i, 26.

bottom, a peg on which yarn is wound; v, 52.

bought, the inward part of a joint; i, 196.

box, a container (not necessarily wooden); ii, **154.**

brake, an instrument used for breaking or crushing; ii, **176;** v, **34;** and ix, **14.**

bracks, bracken; vii, 19.

brawn, flesh or muscle; ii, 80.

bray, to beat or crush to powder; ii, 161.

bream, a fresh-water fish similar to the carp; ii, 52.

broach, to pierce; ii, 60; a spindle; v, 20.

brockelhemp, brooklime; i, 90.

brooklime, *Veronica beccabunga*, a species of speedwell; i, **90** and i, **95.**

broomwort, probably an error for "brownwort"; i, 33.

bryony, *Bryonia dioica*; i, 182.

bullace, black, *Prunus institia*, a wild plum related to the sloe; iv, 31.

buck, lye in which linen, yarn or cloth is steeped as the first step in the process of bleaching; v, 51.

bugloss, a name given to various plants which have leaves resembling an ox's tongue; ii, **4** and i, **27.**

bun, the pith of the stalk; v, 24.

bung, to cork or seal; iii, 31; a cork or wooden plug; iv, **2.**

burl, a small knot or lump in wool or cloth; v, 22.

burnet, properly *Poterium officinale* (*Sanguisorba officinalis* L), also know as bloodwort, but applied to several other plants; i, 98.

butt, a barrel; iv, **3.**

by-dish, a side-dish for scraps; ii, 14.

*calafine, colophony; see i, 168. A variant not recorded in *OED*.

calamint, *Calamintha officinalis*, an aromatic herb; i, 27.

calamus aromaticus, an aromatic reed, or a substitute resembling it; iii, **25.**

camomile, *Anthemis nobilis*, an aromatic creeping herb; i, 29.

Candy, a variety of malmsey (q.v.); iv, **11.**

canker, a persistent, spreading sore or ulcer; i, 50.

capillus veneris, *Adiantum cappillus-veneris*; iii, 10.

caper, the pickled flower-bud of *Capparis spinosa*, still used as a condiment; i, 13.

capon, a castrated fowl; ii, 39.

caprifoil, "goat-leaf," an old name for honeysuckle or woodbine; i, 208.

caprik, a sweet white wine of uncertain origin; iv, **38.**

carbonado, meat boiled upon coals; ii, **95.**

card, an implement used to part, comb out, and set in order the fibres of wool; v, 17.

carduus benedictus, *Carbenia benedicta*, the "blessed thistle"; i, 170.

castoreum, a strong smelling substance obtained from a gland in the beaver; i, 162.

cat's tails, the flowers of *Typha latifolia*; i, 208.

caudle, a warm gruel mixed with wine, herbs and spices; i, 104.

celandine, *Chelidonium majus*, also called swallowwort or tetterwort; i, 21.

centaury, greater, identified since the sixteenth century as *Centaurea rhaponticum*; i, 98.

ceruse, white lead; i, 214.

charger, a platter; ii, 47.

chawdron, a sauce consisting of chopped entrails, spices, etc.; **ii, 88.**

cheat bread, bread of medium quality; cf. *manchet* **ix, 16.**

cheeselip bag, the stomach of a young suckling calf, used in making cheese; vi, 36.

chervil, *Anthriscus cerefolium,* a garden pot-herb; i, 50.

chewet, a pie made with minced meat; **ii, 127.**

chibol, a mild onion, *Allium fistulosum;* **ii, 9.**

chick-weed, *Stellaria media;* i, 107.

chire, a slender, young sprout of grass; vi, 36.

chine, to split open; ii, 76; a joint of meat; **ii, 39.**

churm, a dialect variant of churn; vi, 22.

cinquefoil, *Potentilla reptans,* the "five-leaved herb"; i, 139.

civet, a musk perfume obtained from the glands of the African civet-cat; iii, 34.

clary, *Salvia sclarea,* formerly used as a pot-herb; i, 165.

clew, a ball of yarn or thread; v, 20.

clout, a cloth; i, 44.

cob-iron, one of the irons upon which the spit turns; ii, 59.

codling, an unripe apple; ii, 123.

cod, a pod; ii, 11.

*coffin, the calyx of a flower; **ii, 18** (pre-dates *OED* entry); crust of a pie; ii, 109.

colewort, name applied to any plant of the cabbage family; i, 53.

collop, a slice of meat, usually bacon; ii, 21.

columbine, *Aquilegia vulgaris;* iii, 14.

come, the sprout which withers and separates from the grain in the making of malt; vii, 6.

comfrey, *Symphytum officinale,* a member of the borage family; **i, 144.**

comfit, a sweetmeat or candy; ii, 113.

conceit, anything elaborate, fanciful, or ingenious; ii, 10.

conduit water, running water; iv, 3.

cony, a rabbit; ii, 54.

continent, content; vii, 25.

copperas, green, iron sulphate; i, 22.

copperas, white, zinc sulphate; i, 73.

cordial, a restorative; **i, 104.**

costive, constipated; i, 20.

couch, a heap of sprouting grain; **vii, 25.**

country, county; vi, 5.

course, layer; ii, 13.

coverlid, coverlet, quilt; v, 2.

crop, the head of a plant; iii, 4.

crowfoot, various species of *Ranunculus* (buttercup); i, 247.

cuit, unfermented grape juice concentrated by boiling; iv, 9.

dace, a small fresh-water fish akin to the roach; ii, 102.

damson, *Prunus damascena,* a plum; iv, 31.

dauke, *Daucus carota,* the wild carrot; i, 117.

deer, fallow, deer of a red-brown hue; ii, 111.
defensative, protective; i, 229.
*****dewition,** distillation; **i, 20** i, **34; i, 179.** Not in *OED.*
de minio, a plaster containing red lead; i, 195.
dock, red, *Rumex sanguineus,* valued medicinally because of the association of its colour with blood; i, 55.
dock, wild, the coarse herb *Rumex obtusifolius;* i, 55.
dog-fennel, stinking camomile, *Anthemis cotula;* i, 166.
doucet, a spiced custard pie; ii, 113.
dragon, gum, see gum dragon.
dragon water, water distilled from an infusion of gum dragon (q.v.); i, 14.
dragon(s), the herb *Dracunculus vulgaris;* **iii, 2.**
dram, one-sixteenth of an ounce, or approximately 1.8 grams; i, 33.
draw, clean; take from the oven or the spit; ii, 107.
dredge, powder; i, 36; **ii, 64.**
dress, clean from dirt; v, 44; season (meat); ii, 60.
dresser, a sideboard, from which meat was served; ii, 191.
dropsy, a sickness characterized by the collection of fluid in the cavities of the body, the swelling of extremities, and a loss of colour from the skin; **iii,** 8.
dug, teat; vi, 9.

eager, sour or vinegary; iv, 7.
earning, rennet; ii, 123.
eddish, aftermath; the late grass which grows after harvest. Eddish cheese is made from the milk of cows fed on the eddish; vi, 44.
elecampane, *Inula helenium,* horse-heal, a perennial composite; iii, 4.
election, choice; iv, 2.
electuary, a medicine, made of powder mixed with syrup; i, 36.
enable, assist; ii, 2.
endive, *Cichorium endivia,* a herb closely related to succory; iii, 2.
eryngo, candied root of the sea holly, *Eryngium maritimum;* **ii, 115.**
eye-bright, *Euphrasia officinalis,* euphrasy; **i, 80.**

falling-sickness, epilepsy; i, 37.
fallow, pale red-brown, and hence a deer of that colour; ii, 47.
farce, to stuff or dress meat; ii, 57.
*****farmes,** cleaned intestines, used for making sausages; **ii, 32.** Markham's passage is recorded in *OED,* but wrongly defined.
feaberry, the northern dialect word for gooseberry; ii, 86.
featherfew, *Chrysanthemum parthenium,* feverfew; i, 23.
feltering, a tangle; **v, 2.**
felwort, *Gentiana lutea,* a species of gentian; i, 175.
fever, pestilent, the plague; i, 9; **i, 20.**
fever, quartan, a fever occurring every third day; i, 9.
fever, quotidian, a fever either continuous or peaking daily; i, 9.
fever, tertian, a fever occurring every second day; **i, 9**
filipendula, *Filipendula vulgaris,* also known as drop-wort; i, 149.
fine, to clarify, to become refined; iv, 4.
firefanged, fire-siezed, scorched; vii, 19.
firkin, a small cask, one-quarter the size of a barrel; ii, 181.

fistula, an ulcer; iii, 2.

flag, a reed or a rush; now applied to irises; **vii, 17.**

flammery, a food made from grain boiled to a jelly; in modern use, a sweet custard or jelly; **viii, 9.**

flavour, to give wine an artificial bouquet; **iv, 3.**

fleet, to skim; ii, 119; to float; iii, 5.

flower-gentle, floramour, *Amaranthus spp.*; ii, 4.

flowers, menstruation; i, 177.

flummery, see flammery.

flux, flow; diarrhoea; i, 40.

frankincense, an aromatic gum; i, 56; see note on olibanum; i, 258.

fricassee, a stew; ii, 20.

fuller, one who "fulls" – cleans and thickens – cloth; v, 22.

galantine, a sauce made from blood; **ii, 88.**

galbanum, an aromatic gum or resin; **i, 227.**

galingale, *Cyperus longus*; a plant with pungently aromatic roots, frequently used as a substitute for ginger; i, 124.

gallipot, a small earthenware pot, usually used for ointments or medicines; ii, 17.

gammon, hind-quarter of ham or bacon; ii, 119.

garner, a container for grain or malt; **vii, 20.**

garth, a wooden hoop; vii, 22.

Gascon, a wine from the Bordeaux area; **vi, 12.**

gauge, measure; iv, 2.

Genoa, paste of, baked sweetmeat of quinces, spices, and sugar; **ii, 174.**

germander, *Teucrium chamaedrys* (Turner, *Names*) and other species of *Teucrium*; i, 210.

gigot, "leg or haunch" (*OED*); **ii, 68.**

gillyflower, *Dianthus caryophyllus*, a clove-scented flower often used in salads; ii, 3.

goldsmith's stone, a smooth, dark stone used to test the quality of gold; a "touchstone"; iii, 15

*goodinyake, codiniac or quiddany, a sweetmeat made from quinces; **ii, 142.** Variant not recorded in *OED*.

goose, stubble, a goose fed on stubble; **ii, 86.**

grain, dyer's, the dried bodies of the coccus insect, once thought to be a berry, gathered from the evergreen oak of southern Europe and used to make a red dye; i, 72.

grains [of paradise], the pungent spice, cardamom; i, 136 iii, 8.

gravel, stones in the bladder; iii, 2.

great, whole; iii, 7.

green, young, raw; i, 226.

green sickness, anaemia, as suffered by young women; chlorosis; **i, 170.**

grits, coarse hulled grain; **viii, 8-10.**

gromwell, the herb *Lithospermum officinale*, the hard, stony seeds of which were widely used medicinally; i, 74.

groundsel, the weed *Senecio vulgaris*; i, 202.

gudgeon, a small fresh-water fish; ii, 102.

gum dragon, Tragacanth gum; **ii, 164.**

gurnet, fish of the genus *Trigla*; the gurnard; ii, 55.

gyle, fermenting wort (malt liquor); **ix, 5.**

hade, a strip of land left unploughed as a boundary line; v, 24.
hap, cover over (dial.); vii, 32.
hard, vinegary; **iv, 16.**
harden, harding; a coarse cloth often made with leftover fibres; v, 39.
hards, coarse fibres of flax; **v, 39.**
hartshorn, powdered or calcined harts' horn; **i, 67.**
hart's-tongue, usually identified as the fern, *Scolopendrium vulgare*; i, 27;
  a mistranslation of fenugreek; ii, 4.
haslets, giblets; ii, 61.
heck, rack; vi, 39.
heckle, a fixed comb used for separating the fibres of flax or hemp in preparation for spinning; iv, 21.
hedge-wine, probably an inferior, acidic wine from wild grapes grown in
  hedgerows; iv, 21.
height, viscosity (of candy); **ii, 189.**
henbane, *Hyoscayamus niger*; **i, 184.**
herb of grace, rue, *Ruta graveolens*; **i, 22.**
hern, heron; **ii, 88.**
hillwort, a herb of doubtful identity; **i, 80.**
hind, a lesser household servant or farm labourer; ix, 13.
hippocras, a spiced, sweetened wine; **ii, 150.**
hip, the fruit of the wild rose; ii, 170.
hogshead, a small barrel containing forty to sixty gallons; iii, 31.
holland cloth, linen of the finest grade from the province of Holland in The
  Netherlands; v, 46.
honey, life (live), liquid honey; **iv, 7.**
honey, stone, chrystallized ("candied") honey; **iv, 7.**
hook, sickle; v, 28.
horehound, the herb *Marrubium vulgare*; **i, 88.**
horse-mint, wild mint, *Mentha sylvestris* or *M. aquatica*; i, 89.
horseshoe, horseshoe-vetch, *Hippocrepis comosa*; iii, 5.
houseleek, the evergreen herb, *Sempervivum tectorum*; i, 48.
humour, one of the four fluids of the body, thought to determine physical
  and mental qualities; melancholic, choleric, phlegmatic, and sanguine; **i, 34.**
hurdle, a large wooden frame; v, 35.
hutch, a chest-shaped container; vii, 20.
hyssop, the aromatic herb, *Hyssopus officinalis*; i, 31.

iliaca passio, a painful disease ("passion") of the ileum, the small intestine;
  i, 93.
impostume, an infected swelling or abcess; i, 207.
ireos, orris (q.v.), an aromatic powder, made from the root of the Florentine
  iris; **iii, 25.**
isinglass, gelatin obtained from fish; ii, 113.

jannock, an oatcake; **viii, 9.**
juniper, *Juniperus communis*, the berries of which are used to flavour gin;
  i, 74.

kimnel, a tub used in the preparation of bread, salt meat, brewing, or the making of cheese; vi, 39.

King's evil, scrofula, tubercular swelling of the glands about the neck; a disease once thought to be cured by the touch of the reigning monarch; **i, 55.**

knitwort, comfrey (q.v.); **i, 243.**

knop, the bud or seed vessel of a flower; ii, 167.

knot, knops or buds; ii, 12.

knotgrass, the weed *Polygonum aviculare*; i, 241.

labdanum, an aromatic gum; iii, 25.

lag, lack; iv, 23.

lags, lees; iv, 8.

langdebeef, *langue de boeuf,* ox tongue (*Picris echioides*); see "bugloss"; **i, 27.**

lap, wrap; iii, 11.

lapis calaminaris, calamine; zinc carbonate or zinc silicate; i, 227.

lard, in cookery, to thread strips of bacon or other fat into meat; ii, 111.

lark-heel, larkspur or delphinium; ii, 3.

latten, an alloy similar to brass; iii, 14.

lavender cotton, the ground cypress, *Santolina chamaecyparrisus*; i, 249.

lawn, fine linen; iii, 22.

lax, diarrhoea; i, 129.

lea, a measure of woven thread; **v, 47.**

leach, a dish, usually of jellied meats, sweets, or fruit; **ii, 152.**

lead, a cauldron or large kettle; ix, 5.

leaded, lead-glazed; vi, 20.

leaven, yeast; i, 185.

lettuce, cabbage, head lettuce; **ii, 4.**

limail, metal filings; iii, 14.

limbeck, the "helm" or upper part of a still in which the vapour condenses; i, 76; see Introduction p. xlii.

line, flax; v, 27.

ling, a saltwater fish, frequently salted and used in Lent; ii, 21; heather; vii, 19.

link, a sausage; ii, 39.

list, a strip of cloth; i, 114.

litharge of gold, the scum that rises when lead or silver is refined; impure lead oxide; ii, 186.

lithe, soft; ii, 109.

loblolly, thick gruel; **viii, 10.**

lockram, a linen fabric; i, 239.

long, heavy or viscous; iv, 25.

lovage, the herb *Levisticum officinale*; i, 68.

lupin, a leguminous plant grown for fodder; **i, 117.**

lute, to seal; iii, 5.

lye, urine; i, 241; a strong alkaline solution used for bleaching; **v, 51.**

madder, a source of red dye, *Rubia tinctorum*; **i, 213.**

made (of medicines and dishes in cookery), prepared; compound, complex; i, 230.

maidenhair, properly the fern *Adiantum capillus-veneris*, but often used of English maidenhair, *Asplenium trichomanes*; i, 80.

malkin, a type of rag mop used to clean an oven; ix, 18.

mallard, the common wild duck; ii, 46.

mallow, used of *Malva sylvestris*, or *M. alcea*, wild mallow and vervain mallow respectively; i, 26.

mallow, small, dwarf mallows, *Malva borealis* (*M. rotundifolia* L).

malmsey, a sweet dessert wine; iv, 10.

manchet, a loaf of white bread; ix, 15.

mange, food; viii, 5.

marchpane, marzipan; ii, 173.

marjoram, coarse, the herb self-heal, *Prunella vulgaris*; i, 42.

mastic, the gum or resin from the tree *Pistacia lentiscus*; i, 258.

matrix, the uterus; i, 179.

may-weed, *Anthemis cotula*; i, 45.

mead, a strong drink made of honey and water; ix, 2.

meal, the flour of grain or pulse; i, 99; quantity of milk; vi, 7.

meat, in the general sense, food; vii, 25.

megrim, migraine; i, 63.

melilot, the yellow melilot, *Melilotus officinalis*, from which plasters were made; i, 22.

melting, the process of making malt from barley; vii, 25.

mere sauce, marinade; ii, 111.

metheglin, a strong, sweet drink made from fermented honey and water, and flavoured with aromatic herbs; ix, 2.

mithridate, a medical compound; i, 14.

mint, red, *Mentha aquatica*; i, 27.

morel, nightshade, *Solanum nigrum*; i, 144.

morel, great, the morello cherry; i, 240.

morphew, a name given to diseases which cause the skin to scale; i, 186.

*moss, mousse; iv, 9. Not recorded in *OED* before 1892.

mote, speck; iv, 7.

mother, the uterus, hysteria; i, 97 the crust of yeast that forms on the top of fermenting ale; ix, 5.

motherwort, *Leonuris cardiaca*; i, 176 (note to "mugwort").

mouse-ear, hawk-weed, *Hieracium pilosella* and other plants; i, 52.

mugget, the herb woodruff, *Asperula odorata*; ii, 4 (in cookery) entrails, chitterlings; ii, 37.

mugwort, *Artemisia vulgaris*, but see "motherwort," with which Markham confused it; i, 23.

murrey, purple-red; ii, 92.

muscadine, a fruity, sweet wine; iv, 3.

naughty, evil; v, 29.

near hand, nearly, almost; ii, 33.

nearer, easier; ii, 87.

neat, cattle; ii, 192.

nerval, an ointment for the nerves; i, 196.

nep, catmint, *Nepeta cataria*, but see i, 188, note to "wild nep."

oak of Jerusalem, an aromatic herb, *Chenopodium botrys*; iv, 34.

olibanum, frankincense; i, 258.

olive, in cookery, a dish made from stuffed slices of meat; **ii, 61.**

*olla podrida (olepotrige), a stew of mixed meats, cooked until the meat disintegrates; **ii, 47.** "Olepotrige" is not recorded in *OED*.

ooze, the liquor from a tanning vat; **i, 130.**

opopanax, a resin obtained from the plant *Opopanax Chironium*: **i, 227.**

orach, a tall annual herb, *Atriplex hortensis*, known as garden orach or mountain spinach; **ii, 6.**

order, manage; **iv, 12.**

organy, wild marjoram, *Origanum vulgare*; **i, 242.**

orpine, *Sedum telphium*, a succulent herbaceous plant; **i, 169.**

orris, a powder made from the aromatic root of the Florentine iris; **iii, 25.**

osey, a sweet white wine; **iv, 8.**

osier, willow; **v, 51.**

oxycrate, a mixture of vinegar and water; **i, 189.**

osmund, the fern *Osmunda regalis*; **i, 144.**

overdraw, to draw from the top; **iv, 5.**

painful, painstaking; **v, 17.**

pale, a paling fence; **v, 32.**

palma Christi, Ricinus communis, the plant from which castor oil is derived; **i, 4.**

palsy, any disease which produces involuntary trembling of the limbs; **i, 34.**

pancheon, "a large, shallow earthenware bowl or vessel, wider at the top than bottom" *(OED)*; **vi, 25.**

panperdy, i.e. *pain perdu*, "hidden-bread," a dish resembling the modern French bread; **ii, 28.**

pap, pulp; **i, 106.**

parel, the ingredients used in "fining" or clarifying wine; **iv, 3.**

passion, painful disease or affliction; **i, 97.**

peahen, the female of the peacock; **ii, 51.**

pearl, an opacity or cataract in the eye; **i, 45.**

pearl, seed, a minute pearl; **iii, 4.**

peck, a variable measure equivalent to one-quarter of a bushel or two gallons; **ii, 171.**

peel, a baker's shovel, used to take bread in and out of the oven; **ix, 18.**

pellitory, *Parietaria diffusa*, also known as "pellitory of the wall"; **i, 153.**

pennyroyal, *Mentha pulegium*, a variety of mint; **i, 109.**

pepper, case, a pungent spice obtained from the dried fruit of the *Capsicum* species; **i, 43.**

pepper, long, a variety of pepper (not now in general use) derived from the fruit of *Piper longum*; **i, 136.**

perry, the fermented juice of the pear; **ix, 2.**

pessary, a substance to be inserted into the vagina or anus; **i, 178.**

pettitoes, (of pigs) feet, trotters; **ii, 29.**

pewit, the lapwing; **ii, 191.**

phthisic, consumption; **i, 88.**

pimpernel, the name previously given to great burnet, *Sanguisorba officinalis*, and burnet saxifrage, *Pimpinella saxifraga* as well as to the red (or "scarlet") pimpernel; **i, 107.**

pimpernel, red, *Anagallis arvensis*, pimpernel; **i, 67.**

pin and web, types of cataracts or opacities in the eye; i, 78.

pinion, the end joint of a wing; ii, 76.

pipe, a barrel of the same capacity as a butt (q.v.); iv, 3.

piping, steaming; ii, 65.

pipkin, "a small earthenware pot or pan" (*OED*); ii, 14.

pippin, a cooking apple; ii, 129.

plantain, *Plantago major*; i, 77.

plaster, a medicinal concoction spread upon leather or cloth and applied to the body; i, 22.

pledget, a pad of absorbent material; i, 48.

*plug, not recorded by *OED* before 1627; Markham's use dates it 1623; vii, 22 and 19.

poise, weight; vii, 24.

polypody, the fern *Polypodium vulgare*, often differentiated in terms of its place of growth; i, 93.

pomander, a perfumed ball carried as a supposed protection from disease; iii, 28.

pomecitron, a citron; ii, 187.

pomwater, pomewater, a variety of cooking apple; i, 248.

populeon, ointment of poplar-buds; i, 196.

porret, a young leek or onion; i, 191.

poss, to pound, to toss; v, 50.

posset, spiced milk curd made by pouring hot milk into ale; i, 10.

pot, a sausage; viii, 10.

pottage, soup; ii, 40.

pottle, a measure consisting of two quarts; i, 69.

powder, to salt; vi, 29.

precipitate, mercuric oxide; i, 203.

present, immediate; i, 47.

prick, a word used to describe wine in the process of becoming too acidic; iv, 9.

prick up, set upright in a decorative manner; ii, 113.

prune, damask, *Prunus damascena*, the damson plum; i, 165.

puke, a deep purplish brown; v, 9.

puler, a young bird or fledgling; ii, 85.

pulse, a general name for peas, beans, lentils, etc.; ii, 30.

puncheon, a cask of variable measure; a tool for punching holes; iv, 22.

*purge (of a liquid) to clarify; ix, 5.

purslane, the herb *Portalaca oleracea*; i, 15.

pursy, fat, corpulent; i, 120.

purtenance, appendage; the "pluck" of an animal; ii, 56.

quarter, a measure of grain equal to eight bushels; vii, 14.

quelquechose, literally a "something" a dish consisting of the mixture of many things; ii, 29.

*quenebit, cubeb; a berry, native to Java, with a spicy flavour; iii, 5. This variant not in *OED*.

quick, alive; i, 39.

quinancy, a variant form of "quinsy"; i, 52.

quinsy, any disease involving inflammation of the throat; i, 52.

rack, the neck or the forepart of the spine; ii, 40.

raddle, reddle or ruddle; red ochre; viii, 5.

ragwort, the common ragwort, *Senecio jacobaea*; **i, 211.**

rail, a name given to various varieties of small birds; ii, 47.

range, strainer; ii, 131.

rear, of an egg, coddled, half-cooked; i, 177.

ree, to clean or sift by rotating the contents of a sieve; vii, 28.

*reese, to become reasty or rancid; vi, 29. Pre-dates *OED* entry.

reins, kidneys; i, 13.

rend, rendered; melted and clarified; v, 15.

Rhenish, wine from the region of the Rhine; **iv, 18.**

rheum, any disease which caused running nose and eyes; usually the common cold; i, 40.

ribwort, ribgrass, the narrow-leaved plantain, *Plantago lanceolata*; i, 249.

rid away, to purify, to rid of rubbish; of wine, to extract the drinkable portion; **iv, 8.**

right, true, genuine; i, 227.

roach, a small fresh-water fish; ii, 102.

roche alum, rock alum; **i, 50.**

Rochelle, a wine exported from the seaport of La Rochelle in the Bordeaux region of western France; **iv, 21.**

rochet, the red gurnard; ii, 55.

rock, a distaff; a cleft staff on which raw yarn was held while it was being spun by hand; v, 47.

rocket, the salad herb, *Eruca sativa*; ii, 4.

roe, a species of small deer; ii, 192.

rope (of a liquid), to become clotted, viscous, or stringy; hence also "ropy"; i, 209; iv, 14.

rosa solis, more properly *ros solis*, sundew, *Drosera rotundifolia*; **i, 254.**

rusty, rancid; i, 216.

sack, a sherry-type wine; **iv, 2.**

sad, dark, sombre (of colours); v, 14.

sal gemma, rock salt; iii, 11.

sallat, salad; **ii, 11.**

salt, bay, see bay salt.

sallow, willow; iii, 27.

salve, an ointment; i, 32.

samphire, the herb *Crithmum maritimum*, used in salads; **ii, 4.**

sandragon, "dragon's blood": mercuric sulphide, known as cinnabar or vermillion; i, 70.

sanders, sandalwood; red, yellow, and white varieties of this aromatic wood were known as sanders; **iii, 33.**

sarcenet, sarsenet; "a very fine and soft silk-like material" (*OED*); ii, 167.

savin, a drug derived from the shrub *Juniperus sabina*; **i, 135.**

saxifrage, the name (from Latin) means "rock breaking," and was given to various plants which grew in the clefts of rocks; **i, 148.**

scabious, the plant *Centaurea scabiosa*; i, 23 (note to "maleselon").

scotch, to score, cut deeply; ii, 97.

scruple, a measure equivalent to 20 grains, 1/24 ounce, or a little more than a gram; iii, 22.

seam, clarified animal fat; ii, 25.

searce, to sift; i, 13; a sieve; ix, 18.

selvage, the woven edge of the cloth; iii, 54.

sengreen, the evergreen houseleek, *Sempervivum tectorum*; i, 225.

senna, *Cassia senna*, a strong purgative; **i, 149.**

serpentary, a retort or still; i, 158.

serpigo, a creeping skin disease; **i, 221.**

sester, a small measure of wine containing three or four gallons; **iv, 24.**

setwall, a variety of valerian, *Valeriana pyrenaica*; **i, 144.**

several, separate; v, 39.

sewer, server; the attendant who supervised the arrangement of the table; **ii, 191.**

shambles, slaughter-house; vi, 3.

shearman, one who shears woollen cloth by cutting off the superfluous nap; v, 22.

sheldrake, a variety of wild duck; ii, 85.

shepherd's-purse, teasel, *Capsella bursa-pastoris*; i, 105.

shield (of brawn), the skin of a boar filled with jellied meat; **ii, 192.**

shift, to change the liquid in which something is soaking or marinating; i, 250; to engage in fraud (adulteration); iii, 11.

shive, a slice; ii, 122.

shiver, a fragment; v, 38.

*short, stiff, frothy (of egg whites); **iv, 5** (this sense not recorded in *OED*); friable (of pastry); ii, 108; non-viscous (of wines); iv, 25.

shoveller, spoonbill; **ii, 76.**

sicklewort, self-heal, *Prunella vulgaris*; i, 211.

sile, the action of straining; vi, 17.

siledish, a dish used for straining milk; vi, 17.

simple, medicinal ingredient; i, 223.

sippet, a small slice of bread, toasted or fried, used to sop up gravy or broth; ii, 14.

skirret, a species of water parsnip, *Sium sisarum*; i, 36.

slay, on a loom, the device with evenly spaced notches through which the warp threads run; now called a "reed"; v, 19.

sleight, to rip up (material); i, 198.

slender, thin, lacking in character (of wine); iv, 18.

slice, spatula; ii, 148.

slighting, the action of levelling and smoothing the soil; **v, 26.**

slipping, a skein of yarn; v, 48.

sloe, the fruit of the blackthorn, related to the plum; i, 129.

small, mild (of beer); **ix, 5.**

smallage, *Apium graveolens*, also called wild celery or water parsley; i, 26.

smith's slake water, water in which steel is tempered by being rapidly cooled; i, 213.

smored, simmered or braised in a closed vessel; ii, 54.

smug, neat; vii, 28.

snipe, a marsh bird, characterized by a long bill; ii, 76.

snow, whipped white of eggs; **iv, 5.**

soak, to keep a kiln or fire at a steady temperature for an extended period; i, 211 and **ii, 24**.

sodden, boiled; i, 240.

soil, mixed, loam; vii, 2.

sop, a large sippet (q.v.), slice of bread or toast soaked in a sauce; ii, 91.

sorrel, a herb used in salads and sour sauces, *Rumex acetosa*; i, 15.

soul, centre; ii, 115.

sound, to swoon; i, 183.

souse, to pickle; ii, 101.

southernwood, the aromatic shrub, *Artemisia abrotanum*; i, 187.

sovereign, of superior effectiveness; i, 73.

sparrow-tongue, knotgrass, *polygonum aviculare*; i, 151.

spend, expend, use; ix, 1.

spermaceti, a waxy substance found in the whale; **i, 90**.

spigot, a small peg acting as a plug; v. 50.

spike, French lavender, *Lavendula spica*; i, 249.

spikenard, sarsaparilla, *Aralia racemosa*; i, 149.

splatted, split open; ii, 68.

squinancy, quinsy; **i, 52**.

stackyard, hay-stack yard; v, 24.

staddle, the base of a stack of hay or corn; vii, 22.

stamp, to pound, as with a mortar and pestle; i, 25.

staple (of wool) the quality of the fibre; v, 18.

stay, stop; i, 40.

stillatory, a still; iii, 3.

stint, a sandpiper; ii, 76.

stock-cards, coarse combs fastened to a stock (support), used in the preparation of wool; **v, 14**.

stock-dove, wild dove; ii, 76.

stonecrop, *Sedum acre*, or *Sedum reflexum*; **i, 92**.

stool, bowel movement; i, 139.

stop, stuff (of poultry, etc.); ii, 66.

storax, an aromatic gum; see note to "benjamin," ii, 168; iii, 25.

strait, narrow; i, 4.

strangury, a disease which prevents the easy flow of urine; i, 158.

strike (of flax or hemp), a bundle of coarse fibres; **v, 36**; (of grain) a variable measure, usually equal to a bushel; vii, 13.

strom, in brewing, an oblong wicker basket placed over the bung-hole in the mash-tub to prevent the grain and hops passing through as the liquor drains off; ix, 5.

stubwort, wood sorrel, *Oxalis acetosella*; i, 203.

sturdy, a brain disease which causes an animal to turn continually in one place; **vi, 111**

succory, a salad herb, *Cichorium intybus*, closely related to the endive; i, 20.

sucket, a piece of fruit candied or preserved in sugar; ii, 187.

sugar, plate, a confection of flavoured sugar, formed, or "printed" in various shapes; **ii, 170**.

sward, rind (of bacon); ii, 22.

swinge, to beat or whip; ii, 187.

swingle, to "swinge" or beat flax or hemp in order to separate the skin from the fibre; **v, 38.**
swingle tree, a bench on which flax was swingled; **v, 38.**
swingle tree dagger, a wooden lath used to beat flax; **v, 38.**
symbolize, to blend; i, 20.

tansy, the herb *Tanacetum vulgare*; **ii, 24.**
tansy, wild, *Potentilla anserina*; i, 191.
tare, a variety of vetch; vii, 2.
taster, a small, shallow cup of silver for tasting wine; iv, 10.
teal, a small fresh-water duck; ii, 49.
tear, a fibre of a quality fine enough for spinning; **v, 38** and see note to "hards," v, 39.
tench, a fresh-water fish similar to the carp; ii, 105.
tent, a rolled bandage used to probe wounds; ii, 205.
terms, menstrual period; iii, 16.
tetter, an ulcer; **i, 221.**
thistle, holy, blessed thistle, also known as *carduus benedictus* (q.v.); ii, 4.
thus, frankincense or olibanum; i, 227.
thyme, mother of, the strongly-flavoured wild thyme, *Thymus serpyllum*; ii, 38.
tierce, one-third of a pipe; usually forty-two gallons; iv, 22.
tile-sherd, fragments of tile; vii, 21.
touch, touchstone; iii, 15.
tow, to comb; v, 39; loose fibre; v, 44.
town-cress, garden cress, *Lepidum sativum*, a salad vegetable; i, 168.
toze, to tease (wool) in preparation for carding; **v, 3.**
trencher, a platter; i, 248.
tum, to give the wool a first or second carding (combing) in preparation for finer cards; vi, 17.
tun, a barrel; the action of storing in a barrel; ix, 5; iii, 29.
turnsole, the plant *Chrozophoria tinctoria*, used to make a violet, or deep red dye; **ii, 44.**
turpentine, Venice, turpentine made from *Pinus larix*, the white larch; i, 211.
tutia, tutty, zinc oxide; i, 79.
tutsan, a variety of St. John's-wort, *Hypericum androsaemum*; **i, 179.**
Tyre, a sweet wine; **iv, 37.**

unset, of leeks, not yet transplanted; otherwise a plant which has not yet set seeds; i, 135; iii, 4.

valerian, *Valeriana officinalis* and related plants; i, 249.
vent, sell; vii, 30.
verdigris, copper acetate; **i, 223.**
verge, edge; ii, 138.
verjuice, the juice of sour crab-apples; **iii, 31.**
vetch, the fruit of the leguminous plant species *Vicia*, which includes the common tare; i, 144.
***veil,** membrane or film (on an egg); ii, 156. Pre-dates *OED* entries.
virtue, power; iii, 21.

walker, a fuller (q.v.); v, 22.

walkmill, a fulling mill in which cloth is cleansed; i, 113.

wallowish, insipid or tasteless; ii, 53.

wallwort, *Sambucus ebulus*, also called dwarf or ground elder; i, 117.

walm, boil; ii, 49.

want, lack; ii, 151.

warden, a cooking pear; i, 160.

warp, the fixed threads on the loom; v, 19; the action of setting up the warp; v, 20.

washbrew, a dish, similar to porridge, made from the heart of oatmeal boiled and drained; vii, 11.

wax, grow, become; iii, 11.

web, a whole piece of cloth that is being woven; v, 3.

web, pin and, see pin and web; i, 78.

weft, the horizontal thread, woven by the shuttlecock; v, 19.

whig, whey; **vi, 34.**

whin, a prickly plant, usually gorse or heather; vii, 19.

whitepot, a pudding made with cream, rice, eggs, and spices; **ii, 145.**

wicker, a thin long twig, usually of willow; vii, 17.

widgeon, wild duck; ii, 49.

woodbine, *Lonicera periclymenum*, honeysuckle; i, 72.

woodcock, a migrating bird, related to the snipe; **ii, 76.**

*woodward, the plant called variously woodwaxen, greenweed, dyer's broom, or dyer's weed, *Genista tinctoria*; v, 11. This variant not recorded in *OED*.

wormwood, Roman, *Ambrosia artemisiifolia*, a plant introduced from North America; i, 249.

wort, the liquor made by an infusion of malt in water, from which beer and ale are fermented; **ix, 5ff.**; a general name for a plant; i, 203.

yarrow, properly *Achillea millefolium*, though Markham identified it with the water-violet, *Hottonia palustris*; **i, 24.**

Index